DEALING IN DEATH

The ARMS TRADE *and the* BRITISH CIVIL WARS, 1638–52

PETER EDWARDS

SUTTON PUBLISHING

First published in 2000 by
Sutton Publishing Limited · Phoenix Mill
Thrupp · Stroud · Gloucestershire · GL5 2BU

British Library Cataloguing in Publication Data
A catalogue record for this book is available from the British Library

ISBN 0 7509 1496 3

Typeset in 10/12pt Baskerville.
Typesetting and origination by
Sutton Publishing Limited.
Printed and bound in England
by J.H. Haynes & Co. Ltd, Sparkford.

CONTENTS

LIST OF ILLUSTRATIONS

Between pp. 180 and 181

LIST OF MAPS

LIST OF TABLES

ACKNOWLEDGEMENTS

This book has taken longer to produce than anticipated, mainly because the scope of the subject has grown. Two groups of people, in particular, have been affected by the delay. It is therefore only appropriate that I begin by thanking my family, especially my wife. Apart from putting up with the project for many years she has allowed me to concentrate on the work by not having to think about the distractions of everyday living. The staff at Sutton have been remarkably patient with me, too, as deadlines passed and the book expanded. The 'fault' lies with the Leverhulme Trust and Surrey University Roehampton, whose generous grants enabled me to cover the topic more extensively and in more detail than I would otherwise have been able to do. I am grateful to them both. I was also very lucky that the money bought me excellent research support. Dr Menno Polak covered the Netherlands, Ms Annelies Janssens worked in Belgium, France and Spain and Dr Steve Murdoch looked through the Danish archives. As an unexpected but invaluable bonus, Steve's wife, Dr Alexia Grosjean, supplied me with material on Sweden.

A number of people have read parts of the text and I have benefited greatly from their comments. In particular I would like to thank Dr Martyn Bennett, Mr Claude Blair, Professor Bernard Capp, Professor Mark Fissel, Dr Alexia Grosjean, Professor Jonathan Israel, Dr Steve Murdoch, Dr Jane Ohlmeyer, Mr Gavin Robinson and Dr Ian Roy. Dr Stephen Porter read the entire text and provided me with a number of suggestions for improvement. Aspects of the book have been presented at various seminars: in King's College, London, War Studies Department and to three seminar groups in the Institute of Historical Research, namely on Early Modern British Social and Economic History, Sixteenth and Seventeenth Centuries' British History, and the Low Countries in the early modern period. I have also spoken (twice) at the Gunpowder Research Group's annual general meeting, using the occasions to get answers to technical questions. Although it is customary to say at this point that remarks made by readers or participants at seminars have saved the author from error, it is no less true for being so often stated.

Apart from the research they undertook for me Dr Alexia Grosjean and Dr Stephen Murdoch kindly gave me a preview of their doctoral dissertations before submission. I would like to thank Dr Lenihan for sending me relevant extracts from his dissertation and Drs Lewis, Roy, Sleigh-Johnson and Wanklyn for leave to quote from their theses. Michiel de Jong provided me with information on arms imports from Zeeland ports. The Earl of Dalhousie graciously gave his consent for the use of material in his family records. I am also indebted to Frank Cass and Co. and Cambridge University Press for permission to publish the maps on pages 130 and 156 respectively.

INTRODUCTION

Historians have viewed the period of the Civil Wars from many angles but in essence it was one of military conflict. Success or failure for one side or another depended upon victory in battle and in the capture of towns and territory. The Scots defeated Charles I at Newburn on 28 August 1640 and the Irish Catholics overran much of Ireland in the winter of 1641/2. Parliament overcame the king militarily and then re-established English control in Ireland and Scotland by force of arms. Historians have long recognised this fact (hardly a startling revelation) and, as a result, Civil War military history is one of the most thriving subsections of the whole discipline. Apart from general works, there are a plethora of books on individual battles and prominent military figures. They tell us about the size and disposition of the armies, the tactics adopted and the unfolding of events on the battlefield. What they do not adequately reveal is how the armies acquired their arms and munitions or their uniforms and horses. This is a serious omission for the extent to which they resolved the problem had a considerable bearing on the outcome of the conflict. Without an appraisal of the logistics of arms production and distribution, and an assessment of the degree to which the needs of all sides were satisfied, the reasons why events took the course they did cannot be fully understood. No doubt political considerations were important and have to be examined. In purely military terms, too, one has to take into account tactics, the strength and disposition of the armies, and the morale and skill of the troops. Without weapons, however, the best of soldiers were ineffective.

With this in mind, a number of years ago I started to do the research for a book on the supply of arms to the Royalists and Parliamentarians in the Civil Wars in England. However, it soon became apparent that this was not good enough and that the work had to be extended to deal with the logistical issues connected with the various conflicts that engulfed the British Isles in the period 1638–52. This reappraisal of the subject of my research was partly due to the number of recent studies that dealt with the Irish and Scottish experience or which emphasized the need to see the crisis as one that affected all three kingdoms. It was also due to my own realisation that as, logistically, the conflicts impinged upon each other, it was necessary to put together an integrated account of the system of supply. Even from a narrowly Anglocentric perspective, it is impossible to write in isolation about the provision of arms to the rival armies in England because they were required in other theatres of war, often at the same time. The various parties fighting in Scotland and Ireland had to think about obtaining sufficient military hardware to fight a war, too, whether they were Covenanters, Montrosians, Royalists or Engagers in Scotland or Confederates, Royalists or supporters of Inchiquin, as well as Scottish and English troops, in

Ireland. Their responses to the problem varied and consequently each group has to be looked at separately. On the other hand, there was a certain amount of giving and receiving of *matériel* between the parties, though not as much as was expected or promised. In addition, shifting allegiances, exemplified by Inchiquin's changing loyalties in Ireland, altered the flow of arms and equipment.

Because the native arms industry was concentrated in London and the Home Counties, the side that controlled the capital and its hinterland had access to the bulk of the arms and armaments produced in the three kingdoms. Of course, some arms were made in the provinces and one or two places had particular specialisms. Essential raw materials like timber, saltpetre, ores and minerals were scattered around the British Isles, as were the sources of supply for saddle and draught horses. Locally, too, a considerable quantity of arms, armaments and equipment were stockpiled in town and county magazines or in private armouries. All sources of arms were exploited; existing facilities were developed and new plant set up but, even so, there was a shortfall. War used up supplies at an alarming rate and even Parliament with its control of the south-east could not obtain enough arms and equipment fully to meet its demands. During the years of peace the industries had languished. Moreover, home supplies of some raw materials were inadequate and this affected production of gunpowder, for instance. There was insufficient saltpetre to meet peacetime needs and there was no brimstone at all. All sides, therefore, relied upon imports to a greater or lesser extent, adding a degree of uncertainty to the process. Apart from the problems of dealing with foreign governments, merchants and industrialists, there were the difficulties in ensuring that the goods arrived at their destination. Consequently, each side took care to protect ships going to their ports, while, at the same time, trying to capture those sailing to enemy harbours.

Many people were involved in making arms and equipment or purchasing and moving them from their place of origin to point of delivery. Apart from specialist arms manufacturers, there were others who possessed skills that could be adapted to meet the needs of the wartime economy. This was particularly important for those parties that did not control existing centres of production (especially the London area) and that had to start virtually from scratch or, at least, from a very low base. Conversion was easier in some cases than in others. Tailors and shoemakers needed no additional training and farmers continued to raise horses as they had done before. Smiths, too, could fashion simple iron weapons, though they might need to obtain complex firing mechanisms from a specialist. Plant was a problem but costs varied from item to item, notably between the modest-sized workshops of weapons makers and the larger concerns of the ordnance and munitions manufacturers. Wherever possible, forges, foundries and mills were modified so that they could manufacture military hardware when war broke out. In spite of attempts to poach artificers, the bulk of the specialist workforce did not move and this gave Parliament an enormous benefit. In contrast, the Irish Confederates seem to have had some success in persuading foreigners to migrate to Ireland to work for them. People involved in moving the goods around the country similarly worked for the side which gave them a job, though perhaps under duress. Carriers transported goods overland and trowmen, lightermen and ships' captains sailed them downstream or round the coast.

Many arms dealers were happy to supply any side willing to pay them for their goods and this was certainly the case with foreign merchants. Nonetheless, all sides could rely on the support of a number of partisans in the mercantile community. Sir Nicholas Crispe, a Guinea Company merchant, courtier and erstwhile customs farmer, was one such person. Expelled from the House of Commons as a monopolist in 1641, he put his fortune at the disposal of the king, raising troops, equipping ships and buying arms abroad.[1] In London a radical group of merchants, spearheaded by individuals who had made their mark as interlopers in the colonial trades, engineered the revolution of 1641–2,[2] in which the common council seized power from the pro-Royalist aldermanic clique. Radical in religion and often with a history of opposition to the Crown, they worked in concert both commercially and politically. Stephen Estwick, a girdler and a prominent figure on the influential Committee of Safety, was a typical member of the group. He supplied thousands of garments to the Parliamentarian armies, normally working with a group of like-minded associates such as Maurice Gethin, Tempest Milner, Francis Peck, Thomas Player, John Pocock, and Richard Turner, senior and junior.[3] Tempest Milner and Thomas Player were among the trustees of his estate at the time of his death and a number of Puritan ministers or their widows received bequests in his will.[4]

On the continent expatriates helped to organise the arms trade. If, like Thomas Cuningham for the Covenanters and John Webster for the Royalists, they had settled abroad and had intermarried with local inhabitants, they were particularly well placed to do the job. Cuningham had been born at Veere, the Scottish staple port in Zeeland, where the family played a leading role in the town. In 1625 he had married a Dutch girl, Apollonia de Mysters, by whom he had a number of children, most of whom married into Dutch families. Webster first appears in the Amsterdam notarial records in 1615. Two years later he married Jannetje Lucas at the New Church in Amsterdam. In the 1630s he appears as a landholder as well as a merchant and eventually became Lord of Wulverhorst, Kattenbroek and Schagen.[5]

War materials had to be paid for. Merchants, manufacturers and carriers were more likely to do business with a particular side if they paid promptly and in full. Of course, in the command wartime economy a degree of pressure could be brought to bear and requisitioning and plundering of goods did occur. Even if reimbursed, suppliers might have to wait several years for repayment. Those owed money by the defeated sides had little chance of obtaining it. Nonetheless, if the armies wanted to ensure regular supplies they could not afford to ride roughshod over the people with whom they dealt. Foreign merchants, in particular, had to be well treated and large-scale domestic contractors could not be trifled with. All parties, therefore, had to increase their income. Partisans gave generously to the cause but it soon became apparent that a system of regular taxation had to be imposed. To pay for the cost of the war, far more had to be squeezed out of the population than ever before. The rates at which old taxes were calculated went up and greater attention was paid to an assessment of real income. New imposts were introduced. Such developments had the effect of drawing a growing sector of society into the tax net. Contributions were also solicited from foreign governments or from supporters abroad.

Though this book is primarily concerned with manufacture and supply, it does deal with such themes as tactics, organisation and financial management, as well as with more general issues. In particular, it makes a contribution to the ongoing debate about the 'military revolution' in the early modern period. A key development was the emphasis on fire-power, firstly through the greater use of bows and arrows and secondly, as the technology improved in the sixteenth and seventeenth centuries, by their replacement by firearms. Drill and practice speeded up the reloading process to the extent that in the Swedish army in the 1620s six rows of musketeers executing the countermarch could keep up a constant barrage. As a result, the mass compact squares gave way to more linear formations, a shape that had the added advantage of making the infantry less vulnerable to cannon fire. Even the cavalry was affected, with troopers acting as mounted pistoleers, performing the manoeuvre known as the *caracole*. Fire-power was further improved by the employment of light, mobile cannon on the battlefield. Nor was the traditional role of ordnance as siege weapons ignored and as their power increased, new forms of defensive works evolved to meet the threat. The *trace italienne*, as the system was called, was characterised by the building of low, thick walls and the creation of redoubts, bastions and gun platforms. These changes added to the cost, especially as armies became larger and more professional. Consequently, the State played an increasingly important role in the management and financing of war. To pay for the forces, it exploited the added power and authority gained as a means of extracting additional revenue from the population.[6]

The logistics of the Civil Wars is clearly an important subject but one which has been poorly covered. Professor Kenyon observed in a bibliographical essay in his book, *The Civil Wars in England* (Weidenfeld & Nicolson, London,1988), that 'there is precious little available on the logistics of the Civil Wars.' Some work has been done, of course. For Charles I's problems in the Bishops' Wars Mark Fissel's book, *The Bishops' Wars: Charles I's Campaigns against Scotland 1638–1640* (Cambridge University Press, Cambridge, 1994), is indispensable. An excellent appraisal of the Royalist position is given by Ian Roy in his edition of the Royalist ordnance papers, published in two parts in the Oxfordshire Record Society series (43, 1965; 49, 1975). For Parliament, C.H. Firth's study, *Cromwell's Army*, first published in 1902 (Methuen, London), remains the fullest account and it does contain much of interest. Two unpublished PhD theses cover this general area: D.E. Lewis, 'The Office of Ordnance and the Parliamentarian Land Forces 1642–1648' (Loughborough University, 1976) and J.S. Wheeler, 'English Army Finance and Logistics 1642–1660' (University of California Press, Berkeley, 1980). However, Dr Lewis's work is focused on the administration of the office and Dr Wheeler's thesis is mainly concerned with financial management. While the latter, unlike Dr Lewis, is still active in the field, his interests lie in the interrelationship between finance and logistics in the Interregnum period. He further explores the connection in 'Logistics and Supply in Cromwell's Conquest of Ireland', in Mark Fissel (ed.), *War and government in Britain, 1598–1650* (Manchester University Press, Manchester, 1991), in 'The Logistics of the Cromwellian Conquest of Scotland 1650–1651', *War and Society*, 10 (1992), and especially in a recent book, *The Making of a World Power: War and the Military Revolution in Seventeenth-Century England* (Sutton Publishing, Stroud, 1999).

Of the more general accounts, few give adequate consideration to the supply of *matériel*. The best are Ronald Hutton, *The Royalist War Effort 1642–1646* (Longman, London, 1982), Ian Gentles, *The New Model Army* (Blackwell, Oxford, 1992), Clive Holmes, *The Eastern Association and the English Civil War* (Cambridge University Press, Cambridge, 1974) and Peter Young, *Edgehill 1642* (Roundwood Press, 1967, reprinted by Windrush Press, Moreton-in-Marsh, 1995).

For the Scots and Irish even less has been written specifically on logistics. Pádraig Lenihan does discuss the supply of arms to the Irish Confederates in his PhD thesis, 'The Catholic Confederacy 1642–9: an Irish State at War' (University College, Galway, 1995) and in an article, 'Celtic Warfare in the 1640s', published in a collection of essays edited by John R. Young, *Celtic Dimensions of the British Civil Wars* (John Donald, Edinburgh, 1997). Several contributors to the book, *Ireland from Independence to Occupation*, edited by Jane Ohlmeyer (Cambridge University Press, Cambridge, 1995) deal with the subject and she covers it herself in her study of the Marquess of Antrim, *Civil War and Restoration in the Three Stuart Kingdoms* (Cambridge University Press, Cambridge, 1993), and in an essay, 'The Wars of Religion, 1603–1660', in *A Military History of Ireland*, edited by Thomas Bartlett and Keith Jeffery (Cambridge University Press, Cambridge, 1996). For Scotland, original material covering the supply of arms and equipment to the Scottish Covenanters has been edited by C.S. Terry and published in two volumes as 'Papers relating to the Army of the Solemn League and Covenant', *Publications of the Scottish Record Society*, 2nd series, XVI (1917). Edward Furgol touches on the subject in an essay 'Scotland turned Sweden: the Scottish Covenanters and the Military Revolution, 1638–1651' in *The Scottish National Covenant in its British Context*, edited by John Morrill (Edinburgh University Press, Edinburgh, 1990) and in the introduction to his book, *A Regimental History of the Covenanting Armies 1639–1651* (John Donald, Edinburgh, 1990).

Why then have historians not embraced this vital subject with greater enthusiasm? There is no shortage of documentation, notably in the voluminous archives in the PRO (State and War Office Papers, especially SP 28 and WO 49 and 55). Moreover, the British Library holds various collections of correspondence, which provide information on both Royalists and Parliamentarians. Buried in borough and county record offices is a mass of manuscript material, only a fraction of which is available in print in county record society publications. Some of these sources deal directly with the issue and can be guaranteed to provide hard evidence. Others have to be sifted through very carefully before they reveal anything of interest. In addition, foreign sources have to be looked at and this complicates the process of research. The size of the task is off-putting. Inevitably, the documentary coverage is patchy and while this might lighten the load, it leaves gaps in the record. Thus, while one can find out about virtually anything connected with Parliamentarian supplies and a good deal about the arrangements made by the Royalists, the same cannot be said about the logistical underpinning of the war efforts of the Scottish and Irish. In particular, it is difficult to assess the size of the native arms industries. They did exist and naturally they expanded to meet the demands of war, though negative evidence makes it clear that their general contribution was a modest one, especially in Ireland. It will become obvious when reading the relevant chapters on home supplies that at times I had difficulty in finding any evidence that could be used.

1

ARMS AND EQUIPMENT: A SURVEY

ARMS AND MUNITIONS

E ven if the 'military revolution' changed the type of weapons used by armies and the relative importance of each of them, the authorities had the same aim of providing the soldiers with arms that were reliable and appropriate. They never managed fully to realise these objectives in the British Civil Wars, as is indicated by the record of shortages, accidents and repairs, but they knew what arms and armaments they required for each branch of the army and made efforts to supply them. Given the nature of mid-seventeenth-century warfare, the largest consignments went to the infantry, which normally formed the main component of the army. Conventional wisdom of the time decreed a ratio of foot to cavalry of between two and five to one.[1] The make-up of Parliamentarian armies generally fitted into this pattern, whereas the Royalists tended to have proportionately more cavalry. At times, they had more troopers on the field than infantrymen and even at Naseby, a major battle, they had virtually as many cavalry men as foot.[2] The foot, if up to date, comprised musketeers and pikemen, normally in proportions of two to one.[3] Originally, pikemen had formed the offensive element among the infantry and the musketeers' primary duty had been a defensive one. By the outbreak of the Civil Wars, however, the emphasis on fire-power had led to a reversal of roles and, as a result, the number of musketeers increased at the expense of pikemen.[4]

Each musketeer carried a musket, a firearm 4 ft long and which generally had a matchlock ignition.[5] To fire such guns, a length of lighted match was inserted in the cock and brought down onto the fine powder in the flash pan. This, in turn, ignited the coarser charge in the barrel, which fired the bullet.[6] They were cumbersome, slow to load and inaccurate, but cheaper and easier to make than the more complicated snaphances, which used flint ignition. Moreover, as the snaphances were a comparatively new invention, many gunmakers had still to perfect the art of fabricating them. As the Company of Gunmakers of London noted in a letter to the Privy Council in January 1640, 'These arms having not been many years in use here, nor long made, but we expect hereafter upon encouragement to be more ready in making them, and so shall make them more cheaply.'[7] Many of the carbines bought in the Bishops' Wars had Spanish locks on them.[8] The only detachment routinely issued with snaphances was the so-called fireguard which, because it protected the gunpowder, could not use burning match.[9]

Cost and ease of production were especially important at the beginning of the conflict, when all sides were striving to build up stocks as quickly as possible.

Non-specialist craftsmen like blacksmiths were pressed into service and they would have been capable of making matchlocks. While far fewer of them could have fashioned snaphances, the locks could be obtained from specialists or purchased abroad. The different level of workmanship required to make the various types of muskets is reflected in the prices paid. In November 1643 Mr Watson, a London gunmaker, delivered to the Earl of Essex 200 matchlocks at 18s 6d and 50 snaphance muskets at £1 2s 0d.[10] Expertise was gained over time but matchlocks still retained their pre-eminence. The New Model Army, for instance, purchased at least 19,872 muskets in the months from April 1645 to December 1646 and of these, 17,324 (87.2 per cent) were matchlocks. In the late 1640s the committees for the Parliamentarian army continued to order mainly matchlock muskets.[11] The same was true in Scotland, but snaphances were used and as highly valued as they were in England. In December 1644 the Laird of Glenorchy, asking his son to obtain weapons, said what were most needed were 'snapwarke muskats wth somme swords and halfe pickes'.[12]

The standard musket was not very accurate: the limit of its effective range was about 400 yd, though in battle most musketeers shot their weapons at much closer quarters than that.[13] The only guns which had any real accuracy were the rifled birding and fowling pieces donated by gentlemen, who had used them for sporting purposes. Mr John Collabine, for instance, delivered three great fowling pieces and one small birding piece as part of his contribution to the Propositions. At Oxford, Captain Elms gave in five birding and one fowling piece in April 1643. In 1639 the Scottish Covenanters possessed a number of them.[14] While far too expensive to put into the hands of ordinary soldiers, they were used to good effect by snipers. George Monck, writing in about 1646, recommended that six soldiers in each company should be armed with such a weapon and employed for this purpose – and they were. In one incident in 1642, a marksman at Sherborne Castle shot several officers of the Parliamentarian besieging force.[15]

Across their shoulder musketeers wore a leather bandolier from which hung a dozen or more cartouches (known as chargers), small leather, tin or wooden containers, in which the powder was stored. In the years before the conflict the size of the optimum charge was a matter of debate: according to an order of the Council of War on 24 January 1640, ½ oz of powder was adequate.[16] Musketeers, therefore, carried about ½ lb of powder with them, apart from priming powder, kept in a horn. Calculations made might indicate that the soldiers were allotted greater amounts than this but this allowed for replacing powder used up in action. Thus, a report of January 1642 included the instruction that each musketeer in the trained bands should be provided with 2 lb of powder and a proportional amount of match and shot.[17] Bandoliers were cumbersome pieces of equipment to wear. The cartouches swung to and fro and rattled or jangled as the wearer moved. Apart from the danger that the noise might advertise one's presence, there was always the possibility that a spark might explode the entire belt and blow up the soldier with it. To counteract the problem, Lord Broghill recommended the use of cartridge boxes, worn round the waist.[18] The tin boxes that came with the 200 snaphance muskets, belts and swivels, delivered to the magazine at Stafford in 1644, may have been of this type. The purses, bought one to four dozen at a time by the garrison at Nottingham Castle 'instead of bandoliers' in 1644–5, served a similar purpose.[19] Musketeers also needed a bullet pouch and a priming flask in which the fine powder for the flash was kept.[20]

Musketeers were encumbered with other devices to help them maintain and fire their weapons. Firstly, they required instruments, such as worms, scourers and gunsticks, to load and clean the musket. Secondly – if only in the opening years of the war – they carried a rest, used to bear the weight of the gun when fired. They had been discarded by the end of 1644 in line with continental practice. The New Model Army certainly did not have any. In this respect, a consignment of eighteen rests delivered to the Ordnance Office in May 1649 appears as a stray order.[21] Presumably, by the mid-1640s musketeers could cope with the unsupported weapon, suggesting that muskets had become lighter, probably by being shortened.[22] Often the muskets were sold with their accoutrements and this raised the price. In May and June 1644 matchlock muskets for the Eastern Association army cost 15s and those with gunsticks, worms and scourers 1s more. A bandolier added about 1s 6d to the price (1d–2d more if tin cartouches were used) and a rest a further 1s. To complete the ensemble, musketeers might be equipped with Swedish feathers, stakes about 5 ft long with a pike head at each end. Driven into the ground in front of a line of musketeers, they offered them greater protection against cavalry. At times, they were combined with a musket rest. Of the 265 Swedish feathers in the Earl of Denbigh's magazine in February 1645, eighteen were dual-purpose implements.[23] In another attempt to improve the defensive capabilities of the musketeer, some were issued with half-pikes.[24] They also carried a short sword.

Among the musketeers, dragoons formed a distinct group and not merely because they rode to the field of battle before dismounting to fight. Their name derives from the dragon, a short firearm 16 in long, with a full musket bore and a snaphance mechanism. It was hooked onto a shoulder strap by means of a swivel affixed to the gun.[25] Such weapons did not define the soldier, however, for they might be armed like an ordinary musketeer. In practice, they were more likely to possess a snaphance musket or a carbine, similarly attached by means of a swivel. These fittings might be supplied with the gun, too, adding 2s to the price. Dragoons were often given special jobs to do; they might be sent on ahead to secure bridges or be posted on the flanks of the army, from where they could fire on the opposing cavalry. They might also fight as cavalry, as John Okey's regiment did at Naseby.[26] To do so, they certainly had to have snaphances, since matchlocks were too unwieldy to use on horseback. They could not readily be converted into troopers, however, because they rode far inferior horses.[27]

Pikemen were paid less than musketeers but were deemed to have a higher status.[28] The pike was usually made of ash and, apart from the half-pikes, were supposed to be at least 16 ft long. Some were. On 18 January 1643 the king received a consignment of 202 pike staves, 15½ ft long, which, when the steel head was added, would have brought them up to the requisite size. In practice, there was little conformity for, as in the manufacture of other weapons, under-sized and ill-sorted arms were produced. In October 1645 the New Model Army received 550 15-ft long Spanish pikes.[29] In addition, because they were so awkward to carry, many soldiers cut a couple of feet off the end. They might suffer for this in battle; at the Battle of Benburb in 1646 the Irish Confederacy army under Owen Roe O'Neill defeated the Scottish Covenanters partly because they possessed longer pikes.[30] At the same time, enemy soldiers were trying to hack off the other end. After a Royalist excursion into Hampshire in July 1643, most of the 112 pikes returned to the king's magazine were unheaded.[31] To prevent this occurring steel languets (metal plates) might be added to the head.[32] The foot of some pikes was strengthened by being encased it in brass or iron, a measure which incidentally might have discouraged the pikemen from shortening the weapon. Of the 1,000 pikes Captain Charles Bowles, the Kent commissary officer, bought in 1644–5, 400 had iron feet and 100 had brass feet, costing 5s 4d and 5s 6d respectively. The 500 unshod pikes cost 4s 8d and 5s 0d. The seller, Elizabeth Thacker, a London pikemaker, charged 4d each for the 45 pikes she footed with iron.[33] Pikemen, like musketeers, also possessed a short sword, used for close-quarter work and, infuriatingly, for cutting down branches.[34]

The 'military revolution' might have brought firearms to the fore but older forms of weaponry were not discarded overnight, even among commanders in tune with contemporary developments. Scottish archers saw service in the Swedish army in the 1630s[35] and then in the British Civil Wars. In England a commission of 1619 recommended the removal of several thousand bows from the stores but nonetheless, the Ordnance Office was still employing a bowyer and a fletcher in 1643.[36] Indeed, the value of bowmen was still a matter for discussion in England during the course of the Civil Wars (though perhaps mainly by armchair strategists). A Parliamentarian observer, writing in *Mercurius Civicus* on 28 September 1643, emphasised their effectiveness against cavalry, claiming that 'the flying of the Arrowes are farre more terrible to the horse then bullets, and doe much more turmoyle and vex them if they enter'. The writer advocated that they should be supplied to pikemen, thereby improving their offensive capabilities and allowing them to play a more positive role in battles. This is a point taken up in a booklet published in 1647. As the writer noted, a pikeman was only of value as a means of warding off cavalry and was vulnerable to musket fire. With a bow, however, 'hee may not only doe that service but farther off than the musket can reach, wound the enemies in all their ranckes both of horse and foote with his barbed Arrows, which are farre worse then any bullets'.[37] The same point was being made in Scotland, Archibald Campbell observing in April 1639 that his sons used 'bowis and arrowis with the pike to persew and defend againes horsemen'.[38]

All sides in the British Civil Wars used bows and arrows to some extent. In March 1639 Charles I specifically included archers among the soldiers to be levied to fight the Scots.[39] In September 1643, reportedly, the Royalists had two regiments of archers, though nothing is known of them. The writer, recalling past victories, hoped that Parliament might use them.[40] In fact, Parliament was already deploying archers, especially in the London militia, perhaps an indication of a shortage of firearms. On 13 December 1642 a warrant was issued to pay Colonel John Holmstede £800 for 800 London muskets and £25 for 100 dozen arrows and cases. In January and April 1644 William Molins, the Comptroller of Ordnance for the City, received large consignments of archery ware, including longbow arrows, bowstrings, bow cases, leather quivers, shooting gloves, bracers and musket arrows.[41] Musket arrows, as the name implies, were fired from a musket and the device seems to have represented an attempt to harness modern technology to a traditional weapon, especially one that engendered so much trauma. In 1643 they were said to cause 'terrible execution'. David Powell, the Ordnance Office's fletcher, was making them at the beginning of the war in England.[42]

Archers played a more important part in Celtic warfare. In 1639 most of the Highlanders in the Covenanting army were equipped with bows and arrows, which they could use to deadly effect. A commentator noted in 1641 that they 'are so good markes-men that they will kill a deere in his speed, it being the cheifest part of their liuing'.[43] When the Marquess of Antrim drew up a list of arms he required for his invasion of the Western Isles in 1639 it not only included weapons for his musketeers and pikemen but also 500 longbows (each with four strings and twenty-four arrows) for the Highlanders he expected to recruit upon landing.[44] In Scotland the Royalist Marquess of Huntly, whose power base lay in the north-east, asked Hamilton for 1,000 bows, with arrows, in January 1638.[45] At the same time the Covenanters were arming themselves in like manner. The Campbells of the western Highlands, for instance, were buying up stocks and gathering together archers. On 29 May 1639 Sir James Campbell of Lawers wrote to his kinsman, Sir Colin Campbell of Glenorchy, for thirty of his ablest men, well armed with bows and arrows and hackbuts, to join others already with him. He also asked for as many arrows and arrowheads as he had or could obtain. Five and a half years later the same joint use of musketeers and archers can be seen in the consignment of bowstrings, gunpowder and match that the Earl of Argyll sent his cousin, the Laird of Glenorchy.[46]

Among the Gaels the sword traditionally was the main offensive weapon, used in the Civil Wars to scythe through enemy lines at the end of a headlong charge. Indeed, at the king's review of the Covenanting army in August 1641 the Highlanders carried 'a broad slycing sword' at their side. To ward off the thrust of pike, sword or dagger a targe (or buckler) was carried. In the initial stages of the rebellion in Ireland, the insurgents followed the same tactics and wielded swords and other weapons for close-quarter fighting. According to a contemporary, their weapons consisted mostly of 'swords, targetts, pikes, skenes, forks, staves and whatsoever comes to hand'.[47] However, Lenihan has suggested that this continuity was more apparent than real and rather reflected a rational response to existing logistical problems, namely a shortage of firearms and gunpowder. As imports came in and as Irish soldiers returned home from the continent, trained in musket and pike tactics, the field armies of the confederates became more conventional in composition and in the tactics they employed.[48] However, the charge could still defeat musket/pike formations, especially if the latter comprised raw or inexperienced troops. As executed by Alasdair MacColla MacDonald and his Redshanks, it helped win a succession of battles for

Montrose in Scotland against Covenanter forces organised on continental lines. One refinement he adopted was the device of firing a single salvo of musket fire, after which the attackers dropped the weapon and ran at the enemy with swords drawn. This tactic had Swedish antecedents and was used by Scottish forces under the command of the king, Gustavus Adolphus.[49] MacColla's men were also far more disciplined than those who had used the tactic before, re-forming after unsuccessful charges and, if necessary, awaiting attacks with patience.[50]

For most of the century before the Civil Wars the regiments of foot had dominated the battlefield.[51] The cavalry, nonetheless, looked upon itself as the superior arm, an élitist attitude which reflected the greater costs involved and the background of its members. In the early seventeenth century, moreover, the cavalry staged a comeback, especially as tactical innovation gave greater prominence to their use as an instrument of shock. The success of the Swedish king, Gustavus Adophus, in the Thirty Years' War, who trained his cavalry to charge at the enemy with swords drawn, hastened the process.[52]

In England the old tripartite division of the cavalry into heavily armoured lances/demi-lances, light horsemen and petronels had disappeared by mid-seventeenth century. Cavalrymen disliked the weight of full armour, finding it difficult to move and vulnerable if unseated. Horses strong enough to carry them seem to have been hard to find too.[53] In addition, in England the harquebus, a firearm and the main offensive weapon of the petronels, superseded the lances and spears of the other two divisions. On 13 March 1643 four rotten horsemen's lances were included in a consignment of arms from the Oxford trained band which was handed in to the king's magazine there. This description suggests that the weapons were old and had not been used for some time.[54] Some units of lancers did see action, especially among the Scots, who used them in every theatre of the war. In Ulster the lance was their main cavalry weapon against the insurgents[55] and even 'British' troops may have used them there. In July 1643 1,000 lance staves were delivered to Sir John Clotworthy and William Jephson for the forces in Ireland.[56] Their last appearance on the battlefield appears to have been in the Scottish army at Dunbar in 1650 where the front rank of the Ministers' horse carried lances. These troops did enjoy a modicum of success, as at Marston Moor, where Lord Balgonie's regiment caused considerable damage.[57] A few cuirassiers, clad in full armour, also made an appearance. Hesilrige's 'Lobsters' are the best known and they made an initial impact, on account of the weight of their armour and the protection it provided them.

In essence, the Civil War cavalry were harquebusiers, though harquebuses, as such, were giving way to carbines. Both firearms were about the same length, ranging from 2 ft 6 in to 3 ft 3 in and differing from each other merely in the size of the bore (harquebuses and muskets had a larger bore). Like dragoons, troopers attached their carbine to a swivel, fastened onto a belt slung over a shoulder. They also possessed a brace of pistols. A sword, and perhaps a small poleaxe, completed their arms.[58] Captain Greathead, who served in Lord Fairfax's regiment from May 1644, equipped his men in typical fashion. According to his cornet, the company, sixty troopers plus officers, was well armed with carbines, pistols and swords.[59] Firth suggests that pistols gradually took over from carbines as the main offensive firearm of the cavalry, citing the absence of carbines in the Eastern Association and New Model armies and probably among the local Parliamentarian forces too.[60] While there was most likely a change in emphasis, reflecting the growing importance of Swedish 'shock' tactics, the switch was not that clear-cut. The records confirm that the Eastern Association was not supplied with many carbines and that the New Model Army only acquired a few. These could have been bought for the dragoons rather than for troopers; in a list of horses, arms and equipment purchased for 500 light horse in the period September 1645 to July 1647 no reference is made to carbines. On the other hand, several retrospective company and regimental accounts, drawn up on disbandment, reveal that cavalry regularly used carbines.[61]

Because cavalry could not handle matchlock weapons on horseback, they were issued with snaphances or wheel-locks. Snaphances were cheaper, less complicated and more reliable than wheel-locks and they were used in greater numbers. Wheel-locks were fired by the action of a steel wheel with a serrated edge rubbing against a piece of iron pyrites. The wheel first had to be spanned (wound-up), using a spanner.[62] If spanned too soon, the mechanism might become stiff and not work. At the siege of Wardour, Edmund Ludlow had to use his sword, observing, 'My pistols being wheel-locks and wound up all night, I could not get to fire.'[63] Nonetheless, they were appreciably more expensive than other firearms. When Lord Brooke purchased arms and munitions in the winter of 1642/3 he paid £2 10s 0d for a pair of snaphance pistols and £3 for a pair of wheel-lock (written as firelocks). His carbines cost £1 4s 0d and £1 16s 0d respectively. Gentlemen officers like Lord Brooke often spent a good deal on their own personal arms, notably on pistols. Thus, among his purchases there was a consignment of valuable pistols from William Watson, a leading London gunmaker. He paid the most (£5 10s 0d) for a pair of silvered pistols with hardwood stocks which fitted into holsters faced with plush and laced with gold. In 1642 the Earl of Cumberland paid a cutler £12 for a sword.[64]

Cannon for the artillery were cast in bronze (called brass) as well as in iron.[65] In the Civil Wars iron ordnance tended to be used for defensive purposes – in garrisons, for instance – while the lighter brass guns were preferred for the navy and as field pieces for the army. Tactical innovations stressed mobility, in accordance with the general principles advocated by strategists such as Maurice of Nassau and Gustavus Adolphus. Their success influenced others to adopt their methods.[66] Consequently, greater prominence was given to light, manoeuvrable field guns rather than to the more cumbersome heavyweight ordnance. These small pieces ranged from the saker, which fired a 5–6 lb ball, through the falcon and falconet, to the rabinet and its ¾-pounder. Contemporaries called the sakers and the smaller cannon galloping guns because they could be moved around the battlefield.[67] In general, these pieces required no more than four or five horses to pull them. At the same time, the practice grew of distributing such guns among the infantry regiments.[68] The larger field pieces, the demi-culverin and the occasional culverin, were more powerful, firing balls of 9–12 lb and 16–20 lb respectively. They were hardly manoeuvrable, however, and on the battlefield were positioned in fixed batteries. Culverins might require a team of seventeen horses to move them.[69]

Included among the smaller field pieces were the so-called leather or engine guns, consisting of bronze tubing, strengthened with iron and bound with rope and leather. At Zurich in 1622 Melchior von Wurmbrandt claimed to have perfected the technique but others working in the same field were quick to point out deficiencies in the design.[70] One of Wurmbrandt's rivals, Robert Scott, a Scot and Quartermaster General in the Swedish army, developed an improved model, which successfully passed a test firing in front of the Swedish king in 1627. Scott asked for 20,000 riksdalers for the invention but when Gustavus Adolphus refused, he resigned and joined the Danish army as general of artillery.[71] In 1629 he became a Gentleman of the Bedchamber to Charles I and seems to have established a foundry at Lambeth where he manufactured leather cannon.[72] Another Scot, Alexander Hamilton, was also associated with the development of leather guns. He, too, worked for Gustavus Adolphus but, unlike his compatriot, remained in the king's service and produced ordnance for him, including leather cannon. In 1630, for instance, he had been employed at Orebro making cannon and incendiary devices. He had also served in the artillery train on active service in Germany and was well known to General Leslie.[73] In his assessment of the value of leather guns Professor Parker has concluded that they were of little use, asserting that they did not work very well and were dangerous to handle. However, this is too sweeping a statement, for in certain circumstances they were devastating weapons. On the battlefield they were highly manoeuvrable, for they could be carried on horseback or drawn between two animals. The Scottish Covenanters, in particular, used them to good effect in the Bishops' Wars. Montrose employed them successfully against the Royalist Marquess of Huntly in 1639 and they proved crucial in the victory over Charles at Newburn in 1640. The Parliamentarians later deployed them too.[74]

Of course, cannon were the principal weapon employed in sieges. For the defenders the *trace italienne*, if constructed wholly or in part, improved their defensive capabilities and through the provision of gun platforms a greater offensive capacity too. Attackers might use some of the larger field cannon such as the demi-culverins and the whole culverins; in September 1643 George Monck wrote that he expected to clear out Irish rebel garrisons as soon as the expected culverin arrived. Sometimes they met with success: in 1645 a 9-pounder made breaches in the wall at Sligo.[75] In general, however, they were not heavy enough to do much damage to town or castle walls, especially if redesigned to the new standards or packed with earth and sods. Even culverins might prove ineffectual. Thus, the largest ordnance pieces of all, demi-cannon, cannon and cannon royal, firing upwards of a 27-lb ball, were preferred. The huge cannon royal weighed about 8,000 lb and threw a 66-lb ball.[76] On land, up to seventy draught horses were needed to pull it. Not surprisingly, wherever possible, siege cannon were transported by water! The artillery also deployed mortars firing shells of various sizes. At the Royalist siege of Gloucester grenades of up to 60 lb were lobbed into the city, and even larger ones were made.[77]

An indication of the variety of artillery pieces used by the armies can be seen in a list of cannon from which the Royalists drew their ordnance to fight at Edgehill. On 4 October 1642, the army, then at Shrewsbury, possessed 24 guns: 2 demi-cannon, 1 culverin, 3 demi-culverins, 1 saker, 1 minion, 2 3-pounders, 6 falcons, 5 falconets and 3 rabonets.[78] The details can be compared with an inventory, drawn up three weeks later on their return to Oxford after the battle. It included several Parliamentarian pieces captured at Edgehill. Of the 27 pieces, 21 of them could be classed as mobile field guns. The largest pieces comprised 2 demi-cannon, 2 culverins and 2 demi-culverins and there were also 4 brass mortars. When another survey was taken in the following May, the situation had improved a little. At Oxford 24 brass pieces were listed, together with 4 iron sakers, 4 small pieces manufactured by Mr Lanyon and 4 brass mortars. Moreover, the garrison at Wallingford possessed 7 mixed pieces, Abingdon 8 pieces and a mortar and Banbury 3 pieces.[79]

To convert the firearms and cannon into offensive weapons soldiers required bullets, cannonballs and mortar shells, as well as gunpowder to propel them. For hand guns, bullets, also known as shot, were needed in tens of thousands and in different sizes, according to bore. Musket bullets, at $1\frac{1}{8}$–$1\frac{1}{4}$ oz, were heavier than carbine and pistol shot. There was, however, a good deal of variation. Because of the multiplicity of small craftsmen working in the gunmaking trade it was difficult to standardise firearms and, consequently, the wares tended to be described according to their bore.[80] Certainly, contemporaries often found it difficult to make bullets of the correct size, a problem that had operational implications. Lord Broghill described an occasion when his musketeers' bullets were too large for the barrel, forcing them to gnaw or cut off some of the lead. This not only reduced the range and accuracy of the bullets but also caused delays, making the enemy think that they had lost their courage. In addition, firearms required a medium to create the spark. Flints and pyrites were used in wheel-lock firearms but for the far more common matchlocks, match was needed.

Cannonballs, called round shot, were made of iron, and produced in different sizes to fit a particular type of cannon. Artillery pieces also fired case shot, that is, tin or wooden canisters full of musket balls. The effect was similar to that of a later twelve-bore shotgun, in that the balls spread out in an arc after leaving the cannon and cut down everything in their path. It had a devastating impact if fired upon tightly packed formations at close range.[81] Mortar shells were designed as fragmentation bombs or as incendiaries. A besieging force might also attempt to blow in the gate by affixing a petard – a metal container filled with gunpowder – to it. These explosive devices were difficult and dangerous to use and skilled 'fireworkers' and 'petardiers' were often employed to handle them. They were essential personnel in an artillery train. A Parliamentarian memorandum stated in March 1645 that 'you cannot gett Gonners that are able to make fire workes & apply Petards, unlesse they haue that wages allowed. For to apply Petards is desperate seruice, & to make Fireworkes is a thing that few doe know.'[82] Bartholomew La Roche, the Royalist master fireworker, regularly supervised operations in person.[83] Such weapons could prove very effective. At Chester in 1645 a Royalist deserter spoke of the havoc mortars had caused, destroying houses, killing people and terrifying many others.[84] The panic induced by the sudden and seemingly indiscriminate nature of the attack and the difficulty of finding cover against them was part of their appeal. When grenades started to explode above the castle at Devizes the Royalist governor quickly surrendered.[85]

HORSES, CLOTHING AND EQUIPMENT

To protect themselves many soldiers wore armour, though there was a general trend towards a reduction in the amount worn.[86] The demise of the cuirassier illustrates this development. The plate armour that such troops wore did afford added protection as Sir Arthur Hesilrige found out at Roundway Down in 1643.[87] On balance, however, the disadvantages outweighed the benefits and few followed his example. The normal cavalry armour comprised a steel helmet known as a pot, and a corslet (a back and breastplate). Helmets were either of the three-barred type or made with a single movable noseguard.[88] The latter style was a Dutch fashion, though both types seem to have been manufactured there. In one consignment from Holland, Commissary Bowles obtained 176 sets of harquebusiers' arms, including 'treble barred potts'.[89] Some cavalrymen might have worn gorgets and gauntlets to protect their throats and forearms but there are few references to them. Those that are listed are often described as old, defective or decayed, suggesting an archaic piece of equipment found in the darker recesses of armouries.[90] Pikemen had similar armour to the troopers, namely a helmet called a combe-cap and a corslet. Earlier in the century they had also worn gorgets and thigh pieces known as tassets but these had largely been discarded by the Civil War.[91]

Musketeers did not wear any armour at all and troopers and pikemen tended to follow suit. Pikemen, in particular, suffered on the march; apart from their armour and weapons, they toted a knapsack around with them, in which they kept their food and spare clothing (if they had any). Altogether, their burden might amount to 50–60 lb.[92] As one soldier remarked, 'long and quick marches in hot summer weather cannot but be wonderfully burdensome'.[93] In place of their armour, troopers and perhaps some pikemen wore buff coats of leather, strong enough to deflect a sword thrust. The coats were expensive; according to John Turbervill, writing in September 1640, there was 'not a good one to be gotten under ten pounds, a very poor one for five or six pounds'.[94] This was an extravagant rate – various army accounts indicate that they could be obtained for far less than this. Sir Thomas Martin, who captained a troop of horse in the Eastern Association army, noted that one had cost £7, two others about £2 and a fourth, taken by the quartermaster, 13s 4d.[95] Most seem to have been bought for about £2. In August 1642, for instance, it cost £100 9s (£1 18s each) to clothe a troop of fifty-three horse raised by the town of Watford with buff coats with sleeves (5s 0d was abated because one coat did not have sleeves). In January 1646 Lieutenant-Colonel Thorp paid £4 10s 0d for buff coats for three of his soldiers.[96] The cost was still considerable. They were more expensive than suits of armour; for example, infantry armour cost up to 17s and cavalry armour from a few shillings more. References to armour in the accounts are certainly far more common than those to buff coats, though the latter were often bought privately by those kitting out soldiers.[97] In Scotland, the Covenanters' cavalry and dragoons seem initially to have worn either a jack or secret or a buff coat, with the latter becoming more common as the war progressed.[98]

What the ordinary soldier wore is well known because of the amount of extant material available to us. In September 1642, for instance, the 7,500 suits of clothes that were to be sent to the infantry in Ireland consisted of a cap, doublet, cassock, breeches, two shirts and two pairs of stockings and shoes.[99] Lowland foot regiments in the Scottish Covenanters' army in Ulster were issued with suits of woollen cloth, grey in colour. Highland infantry, on the other hand, wore woollen waistcoats and the *filleadh mor*, a plaid wrapped round the waist and slung over a shoulder, or the *filleadh beag*, in which the plaid was cut into two and worn separately. Some Highlanders wore trews.[100] Cassocks were long cloak-like outer garments, the forerunner of the army greatcoat. In some orders coats were substituted for them.[101] By the time that the Irish and Scottish expeditionary forces of 1649–51 were being clothed, some soldiers, notably the officers, were wearing cloaks.[102] At the beginning of the war the headgear of most foot soldiers was probably a Monmouth cap, the most popular alternative to a helmet.[103] Later in the conflict a broad-brimmed hat called a montero became more common. By the time that the forces in Ireland were being equipped in 1647–8, hats were the norm. Some 16,000 hats for the foot soldiers were ordered at 1s 10d and 4,000 for the cavalry at 2s 2d.[104] In Scotland both Lowlanders and Highlanders typically wore a flat round blue bonnet.[105]

For footwear, the infantry wore shoes, or in Ireland, as an alternative, brogues. Highlanders wore pumps and hose, if they did not go barefoot.[106] The cavalry donned thigh boots to protect their legs in action. Boots were more expensive than shoes; in one consignment sent from Northampton to Ireland in 1642 the boots cost 7s 0d a pair and the shoes 2s 4d.[107] Boots and shoes were often waxed to make them waterproof, though this increased the price.[108] For an army on the march comfortable well-fitting shoes were essential and if the soldiers did not always enjoy that luxury, contracts do reveal that footwear was made in different sizes. In June 1642, the terms of an agreement for 10,000 pairs of shoes (some black and some russet) stipulated that they should be made of well-conditioned leather in five sizes: nine to thirteen, half with three soles and half with two. Most soldiers were expected to have middling-sized feet, for only 500 pairs each of nines and thirteens were to be made.[109] Initially, soldiers probably obtained their clothing and footwear from the recruitment officers or, if impressed, from their parish. Thereafter, they generally bore the cost of replacement garments themselves, the sum being stopped (defalked) out of their wages.[110]

Did these clothes constitute a uniform? To a certain extent they did, but uniformity only developed over time. At the beginning of the war the situation was somewhat mixed. Individuals raising and equipping their own troops naturally tried to clothe their men in the same garb. Similarly, as contractors fulfilled large-scale orders for the armies, often at the regimental level, there would be hundreds of soldiers dressed in identical clothes. As a result, the Earl of Essex's army at Edgehill had a rainbow appearance, even if individual regiments might be identifiable. The presence of regiments with no coordinated colours only served to increase the confusion.[111] For some time colours continued to be determined at a regimental level. Among the Royalists at Marston Moor Prince Rupert's regiment wore blue, Colonel Tillier's, green and the Duke of Newcastle's foot, white. Parliamentarian forces were similarly mixed. In the Eastern Association army, the Earl of Manchester might use green for his own men but other units wore red.[112]

Both colours feature prominently in an account of work done for the Eastern Association army in early 1645 by Thomas Buckley, a Cambridge tailor. For the facing of the coats he used a variety of colours.[113] Essex's own troops wore orange; in April 1643 Thomas Bushell, the captain of the commander's company of foot, received sixty orange coats, together with the same number of shirts, pairs of shoes and knapsacks. The colour was also incorporated into the uniforms of his lifeguard. Although the coats were predominantly grey, they were trimmed in orange and had orange and silver buttons. Altogether, they cost £136 8s 4d, about nine times the price of an infantryman's coat.[114] Unfortunately, these examples do not tell us if other regiments in the army were dressed in the same colour uniforms. It was only when the New Model Army was being equipped that any measure of consistency was achieved. On 7 May 1645 it was reported in a newspaper that the 'men are Redcoats all, the whole army only are distinguished by several facings of their coats'.[115]

Until uniformity was achieved, some other means had to be employed for identification of soldiers on the battlefield. The device adopted was the coloured scarf, sash, ribbon or plume.[116] At Edgehill the Parliamentarians wore scarves of orange, the colour favoured by the Earl of Essex. We can see him buying them too; on 11 August 1642 he authorised the payment of £50 to Sir Philip Stapleton for 100 scarves for his own troop of cuirassiers.[117] The Royalists wore a red sash at the battle. The Scottish Covenanters adopted a blue ribbon as their mark in March 1639.[118] Standards not only served the same purpose of identification but also helped to foster an *esprit de corps*.[119] Each foot company or cavalry troop had its own banner, its design a variant of the regimental colours. These were made out of rich material, normally taffeta, and embroidered with suitable devices and edifying mottoes.[120] Gilded and adorned with tassels and trimmings, they were expensive items, especially if bought ten at a time for each regiment. In 1642 Essex's army acquired them at £4 each.[121] The New Model Army paid £2 1s 6d for theirs.

Trumpets and drums, which also had a utilitarian function, were similarly embellished. Trumpets might have banners attached to them: two black taffeta trumpet banners cost Sir William Brereton £5 in 1644. He also paid £4 10s to have arms painted on twenty drums.[122] Colours, drums and trumpets were often bought as part of a package, which included devices denoting status, notably partizans and halberds. In the spring of 1645 a number of regiments in the New Model Army acquired their own sets. Thus, on 7 April Colonel Rainsborough received £60 1s 0d for the 10 partizans, 23 halberds, 10 colours and 22 drums he had purchased.[123] A partizan was a short spear held by infantry officers, while sergeants wielded a halberd, a weapon with a combined spear and axe-head.[124] Lieutenants might possess a poleaxe, a hand weapon with axe- and hammer-heads, and a captain, a leading staff. Their ceremonial role is indicated by the references to poleaxes and halberds bedecked with fringe. Widow Thacker, for instance, charged Commissary Bowles £1 16s 0d for cleaning six halberds and putting new fringe on them.[125]

To carry them into battle cavalrymen required 'serviceable' horses, that is, mounts of a certain size and strength. Although ideally at least fifteen hands high, in practice many of them were smaller by one or two inches.[126] As a result of cross-breeding with foreign stock, notably horses from North Africa and the Near and Middle East, improvements in the native breeds had occurred in the period before the Civil War, and when it broke out a reasonably large pool of suitable animals was available.[127] This development reflects the changes in cavalry tactics taking place: sheer bulk now counted for less than mobility and the traditional 'great' horses were replaced by lighter, more nimble animals. The Duke of Newcastle, drawing on his experiences in the Civil War, believed that middle-sized horses were the best, observing that they had 'for the most part both strength, spirit and agility and not one in a hundred but proves well when of large horses not one in a thousand does'.[128] General Monck's comment that horses large enough to mount cuirassiers were hard to find is a further indication of the process of change.[129] Incidentally, these innovations must have made it difficult for dragoons to operate as supplementary cavalry on the occasions when they did. Because they employed their mounts primarily as a means of transport, less attention was paid to quality or to attributes such as speed or agility. This is shown in the respective prices paid for troop and dragoon horses. The dealers who supplied the New Model Army with horses charged £7 10s 0d for a trooper's mount and £4 for a dragoon's horse.[130] Once they had been given their horse, troopers and dragoons had to bear the cost of looking after the animal and were answerable if anything happened to it. This partly explains the higher rates of pay that they enjoyed over the foot soldiers.

Strong horses were required for draught work. Fortunately, English draught horses, like the saddle mounts, had also improved in quality as a result of the admixture of foreign blood.[131] Draught horses were needed in large numbers, especially whenever a field army set out on the march. Apart from drawing the cannon, they pulled wagons loaded with arms and ammunition, provisions, equipment and even the personal effects of the officers. Because the roads were unmetalled, bad weather compounded the problem. Normally, culverins had teams of fifteen to seventeen horses but at Lostwithiel in the aftermath of the disastrous Parliamentarian defeat, the narrow lanes were 'so extreme foul with excessive rain' that teams of thirty horses could not move three demi-culverins and a brass piece.[132] Oxen sometimes replaced horses, especially in those parts of the country where they were the main draught animals. In pastoral areas with heavy soils their slower but steadier pace was better suited to the conditions. Fodder cost less too. Thus, they could be found at work in parts of the north and south-west and in Ireland. In July 1643, for instance, sixteen oxen were recorded, drawing a great siege piece of the Irish rebels.[133] Wherever possible, however, horses were preferred. In March 1644 the king's council ordered the sale of fifty-three oxen, then in the artillery train, so that draught horses could be bought with the proceeds.[134]

Horses involved other expenditure. Cavalry and dragoons required saddles and bridles, while the baggage and artillery trains needed harnesses and collars for their draught horses (and yokes for any oxen) and pack saddles and panniers for their packhorses. Cavalry saddles had to be of better quality than dragoon saddles because the troops rode on them into battle. The armies of Essex and Manchester acquired them for about £1, whereas the New Model Army only paid 15s 0d. On average, they cost twice as much as dragoon saddles. The range of saddlery available was quite considerable. In 1644, William Pease, a leading London saddler, supplied the Kentish forces with a great saddle, furnished, at £1 15s; 132 cantle pads, furnished, at £1 5s each; 73 ordinary pad saddles, furnished, at £1 each; 4 scout saddles at 16s each; and 2 saddles for trumpeters at 13s each. He also supplied 6 dozen girths at 3s 6d a dozen; 26 troop horse bits and bridles at 3s 4d each; and a headstall and reins at 1s 8d each.[135] Troopers carried their pistols in holsters across their saddles.[136] Longer holsters had to be made if the pistols were French. On one occasion William Botterell, the Clerk of the Stores at King's Lynn, received sixty pairs of French pistols from Thomas Toll and had to have holsters specially made for them in London.[137]

Horses also had to be cared for properly, if they were to perform effectively. In particular, they had to be shod and fed and treated when sick. Shoeing used up valuable supplies of iron and required the services of a blacksmith. The cost of feeding horses was the single most expensive item, however, and because of the large numbers involved, the search for fodder presented the armies with one of their most serious problems.

Apart from the supply of arms and equipment, a note should be made of the consideration that had to be given to the soldiers' diet because of its effect on their morale and loyalty. The standard diet of troops on the march was bread or biscuits, cheese and beer, though this might be augmented from time to time by meat bought or taken from the local population. Infantrymen seem to have carried about a week's supply of food in their knapsacks.[138] On Cromwell's Scottish campaign of 1650–1 the daily ration of the soldiers consisted of 1–1½ lb of bread and 8–12 oz of cheese and this was typical fare.[139] Soldiers in garrisons might do much better, benefiting from a more varied and plentiful diet; the Parliamentary troops at Lyme Regis, for instance, were reputed to have had 2 oz of meat a day.[140] This was by no means certain, however; much depended upon the resources of the locality, as well as on the attitude of the inhabitants. Sir William Brereton, while besieging Chester for Parliament, experienced great difficulty in provisioning his men, putting it down to the impoverishment of the area and the malignancy of the population.[141]

CONCLUSION

The arms and equipment employed in the British Civil Wars reflected military developments in Europe during the course of the early seventeenth century. This is hardly surprising, given the number of officers who had fought in the Thirty Years' War and who brought to the domestic conflict the experience they had gained overseas. Of course, there were differences between the armies – the Royalists possessed more cavalry than the norm and the Irish Confederates more infantry – but all sides took account of contemporary military practice. In terms of arms and equipment, some items were easier to find than others. At the beginning of the war, suitable cavalry horses were more readily available, especially to the Royalists, than were certain weapons like flintlock muskets and munitions such as gunpowder and match. Changes also occurred during the Civil Wars in terms of tactics and equipment. To a certain extent, many of the problems were caused by the lack of preparation and by the time it took to gear up native industries to supply the requisite arms and armaments. At the outset, some soldiers were not adequately equipped and there was an amateurish air about proceedings. As time wore on not only did the armies become more 'professional' but they were also more likely to be given the proper tools to do the job, shortages notwithstanding.

2

ADMINISTRATION AND SUPPLY

At the centre of the system of supply was the Ordnance Office, located in the Tower of London. With the Armoury, similarly situated there, it dealt with all matters relating to arms, munitions and ordnance: with quality control and standardisation of weapons, as well as with purchase, storage and distribution. The names of the two branches suggest the division of functions but in practice by 1638 the Ordnance Office was expanding its work at the expense of the Armoury. The office set up outposts at Chatham, Deptford, Rochester and Woolwich, specifically to cater for the needs of the navy.[1] The Armoury also established several smaller bases, notably at Greenwich, Portsmouth and Woolwich. Ireland had its own Ordnance Office at Dublin Castle. Scottish Covenanters and Irish Confederates had to create their own system when they rebelled against Charles I. Apart from the arms, armaments and equipment stockpiled in the main centres, war materials were also stored at local arsenals scattered throughout the three kingdoms. The Ordnance Office itself supplied much of the *matériel*. These magazines might be in private hands or be parish-, town- or county-based. At the centre, the ordnance officers were under the control of a superior body, which authorised them to issue arms, even if in the localities the local officers seemed to have acted with a greater degree of freedom. During the Civil Wars, the armies developed their own organisation, the commissariat, as a means of obtaining supplies.

THE ENGLISH ORDNANCE OFFICE

The titular head of the Ordnance Office was the Master of the Ordnance, a post filled by the Earl of Newport between 1638 and 1642.[2] In practice, the work was carried out by his deputy, the Lieutenant. In 1638 the incumbent was Sir John Heydon; he had a large and varied staff under his control, including officers, clerks, artificers and labourers.[3] There was even a ratcatcher.[4] The leading officers had their own area of responsibility, though there was some overlap, notably in the determination of quality and price and in the issue of stock from the stores.[5] This led to some duplication in record keeping.[6] Three of the officers specifically dealt with the goods themselves: the Surveyor was charged with quality control, the Master Gunner with proving ordnance and the Keeper of the Stores with looking after goods while in the Ordnance Office's hands. The functions of the Clerk of the Ordnance and the Clerk of Deliveries were essentially clerical, though vital if waste and loss were to be avoided. The former was mainly concerned with internal bookkeeping, entering into the quarter books (the permanent record of the office's business) the information given to him by the junior officers. The Clerk of Deliveries maintained a record of issues and was responsible for the return of equipment no longer required at the end of an expedition.[7] The Armoury had a separate, albeit smaller, workforce, consisting of a master, a deputy master and a clerk, as well as a team of craftsmen. The Keeper of Small Guns and the furbishers maintained the firearms there.[8] The largest provincial arsenals might have a keeper, a clerk and a few artificers and labourers but most of the magazines probably had to make do with a single official, the arms being maintained by local craftsmen.

The Ordnance Office employed a number of artificers, who provided the necessary craft skills to make essential equipment and to maintain the stock in good working order. On the eve of the conflict they comprised two furbishers (gunsmiths), a plumber, ladlemaker, bowyer, fletcher, smith, carpenter, wheelwright and cooper.[9] In most cases the individual had to adapt his skills to the highly specialised needs of the office. Thus, the ladlemaker made pieces of equipment for the ordnance and the plumber dealt in lead shot. Similarly, the carpenter constructed field carriages for the cannon and wooden chests for weapons.[10] The wheelwright fashioned wheels for wagons and gun carriages, as well as making the vehicles themselves, and even wheelbarrows. Because of their craft background the artificers tended to be drawn from the London livery companies.[11] Though paid a salary by the Ordnance Office, they also received money for any arms or equipment they made or refurbished. The artificers who provided equipment or shot produced the bulk of the ware but outsiders made most of the weapons.

Many of the staff and Ordnance Office contractors lived, as well as worked, in and around the Tower, the amount of business generated by the Office acting as a magnet to them. Thomas Hodgskin, the master smith, lived at the Mint in the Tower and there were lodgings for the senior officers there too, including the Master, the Lieutenant , the Surveyor of the Ordnance and the Keeper of the Stores.[12] Others lived in the surrounding streets. Sir John Heydon, the Lieutenant, and George Fisher, one of the furbishers, had houses in the Minories.[13] The Minories had long been noted for its arms manufactories. At the end of Elizabeth I's reign Stow noted that on an old abbey site there 'is now built divers fair and large storehouses for armour and habilments of war, with divers workhouses, serving for the same purpose'.[14] Robert Steadman, the other furbisher, lived nearby in St Katherine's Street, as did Lawrence Bromfield, a major supplier of swords.

Before the arms were paid for and accepted into the Ordnance Office, they had to be tested. This was a vital precaution not only to prevent accidents but also to ensure quality control. Some items did not pass. In March 1639 a demi-culverin broke in the trial and later in the year a culverin failed.[15] The Keeper of the Small Guns, in conjunction with the two furbishers, tested firearms in the Proof House in the Tower.[16] The Proof Master, working under the master gunner, proved ordnance. Items might be tested locally in the Artillery Garden or close to the foundries in Kent, conveniently sited for the naval ordnance depots at Rochester, Deptford and Chatham.[17] In May 1638, for instance, ordnance officers went to John Browne's foundries at Brenchley and Horsemonden to prove a hundred cannon, earmarked for the king's ships, the *Royal Sovereign* and the *Sovereign of the Seas*.[18] Once approved, the Mark-Master stamped the arms with a distinctive symbol that served to identify ownership. The Crown had various marks, which corresponded to different branches of the armed forces. In January 1639 John East, engraver, made ten stamps for marking muskets, carbines and pistols; four of the dies had CR on them, two CR and an anchor, three a crown and one an anchor.[19]

The practices of the Ordnance Office were not above suspicion and it had its critics both at the time and among historians. Inquiries undertaken in 1630–3 and 1639 unearthed various abuses and shortcomings in the conduct of its affairs.[20] Personal disputes and a lack of cooperation between the senior officers bedevilled relations among the staff. In 1639 Newport complained that he was not being kept informed and that important decisions were being taken without his knowledge.[21] Heydon clashed with his subordinates and both sides made accusations against each other.[22] Some malpractice might be explained away[23] but accounting procedures were lax, leading to problems such as the loss or misappropriation of stock; the receipt of sub-standard ware; the failure to check on the delivery of goods ordered on credit; and even to double payment for weapons sent out for repair. A major cause of the trouble was insufficient funding. The annual budget of £6,000 was totally inadequate and this made it difficult for the officials to obtain vital stores. Because they often had to make the suppliers wait for payment, the latter recompensed themselves by charging high prices. Within the office, low salaries led to corrupt practices. Officials claimed excessive travelling expenses and demanded fees to prove goods delivered to the Tower and to process the paperwork. This annoyed the suppliers. On the other hand, they were accused of conspiring with the officers, who were paid a percentage of the sums disbursed, to raise prices. One or two officials were undoubtedly corrupt, having been found guilty of embezzlement, and there may well have been others.[24]

Proving weapons offered an opportunity for collusion between ordnance officers and manufacturers, or at least created a potential clash of interests. This became apparent in the Bishops' Wars when in 1639 a large consignment of arms from Hamburg was rejected as unsatisfactory. The appraisers were three prominent members of the Gunmakers' Company, who clearly had a vested interest in damning these goods. In the Tower the officers refused to receive the weapons, let alone maintain them in working order.[25] At the same time, the testing of swords was hampered by the squabble between Benjamin Stone and the Cutlers' Company. Stone, a renegade member, strove to break the company's virtual monopoly of Ordnance Office business by impugning the quality of their weapons. He was so successful that he was appointed the office's official cutler and supplied it with large numbers of blades.[26] This made it easier for him to get his own swords passed and those of the Cutlers' Company rejected. In the event, Stone could not hope to supply blades in the quantities required and members of the Cutlers' Company did gain a proportion of the business.[27]

The Bishops' Wars, 1638–40

The organisational ability of the Ordnance Office was put the test in 1638 when the king resolved to deal with the rebellion in Scotland, sparked off by the imposition of the English prayer book there. At first glance it clearly failed in its task.[28] In both campaigns the king's forces had insufficient arms, ordnance and munitions to meet their needs, a problem which had a serious effect on the final outcome. In the first war, lack of arms, as well as men and money, prevented the English army from taking the initiative. On 10 May 1639 Sir Edmund Verney, the standard bearer, wrote, 'Our men are verry rawe, our armes of all sorts nawght, our vittle scarce, and provision for horses woarce; and nowe you maye judg what case wee are in, and all for want of monny.'[29] Ironically, by the time that negotiations between the two sides started, war materials were beginning to get through.[30] In the second war, attempts were made not to repeat the strategic mistakes of the first one but all this did was to spread slender resources more thinly. At the decisive Battle of Newburn, fought on 28 August 1640, many of the English soldiers had no firearms.[31] They also lacked artillery, the weapon that decided the outcome of the battle and with it the war. Whereas the Scots deployed up to eighty cannon, mostly demi-culverins, on the field, Conway, the English commander, possessed only eight, none larger than a saker. At the time, the artillery train was at Hull and shiploads of arms were still in transit.[32]

Those arms that did arrive were often inadequate. Many of the imported weapons were deemed to be unusable, though the appraisal was not totally unbiased.[33] Shortage of money also meant that the government tried to obtain weapons at home as cheaply as possible. Orders were placed with arms manufacturers but by calling out the militia to fight the Scots the king expected the counties to provide the weapons and equipment as well as the soldiers. Not only were the counties reluctant to see men and military hardware being deployed outside the county, and having to spend money to do so, they were also unable or unwilling to provide them with decent arms.[34] Not surprisingly, some of the worst weapons were those belonging to the county militias and this was a matter over which the Ordnance Office had little control. Arms from Cambridgeshire, for instance, were said to be outmoded and unserviceable, while some of the arms received were so rotten that they could be pierced with a bodkin. On 17 January 1639 Sir Thomas Morton reported that the Durham trained bands were short of arms and that the corslets had no taces (tassets).[35]

Nonetheless, there is another side to the picture and any fair appraisal of the Ordnance Office's activities has to take into account what it did accomplish. Its performance, in fact, was creditable, given the scale of the demand and the logistical problems involved. The volume of war materials handled, if not unprecedented, far exceeded the requirements of the expeditions of the 1620s.[36] Large quantities of arms had to be contracted for, acquired and tested before they were distributed to the army. As the office, together with the arms industry, was based in the south-east, most of the arms had to be sent the length of the country. Transport facilities had to be organised on a grand scale. During the course of 1639 62 cannon, 166 lasts of gunpowder and 80 tons of musket shot were dispatched to the north, as were thousands of suits of armour and hand arms. Ships, loaded with war materials, regularly plied between London and Hull, where the main supply depot was established, for transhipment to the rendezvous at York. Some cargoes were taken further north, to Newcastle or Holy Island. For the second war, a smaller amount of *matériel* had to be moved but this was due to the foresight of the Ordnance Office in maintaining magazines in the north, notably at Hull. Even so, ships moved tons of arms, ordnance and munitions.[37]

To have collected and distributed this amount of military hardware was a considerable achievement. It was even more noteworthy because of the constraints under which the Ordnance Office worked. Apart from a shortage of manpower, it had to respond to a government oblivious of the time it took to produce goods on such a scale and with a wildly optimistic sense of the capabilities of a home armaments' industry in decline after years of peace. The provision of ordnance was less of a problem than that of other weapons because the Ordnance Office could deal with a monopolist using local raw materials and who was accustomed to fulfilling large-scale contracts for the government. The artillery train may have been stuck at Hull when it should have been at Newburn but this was due less to deficiencies in the Ordnance Office than to inadequate strategic planning, inept leadership and poor political control. It was particularly difficult to obtain goods in bulk from the hand arms industry because it was fragmented into a myriad of small units. The Ordnance Office could place large orders by contracting with the craft companies of London or with *ad hoc* partnerships but this led to delays and difficulties in quality control, standardisation and delivery.

There were corrupt practices among the ordnance officers but they were being asked to accomplish an impossible task. Their predicament is neatly illustrated when in December 1639 the government thought about putting in an order for a huge quantity of arms as a prelude to fighting the Scots again. The pikes alone would not have been ready until late 1643.[38] The main problem was lack of money. The Ordnance Office's budget of £6,000 per annum, inadequate in peacetime, was a derisory amount with which to equip an army going to war. Normally, the monarch would ask Parliament for a subsidy but because Charles was loathe to recall it, he tried to wage war without the funds which it alone could provide. The failure of the Short Parliament meant that he had to finance the second stage of the war from whatever funds he could lay his hands on.[39] Lack of money fatally damaged the war effort. Dealers and manufacturers were reluctant to do business with the king, even when they did not need payment in order to maintain production, and this affected supply. Without cash, it was far more difficult to procure arms. Moreover, lack of pay had an impact on the morale of the soldiers and made them refractory and disinclined to fight.

For their part, the Scottish Covenanters had no Ordnance Office to organise the purchase, collection and distribution of arms and equipment. Initially, they did not have a central arsenal either, for Edinburgh Castle, the obvious site, was in royal hands. How then did they manage to arm and clothe an army that defeated Charles's forces? They had to rely on imports but they also made full use of home resources. In essence they made the country an armed camp, arguing that in a time of emergency everyone had to contribute, according to their means, either in person or materially. In January 1639 a circular was sent round the counties providing details of a radical scheme that was being introduced to obtain the necessary soldiers, money and arms.[40] At the centre, the provisional government (the Tables) continued to oversee the war effort, but through a hierarchy of war committees it involved people down to the local level in the process. In each county a committee of war was set up, charged with the task of raising and drilling troops and exacting money to pay for wages and war materials. The convenor of each committee had direct communication with the Tables, while representatives from these committees, serving in three-month shifts, met together in Edinburgh, thereby providing a national forum for the views of people in the localities.[41] Membership of the shire committee consisted of representatives of the local war committees that were established in burghs, presbyteries and even parishes. These men, in turn, were answerable to their neighbours for their actions. Working through these local committees of war, the Tables asked for lists to be drawn up of able men (aged sixteen to sixty) and arms available in each parish and, equally important, the weapons these men could buy, willingly or otherwise.[42] Non-contributors were classed as 'anti-Covenanter' and fined, perhaps imprisoned, and their weapons seized.[43]

On 8 June 1640 the Scottish Parliament formally set up a successor to the Tables to oversee the war effort. Justified as a means of dealing with the immediate threat from England, the new body, the Committee of Estates, was only intended to sit until the following session of Parliament. Although conceived as a temporary expedient, it continued to act as the executive arm of the government throughout the course of the Civil Wars. The committee was given wide powers to maintain the army, deal with civic and public order and to raise taxes and loans to finance the war. Like the Tables, it also exercised authority over local and regional bodies and took over its position at the apex of the hierarchy of war committees. Four days earlier a committee for the provisioning of the army had been established with the task of ensuring that the nation's resources were effectively deployed for this purpose. On 15 November 1641 the Parliament set up two financial committees to deal with the postwar situation. The Commission for Regulating the Common Burdens was concerned with re-establishing financial order, while the job of the Commission for the Receiving of Brotherly Assistance was to administer the money paid by the English Parliament in reparation. As rebellion flared up in Ireland, arms had to be raised to equip the expeditionary force sent there from Scotland. On 21 January 1642, therefore, a specialist military subcommittee was created out of these joint commissions with the remit of ascertaining the amount of arms and ammunition to be dispatched to that country, to determine the level of army officers' pay, and to oversee the manufacture of arms and munitions.[44]

There might have been no functioning central arsenal at the beginning of the campaign but it was not an insurmountable problem. Weapons were kept in people's homes, in private armouries and in town and county magazines. The circular of January 1639 ordered the shires to provide a magazine for victuals and munitions within their border and there is evidence to suggest that the burghs, at least, also set about improving their facilities. At Edinburgh an inspection of the armoury was made in June 1638 and decisions taken to keep a proper record of arms in store and to stock only serviceable armour. At the time the armoury contained 200 double and 190 half-muskets, 66 hackbuts, 420 rests and 443 bandoliers, 207 pikes, 219 corslets and headpieces, and 2 bundles of match. In August the armoury was moved to a new location.[45] Because many of the soldiers were raised by county levies this decentralised system had its advantages. Arms were available locally and could be supplied to the troops as and when required. To a certain extent, it could also cope with the storage of arms and armaments that were coming into the country from outside. As returning officers brought caches of arms with them, they could keep them until they needed to be used. Consignments that were being imported separately created a bigger problem and presumably this led to a certain amount of stockpiling of war material, especially at Leith, the main port of entry. In 1639 the Covenanters fortified Leith (and its offshoot, Burntisland, across the Firth) and this increased its appeal as the site of a central magazine. Leith's status was probably formalised in the aftermath of the Pacification of Berwick (June 1639) that ended the First Bishops' War. According to its terms, the Covenanters had to hand back Edinburgh Castle to the king but could retain their heavy cannon and ammunition. As they did not have to dismantle the fortifications at Leith, the site was a perfect one to house the ordnance and any other arms gathered centrally.[46]

Although the English Ordnance Office cannot solely be blamed for the defeat of Charles's army, its performance can still be compared with that of the Covenanters. In the First Bishops' War the Covenanters made good use of the military resources of the country but, like the English militia, they must have acquired many weapons that were old and in need of repair.[47] Imports were far more important as a source of *matériel*. Initially, the English army had been surprised at the apparent size of the Scottish forces but on closer inspection this assessment was shown to be somewhat illusory. Sir Edmund Verney was one of those who changed his opinion, commenting on 11 June that the Scots had fewer men and were not as well armed as were the English forces.[48] He probably did not know the full extent of the military supplies that the Covenanters had received from abroad![49] In the event, their actual strength was not put to the test because Charles's advisers persuaded him to arrange a truce in spite of the fact that supplies were beginning to arrive for his army. While the Scots had kept their nerve and their resolve, the English had neither the determination nor the same commitment to the cause. When, in August 1640, the Covenanters had to fight, they were in a far stronger position than they had been the previous year. Some, if not all, of the gaps in weapons provision, identified in the parish surveys of 1638–9, had been made good. Weapons could be bought in the country, though imports shipped in by merchants or by friendly governments provided most of the arms and armaments required. Their support was particularly valuable in supplying the Covenanters with ordnance and munitions and with the raw materials to manufacture these goods at home. The benefit was seen at Newburn.

During the course of the wars the Scots also had the advantage of operating with shorter lines of communication. Cavalry patrolled the borders to monitor enemy movements and shire levies were put on 24-hour standby to muster, when bidden, complete with arms, equipment and a month's supply of provisions. Actual service was rotated among groups of four men, the person who marched out with the army having to supply himself with provisions for ten days.[50] Moreover, the Covenanters could supply their forces with arms and armaments much more quickly than the English could do, drawing many of their weapons from local and county stores. Even ordnance and munitions, stockpiled at Leith and other centres, could be transported to the army comparatively easily. The contrast with the English army, spread thinly across northern England and with fewer resources than in 1639, is highly illuminating. In addition, Charles's indecisiveness allowed the Scots to take the initiative, letting them assemble and fit out their forces for the invasion of England.[51] At Newburn the Covenanters' fire-power destroyed the English army.

THE IRISH INSURRECTION, 1641–2

Government troops stationed in Ireland were supplied with arms and equipment from the central magazine situated in Dublin Castle. When the insurrection broke out in October 1641 it was particularly well stocked since it was full of the war materials that the Earl of Strafford had collected for Antrim's aborted expedition to western Scotland.[52] Like its parent body, however, it was underfunded. An estimate of expenditure made in spring 1642, taken in the midst of a rebellion, alloted a mere £4,500 per annum for war. A further £300 was earmarked for repairing storehouses, platforms and carriages, £100 for refurbishing arms, £100 for wagons and teams, and £200 for incidental expenses.[53] The staff, though fewer than at the Tower of London, did a similar range of jobs.[54] Because the bulk of its stock came from England it was less involved in contracting for supplies than its English counterpart and was mainly concerned with the receipt, maintenance and dispatch of *matériel*. At its head was the Master of the Ordnance and Munitions, a post that Sir John Borlase filled in 1641. His deputy, the Lieutenant of the Ordnance, was Captain John Russell.[55] The Clerk of the Ordnance was responsible for keeping a record of receipts and issues. His task was made more complicated by the regular practice of shipping arms directly from England to the place or person requiring them. Gentlemen of the Ordnance carried out other administrative work. In addition, the office employed artificers to maintain and refurbish arms in store. John Leland, a blacksmith, probably worked in this capacity for in January 1642 he was paid £5 for searching for arms. He also earned a regular income making pike heads, which he delivered to the stores.[56] The Master of the Ordnance had general oversight of the other magazines in Ireland and in spring 1642 Borlase was given £200 to pay for the cost of auditing their accounts. A list of *c.* 1626 indicates that these magazines were located at Newry, Derry, Carrickfergus, Galway, Athlone, Limerick and Waterford, in each of which a Clerk of the Stores (or Munitions) was appointed to carry out the day-to-day administration.[57]

When the insurrection broke out in Ulster on 22 October 1641 the insurgents were able to make rapid progress because of the element of surprise. As they needed additional arms, they particularly targeted arsenals. On 24 October Viscount Montgomery reported to Ormond, the Deputy Lieutenant, that the Catholics had captured the magazine at Newry where they obtained gunpowder and three cannon. At Tanderagee they seized seventy barrels of gunpowder and a large quantity of arms. As the rebellion spread, the same process was repeated elsewhere in the country. Three more guns were captured at Limerick in June 1642.[58] Not all of the magazines offered rich pickings, however, for many of them had been allowed to run down before the war. When the insurgents appeared outside Cloghouter Castle, Co. Cavan, there was neither gunpowder nor a single working musket. At Galway, most of the pikes and calivers proved to be unserviceable when called upon for the defence of Portumna.[59] In both cases, the Clerk of the Stores was blamed for a lack of care and attention. Unfortunately for the rebels, they failed to take the biggest prize of all – Dublin Castle.

The retention of the magazine at the castle was to prove a vital source of arms for the Royalists in the conflict, not only enabling them to defend themselves but also providing them with the means to take the offensive. According to one account, there was sufficient military hardware there to supply an army of more than 20,000 men. Initially, the Lords Justices were somewhat reluctant to release supplies because of fears for the safety of Dublin, but once the immediate danger had passed, arms and munitions were distributed more freely. Ormond received many requests for arms; in December, for instance, arms were sent to Waterford and Derry.[60] However, because deliveries out of the stores were not adequately replaced, the situation deteriorated during the course of 1642. By the end of August the position was said to be desperate. According to the Irish Council's calculation there remained only 300 barrels of gunpowder and 150 barrels of match in the magazine at Dublin Castle.[61] If true, arms were evidently not getting through from England in the quantities needed. As in Scotland, they appear to have arrived too slowly and in insufficient amounts, suggesting that some of the problems that plagued that campaign continued unresolved. It took time to amass the necessary hardware, especially as finance remained a problem.

Apart from institutional difficulties within the Ordnance Office, the English response became mired in the struggle between the king and Parliament, especially over control of the forces and the armaments to be sent to subdue the rebels. The Ordnance Office found itself in the middle of two warring parties, severely affecting its operational efficiency. A quick reaction to the crisis was required and, taking advantage of the king's absence at the beginning of November 1641, Parliament responded on its own initiative. On 6 November the House of Commons ordered the Master of the Ordnance to deliver to the Lord

Lieutenant of Ireland arms for 1,000 horse and 8,000 foot.[62] The Lords ratified these measures but the king was hardly likely to be pleased at an action taken without his authority.[63] On this occasion he issued his own warrant, confirming the order, but the matter was bound to recur. Thus, an order made by the Parliamentary Committee for Irish Affairs on 1 January 1642 to the Ordnance Office, to issue a large quantity of munitions for the Irish service, was countermanded six days later by the king. In future, they were only to act on receipt of the accustomed authorisation, namely a warrant signed by the king or by six Privy Councillors.[64]

After the king left London, Parliament could act more freely. On 4 April it instructed the Irish Committee to provide clothes, victuals and provender and to find secure storage for them in Ireland. Parliament also told it to provide arms and munitions and deliver them to the Master of the Irish Ordnance Office.[65] Officials in the Tower did exert themselves to raise essential supplies; surveys were made of goods in store and contracts were drawn up with manufacturers to augment supplies.[66] Arms were also moved from important provincial magazines, especially from those in the north. In January three ships, laden with ammunition, arrived from Berwick and in May the entire magazine at Hull was seized by Parliament and whisked off to London.[67] During the course of 1642 the Ordnance Office purchased and transported tons of arms, munitions and equipment;[68] unfortunately, it did take time to collect the arms together and there also appears to have been a bottleneck at the ports. In September the Lords Justices complained about powder and match 'of which there is so great want' lying for weeks at Chester and of clothing and footwear being stayed by the king's warrant.[69] Charles I had his own use for them! By this time, of course, preparations for an Irish campaign had been overtaken by events in England. In August, for instance, pressing needs at home prevented an artillery train from being sent to Ireland.[70] It must have been a frustrating experience for all concerned. Just as the government found itself in a position to crush the Irish rebels – with large numbers of troops deployed in Ireland and war materials stockpiled – open hostility between Crown and Parliament diverted attention back to England.[71]

The Catholics had to create their own administrative structures. Initially, the rebellion had taken the form of a series of uncoordinated attacks, but as the Royalists regrouped and began to inflict defeats on the insurgents, the latter realised the need for some sort of political and military organisation.[72] Between 10 and 13 May a general assembly meeting at Kilkenny agreed to establish a Supreme Council that would take charge of the war effort. It also ordered all Catholics to take an oath of association. The Council met on 11 June and began its work. On 24 October representatives from all four provinces gathered together at Kilkenny and formally established an association that became known as the Confederation of Kilkenny.[73] It also appointed commanders of each of the four provincial armies and made plans for a national or 'running' army under Hugh O'Byrne. This fell through, however, because, Hazlett claims, the Supreme Council did not give O'Byrne sufficient supplies. In the event, it merged with the

Leinster army, which effectively assumed the role.[74] As war materials built up, mainly through imports, the Catholics established magazines in the territories they controlled. Their main arsenal was set up at Kilkenny, their administrative centre, but they continued to make use of pre-existing magazines at ports such as Waterford, Wexford, Galway and Limerick.[75]

THE DRIFT INTO WAR IN ENGLAND, 1642

The breakdown in relations between king and Parliament not only made it more difficult for the Ordnance Office to function effectively but also ensured that it, too, would be fought over. In June the king failed in an undercover attempt to move the stores in the Tower to York or Newcastle in order to prevent their seizure by his opponents. In addition Charles told the ordnance officers only to act on his orders. The Earl of Essex, for his part, put in his own requests for arms. Loyalist officers refused to comply, citing the king's instructions of 7 January, and suffered a short period of imprisonment. After their release, two of them, Richard March and Edward Sherborne, left London and joined the king.

Finally, in September Parliament took possession of the stores in the Tower and the Armoury. As a result, the Royalists had to create their own Ordnance Office at their headquarters at Oxford. They established their central magazine at New College and deposited their artillery in Magdalen College grove. A separate magazine, based on a collection of arms and munitions in Oxford itself, was housed in the Schools' Tower. It also served as the armoury. The county's arms were stored at Peckwater Inn.[76] To help them they had the services of many of the old office's top men. Six of the nine senior ordnance and armoury officers remained loyal and followed the king to Oxford. They included Sir John Heydon (Lieutenant of the Ordnance), Edward Sherborne (Clerk of the Ordnance), Richard March (Keeper of the Stores), Thomas Eastbrook (Clerk of the Deliveries) and William Legge (Master of the Armoury). Their secretaries, who had been personally appointed, went too. Among the workforce as a whole, the response was not as great, even after the king had issued a general pardon in March 1643 as an inducement for them to come.[77] The Ordnance Office's suppliers stayed behind, including John Browne, the gunfounder, who on more than one occasion during the war, was accused of Royalist sympathies; one or two of his men, however, did make their way to Oxford.

The king, therefore, had to recruit most of his workforce afresh, but at least he had experienced men in charge. This undoubtedly helped to minimise the disruption caused by the move. Sir John Heydon was the vital cog. A skilled administrator, he provided the essential professionalism and continuity necessary in such a crucial position, especially as from May 1643 to August 1644 the nominal head was the arrogant but ineffective Henry Percy.[78] Nonetheless, the system set up at Oxford did not exactly replicate that of the original office. The post of Surveyor of the Ordnance disappeared, as did, more importantly, that of Master of the Ordnance, though Percy, made General of the Artillery in May

1643, did an equivalent job. After Percy's dismissal in August 1644 Lord Hopton occupied the post, but as his experience was needed in the field, Heydon was soon put in overall charge again.[79] Initially, the demarcation lines between the various functions were not as clear-cut as they had been in the old Ordnance Office, with Heydon, the Lieutenant, and the two comptrollers, March and Sherborne, all being involved with the keeping and distribution of arms. Over time, a division of function did evolve: under Heydon, March assumed responsibility for the artillery and Sherborne for the army.[80]

Parliament's position was completely different. It gained control of the Tower, but the Ordnance Office, shorn of its leading officials, lacked direction and expertise. Because suitable managerial staff were hard to find, it was forced to employ men who were short on experience. Among those chosen were an army paymaster and a London hosier. It did not have a Lieutenant of the Ordnance until early 1644. While problems over personnel did reduce the effectiveness of the office in the short term, such shortcomings were outweighed by the advantages that Parliament possessed.[81] It could count on one or two officers, including James Wemyss, the Master Gunner of England, as well as on virtually all of the artificers in the Tower.[82] In addition, it could still do business with the office's traditional suppliers. One or two of them went to Oxford, joined by a few others as the war progressed, but virtually all of them readily transferred their loyalties to Parliament. The office had easier access to continental supplies too.

The struggle to secure the nation's military resources spread throughout the whole country. At a county level it focused on the militia. The monarch, as Commander-in-Chief, controlled the trained bands through his representatives there, the Lords and Deputy Lieutenants. However, because of the Irish crisis and fears of what the king would do with the troops, John Pym introduced a measure into the Commons, designed to put the county militias under the control of Lords and Deputy Lieutenants appointed by Parliament. On 5 March 1642 Parliament passed an ordinance to this effect. Charles I responded by issuing Commissions of Array, somewhat shakily based on an unrepealed statute of Henry IV, allowing the monarch to levy troops in the country.[83] In the summer both sides attempted to muster the militias. As a result, many counties experienced the unedifying spectacle of two sets of officials, armed with authorisation papers of dubious provenance, putting pressure on people to make a choice. Many tried to avoid doing so and there was much fence-sitting.[84]

A similar tug of war developed over control of local magazines and this grew in intensity over the summer of 1642 and in the opening months of the conflict. Special attention was focused on the county arsenals. All over the country partisans of both parties struggled with each other to gain possession of the weapons. To justify their actions, they cited as their authority either the Militia Ordinance or the Commission of Array. In Leicestershire in June the Earl of Stamford used the ordinance to defend his appropriation of the county's stock of munitions.[85] Charles I, in turn, told his Commissioners of Array that as part of their duties they were to take possession of all armaments they could find.[86] Important arsenals like those at Hull and Portsmouth were particularly targeted.

On 14 January 1642 the future Parliamentarian commander, Thomas Fairfax, wrote of Hull that its magazine 'is of great importance and had need to be safeguarded which if any sheres rise here will be principally aimed at'.[87] Here, the Parliamentarians acted more quickly than the king, putting in Sir John Hotham as governor before the Royalists could move. When the king arrived to secure the city and its magazine on 23 April, Hotham denied him entrance. Expecting a Royalist attack, the arms were shortly afterwards shipped to London in spite of the king's express orders forbidding it.[88] Portsmouth fell to the Parliamentarians on 5 September. Many of the coastal forts along the south coast similarly came under their control.[89] Moreover, the navy declared for Parliament, bringing with it all its stock of ordnance and munitions. On balance, Parliament fared better, both in terms of mustering the militia and the acquisition of local caches of arms. While there was a good deal of concern about the legality of both the Militia Ordinance and the Commission of Array, the latter attracted little support, even in areas later to be Royalist strongholds.

Private armouries and stables were ransacked too. At Oxford a thorough search for arms was carried out. In November a collection, made at the Guildhall, filled one cart with muskets and another with gunpowder and shot. They were then deposited in the Schools' Tower.[90] In the following March and April two further appeals were made: the second, it seems, because of the poor response to the first one. To these donations should be added others that dribbled in to the magazine in small lots. Both sides appealed to their supporters for arms and equipment and for money to pay expenses. Some gave generously. Wealthy individuals might raise whole regiments and companies of soldiers, equipping them at their own expense. The Royalist, Sir William Pennyman, for instance, maintained a regiment of horse and one of foot in the king's service.[91] More formal methods were also employed. On 9 June 1642 Parliament issued the 'Propositions', asking people to contribute money and plate or to equip and maintain the cavalry with horses and arms.[92] As the horses and arms were brought in, they were to be valued and their owners promised repayment at 8 per cent interest. People living within eighty miles of London had a fortnight to make their donation, and those further away three weeks. On 25 August the city of London was asked to donate 6,000 muskets and 4,000 pikes.[93] The Royalists adopted a similar ploy. In June 1642 a number of peers signed the 'Engagement', promising to protect the king against his enemies and organising the collection of horses, arms and equipment.[94]

Naturally, attempts were made to disarm rival supporters, a move which had the double benefit of augmenting one's own stock while denying it to the enemy. In August 1642 a house-to-house search for arms was made in London. As a result, a considerable amount of arms was confiscated at Lambeth Palace and at the home of the Earl of Dorset, as well as at suspect houses in Westminster and Covent Garden. On 31 October Cornet Wirley plundered the house of the Royalist, Robert Blank, and took away a good deal of weapons. They included one complete suit of armour, together with a hamper of assorted pieces, 47 firelocks with keys, 4 pairs of pistols with keys, cases and moulds, 50 bandoliers, a quarter of a barrel of musket shot,

55 swords, 1 rapier and 58 belts, 3 hand bills, 2 bridles and a saddle, and 48 coats.[95] Unfortunately, soldiers were not always very discriminating, and attacked the homes of supporters and terrorised whole neighbourhoods in their search for weapons. Thus, in August 1642, 500 Royalist troops were reported to be rampaging through the Rugby area looking for arms.[96] Inevitably, those who did not subscribe to requests for war materials were viewed with suspicion and greater pressure put on them. In Shropshire the Royalists asked the bailiff of Ludlow to compel recalcitrant gentry to muster with their horses, arms and equipment at Shrewsbury on 15 December 1642 or face the consequences.[97] Some found it genuinely difficult to make a decision. In Warwickshire, John Fetherston of Packwood wrote to his brother, lamenting his predicament. 'I am in a great Distraction concerninge my Armor beinge altogether vnable to satisfy my self [word indistinct in document] of Judgement & Conscienc what to doe by Reason of the seuerall Commands of the Kinge & parliament my protestacion putts me in mind that I am bound in conscienc to serve both. . . .'[98]

RIVAL ORDNANCE OFFICES AT WORK, 1642–8

When, in August 1642, England was swept up into the conflict, the work of the Ordnance Office not only expanded, it grew in complexity and threw up some unique problems. Two rival offices existed, vying for arms and munitions and operating in a more hostile environment. Because the country was divided into two (unequal) halves, resources were spread more thinly, both in terms of raw materials and in manufactured products. There were also problems of adapting to the specific circumstances of the conflict; the war was largely fought on land and the office's traditional role and expertise lay in provisioning the navy. Officers might take advantage of the wartime command economy, backed up by military force, but the nature of the conflict tended to fragment their authority. Neither side had complete control over the handling and distribution of weapons. Armies possessed a parallel commissariat structure, while secondary arsenals were established or developed. There were certain advantages to be gained from decentralisation but it did make it more difficult to keep a track on supplies. In practice, local officials developed their own semi-autonomous networks and exercised a good deal of independence.

War made effective control of strategic supplies vital and both sides sought to tighten up the system of authorisation. Without the king and the Privy Council as the natural focus of authority Parliament had to establish its own structure. On 4 July 1642 it instituted as its executive arm, the Committee of Lords and Commons for the Safety of the Kingdom, following the example of a similar committee created for the city of London earlier in the year.[99] It remained in existence until 1645 but over time it lost authority to other bodies; the Committee of Both Kingdoms, for instance, took over much of its executive power. Set up in January 1644 as a result of the Scottish alliance, it coordinated the affairs of the two countries. It did do much of the work of the older committee but operated in a more effective way, even though generals often resented its interference in military matters. It comprised five members from the House of Lords and ten from the Lower House, as well as three Scottish representatives.[100] Instructions to the ordnance officers to order *matériel* might originate in the House of Commons or with one of these two committees but other, more specialised, bodies were involved too. The pre-war Committee of the Navy, for instance, continued to order and distribute naval stores. It had no army equivalent, though the Committee of the Army, set up in March 1645, did deal with the task of supplying the New Model Army. In June 1645, in response to shortages in the supply of munitions, a Committee for Powder, Match and Shot was formed. The work of these committees was not mutually exclusive; indeed, the Committee of the Navy often supplied munitions to the army. There was a similar overlap in personnel.[101]

The Royalists attempted to impose greater control. To issue arms, a signature from the king, the main army commander or the commanders of the horse and foot regiments was normally required. In practice, it was not quite that straightforward. At Oxford, the queen's stores, although deposited in the New College magazine, remained semi-detached and her nominees were able to issue arms from it. To obtain stock from the Ordnance Commissioners' stores in the Schools' Tower a royal warrant was necessary. In June 1643 the commissioners had to be ordered to yield authority to Henry Percy, the newly created General of the Artillery, and thereafter he transferred arms by countersigning royal warrants.[102] In addition, the governor of Oxford, as commander of the garrison, used his position to draw *matériel* from the main magazine. On 9 April 1643, for example, he asked Heydon to deliver half the normal proportion of match to an officer from Colonel Gerrard's regiment. Heydon did so but under protest. After the king left Oxford in June 1644 the situation grew worse.[103]

There were other problems. For example, the decentralisation of production made it difficult for ordnance officers properly to supervise the ordering and dispatching of arms and equipment. Moreover, local governors and commanders did not always heed instructions from Percy. They might, for instance, help themselves to imported arms being taken to Oxford. In January 1644 John Strachan, the keeper of the magazine at Weymouth, told Percy that 'ye Governors heere in the west were all like kings in theire owne parts where they governe'.[104] Keepers of regional magazines experienced the same problem. At Bristol Richard March complained that Sir Francis Hawley, deputy governor of the city, was attempting to acquire arms on his own initiative. On 24 January 1644 he informed Percy that Hawley was illegally trying to obtain gunpowder from Weymouth and asked him if he would assign all gunpowder going to Bristol to him.[105]

Perhaps surprisingly, given the upheaval, the Royalist Ordnance Office became operational quite quickly, a tribute to the skill and experience of its personnel. Initially, nominated Ordnance Commissioners, charged with looking after the artillery train, carried on the administration, but from December the pre-war staff were back in place. The record of receipts and issues, probably the work of Sherborne, the old Clerk of the Stores, dates from this time and shows a fully working system. The office was mainly concerned with supplying ordnance and munitions to its clients, whether field armies, smaller detachments or garrisons and most of the issues refer to ordnance, musket- and cannonballs, match and gunpowder. Normally, quantities allocated to the artillery train were listed separately from those earmarked for the horse and foot regiments. Side arms were supplied but rather infrequently.[106] The preponderance of ordnance and munitions in the magazine is indicated in the inventories, suggesting that weapons were generally issued separately, perhaps out of the armoury in the Schools' Tower. The pattern of its deliveries reveals that it did restrict itself to southern England. In the north the Earl of Newcastle established a separate Ordnance Office, making his son, Viscount Mansfield, the nominal head as General of the Ordnance, and Sir William Davenant, the Lieutenant-General of the Ordnance.[107] It received supplies from private armouries as well as from northern manufactories but the bulk of the *matériel* probably came in as imports, chiefly from the Low Countries, from summer 1642 onwards.[108] In turn, convoys of munitions from the north brought welcome relief to Oxford.[109]

The Parliamentarian Ordnance Office, on the other hand, took some time to get going. Initially, its main function appears to have been as a provider of ordnance and shot to Essex's army and to towns and fortresses under Parliamentary control.[110] Until 1644 other war materials were largely purchased elsewhere. As before the war, the Ordnance Office was hampered by a shortage of money and delays in acquiring and replacing stock. Typically, the purchases made tended to go to the navy and the land forces suffered.[111] Because the navy was given such preferential treatment, it was often asked to make available some of its stock to the army.[112] In 1644 attempts were made to improve the situation and supplies did begin to flow in greater quantities. However, it was the creation of the New Model Army in 1645 that really transformed the fortunes of the Ordnance Office. Parliament recognized the fact that, if the hopes pinned on the new army were to be realised, it had to finance and equip it properly. As the major supplier, the office benefited. In 1645 and 1646 it provided the bulk of the arms and munitions, as well as the ordnance. A separate magazine for the army was established in the Tower and *matériel* diverted to it.[113] When the army began its western campaign after the Battle of Naseby, the arms and equipment were moved to a new magazine at Reading. William Botterell, who had previously been clerk of the Eastern Association's arsenal at King's Lynn, was put in charge.[114] Fully occupied, the Ordnance Office had little spare capacity to supply the other armies or local forces and garrisons.

Clearly, the rival Ordnance Offices did not monopolise the distribution of war materials to the forces. Indeed, among the Royalists, the trend was towards decentralisation. An early example was the use of stock from Oxford to establish an arms depot at Reading in November 1642. More importantly, Bristol, after its capture in July 1643, was developed as a manufacturing and distribution centre. So vital was the city to the Royalist war effort that Richard March was sent to take charge there. He seems to have had a general supervisory role over the whole of the south-west, for he communicated with individuals at ports in the region and was occasionally away from Bristol, presumably on business.[115] Bristol did send arms and munitions to Oxford but it also supplied goods directly to other forces. During the course of 1644 Bristol's importance relative to that of Oxford increased, though it never completely supplanted it. At a Council of War held in April 1644, Rupert, conscious of the exposed position of Oxford, recommended that Bristol should become the main centre for the arms and armaments industries.[116] Weymouth and Worcester also possessed well-stocked arsenals, the one based on large-scale imports and the other on local manufactories. Like Bristol, they had their own distribution networks, although arms were sent to Oxford or passed between them.

Parliament moved in the opposite direction, with the Ordnance Office achieving greater prominence with the provisioning of the New Model Army in 1645 and 1646. In the early stages of the war the magazine, assembled for the Committee of Safety by Owen Rowe and John Bradley, helped fill in the gaps. It provided weapons for Essex's army and was the probable source of many of its arms.[117] Samuel Cordwell and John Berisford, the leading Parliamentarian gunpowder manufacturers, initially deposited their stock in this magazine and only seem to have begun dealing with the Ordnance Office well into 1644.[118] Arms could be drawn from one or two other magazines in London. The city militia's magazine lay at Leadenhall and while its main function was to supply arms for the defence of the capital, it served as a useful reserve pool of weaponry for dispatch elsewhere, if necessary. Similarly, the contents of the magazine of the Irish Adventurers were at times diverted for other uses. Some of the bigger provincial magazines had independent sources, even if they did acquire some munitions from central stores. Thus, the Eastern Association's arsenal at King's Lynn was largely stocked with *matériel* obtained from merchants, who had either bought it locally, in London, or abroad. In early 1644, for instance, Bartholomew Wormall, a King's Lynn merchant, brought over from the Netherlands arms worth almost £8,000.[119] Smaller magazines might utilise local supplies. At Coventry the keeper dealt with a number of artificers, who provided some of the militia's requirements in arms and munitions.[120]

Arms flowed through the system at all levels. War materials percolated down from the central arsenals, and well-stocked local magazines, like the one at Stafford Castle, distributed goods as well as received them. On 16 May 1644 the keeper of the stores there took delivery of a large consignment of arms, munitions and ordnance and in the following months doled them out in small lots to garrisons and forces operating throughout the West Midlands.[121] The strategic importance of the commodities concerned created a certain tension in the minds of the persons controlling them. On the one hand, commanders and governors, conditioned by the instinct for self-preservation, were loathe to relinquish their hold on valuable *matériel*. In April 1643 the authorities at Gloucester justified their refusal to send arms to Bristol with the excuse that the inhabitants had provided them solely for the defence of their city.[122] On the other hand, the war had to be won and the ebb and flow of battle made it essential that scarce supplies should be moved to places where they were needed. When, in April 1644, Lord Loughborough, the Royalist commander in the East Midlands, informed the king of his inability to supply his forces and garrisons with gunpowder, Charles asked Prince Rupert if he could send him some barrels from the stores at Dudley Castle. In return, he promised to replace them out of the New College magazine.[123] This was such a typical practice that the carriage of munitions from one magazine to another at times resembled the movement of pieces on a chessboard.[124]

Because of the increase in the number of magazines and in the amount of business being conducted, more people were needed during the war to administer the system and to maintain the arms and equipment. This might spread resources more thinly. At Banbury the Royalists had fewer than six cannon but they still needed a keeper and a gentleman of the ordnance, fourteen gunners and matrosses, and a gunsmith and his mate to look after them.[125] Officers, moreover, could not merely mothball the arms but had to keep them in readiness for immediate use.

The rival Ordnance Offices had the biggest problem in keeping the weapons in good repair. At Oxford, gunsmiths were brought into the city and housed in the Schools' Tower, which served as a workshop as well as an armoury. In London officials took advantage of the established arms industries there to put out much of the work to outsiders, though the furbishers did share in it. Between 1642 and 1649 Robert Steadman earned £197 16s repairing swords, pikes and firearms. In the years 1642–7 George Fisher did £182 16s 10d worth of work. Typically, they had to wait several months before being paid. Owen Rowe and John Bradley similarly employed a large number of artificers, mostly at piece rates, to refurbish the weapons and accoutrements in their magazine. Local arsenals were involved in the same process, though the arrangements made differed from place to place. At Arundel the armourers worked in the castle, maintaining the arms of the magazine there.[126] At Coventry, some were put on a retainer and paid a wage, while others worked at piece rates. It is often possible to identify those 'on the staff'; apart from the wages, they worked more regularly than others. At Coventry, they included men like John Guy, the gunsmith, and Nicholas Jackson, the pikemaker. Obviously, there was less work to do in the smaller magazines than in the bigger ones, but in the aftermath of an engagement, a campaign or the return of a body of soldiers, the amount of business might suddenly grow.

The war also stimulated production at magazines. At Oxford, the Ordnance Commissioners, Sir George Strode and William Wandesford, steadily encroached on the work of the artificers during the course of 1643. By the end of the year they were involved in the manufacture of gunpowder, swords, pikes, ordnance, match and shot.[127] Nationally, Parliament tended to continue using the traditional method of contracting out for supplies. The furbishers, Robert Steadman and George Fisher, and the plumber, Daniel Judd, did sell goods to the Ordnance Office but as independent manufacturers. Locally, however, some Parliamentarian magazines were engaged in making arms and armaments. They often did so as a means of making good deficiencies in stock; there was never enough military hardware to go round and smaller garrisons, put at the back of queue, were less likely to be served.[128] At Nottingham, firearms, swords and pikes were being made in the castle.[129]

The armed forces, through the commissariat, also dealt direct with the suppliers of war materials. Each army had its own set of commissary officers, charged with acquiring a wide range of goods and services. At the head of the commissariat were the commissary-generals and below them a number of regimental and company officers. Each troop had a quartermaster.[130] Traditionally, they were responsible for obtaining goods such as victuals, clothing, draught animals and fodder, items not covered by the Ordnance Office. However, they did deal in arms and munitions too. John Phipps, for instance, was Commissary of the Ammunition in the New Model Army.[131] Because they requisitioned goods and enforced free quarter, commissary officers were not very popular with the local residents. Nevertheless, they brought some semblance of order to the system, which was preferable to the free-for-all that would have occurred (and did occur) if individual officers were allowed to act on their own initiative. Colonel Fraser of Parliament's West Midlands Association army certainly thought so. In May 1644, he wrote to his commander, the Earl of Denbigh, to complain about the soldiers, who committed 'such incivillities and wrongs . . . by taking of horses monie and clothes from cuntrie people who are our freinds. . . .' With this in mind, he claimed that a commissary officer would do less harm to the country than captains sending out their soldiers to bring in provisions.[132]

Commissary officers might buy goods privately or in the open market. Some of the supplies came from local sources. Thus, entries in the accounts of John Cory of Norwich, high collector of the weekly assessment for the Eastern Association, refer to consignments of various sizes as, for example, the purchase of eighty swords from Sam Calthorne, £44 worth of arms from James Brockden and seven swords and two belts from Thomas Browne.[133] Commissary officers might spend large sums of money; one such man was Lieutenant Russell, employed by the Eastern Association to buy horses. During 1644 he visited such noted centres as Bedford, Bury St Edmunds, Huntingdon, Northampton and Stamford and spent a total of £6,112 18s 8d.[134] Cargoes also came from London. In early 1644, the Eastern Association employed Captain West as an agent there. In less than three months he bought £6,665 worth of arms in the capital, much of it from Edward Barker of Coldharbour.[135] County militias had their commissary officers too. In Kent Captain Charles Bowles was Receiver-General and treasurer to the committee, as well as County Commissary. For repairs he used local people but he made his purchases in London, where he dealt with leading contractors.[136] At Stafford Mr Flower combined the posts of Keeper of the Magazine at the castle and Commissary for the Ammunition.[137]

SCOTLAND AND IRELAND, 1642–52

In Scotland the Covenanters continued to manage affairs in the same way as they had done during the Bishops' Wars. The Committee of Estates directed the war effort, specifically through its army and financial committees.[138] On 26 July 1644 at the inaugural session of the First Triennial Parliament a new commission was given to the Committee of Estates, and on 10 January, following a sessional committee, the Committee for Managing the War was established to oversee the war in the three kingdoms. It only sat during the Parliamentarian session and was replaced by a similar committee on 8 July. Both were subject to Parliament's authority. At the fourth session, on 29 July, two new committees – the Committee for the Prosecution of the War and the Committee for Provision of the Army – took over. In turn, the Committee of Dispatches, set up on 1 December, continued the work. The split in the Covenanter ranks caused by the Engagement of 1648 led to the exclusion of its supporters from government as well as the army, when the Kirk party regained control. This is reflected in the composition of the Committee for the Affairs of the Army, appointed on 27 November 1650 and charged with the task of unifying, strengthening and supplying the army in the face of Cromwell's invasion of the country.[139] Subsequently, after the defeat at Dunbar in September 1650, Royalists could no longer be excluded from army and administrative posts and on 25 March 1651 a new committee, the Committee for Managing the Affairs of the Army, was created to accommodate them. Although it had an uneasy relationship with the Kirk-dominated Committee of Estates, it worked hard to raise men, money and supplies for the army.[140]

In the shires local committees of war still supplied recruits, arms and equipment. On 18 August 1643 the Committee of Estates ordered that all able men between the ages of sixteen and sixty should be prepared to muster, fully armed and equipped, with forty days' provisions, within two days' notice.[141] A further order of 6 March 1645 prescribed penalties for non-compliance and made provision for those who did not have the means to acquire the requisite weapons.[142] In between these measures, an act of 4 January 1644 fixed quotas on the shires to furnish a certain amount of arms and ammunition.[143] In 1643 the shire committees were also told to provide a secure place for the storage of arms and ammunition. Two years later a further order specified the need to ensure that there were magazines for victuals, arms and ammunition in the burghs.[144] At Glasgow in February 1646 the city council ordered that all gunpowder, shot and other arms and ammunition in the town were to be sent to the tollbooth and put in the charge of Thomas Browne and Robert Mack.[145] Although these magazines were primarily used to store the arms of the burgh or county they served, *matériel* might be moved from one place to another. At the end of September 1648, for instance, 100 muskets from Edinburgh and ½ ton of lead from Glasgow were earmarked for the garrison at Dumbarton Castle and Dunglass House, probably to replace itmes taken from the castle earlier in the month by the Marquess of Argyll's forces. An inventory drawn up in July reveals an assortment of arms, ordnance and munitions, strewn around the castle, many of the items in need of repair.[146]

The central magazine at Leith, described in September 1645 as 'ane great magasen of ammunitioun and cannoun for the defence of the kingdome within the boundis of Edinburgh and Leyth',[147] distributed war materials to the forces in England and Ireland as well as in Scotland.[148] The associated magazine at Burntisland, across the Firth of Forth, facilitated the receipt from and issue of arms to north-eastern Scotland. After the Scots entered England in January 1644 Berwick became an important staging post for the transmission of arms to the forces south of the border. According to the record of issues, the quantity of arms, ordnance and munitions dispatched from Leith between 15 April 1643 and 15 November 1648 amounted to 9 cases of frames (for leather guns) and 8 petards; 157,598 lb of gunpowder, 301,622 lb of match, 45,650 lb of musket shot and 680 grenades; 19,108 muskets, with 20,130 pairs of bandoliers and 500 musket rests; 540 pairs of pistols, 8,851 swords with 7,729 belts, 5,159 pikes, 400 lances and 2,574 Swedish feathers; and 194 corslets.[149] Most of the stock was imported; the consignment that Thomas Cuningham sent from Veere in Zeeland in 1644, for instance, is revealed in the receipt of cargoes from the ships he chartered.[150] James Riddell, an Edinburgh merchant, brought in several consignments too. On 28 October 1645 a warrant was issued to Thomas Hamilton, the commissary officer for the artillery, to receive 400 muskets and pairs of bandoliers and two barrels of gunpowder from Riddell and put them into the magazine.[151] The keeper also took possession of arms and munitions manufactured in the country, especially in and around Edinburgh.[152]

Thomas Glaidstanes was the keeper at Leith with John Acheson as his counterpart at Burntisland, while John Thomson served at Berwick.[153] However, we do not know the size of the staff employed or their specific duties. Glasgow had two keepers of its magazine and they seem to have done all the administration and perhaps the work of refurbishing too.[154] Glaidstanes clearly acted as clerk of receipt and issues but he must have had others to work for him. Local artificers were certainly employed. On 20 February 1645, Thomas Moody, a gunsmith, was paid £1 9s 6d for fixing arms. Similarly, porterage was performed on a casual basis. On 13 July 1645, Captain Dick's men were paid £5 in 'drinkmoney' for moving 140 barrels of gunpowder shipped from Holland by Thomas Cuningham.[155] At an administrative level, commissary officers and commissioners were closely involved in the system of supply. William Thomson, a deputy to Sir Alexander Gibson, the army treasurer, helped administer the movement of arms into the stores and their dispatch to Engand. James Sword, a baillie of St Andrews and a member of governmental committees, was even more prominent.[156] To take goods from the store, the Committee of Estates either gave a warrant to the keeper, Glaidstanes or Acheson, or issued one to the intended recipient or his agent. On 16 February 1649, for instance, a warrant was given to the keeper to deliver 260 demi-culverin and culverin balls, destined for Stirling Castle, to Major-General Holborne or his representative. Not surprisingly, Thomas Hamilton, the commissary to the train of artillery, was the most frequent visitor.[157]

In Ireland Sir John Borlase remained in his post, which was in essence a clerical one. Responsibility for the purchase of *matériel* was carried out in England by the Irish Committee and the goods were sent over to Ireland by commissary officers like William Dobbins. Typically, on 23 June 1646 the Irish Committee told Borlase to test and examine the cannon that were being shipped to Ireland for the artillery train. Two months later he was asked to confirm in writing that the arms and other goods sent over by the contractor, John Davies, were serviceable.[158] Borlase did have money to spend (in the same month he asked for £1,000) but it was mainly used for wages, maintenance of arms and buildings and carrying expenses.[159] Moreover, because of the rift that appeared between the Irish Royalists and Parliament, especially after the cessation of hostilities with the Confederates in September 1643, deliveries declined in quantity and regularity. Apart from giving priority to its own forces, the committee tended to send the arms directly to a commander or a garrison. William Dobbins, for instance, delivered some of the arms and equipment acquired from Davies to officers in Ulster.[160] They also bypassed the Irish Ordnance Office by dealing with commissary officers in the country like Tobias Norris, the Commissary of the British Army in Ulster. On 15 August 1646 he was told to go to Chester and Liverpool to take charge of the arms sent there *en route* for Ireland. He was to store them at Belfast and distribute them according to warrants presented to him.[161]

For the Confederates the Supreme Council continued to run the war. In June 1644 reformers proposed that men with military experience should attend supreme and local council meetings 'for the better management of military affairs'.[162] They also advocated the creation of a war council, drawing its members from the same sources, with the brief 'to determine all military causes and to give their opinion and advice for the management and conduct of the armies and war'. Nothing seems to have come of this scheme nor of the one to create a national army. In early 1646 the papal nuncio, Rinuccini, complained that in spite of its inexperience in military matters, the Supreme Council took the decisions. Nevertheless, when he was in charge, he did exactly the same.[163] In this respect, failure to reform inevitably affected the prosecution of the war and mistakes were made. Moreover, the existence of separate provincial armies dissipated the war effort, even if Ó Siochru believes that the system did have certain advantages. In practice, the commanders enjoyed considerable independence of action, for once the campaigning season had started, political control tended to evaporate.[164] A national army, operating under the control of a war council, might have been able to utilise its resources more effectively.

At the provincial level councils exercised control of its forces through an army subcommittee, so surviving records, like those of the committee for the Leinster army in 1647, allow us to see how they were run. During the course of his negotiations with the Confederacy in 1646 Ormond asked for details of this army, including the amount of ammunition, match and spare arms it had in store or which could be readily obtained. In reply, he was told that there were 27 barrels of gunpowder at the castle in Kilkenny and a further 20 barrels at Kilkea. Some 2 tons and 13 cwt of match and 7 cwt of lead shot were also stored at Kilkenny but there were no spare arms. A further 120 barrels of gunpowder and 5½ tons of match were available for purchase from merchants.[165]

The Clerk of the Magazine was James Preston, who was in sole charge, though he made use of other people as and when required. As the inventory suggests, Preston was mainly concerned with receiving and issuing munitions.

Consignments were reasonably large; deliveries of gunpowder in July 1647 included two loads, totalling 109 casks, and a third weighting ½ ton.[166] Merchants were among those who provided him with war materials; also in July 1647, Patrick Archer, a Kilkenny merchant, brought a consignment of thirty-four casks of gunpowder that had been purchased from Matthew Everard.[167] In contrast, in the same month Preston went to Thomastown to obtain another consignment of gunpowder from Edmund Arlond, the 'sovereign' there. On this occasion he paid Arlond to transport the goods; at other times, he made use of Charles Kinsella, the army's carriage master, or hired a carrier.[168] From his stores Preston made deliveries to a number of army units and supplied *matériel* for the siege of Carlow. Jenico Preston was made the Clerk of the Stores for this travelling magazine.[169] The Leinster army, of course, had its own commissary officers, who might obtain arms from James or Jenico Preston or receive them direct from the suppliers. In June 1647 its roster included a commissary-general of the victuals, with two clerks; commissaries for the field and magazine, for arms and for clothing, each with their own clerk; a store-keeper; and a carriage master.[170]

THE ORDNANCE OFFICE AND CONQUEST OF IRELAND AND SCOTLAND, 1649–52

Action in Scotland and Ireland bracketed the central conflict between Crown and Parliament, giving a semblance of symmetry to the events of the Civil Wars. However, the final outcome was completely different. Between 1649 and 1652 Cromwell inflicted crushing defeats on the Irish and Scots, thereby reversing the outcome of 1640 and 1641. Of course, he was in a stronger position than Charles I had ever been. By mid-1649 the Royalists and their Scottish allies had been defeated and the king executed. Within the Parliamentarian ranks the army's supporters, the Independents, had emerged successful in the power struggle in Parliament with the Presbyterians. This ensured that the needs of the army would be more closely attended to and the money found to meet them. At last, the Ordnance Office had the means to provision the expeditionary forces, and the freedom of the market place too. No longer did they have to share the raw materials of the country or the product of the nation's armaments industry with their enemy. Superior planning and effective logistical support helped determine the outcome of the campaigns and indicates what the Ordnance Office was capable of when given adequate funding to do the job. With the money that was made available it was able to buy arms and armaments in bulk and to transport them to where they were needed. As a result, the Parliamentarian armies in Ireland and Scotland did not suffer from shortages in arms and munitions and this gave them a great advantage over their enemies.[171]

In Ireland, from the summer of 1649 supplies flooded in.[172] Ordnance was a priority. The country contained numerous fortified towns, all of which had to be conquered, and to make the task harder the defences of these places had often been strengthened over the years of conflict.[173] Cromwell's artillery train, shipped out in July 1649, seems to have comprised eleven siege guns and twelve field pieces; in size and fire-power it was superior to the combined ordnance of all other armies operating in Ireland.[174] The siege guns quickly proved their worth at Drogheda and later at strongholds such as Clonmel, Kilkenny and Wexford.[175] John Browne, the founder, furnished the forces with round shot and grenades, fulfilling a contract made on 8 May 1649. In three consignments, delivered in July, August and October, he provided 10,796 cannonballs (for cannon of eight, down to falcon), 1,299 mortar bombs (12 in and 14 in) and 800 hand grenades, weighing in total 178 tons, 1 cwt, 2 qr, 80½ lb.[176] The supply of other necessities was also carefully organised. Between June 1649 and February 1650 food valued at £51,375 was sent to the troops.[177] They also received, while at winter quarters from November 1649 to February 1650, clothing, shoes and tents, worth £32,952.[178]

The forces sent north to suppress the Scots were also well equipped and effectively resupplied by the Ordnance Office. Between July 1650 and August 1651, £29,985 was spent on *matériel*: 3,848 barrels of gunpowder, 170 tons of match, 27 tons of musket shot, 6,565 matchlock- and 514 snaphance-muskets, 2,400 carbines, 3,000 swords and 5,667 bandoliers.[179] Cromwell's artillery train consisted of 50 pieces. The Ordnance Office furnished it with large consignments of gunpowder and shot, partly for its own needs and partly for those of the rest of the army.[180] Although ordnance did not play the same dominant role as in Ireland, it was deployed to good effect in the field and at sieges;[181] George Monck, the General of Artillery, was particularly adept in the use of mortars.[182] As in Ireland, food, clothing and tents were supplied: £85,706 worth of food was shipped to the soldiers between September 1650 and July 1651, providing them with the bulk of their nutritional requirements. This not only enabled Cromwell to overcome the Scots' scorched earth policy but allowed him to keep his army in the country during the winter.[183] Most of the clothing came from England too. Between July 1650 and September 1651, 14,000 pairs of stockings, 12,824 shirts, 3,800 cassocks and breeches, and 3,002 cloaks were sent. The 33,400 pairs of shoes and 10,480 pairs of boots, delivered over an eleven-month period, allowed for two changes of footwear. In addition, the army was adequately equipped with sheltering facilities, should it have to camp in the open. When it invaded Scotland in July 1650 it took 3,000 tents with it. Furthermore, 3,050 tents and tarpaulins and 36,000 ells of tent canvas were delivered between February and May 1651 for use in the spring and summer campaigns of that year.[184]

CONCLUSION

In England, the picture of the Ordnance Office (or Ordnance Offices during the First Civil War) portrayed here is a positive one. It did have its failings: money was wasted, arms arrived late and officials, at times, were engaged in dubious practices. However, many of the problems were beyond its control. A chronic shortage of money lay at the heart of the matter, especially during the campaigns against the Scots and Irish in the years 1638–42, a weakness compounded by the lack of realism on the part of the government. When sufficient money was forthcoming – as in 1645–6 for the fitting out of the New Model Army, or in the years 1649–52 for the reconquest of Ireland and the occupation of Scotland – the office did its job effectively. During the period 1642–6 the situation was complicated by the existence of two rival Ordnance Offices and by the difficulties in maintaining supplies in the middle of a civil war. The Royalists, having to start from scratch at Oxford, faced particular difficulties but they managed to establish their office remarkably quickly. This reflects favourably on the high level of professionalism possessed by the leading pre-war officers, especially men like Heydon, March and Sherborne, who were instrumental in setting up the system. Parliament, without the same expertise, took longer to get going. Moreover, it did not initially control supplies to the same extent as did its Royalist counterpart, for other magazines – notably those belonging to the Committee of Safety and the Militia of London – were also involved in the collection and distribution of arms. Over time, however, it achieved greater prominence and in 1645 it came into its own.

In the other two kingdoms, all the contenders except the Irish Royalists had to create their own system. This did not mean that the Royalists fared any better than the others, for any advantage that they might have gained from being able to make use of existing facilities and expertise was counteracted by the drying up of their traditional source of supply, the English Ordnance Office. In fact, judging from the constant pleas they made to Parliament for supplies,[185] they suffered greater shortages. As in England, each side established a central magazine, complementing it with a network of local store places. None of the parties had the same logistical problems as faced the English, however, as they operated on much shorter supply lines. The contrasting experience of the Covenanting and the English troops in the Bishops' Wars partly reflects this point. They were not so involved with contracting for arms and equipment either, because their home industries could do no more than supply a small proportion of the goods required. In general, the organisation was more rudimentary too. Apart from the establishment at Dublin Castle there were no Masters of the Ordnance, and the Clerk of the Stores dealt with receipts and issues and looked after the stock while it was in the stores. Artificers, carriers and labourers were employed, when needed, rather than being put on the staff. Although the available evidence does not allow us to look at their organisation in detail, the Covenanters and confederates at least managed to perform creditably for most of the period. It was only when England was able fully to exploit its superior resources that the inherent weakness of their position became apparent.

3

THE SINEWS OF WAR: FINANCING THE WAR EFFORT

Financial considerations clearly are very important in an account of the arms trade in the British Civil Wars or, indeed, any conflict. If most of the money needed was spent on soldiers' pay, considerable sums still had to be disbursed on arms and equipment. Soldiers could not fight without weapons, but they would have had difficulty in obtaining them, if they were not provided with 'the sinews of war'. All of the various conflicts fought in Britain in the years 1638–52 involved real issues of principle and, without doubt, activists felt the need to uphold them, even if it meant going to war and spending money. Moreover, calculations of cost, if made, were tempered by the widely held belief that hostilities would not last long and that expenditure could be contained.

Unfortunately, the quick, clinical (and cheap) strike proved illusory. The Irish rebels hoped for success, using the element of surprise, but although they swept through most of the country, they did not quite push the Protestant establishment into the Irish Sea. In England the battle to determine the outcome of the war, fought at Edgehill on 23 October 1642, was indecisive. The king may have won on points but he failed to follow up his success by marching on London. In Scotland, the Covenanters certainly sent Charles I and his prayer book packing but, ironically, in doing so set in motion the chain of events that was to lead to a decade and a half of almost constant warfare in one part of the British Isles or another. 'Voluntary' contributions soon gave way to measures of taxation and at a high rate. Because the money tended to come in slowly, it was often used as security to obtain a loan. Nonetheless, the war bankrupted all sides. Even Parliament, which possessed the greatest resources, could not match expenditure with income. In Scotland, by the time that the wheel had turned full circle in 1651 with the defeat of the Covenanters at the hands of an English army, the country owed many millions of Scottish pounds.[1] Ireland was even more devastated.[2]

FINANCING THE WAR AGAINST THE SCOTTISH AND IRISH REBELS

Charles I had managed to cope financially during the years of peace in the period of personal rule by exploiting all the resources at his disposal. When war loomed against the Scottish Covenanters in 1638 he was confident that he needed only a modest outlay to fight the war, passing on a good deal of the cost to his subjects through their militia obligations and by achieving a quick victory. He may have calculated that the mere show of force would be sufficient to bring the rebels to heel. In the summer he heard from Juxon, the Chancellor of the

Exchequer, that the required £200,000 would be available to him for start-up costs and went ahead with purchasing arms.[3] The imposition of coat and conduct money on the counties transferred some of his expenses to others, though it caused a storm of protest and a significant number of people refused to contribute to it. Nonetheless, most of the gentry and nobility seem to have paid; even such a staunch Parliamentarian as Sir Gilbert Gerrard at Harrow-on-the-Hill.[4]

Loans and tallies were sought to cover the gap between expenditure and the receipt of money into the Exchequer. Unfortunately, because of Charles's poor credit-worthiness among the financiers, it was difficult to obtain loans and at first only £110,000 could be raised.[5] Even the full amount would have been insufficient to buy all the arms and equipment needed for an army of the size envisaged. Over winter, moreover, funds came into the Exchequer very slowly. On 25 February 1639 the Venetian ambassador reported that the king's ability to buy arms was being hampered by a lack of money and the ill will of the people. When the army was being assembled in the north in spring 1639 it was, therefore, short of pay and weapons. To the king's surprise, his subjects were no more inclined than before to bail him out with loans. Although almost £750,000 was spent in cash and tallies in 1639, it did not come in early enough and in sufficient quantities to be of much use.[6]

For the Second Bishops' War lessons were learned. Charles asked for an initial sum of £300,000 and hoped to underpin the cost of the war by calling on Parliament to vote him taxes.[7] To obtain ready money he had to lean heavily on those around him, specifically his councillors, officials and courtiers.[8] Coat and conduct money was imposed again, causing an even greater outcry than in the First Bishops' War and adding to the grievances clamouring to be heard when the Short Parliament met on 13 April 1640. Sir John Finch, the Lord Keeper, was not well received, therefore, when in his opening speech he emphasised the pressing need for money and stressed that this matter should be dealt with before the hearing of grievances.[9] Parliament's failure to deliver the needed subsidies led to its dissolution within three weeks and a crisis of funding for Charles. As in 1639, a considerable amount of money did eventually pass through the hands of the tellers in the Exchequer (£953,984 in cash and tallies) but it, too, took too long to collect and deliver to the front.[10] Lack of pay, insufficient weapons (many substandard) and a shortage of provisions sapped the morale of the Royalist troops and made them mutinous.[11] The decisive victory that the Scottish Covenanters won at Newburn on 28 August was partly due to the superior tactical sense of its commander and better logistical support, but was also facilitated by the abject state of the king's army. As a result of their success, the Scots took Newcastle and occupied north-eastern England down to the River Tees.

Defeat by the Scots cost England even more money and forced Charles to call Parliament again. The Long Parliament assembled on 3 November. If Charles had any plan, he might have hoped that defeat at the hands of the old enemy and the occupation of a part of the country would rally support to him. Specifically, he expected Parliament to vote him taxes to fight a third war and to do so before members could discuss grievances![12] In the meantime, the Scottish demands had to be met. At the peace negotiations held at Ripon the Scots insisted that their army be maintained at England's expense. Eventually, on 16 October, they accepted £850 a day. The Scots also claimed compensation for expenses incurred during the war, calculated at £515,000. On 22 January 1641 Parliament agreed to pay £300,000 sterling in 'brotherly assistance'. Collection of the £850 a day began on 23 October and in the interim period before a parliamentary levy could be raised, the money was exacted from Durham, Northumberland and the borough of Newcastle. At the same time London merchants were asked for a loan to cover the Scots' immediate requirements, though by mid-December there was still no sign of the money.[13] On 10 December Parliament did grant a double subsidy but because it proved insufficient to meet the needs of the Scottish and English armies, it had to do the same again less than two weeks later. Two more subsidies were voted through in May.[14] By the time the Scots army left England on 25 August 1641, £80,000 of the brotherly assistance had been paid and the rest promised in two instalments, due at midsummers 1642 and 1643. The daily maintenance, totalling £266,050 sterling, had also been discharged, though £38,000 was owed to the two north-eastern counties.[15]

In Ireland the rebellion came as a complete surprise when it broke out in October 1641. Typically, the initial response of the English government was to borrow money from London merchants in order to raise money quickly for soldiers and arms. In November 1641 the city pledged £50,000, albeit reluctantly; this reticence was due not only to cynicism about the prospects for recompense but also to the amounts allocated to individual livery companies. The vintners had to borrow £1,000 to raise their contribution of £5,000. In December the Merchant Adventurers put up £100,000.[16] By the following May more money was needed to purchase arms, equipment and provisions and on the 30th the Committee for Irish Affairs asked Parliament to persuade the city to loan a further £150,000. In June the livery companies were induced, again with difficulty, to subscribe £100,000. Smaller amounts came in from various other bodies.[17] Some of the money was sent over to Ireland to cover expenses there. On 7 June the Irish Council reported to the Earl of Leicester, the Lord Lieutenant, that £11,500 had arrived but added that a far greater sum was needed fully to meet the costs of the army.[18]

In February 1642 a group of London merchants floated a scheme that they claimed would cost the government little but which would raise sufficient funds to pay for a force to crush the rebels. In return for putting up the money to pay for the troops and purchase arms, they would receive confiscated rebel land. By the terms of an act passed in March the 'adventurers' were to obtain 2.5 million acres of land at the rate per 1,000 acres of £200 in Ulster, £300 in Connaught, £400 in Munster and £600 in Leinster. The goal of £1 million was wildly optimistic, given the level of risk involved. In the event, £306,718 was raised in 1642, with more coming in later. The same group of people subscribed to the 'sea adventure' of summer 1642: fifteen leading London merchants and their associates advanced money for a seaborne invasion of southern Ireland in return for additional allotments of land in the country.[19] As the situation in England deteriorated, much of the money, as well as the soldiers and arms, was diverted to home use.[20] A similar fate befell the tax authorised by Parliament in March 1642 to help meet its debts and to pay for the war in Ireland. The act allowed for £400,000 to be raised by fixed quotas on counties and some boroughs and provided for the appointment of assessors and collectors in each area.[21]

PARLIAMENTARIAN FINANCES

When Parliament went to war with the king it was, financially speaking, a novel experience. Instead of scrutinising carefully all requests for taxation from the government, members found themselves in the position of having to raise and spend large sums of money. Costs were huge, although expenditure did fluctuate according to need and circumstance. Between August 1642 and 24 March 1645 the Treasurers at War spent £1,105,826 on Essex's and Waller's armies alone, an average of £35,671 a month. If the figures for the Eastern Association and northern armies were added, the sum would be far higher. More comprehensively, the treasurers disbursed £7,323,718 between 25 March 1645 and December 1651, that is, a mean of £90,416 a month.[22] This was the period in which the New Model Army was raised and the conquests of Ireland and Scotland accomplished. The navy had to be provided for too. The Navy Commissioners paid out £1,552,672 in the years 1642 to 1647, with peak expenditure in the period from 1 January to 7 August 1643. In the four following years, 1648 to 1652, they spent a further £1,446,228, with maximum outlay similarly coinciding with the Irish and Scottish campaigns. In the period from 13 May 1649 to 31 December 1650 outgoings per month averaged £10,000 more than the peak months of 1643.[23]

Income never matched expenditure; between 1645 and 1649 the average annual deficit was running at £0.7 million and by the end of the decade Parliament was over £3 million in debt.[24] There were serious financial crises in 1643 and 1644, and between November 1646 and early 1649. The first was caused by the failure of the main sources of Parliamentarian revenue to come 'on stream' quickly enough at a time of rapidly increasing military expenditure. Ironically, the second occurred at the end of the First Civil War, a time when costs should have gone down. Unfortunately, in late 1646 the Treasury was virtually empty; many taxpayers refused to pay for a war perceived to be over and the House of Commons did not renew the main tax, the assessment, after October 1646.[25] Yet Parliament had debts to pay, including arrears to the soldiers and money owed to the contractors, as well as funding campaigns in Ireland and Scotland.[26] In spite of these problems advances were made in financial management in the 1640s, especially from spring 1645, when arrangements were being made to create and fund the New Model Army.

At first, Parliament tried to finance the war in England through loans and contributions. In London Parliament expected the City to continue to serve as a source of loans. Royalist sympathisers tended to leave the capital after the radicals had seized control in summer 1642[27] but as remaining merchants were not all partisans of Parliament, they were not necessarily eager to venture their money, and with good reason. Between 1640 and 1645 the Drapers' Company lent £150,000 to various governments, accumulating a debt of £14,000 and receiving only £425 in interest.[28] Merchants were also asked to use their contacts abroad; in March 1644 the Committee of Both Kingdoms hoped to persuade some of the richest London merchants to borrow £300,000 in Holland. Sympathisers living in the United Provinces separately sent £31,215 in aid in the years 1643-8.[29] Symptomatic of the growing wariness over the extending of credit for the purchase of arms was the comment of Sir Oliver Luke who told his son, Sir Samuel, in November 1644 that 'there is none to be had without ready money for they will not trust the State with any more'.[30] City merchants still provided loans but increasingly sought concessions as, for example, the right to appoint nominees to oversee the nation's finances.[31] Their involvement brought a greater professionalism to the job of financial management. Eight of their number were appointed to control the receipt and issue of the new monthly tax of 1645, for instance, and this made the mercantile community more willing to subscribe to the £80,000 loan secured against it. With the loan Fairfax was able to equip and arm the New Model Army.[32]

Parliament also sought to obtain money and materials by asking for contributions from the public at large. The Propositions, issued on 9 June 1642, called for money and plate, as well as horses and arms.[33] According to Wheeler, the response was impressive. In the years 1642–5 over £1 million was raised in this way.[34] However, the level of contributions did vary from place to place; in north Somerset large amounts were raised, whereas in Kent, Staffordshire and Warwickshire receipts fell far short of expectations.[35] Parliament certainly thought that more should have been given and in May 1643 it imposed a tax of one-fifth on the personal estate and one-twentieth on the real estate of non-contributors.[36] In 1643, £1,418,299 was levied on defaulters but by March 1644 less than one-fifth (£260,306) had been raised. Money continued to come in for years; in the region controlled by the Eastern Association, for instance, £87,340 had been collected by 1650.[37]

The patchy response to the Propositions, coupled with the realisation that the war would not end quickly, made Parliament aware of the need for regular taxation. In this respect, it acted more decisively than the king. Moreover, starting from scratch, it could mould the system to its own design. In its anxiety to prevent an abuse of power, separate treasuries were created to administer individual sources of income and each of them was kept distinct and out of the control of money-raising bodies. Most of the money was assessed and collected locally, working through the financial subsection of the county committees.[38] At the centre the Committee of Safety was established as a military executive and among other functions acted as a link between the commander and the separate military and civilian organisations in the provinces. As noted above, when the Scots joined the war the new Committee of Both Kingdoms more effectively carried out the work.[39] To tighten up control of finances Parliament set up the Committee for Taking the Accounts of the Kingdom in February 1645.[40]

On 24 February 1643 Parliament made the first of its orders for a weekly assessment, initially for a three-month period.[41] The tax was assessed in the same way as ship money and the impost of £400,000 for Ireland had been, and had the same coercive powers. Income increased dramatically, along with the size of the taxpaying group. Dr Morrill has likened the weekly assessment ordinance of February 1643 to the voting of a Parliamentarian subsidy every fortnight.[42] Even so, it proved insufficient to pay for the main field armies. Only £129,819 had come into the central Treasury by March 1645, though much more had stuck to the hands of county treasurers.[43] To increase the income John Pym tried to introduce an excise but it met with considerable resistance; after all, it had been denounced in the Grand Remonstrance and was unpopular among the people. It was eventually passed on 22 July 1643 under the title of the 'new impost' so as to reduce opposition to it.[44] This did not make it any more popular than before. At first, the ordinance put a duty on tobacco and alcohol and on a variety of imported groceries and luxury goods. Over the course of the next two years other commodities were added to the list, including meat and salt in January 1644.[45] Customs dues, which had been an important source of income for Charles during the eleven years of personal rule, continued to be exacted and were specifically earmarked for the navy.[46] Between August 1643 and May 1649 this source provided it with £1.1 million, 74 per cent of the sum spent.[47]

Sandwiched between the assessment and the excise was Parliament's sequestration ordinance of 27 March 1643, allowing for the seizure of enemy property. The task of administering the confiscated land was carried out locally by agents appointed by county committees.[48] An ordinance of 18 August eased the hardship by allowing up to one-fifth of the estate to be retained. Moreover, many agents, who often knew the victims, adopted a moderate stance.[49] In practice, too, Royalists may have been able to compound for their estates, a development that gradually expanded and became law in August 1645.[50] Between 1643 and 1652 the central treasuries received £377,535 from sequestration and £1,285,205 from compounding.[51] In order to meet the financial crisis of the late 1640s land was sold off. Sales of episcopal land, initiated after bishoprics were abolished in October 1646, enabled Parliament to secure loans and over time reduce the debt burden. The process was slow but by 1655 it had paid off £676,000.[52] In spring 1649 Dean and Chapter land was put on the market, most of it being sold or contracted for by September 1650. Proceeds helped to boost the government's credit among the arms and provisioning contractors, then being asked to supply the Irish and Scottish expeditionary forces.[53] In July the royal estates were disposed of in order to meet the soldiers' arrears, a necessary prerequisite before the army could set out for Ireland.[54] In March 1650 the sale of fee farm rents helped to meet the cost of continuing military action in Ireland and the purchasing of supplies for the invasion of Scotland.[55]

In the first two years of the war the excise provided the main source of income for the field armies.[56] The Ordnance Office was given specific allocations out of the tax for arms and ammunition: £3,008 on 4 July 1644 and six monthly payments of £2,000 from August onwards.[57] Revenue was often used as security for loans (as was the assessment). Between September 1644 and September 1645, for instance, at least £156,000 of anticipated revenue from the excise was spent on the army, and £281,000 the following year.[58] In 1645 the excise was replaced by an improved assessment, now collected monthly, as the basis of funding. It was calculated to bring in £53,436 a month. In the long run, it did provide the bulk of the income acquired by the Treasurers at War but because the cash came in slowly, roughly one-quarter of the immediate revenue had to be obtained from loans and composition fines.[59] Nonetheless, the Ordnance Office continued to receive funds from the excise, as did the Committee for Powder, Match and Shot.[60]

Where imposts were assessed and collected in the counties, officers at the central treasuries regularly had difficulty in getting local officials to hand over the money. In Staffordshire, they ignored the instruction to send the assessment money to the capital, choosing instead to distribute it to commanders and garrisons in the county. In the Eastern Association much of the money collected on the Propositions and the weekly assessment was spent locally.[61] Tensions also existed between various Association treasurers and those of the constituent counties. The Earl of Denbigh, commander of the West Midlands' Association, for instance, had trouble with the Warwickshire committee.[62] Apart from squabbles about military authority, the deployment of the troops and the allocation of scarce resources, there were political and social differences too. Denbigh, a moderate, was worried that the conflict was destroying the established social order and disparagingly said of committees, 'they are not born to it'. County officials were unhappy with the procedure for collecting composition fines which, unlike sequestration, was dealt with centrally and therefore was out of their hands. For this reason they disliked the monthly assessment, introduced to fund the New Model Army, because London merchants ran it rather than, as before, county officials.[63]

Paper calculations of revenue did not always match the sums actually raised. In spring 1643 the Eastern Association army faced a financial crisis, with little money available for pay, arms or equipment. Royalist agents in London reported that Parliament 'want money for their Army extreamely'.[64] At Newport Pagnell, Sir Samuel Luke, the governor and Parliamentarian Scout-Master-General, constantly badgered those county committees, whose funds maintained this vital outpost, to pay their dues. Bedford was particularly recalcitrant. In his letters to London, which have to be read with due attention paid to special pleading and embellishment, he painted a terrible picture of a mutinous and demoralised soldiery, without pay or adequate food and clothing and with no money to buy arms.[65] Sir William Brereton, the Cheshire commander, also complained about the shortage of money to buy arms. In spring 1645, having just failed to take Chester, he wrote to the Committee of Both Kingdoms, asking for money and backing up his plea with accounts of his troubles. On 12 April he got what he wanted, £5,000, loaned from the London livery companies on the

security of the excise. Three weeks later Parliament granted him £835 from the
Court of Wards and Liveries, a portion of the £2,125 given to him to buy 500
sets of cavalry armour, pistols and saddles. In September, preparing to invest
Chester again, he obtained a further £10,000 out of the excise. Even so, at the
end of October Brereton complained that he had only received £2,000 and that
£1,600 had already been spent on ammunition.[66] Brereton appears to have done
particularly well because he was needed to spearhead the assault on Chester. The
city, a Royalist stronghold and arms centre, was a vital link with Ireland and
could be used to bring soldiers and arms into the country. Its importance grew
over time, as the Royalists were forced back into their western heartland, and its
capture was of great strategic importance.

Most of the expenditure made on the army went on pay and it is not always
easy to discern the proportion devoted to the purchase of *matériel*. In 1644 the
Eastern Association spent on average £6,197 a month on munitions and horses,
a similar proportion to the sum earmarked for the New Model Army.[67] In 1645
the wages bill of the New Model Army was expected to total £45,000 a month,
which would leave over £8,000 for the purchase of arms and equipment.[68]
Unfortunately, the sum proved insufficient, even for the soldiers' pay, though the
money set aside for arms was a reasonable one. On 10 March the Commons had
agreed to allocate £31,989 for the purchase of arms, equipment and clothing for
the horse and foot regiments and £4,406 for the artillery train. Between April
and August contracts were issued, totalling £31,233 16s 0d.[69] The expense of
equipping soldiers was considerable and even at troop level costs soon mounted.
When the accounts of a troop of horse in the Earl of Essex's army were drawn up
in July 1644 it was revealed that £2,033 16s 0d had been spent on horses,
firearms, armour and saddlery.[70] Many officers, therefore, had to dig deeply into
their pockets to equip and maintain units of soldiers and the expenditure they
had made was emphasised in their accounts, when presented for auditing.

A lack of money inevitably had the greatest impact on the pay of the soldiers,
but suppliers suffered too. Delays in repayment affected their cash flow,
hindering the purchase of essential materials and putting some of them out of
business. Many were recompensed within a reasonable space of time but at the
end of the Second Civil War they were still owed thousands of pounds for arms
and equipment. The worst affected were those who had dealt with the
Committee of Safety, the London militia and various local forces in the early
stages of the war. Some suppliers who delivered goods in 1642 were not paid
until 1644.[71] Although the situation improved, the problem remained. Between
1644 and 1648 the Ordnance Office issued warrants with a recorded value of
£46,142 11s 5¾d and at the end of the period £18,327 4s 0¾d remained unpaid
(mostly from 1645 to 1646).[72] Those who contracted with the Army Committee
did better. Its treasurers paid out nine-tenths (89.4 per cent) of the £104,682 13s
5¼d owed in the period from March 1645 to December 1648.[73] Even the largest
contractors at times had to wait. At the end of 1648 John Berisford and Samuel
Cordwell, the leading gunpowder makers, were owed about £5,000 and over
£2,000 respectively. Thomas Steventon and John Freeman were similarly owed

large sums for match.[74] In such circumstances Parliament tended to adopt an *ad hoc* arrangement, plundering whatever account had money in it. At the beginning of 1650 Daniel Judd, the main supplier of lead shot, possessed three warrants, issued between February 1648 and June 1649, for the payment of £1,885 out of the £12,000 allocated to the committee from the excise. However, because other large bills had to be settled first, he could not be paid from this source. The Army Committee, anxious to satisfy such an important contractor, ordered Sir John Wollaston, one of the Treasurers at War, to give him £125 from Hampshire's assessment and £1,760 from that of Kent.[75] Judd was based in Kent and this made the money easier to collect and the county committee more ready to pay. Evidence from 1648 suggests that this was a common practice: Kent paid John Browne, the gunfounder, and Northamptonshire the Northampton shoemakers.

ROYALIST FINANCES

When Charles went to war with Parliament in 1642 he had had a number of years' experience of trying to find sufficient income to fund his government. War brought extra expense and obviously could not be paid for with a Parliamentarian subsidy! The loss of London, its taxpayers and customs receipts was a particular blow. On the other hand, he had the support of many of the richest peers in the country and they were willing to supply him with money. Moreover, he could use the pressure of war to exact greater sums than ever before, even when backed up with Parliamentarian sanction. In addition, he had the example of Parliament to provide him with ideas for ways of raising revenue. The contribution, excise and sequestration all had Parliamentarian precedents and he continued to draw from the customs what income he could. Somewhat ironically for the monarch who had imposed ship money, he was worried about the legality of imposing taxes unilaterally. Thus, contributions, the Royalist equivalent of assessments, were first described as loans and voted in by grand juries or groups of freeholders. For some time he was reluctant to sequestrate the estates of his opponents, viewing the measure as an attack on property rights.

Initially, control of Royalist finances was given to John Ashburnham, Treasurer at War from November 1642. He did not enjoy sole authority for long, however, for on 27 December Charles I issued a proclamation, removing the Exchequer of Receipt and the Office of First Fruits and Tenths to Oxford. About a dozen Exchequer officials transferred there and with their help, the Exchequer began operations on 12 February. Edward Hyde became Chancellor on 3 March. The dual system led to friction between the two offices and to problems with auditing, and undoubtedly it hampered the Royalist war effort.[76] According to Wheeler, Royalist financial and administrative shortcomings constituted their greatest weakness and the single most important reason for their defeat.[77] In the counties, administration was in the hands of the Commission of Array or, where replaced, by new commissions reconstituted as committees 'for the guarding of the county'. The primacy of their financial role is revealed in the instructions that the king gave to the latter committees in 1643. In essence they had to raise a county tax to pay for the local forces; obtain a voluntary contribution from the wealthier inhabitants and dispatch it to Oxford; and make a list of Parliamentarians and the value of their estates, for future reference.[78] The earmarking of distinct sources of revenue for local forces and the field army neatly sidestepped the problem that the Parliamentarians faced but it did not ensure that all of Oxford's proportion was sent there.

The king began soliciting donations from the nobility and gentry in summer 1642 and continued to ask for help thereafter. In September he pressed the Earl of Kingston for a loan of £5,000, promising to repay it 'as if you had all my Crown land engaged for it'.[79] The list of subscribers is impressive and the money they gave provided the king with the means to recruit an army and equip the soldiers. The support of men like the Marquess of Worcester, the richest peer in the kingdom, and his son Edward, Lord Herbert, was particularly welcomed. As early as July 1642 Herbert sent £5,000 to the king and with the money Charles raised his first cavalry regiment. The family's money also financed and equipped the Marquess of Hertford's troops when they secured much of South Wales and the southern March in autumn 1642. By the end of the war the Marquess of Worcester had spent nearly £1 million on the Royalist cause, as had the Duke of Newcastle.[80] The king could also borrow money from financiers such as Sir Nicholas Crispe, who had joined him at Oxford. Richard Lloyd later recalled that he knew 'some Londoners of greate estates that continued at Oxford and diueres other monied men'.[81] The universities contributed £25,000.[82]

Invitations to contribute soon gave way to forced loans. In September 1643, for instance, the king demanded a loan of £4,000 from Worcester and a further £3,000 from the county.[83] The following year, he issued the so-called 'Privy Seal letters', asking wealthy individuals for specific sums of money, a measure which he hoped would raise £100,000. [84] He also sought help abroad. The queen, who left for the continent in February 1642, was particularly active, pressurising her relatives in the United Provinces and France for money and arms.[85] Shortly after her arrival at The Hague, the stadtholder, Frederick Henry, obtained a loan of 300,000 guilders for her on his own credit. Similarly, he put himself forward when it became clear that the queen's attempt to pawn the crown jewels would founder unless he lent his name to the transaction.[86] The Amsterdam merchant, John Webster, was involved in the affair and along with a number of Royalist expatriates, negotiated other financial deals too.[87] The money was used to bring in shiploads of arms.

Charles wrung money out of whatever sources of income he had to hand. He sold titles and honours: sixty-seven new baronets were created in the years 1642–4. In September 1642, while at Shrewsbury, he raised Sir Richard Newport to the peerage for £6,000. In March 1643 the Earl of Worcester bought a marquisate for more than £100,000 in cash and arms.[88] Roman Catholics were asked for an advance on their recusancy fines and this netted nearly £5,000.[89] The Court of Wards, though reduced in circumstances, yielded £12,570 in the period from February 1643 to June 1646. Clerical taxation in the form of first fruits and tenths added a further £9,064. This source of revenue, though modest, was particularly useful in the first year of the war. In Easter Term 1643 it provided over two-thirds (68.1 per cent) of the £6,784 received into the Exchequer.[90] Plate was melted down and minted as coins. While at Shrewsbury the king summoned Thomas Bushell, the master of his mint at Aberystwyth, to coin plate that Sir John Byron had brought from Oxford. When the king moved to Oxford later that year the royal mint was established in the city in New Inn Hall Street with Bushell in charge.[91] Further appeals were made for plate. At Shrewsbury in September, the king urged the gentry to make donations, offering to melt down his own plate first. Over the winter, Oxford colleges were again asked to contribute. In Cornwall, the gentry sent in plate worth £3,000 in April 1643. On 22 May 1644 a mint was established at Worcester.[92]

Like Parliament, the king soon realised that he would have to introduce some form of regular taxation. The process of giving contributions began in Oxfordshire on 21 December 1642 when the gentry agreed to make regular payments to support the field army stationed there. Because each county had to give its consent, it took time to get overall agreement. Denbighshire gentry did not fix a rate until July 1643, having refused to make one the previous month.[93] The caucuses that decided the matter did not have that much choice; apart from the evident need to raise considerable sums of money, the alternative was an unregulated free-for-all in which the forces took what they wanted.[94] In Yorkshire, Newcastle levied the 'Great Sess'. Introduced in April 1643 to raise £90,000 in three months, it was then reissued at the rate of £30,000 a month.[95] Altogether, the fifteen counties under Royalist control contributed £6,700 a week, £6,000 of which was spent on the army.[96] In Gloucestershire, taxpayers were allowed to pay up to half of their assessment in kind at fixed rates and this option was a common one.[97] The Royalists also followed Parliamentarian precedent when they introduced an excise tax in May 1644. Committees were set up in a number of English towns and counties. The returns were variable, generating a good deal of income in Worcester but little in Welsh border counties. In the north and the north Midlands it had little effect because it was brought in at a time when the Royalist cause was in decline in the region.[98]

The king, after some hesitation, allowed his officials to sequestrate opponents' land, when in January 1644 he permitted the Gloucestershire committee for the guarding of the county to act on its own initiative. As unsanctioned seizures of enemy property had been made for some time, it was hardly a new departure. The value of sequestration to the Royalists is hard to assess because of the lack of evidence; all that we have is material on individual estates. In Herefordshire, for example, the Harley estate brought in £2,250 in 1643 and in Warwickshire the Earl of Middlesex's estate produced £600. In Glamorgan the committee exploited the mineral resources of sequestered land.[99] Customs receipts further augmented the king's income. Trade through Newcastle and Bristol was particularly valuable but south-western ports such as Dartmouth, Exeter and Falmouth also provided much needed income. Some of it was sent to Oxford; between February 1643 and June 1646, £13,760 was paid in.[100] Most of the customs receipts were spent locally, however. At Bristol they helped finance the garrison.[101] In February 1644, the Earl of Marlborough, the Royalist admiral, was able to fit out a number of his ships with £1,000 that he had received from the customs officials in the western ports.[102] To encourage foreign merchants to import arms customs duties might be waived.

The area under the control of the Royalists was not, in general, as prosperous as Parliament's but they made good use of their resources. The income raised was proportionately on a par with the revenues received by Parliament. They did this by adopting the same fiscal devices and the same persistence towards defaulters. There were signs in 1643 that within their sphere of influence, the administration was settling down and beginning to operate with increasing efficiency. In Worcestershire, this is reflected in the reduction in the amount of unpaid tax. On 25 May 1643 more than half of the £12,000 due for the first four months of the year remained unpaid but a breakdown of the monthly totals reveals that the money was gradually coming in. Whereas only £54 had been paid of April's instalment, £1,361 of March's had been received, £2,055 of February's and £2,343 of January's.[103] This suggests that, as in Parliamentarian counties, the administration carried the arrears forward and maintained the pressure on the refractory. In early 1645, too, there was a resurgence in counties like Herefordshire and Monmouthshire.[104] In frontier zones, of course, there was no stability and this prevented the Royalist administration from operating from a secure base. As the Royalist territory shrank, they were compelled to raise an increasing amount of revenue from ever-diminishing resources. Inevitably, arrisons encroached on each other's preserve; in 1644 Colonel Leveson, the governor of Dudley Castle accused Colonel Bagot, his counterpart at Lichfield, of interfering with the collection of his tax.[105]

Supplies for the main field army, based at Oxford, were paid for by grants from the Exchequer or War Treasury, with revenue drawn from various sources: donations, the Privy Seal letter money, and income derived from the excise and sequestration, as well as irregular levies imposed while on campaign.[106] In February 1644 William Legge, Master of the Armoury, was allowed £2,000 out of the Exchequer to pay for swords and belts produced in Oxford.[107] Most of the business, however, was conducted through the leading Ordnance Commissioners, Strode and Wandesford, who dealt with the manufacturers and received money to pay them. In October 1643 they purchased arms and munitions with £5,000 drawn on the Exchequer.[108] Bristol, as a major arms centre and one that supplied the field army, obtained some money from central funds. Nonetheless, it was a prosperous port and thus expected to finance its own operations, using customs receipts and the contributions raised in the Bristol area. In 1644 £200–300 a week was set aside for supplies, rising to £350 in November.[109]

For the local forces, county contributions provided the principal source of funding for the purchase of war materials. At Worcester, the governor, Sir William Russell, paid out over £1,000, mainly for saltpetre, gunpowder, ordnance and ammunition, in the ten months from 10 December 1642. A special county levy had to be imposed in spring 1643 when the king ordered gunpowder mills to be made in the city. The mill near Totnes was similarly financed.[110]

At Lichfield Castle, expenditure in the period from 22 April to 16 December 1643 totalled £8,727 8s 6d, out of which almost two-fifths (£3,316 14s 0d) was spent on soldiers' pay. War materials accounted for £751 5s 0d (8.6 per cent). The money paid for the building of a gunpowder mill and a furnace in which to boil saltpetre liquor, as well as the running costs of making saltpetre, gunpowder, match and lead shot. The garrison also made ordnance, weapons and uniforms and bought cannonballs, swords, firearms, bandoliers, halberds, drums and saddlery. Facilities were available for repairing arms and ordnance.[111]

At the parish level the constables' accounts reveal the part played by local inhabitants in provisioning the county forces. Apart from their contribution money, they supplied all manner of war materials. At Upton, Nottinghamshire, the constable paid for repairs to the parochial armour and weapons and bought match, gunpowder, boots and saddlery ware. Because commissioners had to find draught teams when goods passed through their county, naturally inhabitants like those at Upton were involved. On one occasion James Bloomer's servant was paid 4d to buy cording to tie round the arms brought from Newark.[112]

Recorded figures suggest that the king had insufficient financial resources to pay for his army and their weapons. Between 11 February 1643 and 28 March 1646, Hyde accounted for £97,832 at the Exchequer. Ashburnham, as Treasurer at War, administered greater sums, including money that ought to have gone to the Exchequer. In the first year of his office, November 1642 to October 1643, he received £180,768 from various sources, of which £117,000 was used by the army.[113] Of course, these figures do not include county contributions or other sums of money raised and spent locally, but even if one projects War Treasury figures forward, the sums available for the field armies and other heads of expenditure, funded centrally, seem to have been too small. Somehow the Royalists muddled through (with God's providence according to Hyde) but,[114] inevitably, shortages occurred. Strode and Wandesford regularly had to subsidise the operation themselves. In compensation, they were granted rights over various royal parks, manors and woods, out of which they were also to pay off debts to smiths and gunmakers.[115] In autumn 1643 only two-thirds of the weekly sum of £240 due to the artillery train was received from the Treasurer at War. By the following May it was being paid out of the excise but it is doubtful if the allocation was ring-fenced for long. Shortage of money hampered the manufacture of incendiary devices at Oxford. La Roche needed over £70 a week for materials but although the value of his work was recognised, the money was not always available.[116]

Provincial receipts proved insufficient too. At Bristol they failed to come up to expectations. In November 1644 a committee had recommended that arms supply should be given top priority and first call on the receipts, yet by 22 May only £2,490 out of a total of £10,150 had been received. Richard March suggested that the excise be used to pay off the debts to the artificers – then £1,200 in arrears – and to ensure regular weekly payments. According to March, the Council faced a stark choice: without the money the arms makers could not continue, but with it they could provide weapons for 20,000 men a year. By July the money had been paid but, presumably, at the expense of other creditors.[117] In negotiations over prices and quantities manufacturers emphasised the need for ready money. In January 1644 March reported that a local plumber would make musket shot for £16 a ton if paid weekly. A gunpowder maker promised to furnish six or eight barrels a week for cash and if this were done, March thought that he could beat the man down from £5 to £4 10s 0d a barrel.[118] Uncertainty of payment also affected business with merchants. According to John Strachan, writing from Weymouth in February 1644, they were reluctant to stockpile foreign gunpowder for resale to the king because Royalist officials acted in a capricious manner, taking the goods at their own convenience and paying for them when they pleased.[119]

COVENANTER FINANCES

Like Charles I and Parliament, the initial response of the Covenanters for money was to ask their supporters for a loan. In the shires the sum was set at one dollar for every 1000 merks of income (£1 6s 8d : £666 Scots) and was based on ability to pay, not merely on land. They continued to ask for contributions too. An appeal for voluntary donations, launched in February 1643, for instance, had netted £168,000 Scots by the end of April. The Covenanters also asked for plate and in 1639 took over the royal mint at Edinburgh, coining about £293,650 Scots there between June 1639 and April 1641.[120] In addition, they negotiated commercial loans in anticipation of revenue. For example, in 1639, while waiting for the results of a valuation, they obtained loans from the mercantile community, especially at Edinburgh, the financial centre of the country. They borrowed 200,000 merks (over £11,000 sterling) from William Dick alone. In August the following year, at a critical moment in the military build-up, the government raised a further £100,000 Scots from Edinburgh merchants because taxation 'came bot slowlie in'. The burghs also acquired money in the same way. At Edinburgh in May 1639, the city council, aware of the gap between costs and income 'in these urgent times', procured a loan of £10,000 Scots from Thomas Wilson, a Leith skipper. To help pay for the Scottish troops, then about to embark for Ireland, the Commissions for Regulating the Common Burdens and Brotherly Assistance authorised the borrowing of £168,000 Scots on 28 March 1642. In August 1643 further loans, secured against future revenue, were needed to buy arms for the troops levied.[121]

The government also made use of their mercantile contacts abroad, notably at their staple port of Veere in the Low Countries. In May 1644 Thomas Cuningham, one of the factors there, was asked to act as an agent to raise money.[122] Although the project was abandoned, Cuningham did find backers for his own dealings on behalf of the Covenanters. Adrian and Cornelius Lampsins, merchants from Middleburg and Flushing, agreed to act as guarantors for the payment of £185,185 Scots worth of arms that Cuningham had obtained on credit. Settlement was due by July 1648. Unfortunately, when the time came the Engagers were in power and because Cuningham refused to supply them with arms, they repudiated the debt. It took several years before he obtained satisfaction.[123]

By spring 1639 voluntary loans were being supplemented by taxes raised at a local level. Town councils, for instance, began to impose stints on their inhabitants in order to meet the cost of their military obligations. In March Glasgow collected over £1,400 Scots for muskets, gunpowder and match and in May Dunfermline raised £400 Scots. Pressure was brought to bear on non-contributors, perhaps by seizing their assets or by imprisoning them. At Edinburgh in April 1640 the council resolved to lock such people up.[124] Assessors, generally local merchants, were appointed to allocate individual sums. At Stirling in 1641 two merchants, Patrick Sword and Robert Young, had the task of dividing up the 900 merks due from the town among the contributors.[125] In addition, forced loans were adopted as a device to secure funds in an ever-worsening situation, at times in the form of a 'blind bond' for an unstated amount, and in association with a tax levy. In June 1640 a loan of one-twentieth of yearly rent was introduced at the same time as a new tax was being devised. Three years later, in July 1643, a loan of £800,000 Scots to pay for the army in Ireland (subsequently diverted to the use of the army in England) was voted in, along with a tax of £200,000 Scots for home defence. Early in 1644 a blind bond was issued, which in five months raised £562,733 6s 8s Scots from 366 donors. Another one was used to pay for troops to fight Huntly in the north-east.[126] At times, there was a penal element to the proceedings, for the government tended to target opponents of the regime, like the defeated Engagers in 1649. Such measures continued up to the eve of the Cromwellian conquest; in May 1651 the Scottish Parliament approved a 'voluntary' loan that netted £50,056 14s 8d Scots. Those who refused were reported to the authorities.[127]

During the course of 1639–40 the Scottish Covenanters introduced an innovatory tax, known as the tenth penny. Using the presbytery as the unit of collection and based on a up-to-date valuation of wealth, it assessed all forms of income and was, therefore, more equitable than previous taxes.[128] As a result, the shire (and therefore the parish) totals could be set at far higher rates than had been possible before the conflict. At Monimail, Fife, the rental value was assessed at 25,261 merks, representing a tax bill of £16,840 13s 4d Scots (over £1,400 sterling).[129] However, as it took time to assess the new valuations, an associated loan of a twentieth helped bridge the gap. Money came in slowly and it was to improve the receipt and administration of incoming revenue that the Committee for Regulating the Common Burdens was set up in November 1641. By the end of 1643 nearly 84 per cent of the tenth penny had been paid and accounted for.[130] A new valuation was made for the tax of £120,000 Scots in 1643 but in its distinction between constant and casual rent, it continued to tax various forms of income. The Treasury had difficulty in getting the counties to release the money and in December 1644 the Committee of Estates complained that the money was being retained locally in excess of what was allowed in levy and transport charges.[131]

In February 1645 the 'maintenance' was introduced, a tax based on the Parliamentarian assessment. Its initial purpose was to raise £108,000 Scots, the sum needed to pay the monthly maintenance cost of the forces mustered to deal with Montrose. Each county and burgh paid a proportion of the amount. The tax was periodically renewed, normally for the same global sum, though in November 1645, for instance, the sum required was £134,940 1s 4d Scots. Using revised valuations, the maintenance remained the principal tax in the country until the Cromwellian conquest, by which time revenue was hopelessly in arrears.[132]

Because of the disappointing returns of the tenth penny and twentieth the Scots introduced an excise as a means of financing their armies in England and Ireland at the beginning of 1644. Moreover, the Excise Committee, set up on 27 January, was given the specific task of obtaining credit to buy arms. It was no more popular in that country than it was in England. The measure was wide-ranging, incorporating what was normally classed as customs revenue: duties were to be paid on beer and wine, tobacco, meat and textiles, as well as on exported coal and on all imported manufactured goods. It did not bring in as much as was hoped, however, and was allowed to lapse, only to be resurrected in March 1647.[133] At the same time, the renewal of civil war in Scotland led to the sequestration of the estates of malignants and the fining of those who submitted. In January 1645 Parliament voted to allow the sale of their opponents' property in order to obtain sufficient funds to meet the threat from Montrose, and a Committee for Borrowing Malignants' Rents was established on 11 January. After Montrose had been defeated at Philiphaugh on 13 September 1645, income from fines increased. By 1646 they provided the largest source of revenue.[134]

It is not always easy to find out how much of the money raised was spent on war materials, as many of the arms were provided by individuals, according to means, and not paid for out of public money.[135] As noted above, the Covenanters, like Charles I, sought to defray some of the cost by getting the counties to arm and equip their levies. In the winter of 1643/4 the burgh treasurer at Edinburgh paid out £12,494 17s 10d Scots, fitting out the city's regiment with arms, equipment and baggage horses. While in England the following spring and summer, the regiment cost about £5,166 Scots a month. In November 1645 John Pearson, one of the city's bailies, was authorised to collect £682 Scots for armour.[136] According to the accounts, in February 1644 clothing and arming the soldiers at Glasgow cost £2,296 Scots.[137]

Nonetheless, the Committee of Estates did spend money on military supplies out of the money raised. On 18 August 1643 it borrowed £40,000 Scots on the security of the £120,000 Scots tax to pay for equipping the army.[138] A certain proportion of the money was to be spent locally to pay for transport and the soldiers' levy. The following June Lord Innerpeffer gave John Cockburn, the routmaster of the College of Justice's troop, £100 Scots, as his contribution to the outfitting of the unit.[139] Later, the maintenance was used to buy arms, payment being made once bonds or tickets had been received from the recipients. On 5 June 1650, for instance, James Cockburn, the subcollector of the maintenance in Berwickshire, received bonds and tickets for 162 muskets and 134 pikes from the various officers who had been issued with them. More were to follow.

Cockburn was to pay for the arms at the rate stipulated by the county's Committee of War out of money collected in tax.[140]

By the time that Cromwell had conquered Scotland in 1651 the cost of fighting wars on several fronts had utterly exhausted the country. The price was far in excess of what a small nation, of modest means, could afford to pay and, in this respect,[141] the Covenanters' biggest mistake had been to believe the promises of English financial support. Parliament had pledged funds for the 10,000-strong army sent to Ulster in 1642, which cost £16,000 sterling a month to maintain. About £70,000 sterling was paid but then hostilities in England interfered with the flow of money. This meant that only half of the £300,000 sterling agreed on in January 1641 was ever paid.[142] Faced with clear evidence of the English Parliament's incapacity (or reluctance) to pay its debts, the Covenanters nevertheless agreed to an alliance and to invade England on its behalf. For their services the Scots were to be given £31,000 sterling a month and the pledge of further sums after the Royalists had been defeated. It never materialised in the amounts promised. By Parliament's reckoning the Scots had only received something over £15,000 sterling a month for the period from 6 October 1643 to 1 November 1645.[143]

The army could at least tax those parts of the country it controlled. It took over the Great Sess in the north and collected assessment money further south. Between November 1645 and May 1646, while besieging Newark, the army obtained £48,519 17s 2d sterling, three-quarters of which came from Nottinghamshire.[144] During the protracted negotiations for the withdrawal of the army in England, Scotland claimed almost £2 million sterling in costs, while Parliament calculated its receipts at almost £1½ million. Scotland accepted £400,000 sterling, half to be paid before the troops left.[145] Scottish involvement in the Second Civil War provided Parliament with the excuse to cancel the debts still owed, probably nearly £1 million sterling.[146]

On 9 July 1640 Sir John Cochrane, while on a mission to Sweden to obtain arms and armaments, specifically stated that the Covenanters sought neither money nor soldiers.[147] With the decisive battle of Newburn only a month and a half away, their confidence was not necessarily misplaced but evidently they did not envisage a further eleven years of war! Between 1639 and 1651 twelve Covenanting armies were raised, ranging in size from 2,000 to 24,000 men.[148] To arm, equip and pay so many soldiers was a costly business and clearly the money had to stretch a long way. Accounts such as those made by Sir Adam Hepburn, the treasurer of the Army of the Solemn League and Covenant, indicate that large sums were disbursed on arms, equipment and clothing [149] The Committee of Estates also responded to requests for money from commanders. Nonetheless, difficulties in securing adequate finances did affect supplies to the army and the problems grew over time. In November 1643 there were few arms in the central magazine and because the English Parliament had not delivered the money due, there was no cash to buy any or to reimburse the counties for the arms they had been asked to get.[150] The troops in Ireland also suffered from the failure of the English to honour their promises. In November 1643 the English commissioners assured their Scottish counterparts that they were shortly going to send over £10,000 sterling in cash, 10,000 uniforms and pairs of shoes, and 10,000 bolls of meal, part of the £60,000 sterling owed. The following April the Scots told the Speaker that nothing had been received from England for twenty-two months. Circumstances had not improved in 1645, though, as before, some supplies were sent from Scotland; £10,000 sterling was dispatched, together with clothes and provisions, but, as Loudon, the Chancellor, observed, 'unless the English Parliament send money, victuals and ammunition they [the troops] will be forced to relinquish that kingdom'.[151] Up to 1649 Parliament had paid a mere £360,000 sterling to maintain the British and Scottish troops in Ireland, whose cost in summer 1643 has been calculated at £525,000.[152] In Scotland, arrears mounted up over the years and money was harder to come by. By 1651 the situation was desperate. Symptomatic of the problem were the difficulties experienced by the Army Committee in finding money to pay for urgently needed lead shot. In April the committee contracted with James Menteith for 30,000 lb of musket and pistol shot but admitted that it had no means of paying him. It was, therefore, forced to recall the £10 Scots levy for each soldier, then in the hands of the colonels.[153]

FINANCING THE IRISH ROYALISTS AND CONFEDERATES

In 1642 the Royalist forces cost £607,452 to maintain, seven times the annual income of the country in 1640.[154] Constant references to shortages of arms and equipment, together with the cash to pay for them, suggest that they had severe problems with funding. The Royalists continued to press Parliament for money (especially from the £400,000 tax earmarked for Ireland), setting out their case in harrowing terms. On 11 July 1643 the Council wrote to the Speaker that the army could not take the field against the rebels for 'want of means to furnish themselves with necessaries for their accommodation, the horsemen wanting money even to shoe their horses, or mend the defects of their furniture and arms, and the foot also wanting means to fix their arms . . .'.[155] Some arms and money were sent but too little to be effective. The cessation of hostilities with the Confederates on 15 September 1643 eased the situation, if only temporarily. Ormond not only received cash and cattle from the Catholics but could also save money by demobilising some of his troops. Conversely, the truce reduced the prospects of help from the English Parliament.[156] Parliamentarian money for Ireland, like the weekly levy introduced by an ordinance of 18 October 1644, went to the 'British' forces rather than to Ormond's troops.[157]

The Confederates also incurred considerable military expenses; in 1647, for instance, it cost over £10,000 to keep the army in the field for a six-week period. Finding sufficient cash to foot such bills was always a problem, even though they controlled most of the country.[158] In 1643 the Supreme Council observed that 'although the people contribute cheerfully what they have, yet the stock of money now in the kingdom answers not their desires.'[159] It pinned the blame on the greed of the country's former governors, but it wasted money too.[160] Even contemporaries commented on the Confederates' over-bureaucratic system of government, described at the time as 'a world of clerks and attorneys, a set number of commissioners in every county, receivers and aplotters . . . a world of money, but the most part, or rather all, was spent in daily wages of the Supreme Council, judges, clerks, and other mechanical men and little or nothing went to the military.'[161] In August 1646 it was admitted that of £18,000 due to the army, up to £10,000 might be lost in officials' fees, waste, non-payment and garrison charges.[162]

One solution was to solicit outside help. As the Supreme Council admitted on 7 April 1643 in a letter to the Franciscan, Hugh Bourke, in Flanders, 'Our wants are money, armes and amunicion; these wee have noe way to provide for, the countrye beinge exceedinglye exhausted unless wee may be assisted by those who wish well unto our cause beyond the seas.'[163] The Confederates could count on the sympathy of Roman Catholic powers and even exert political leverage by playing off the French against the Spanish over the promise of Irish troops and the use of their ports. Unfortunately, these states were embroiled in their own struggles which claimed their attention and resources. In particular, the French and Spanish – enemies in the Thirty Years' War – did not want to alienate England by too openly supporting the insurgents, especially as the outcome of the rebellion was so uncertain. The papacy was not only deeply involved in this conflict but was also engaged in a war with Parma. Nonetheless, it did make the greatest contribution, sending £25,000 in cash and £31,000 in bills of exchange.[164] The money that the papal nuncio, Rinuccini, provided in the months after his arrival in November 1645 was particularly valuable. It enabled Owen Roe O'Neill to recruit more troops for his Ulster army and to pay them regularly for the first time. It was thus instrumental in his victory over the Scots at Benburb in June 1646. France promised 100,000 crowns (about £22,000) but only delivered a third of the amount (nearly £7,300), while Spain contributed a mere £5,000, though mostly in gold coin.[165] A sum of less than £70,000, though welcome, would not sustain the cause for long and in 1647 the Confederate leadership wrote gloomily of 'our expectation of great sums and helps beyond the seas being turned into wind and smoake and despayre.'[166]

Contemplating the poor response of their allies abroad, Richard Bellings, the Supreme Council's secretary, concluded that foreign aid was a sop merely to encourage people at home to give more, rather than a genuine attempt to relieve their burden.[167] As the Royalists received so little external help, too, both sides had to find the bulk of their income at home. Inevitably, supporters were the first to be asked to contribute. For the Royalists, the rapid advance of the rebels in the opening months of the war meant that commanders had to dip into their own pockets to buy arms for their troops, while civilians gave money or extended their credit.[168] In Munster the Earl of Cork bankrolled the Royalist war effort and in Galway the Earl of Clanricard claimed that his entire fortune had been consumed in the service.[169] Merchants provided loans, at times under some pressure. In January 1644 Ormond, needing £600 immediately, drew up a list of Dubliners who could contribute, together with the sums they were to give 'with their own free consents'.[170] Supporters among the mercantile élite of Confederate towns loaned money for the cause. Patrick Archer of Kilkenny was the most prominent: in 1644–5 he consigned goods and money worth £5,000 to the Confederacy and in general underpinned its finances. He also dealt with the Royalists, later claiming to have spent £10,000 without recompense on behalf of both parties.[171] Ready cash was a problem and at Dublin a lack of specie forced Ormond to call in plate and to strike coins from it. The practice, which continued in the following years, was designed to provide cash to pay for troops and arms and, so it seems, to stimulate foreign trade. In November 1642 the general assembly of the Confederacy agreed to establish a mint at Waterford and called for enough plate to coin £4,000. Lord Inchiquin, the Protestant leader in Munster, struck his own coins in 1643.[172]

Existing sources of revenue were utilised and others developed. The Confederates allocated two parts of the profits of tithes and church livings to the maintenance of the army and also taxed people on one-third of their freeholds and one-tenth of their movable goods. In addition, they also ordered individuals to contribute one-quarter of their estates to the war effort.[173] The inadequacy of these measures, however, led to the development of the applotment, a tax based on county quotas, which, like others of the kind (the tenth penny, for example), more effectively tapped local wealth.[174] The bulk of the income came from Leinster and Munster.[175] In the residual Royalist areas the main assessment, the cess, was based upon the ploughland (notionally 120 acres of arable land). Towns paid too; in February 1643 forty-three people at Youghal contributed £614 to that month's cess. At Dublin income from St John's parish declined from £75 8s 0d in 1638 to £47 in 1646, reflecting the impact of depopulation on the city's taxable wealth.[176] Cromwell was later substantially to increase the returns by applying greater pressure on taxpayers. In 1651 Ulster's portion of the half-year bill for the army amounted to £5,430 and the following year the whole country was rated at £24,770 in cess and £6,495 5s 0d in forage. As in England, the property of opponents was sequestered. In one ten-month period in 1646–7, £627 10s 0s was obtained in rent in County Carlow alone and in 1649 the rent roll of potential victims in counties Carlow, Kildare and Wexford amounted to £2,700.[177] After the war, of course, the adventurers claimed their prize out of Catholic land.

Customs' receipts were affected by the dislocation of trade, the confusion of war and the common practice of waiving duty on war materials and provisions. At Dublin the customs, worth almost £5,000 a year in the early 1630s, had fallen to £1,400 by 1644–5 and to no more than £600 by 1647. At the beginning of 1645 the customs at Derry had not been collected for three or four years and although recently resumed by the new governor, Colonel Mervin, they had, at the time of writing, only brought in £5.[178] According to Patrick Darcy, writing in January 1649, the revenue derived from the customs at Confederate ports was inconsiderable. Between 1645 and May 1648 those of Galway had yielded £1,600–1,800 per annum but nothing thereafter because they had been illegally appropriated. In 1648 Limerick had compounded for its customs at £1,000 a year for two years. Waterford's customs generated little income and those at Wexford and Ross far less.[179]

Both sides also adopted the excise. In October 1643 the Irish Council justified the introduction of 'such a thing so unknown to the king's laws and gracious government' by claiming that without it the army would have perished from want. The duty was put on liquor, tobacco and cattle being sold at Drogheda, Dublin and Trim and throughout Munster.[180] In Munster it was not very effective, Hards Waller informing Ormond in February 1644 that it had failed utterly.[181] Nonetheless, a year later Colonel Mervin asked Ormond for permission to introduce the measure at Derry to ease the burden and to pay for more soldiers.[182] The Confederates obtained excise receipts from Leinster and Munster, with counties Kilkenny and Wexford providing the largest sums.[183] The excise was also valuable as collateral; Ormond used it as such to raise the aforementioned £600 in Dublin in January 1644, and in March 1646 the Confederates obtained £3,000 on the security of the excise taken in Clonmel, Galway, Kilkenny, Limerick, Waterford and Wexford.[184]

By the late 1640s, years of warfare had taken their toll and the country was devastated. In 1647 the Confederation lamented, 'our exchequer emptie and altogether hopeless to get in moneys from a country so totally exhausted and so lamentable ruined.'[185] Loans, an essential element in military funding, were increasingly hard to arrange; interest rates were high, few people had the funds and those who did were reluctant to risk their money. Galway refused to lend £1,000 to the Earl of Clanricard in 1647 because he had not repaid his previous loans.[186] In January 1649, Darcy suggested to Ormond various ways in which revenue could be increased. Firstly, he advised that the customs of all those ports that subscribed to the peace should be farmed. Secondly, he stressed the importance of tobacco, claiming that it 'drawes more mony than all the importacions and exportacions of Ireland'. At one port alone over 12,000 cwt was imported and at 3*d* a pound in customs, the income would amount to £16,800. Similar sums might be obtained from other ports.[187] At the time, customs were reputedly bringing in £100,000 a year.[188] With regard to excise, Darcy thought that because of scarcities of victuals, all provisions, except liquor, should not be chargeable. In towns he emphasised the need for diligence in collecting the impost, while in the countryside he proposed that an agreed composition should be made. Finally, he recommended that the tenths of prizes – a tax of one-tenth of the value of all captured ships – should be tightened up. Using this source as security, Ormond was able to borrow £4,000 from Waterford, nearly £1,500 from Wexford, and £750 from Ross.[189] Hardly had these suggestions been mooted when Cromwell's invasion force landed in the country.

CIVILIAN REACTIONS

Initially, all sides tried to finance their war effort by appealing to their supporters for funds. However, this restricted approach soon foundered as costs mounted and as enthusiasm waned. In England, at least, the authorities had to contend with the massive display of indifference, even hostility, shown towards both sides. The voluntary principle, therefore, gave way to compulsion. As a result, the tax burden not only rose dramatically but also fell on a much wider range of people. Warwickshire was rated at £600 per week by Parliament, as compared with a total of £4,000 a year in ship money or under £6,000 for the £400,000 tax. Royalist Oxfordshire was charged £1,176 a week, that is, £61,152 a year, seventeen times higher than the ship money assessment of 1635.[190] Apart from regular direct taxation, occasional levies were imposed, either nationally or for some local purpose. Goods were taxed through the excise and possessions requisitioned by the soldiers or used up in free quarter. Individuals or whole communities might be plundered. In December 1643 the inhabitants of Essex not only had to pay their assessment of £4,500 but also special levies of £4,500 for the army, £300 for the relief of widows, orphans and invalids and £250 for the establishment of Newport Pagnell garrison. Frontier areas, subject to the exactions of both sides, were particularly hard hit. The inhabitants of Grendon and Wishaw in north Warwickshire claimed that apart from contributing to the Parliamentarian forces and to the Royalist garrisons at Ashby, Dudley and Lichfield, they constantly had their goods and cattle plundered.[191]

It is not surprising, therefore, to find that taxpayers complained that they were unable to pay the sums asked for. When Somerset's rating went up from £1,500 to £2,000 in September 1643, a Bridgwater man grumbled that 'we are squeezed like wax in our weekly payments, still mounting'. On 4 December 1644 the Hertfordshire Committee observed that, 'Taxes are so frequent in the country for one thing and another, that when warrants are issued, the returns are often complaints and tears and not monies as are expected.'[192] While it was clearly in the interests of taxpayers to plead poverty, the piling on of various impositions did lead to genuine hardship. By September 1648, for instance, the inhabitants of Scarborough had had enough. They told the governor that they could no longer pay the assessment, citing the decay in the town's trade and heavy expenditure over the past six weeks in imposts and workmen's wages, quartering soldiers, making defensive works and supplying the garrison with various items.[193]

While few people in the three kingdoms liked paying taxes, the response to them varied. The biggest sums were raised out of the regular direct taxes but by themselves they did not provoke very much hostility. In the Eastern Association area the tally seems to have been one riot and a number of assaults on local collectors, but nothing on the scale of the resistance to the gathering in of ship money in 1639–40.[194] The taxes were assessed by local people and in England and Scotland, at least, appeal procedures were built into the system. In Scotland, moreover, the creation of a hierarchy of war committees from the parish upwards involved ordinary people in the sanctioning and decision-making processes.[195] In England, there is evidence from the north Midlands that the rival parties moderated their demands in areas where their jurisdiction overlapped, and avoided direct confrontation. Even when soldiers collected their allocations, they generally acted in a reasonable manner, though their presence did tend to encourage compliance.[196] Inevitably, there were some rogue units; one such body was van Druschke's Horse, a regiment in the Army of the Solemn League and Covenant, which plundered its way across the north and the north Midlands during the course of 1646.[197]

In this respect, a distinction should be made between troops settled in the district and those passing through. The former had a stake in maintaining the goodwill of the local inhabitants and tended to act accordingly, whereas the latter, with no such constraints, were more likely merely to take what they needed. Of course, garrison soldiers might act in an arbitrary manner, especially if short of funds or provisions. The troops under Colonel Fox, the Parliamentarian governor of Edgbaston House, Warwickshire, for instance, acquired a bad reputation, though this was due rather from necessity than ruthlessness. Inadequately supported either by his commander, Denbigh, or the county committee, Fox had to improvise as best he could. The consequences of alienating the home population can be seen in the response to the depredations of the Royalist Colonel Croker, who commanded one of the Earl of Northampton's regiments in the East Midlands. Deputed to collect contributions in January 1643, within days he had so incensed some Oxfordshire communities that they refused to pay contributions and by May several Warwickshire parishes were seriously in arrears.[198]

People felt particularly upset when the demands appeared arbitrary or unjust, the officials tyrannical or the soldiery intimidatory. The excise was particularly hated. In May 1645 the Derby Committee wrote to the Speaker to tell him of the opposition of local people to it, especially the countrymen and soldiers, 'on whom it will fall the heaviest'.[199] It was disliked because it taxed ordinary products and penalised the poorer sections of society. The uproar that followed the extension of the excise to meat and salt in January 1644 eventually led to their removal from the list in August 1647. In Scotland, the introduction of the excise on 31 January 1643 led to riots in Edinburgh and caused John Spalding to exclaim, 'Thus is this miserabill countrie overburdenit with uncouth taxationis . . . quilk this land is unhabill to beir.'[200] The actions of the officials caused considerable offence. They were appointed centrally, often drawn from outside the area, and, even if local, did not normally come from the ranks of the traditional governors. They were, therefore, not susceptible to local influences and pressures that helped to mediate tensions arising out of the assessment. Apart from their extensive and intrusive powers of search and arrest, they widely reputed to be corrupt and self-seeking. The excisemen were the cause of numerous riots during the war years and after.[201]

Even greater was the hostility felt towards free quarter, whereby units of soldiers were billeted in people's houses, perhaps for days or even weeks on end. Complaints about the intolerable burden of free quarter were heard from early on in the war and the practice did more than anything else to alienate the civilian population from the soldiery. Overall, it may have doubled the amount that people paid.[202] Soldiers were supposed to give vouchers to cover the cost and these could be redeemed from the local treasurer. In settled areas they often were but even here problems arose. Vouchers did not always cover actual expenditure, while money spent on the soldiers reduced the amount of ready cash available to buy essentials or to pay taxes.[203] After the war, Royalist vouchers were worthless! When the soldiers left they might take away items that were of use to them – and vital to the former owners. The loss of draught animals, for instance, prevented farmers from preparing their land and carriers from pursuing their livelihood. In late 1644 and 1645 outrages such as these contributed to the formation of clubmen's associations in a number of English counties, with the avowed intention of ridding the area of the soldiers of both sides. They tended to occur in Royalist areas and it is true that as their territory shrank and with it their ability to raise money, the Royalists were forced to adopt more ruthless tactics to obtain money and provisions. In Glamorgan discontent over arbitrary action and higher taxation led to the emergence of the 'Peaceable Army' in late summer 1645. Yet, in some areas where such conditions existed they did not occur and, as Bennett has suggested, the phenomena were 'individualist in their composition, demands and behaviour'.[204]

CONCLUSION

The cost of paying the soldiers and arming and equipping the armies was huge and posed particular problems to those who had to foot the bill. Various devices were adopted to minimise expense, especially appeals to supporters, but expedients could not guarantee supplies nor the loyalty of the soldiery. All sides quickly realised that they would have to raise taxes. Apart from the tenth penny in Scotland, none of the various financial measures adopted were new; the taxation of personal wealth, the use of loans, sales of land and the imposition of customs and excise duties were integral parts of the fiscal system and were well known to contemporaries. Moreover, the king continued to draw an income from the same prerogative rights that had helped to sustain him in his period of personal rule.[205] Not only did all parties draw upon similar sources of revenue to fund their army but they also based their financial administration on the same units, the parish/kirk and the shire. Inevitably, this led to a tug of war between local and central officials over control of the money. What was novel about the Civil Wars was the scale of the financial demands, the amounts raised and the change in the relationship between the administrative bodies in the locality and those at national level. The threat of force added extra leverage, though a muted one, in England at least, as stress was laid on cooperation with the civilian population.

The war engulfed the whole of the British Isles, and Scotland and Ireland in particular were devastated by it. Scotland, buoyed by the early success against an unpopular and badly supported monarch, was seduced into adopting the role of the militant champion of Protestantism (specifically, Presbyterianism) throughout the three kingdoms, a position the resources of the country could not sustain. In Ireland, it really did have to be all over by Christmas, if the rebellion were to succeed. That the war lasted for so long was due to distractions in England and Scotland, as well as to the various changes of allegiance among the parties to the conflict in the country itself. Four armies fought there and the conflict was waged with greater savagery than in the other theatres of war. When the civil wars in England were over and adequate funds made available for the conquest of

Scotland and Ireland, the fate of the two countries was sealed. In England, hindsight might make it obvious that Parliament, with its superior resources, would win. At the time it was not that clear-cut. Financially, the Royalists had to adopt Parliamentarian practices but they did so effectively and increased their income. In the long run, what really weakened the Royalist war effort was the fact that the war had a greater impact on its territories than on those of Parliament and this made it difficult for the financial machinery to establish itself and bed down. The war had a particularly damaging effect on those areas on which the Royalists depended economically, not only because of the direct action of the enemy forces but also because of the heightening sense of insecurity it engendered. It made people wary of setting out on the road and trade suffered. Revenue fell. This, in turn, necessitated the introduction of various expedients to obtain money and essential supplies, including special levies, free quarter and even outright plunder, which further reduced the ability of taxpayers to pay. As long as the Royalists possessed an army they could exert pressure on the populace but the defeat at Naseby removed this support.[206]

4

HOME SUPPLIES: WEAPONS

The weapons industries were scattered around the three kingdoms but there were obvious concentrations. One or two places had a specific specialisation, for example pistol making in the Perthshire village of Doune. The largest groupings, however, occurred in the vicinity of the central magazine, where demand was the greatest. Because artisans fashioned these items (or parts of them) in a traditional handicraft manner, production levels were not particularly high, even in London. War added to the problems of supply, especially as the business had shrunk during the long period of peace and, in Scotland's case, because of the Union of the Crowns. Charles faced difficulties when preparing to fight the Scots in 1639–40 and all sides in the Civil Wars experienced shortages. To overcome the problem of fragmentation, various devices were employed. The guild structure could be used; in London, orders were placed with the relevant livery company and the contracts shared by a number of its members. On occasion, the craftsmen themselves took the initiative, forming partnerships and negotiating on their own behalf. At other times, a merchant took the lead, putting out work to others. The process of manufacturing arms was also speeded up by the practice of making the component parts individually and assembling them separately. Finally, of course, the demand for new weapons could be reduced if existing ones were kept in good order. Consequently, refurbishing weapons was a task regularly carried out by the employees of the Ordnance Office working in the Tower and by their counterparts elsewhere in the British Isles. In the middle of a war this job took on added importance.

Typically, craftsmen and artificers engaged in making weapons worked in workshops and forges attached to their own home where they fashioned and assembled the various parts. Units of production were, therefore, comparatively small, though leading London operators employed a number of people, including journeymen and apprentices. When Robert Compton, a gunmaker, sorted out the firearms in the Tower in 1639 he and six of his servants did the work.[1] Some mechanisation had taken place, notably in the manufacture of swords, where the largest operators used mills, in which the grindstones were driven by water-power. Pike heads, too, might be made in bulk at forges and sent to pikemakers, who affixed them to staves. Each weapon, in fact, was a composite item and different craftsmen might produce its component parts. Much of the work, therefore, involved the assemblage of parts brought in from elsewhere. On 22 August 1638, for instance, two London cutlers, Robert South and William Cave, claimed £125 for work done for the Ordnance Office, affixing hilts onto 1,000 rapier and sword blades and putting them into scabbards.[2]

The move to greater specialisation was promoted by the growing complexity of weapons technology, especially in the manufacture of firearms. To improve their standards of workmanship was an avowed intention of the London gunmakers, when in the 1630s they sought to establish themselves as a separate livery company. In their drive for incorporation they emphasised their special skills and warned of the dangers of allowing 'Tinkers, Smithes and other Botchers of Armes', to meddle with weapons.[3] Of course, too much should not be read into what was after all an essential part of their argument, the disparagement of their rivals. The gunmakers received their charter on 14 March 1638 but, naturally, their action upset the blacksmiths and armourers, from whose ranks they had emerged.[4] Some of the gunmakers in the livery company were specialist locksmiths and therefore capable of fabricating the more complicated firing mechanisms. Nonetheless, they did come from different backgrounds: Warner Pin, a native of Jülich and an important governmental contractor in the 1640s, was an inlayer of gunstocks. He, like other craftsmen working in the weapons and equipment industries, was able to function by assembling parts made by specialists.[5] Perversely, it was for this reason that some gunmakers also dealt in swords. Robert Steadman, one of the furbishers of firearms in the Tower, for instance, made and repaired hundreds of swords as well as guns in the period of the Civil Wars.

Refurbishing weapons was an important aspect of the work. Arms had to be maintained and, where necessary, repaired. The navy provided a regular source of employment; when ships returned to port, their arms and munitions were sent back to the stores and any repairs carried out. On one occasion in 1638 Robert Compton earned £11 5s for cleaning 270 muskets 'lately returned from ye Seas'.[6] Those with an official post at the Ordnance Office took the lead; George Fisher and Robert Steadman cleaned and repaired muskets and John Edwards and Robert Thacker viewed, sorted and straightened pikes, but so many weapons needed attention that numerous people were involved. On 12 May 1638 twenty-nine cutlers and gunmakers were given warrants, totalling £238 6s 6d, for work done for the navy.[7] Magazines elsewhere similarly employed local craftsmen, if on a lesser scale, stimulating the local arms industries and helping to maintain a skilled workforce in the provinces. The cost of refurbishing a weapon depended on what had to be done to it, each task being separately valued. In 1638 gunmakers charged 10d for putting a new lock on a musket, 18d for cleaning it, 20d for cleaning and repair work and 5s if a new stock had to be put on too.[8]

In wartime the amount of work to be done naturally increased, though levels of activity fluctuated according to circumstances. Before the campaigning season started attention was focused on getting as many weapons and items of equipment into as serviceable a condition as possible. In the aftermath of a battle 'unfixed' weapons were returned for repair. After Edgehill two men brought in a cartload of bullets and broken muskets, while in the days following the Battle of Naseby six men were employed by Parliament to look for arms left on the field.[9] To keep their weapons in good order armies took gunsmiths with them on the march. At the beginning of the war a Royalist document dealing with the issue of 'recovering lost arms, making and procuring new and preserving arms for the future' suggested that every company or troop ought to employ a good gunsmith or at the least that there should be two per regiment. It was sound advice, too, as Richard Grenville, a Royalist officer in Ireland, found out. Writing from Trim in May 1642, he asked Ormond to send him a gunsmith skilled in mending firelocks because his arms were 'all unfixed'. When, two months later, a gunsmith had still not arrived and the greater part of the guns were 'broken and unfixed', he reported that his soldiers could no longer operate as a fighting force.[10]

THE WEAPONS INDUSTRIES OF ENGLAND AND WALES IN THE BISHOPS' WARS

The manufacture of firearms was the most fragmented of all the industries that provided weapons for the king. Each gunmaker could only put together a restricted number of items, especially if he made the lock. To obtain guns for the expeditionary forces to Scotland and Ireland in the years 1638–42, the king had to deal with nearly thirty London gunmakers, sometimes individually but often as a group.[11] The growth in the numbers of wheel-lock and snaphance firearms further complicated the process and some gunmakers took time to master the art. As they explained, 'The afore mentioned carbines and pistolls have not beene here many yeares in use, nor long beene made, and we doubt but here after upon Encouragement we shalbe more ready in the makinge of them and soe shall afford them at cheaper rates.'[12] Nonetheless, they did supply the king with them. On 31 December 1639 warrants were issued to pay the gunmakers for 4,338 firearms, including $400\frac{1}{2}$ pairs of wheel-lock pistols and 216 firelock carbines; 165 carbines had Spanish locks affixed to them. Although a generic term for a type of lock, they were imported from Spain at the time.[13]

Most cutlers made swords 'domestically', forging and edging the blade and attaching the hilt and pommel in workshops attached to the house. Some enterprises, however, were planned on a larger scale and based on a blademill. A major supplier of swords and blades to the Ordnance Office was Benjamin Stone, who produced blades at a mill on Hounslow Heath. In 1638–9 he agreed to deliver 1,000 swords a month to the stores.[14] The mill had been established in 1629 and staffed with bladesmiths from Solingen in Germany, invited over by the king to develop the craft in England. Stone claimed to have spent £6,000 perfecting the art but he clearly benefited from his association with craftsmen from one of the most noted centres of blademaking in Europe. The Germans supervised the proceedings at Hounslow and provided instruction to the Englishmen employed in the works.[15] Stone, as noted above, successfully broke the Cutlers' Company's monopoly on the manufacture of swords and became the king's blademaker. In December 1638 he was provided with a shed in the Tower to grind swords and put hilts on them; presumably this 'domestic' arrangement was intended to allow him to carry out his official duty of refurbishing swords in the stores in need of repair.[16] The king profited from the rivalry between Stone and the company for he could play one side off against

Map 1: Major ports, industrial centres and magazines in England and Wales.

the other. He supported Stone, buying thousands of swords from him, but also gave contracts to members of the Cutlers' Company. On one occasion three cutlers, William Cave, Robert Moore and Robert South, combined to deliver 3,080 swords. In any case, Stone did not have the capacity to provide all the swords needed. One order for 22,503 swords, for instance, was divided between Stone and his competitors.[17]

Pikemakers likewise worked within a handicraft system but apart from the heads forged by bladesmiths, tended to be assemblers of parts rather than manufacturers. They sorted out the wood, straightened the staves and painted them with *aqua vitae*, and then affixed the heads, languets and feet. They bought in the iron parts, some of which came from abroad.[18] An individual could, therefore, make quite a large number. For the Scottish campaign the king bought all his home-produced pikes from three people, overwhelmingly from John Edwards and Robert Thacker, respectively the King's Pikemaker and the Yeoman of the King's Tiltstaves and Lances. They made short, as well as long, pikes and also manufactured musket rests, halberds and partizans. These products, all of which comprised wooden staves with metal attachments, fitted in well with pikemaking. In November 1639, as part of the preparations for the Second Bishops' War, they agreed to deliver to the stores 400 long pikes and 500 rests a month.[19] Like the gunmakers they insisted on money on account (imprest) and payment of the balance on delivery. Edwards and Thacker also helped supply weapons to Ireland in 1642.

Apart from dealing direct with the Ordnance Office, suppliers (and others too) sold goods to gunmakers and cutlers, who in turn could obtain a mark-up for their own goods as 'fully furnished'. In December 1639 seven gunmakers dispatched sixty-three carbines to the Tower, each complete with belt and swivel, cartouches, key, mould, worm and scourer.[20] Individuals might sell items separately. Thus, on 22 August 1638 Benjamin Stone, the blademaker, received a debenture for 1,000 swords and rapiers newly hilted and scabbarded at 2*s* 6*d* each, and Toby Bury, a girdler, another one for 1,000 girdles and hangers at 2*s* each and 1,000 belts at 1*s* 8*d* each. Craftsmen doing work for the Ordnance Office might need to buy in the pieces needed. When Robert Compton fitted 500 muskets with rings, swivels and nails 'in the manner of Carrabynes', the cost of the work included the price of the parts.[21]

Bulk orders tended to be organised through the respective livery companies, which negotiated prices and delivery dates and then allocated the work among their members. The latter, in turn, might subcontract out some of the work if they felt that they could not complete it themselves in time. Deals might also be made with *ad hoc* consortia of artificers. On one occasion the government tried to obtain its supplies more cheaply by bypassing the Gunmakers' Company and bargaining with a group of middle-order gunmakers.[22] The practice of forming temporary associations to fulfil contracts was widespread but particularly noticeable in the fragmented gunmaking industry. On 16 December 1639 twenty-seven gunmakers undertook to produce between them 1,600 muskets a month, besides carbines and pistols. Three months later the company calculated that by the end of May they would have made 10,000 muskets, together with hundreds of carbines and pistols. Thereafter, they hoped to raise production to over 2,000 muskets a month.[23] The king gained from such an arrangement but there were drawbacks too. By negotiating as a group the manufacturers had a stronger bargaining position and they inevitably sought to use it to remedy past abuses, demanding ready money and the ending of the practice of giving fees to Ordnance Office officials.[24] Two weeks after the agreement with the gunmakers, just referred to, warrants were issued to pay them.[25] At least payment encouraged the gunmakers to produce weapons as quickly as possible and in general it seems as though the various groups of arms makers did provide most of the weapons for which they were contracted.

There were people who made hand arms in the provinces; many blacksmiths, for instance, could turn out serviceable, if unsophisticated, weapons if called upon. Birmingham was an important centre for firearms and swords and elsewhere military bases and arsenals supported small knots of workers, who could exploit local opportunities for manufacture and repair. In January 1639 Sir Jacob Astley recorded that there were four gunsmiths at Hull, one of whom made very good firelocks.[26] Astley, who was touring the north to assess its military preparedness for the Scottish campaign, also highlighted deficiencies in the region. In response, the Privy Council, noting the 'great want of armourers, gunsmiths, sword-makers and bandolier-makers in northern parts', ordered the Master of the Ordnance to send suitably skilled persons to York and the twelve northernmost counties.[27]

PARLIAMENT

When the Civil War broke out in England, Parliament benefited from its access to the arms industry of the capital. According to extant material, which provides only a partial picture, London arms makers produced over 30,000 pikes, 102,000 swords and 111,000 firearms between August 1642 and September 1651.[28] This is a creditable performance and to achieve it Parliament was helped by the ease with which the arms makers transferred their allegiance from the king, even if some of them might have seen it as a hard necessity. There is remarkable continuity in the names of the people who supplied weapons to Charles's forces in Scotland and Ireland in the years from 1638 to 1642 and those who dealt with Parliament over the course of the next decade. One or two went through the whole period and several more handed over to a son, normally after a period of working together. A gap signifies death or retirement rather than stout Royalist convictions, though a few individuals did feel strongly enough to make the move.

It did take some time for the manufacturers to gear up to meet extra demand and merchants imported weapons to supplement those being made at home or provided on the Propositions. Home production of firearms, perhaps hit by the decline in shipments of coal from Royalist Newcastle, was badly affected. On 1 December 1642 two Lancashire MPs were told that their warrant for 1,000 muskets for the county force could not be honoured 'for want of Store in the magazin'.[29] By the end of 1642 recorded deliveries to the Committee of Safety's magazine totalled a mere 600 muskets, 87 carbines and 131 pairs of pistols. What, then, were the gunmakers doing in the winter of 1642/3? They certainly did make some firearms for they were selling them on the open market. Lord Brooke bought 935 muskets, 284 carbines and 257 pairs of pistols off twenty-nine London gunmakers in February 1643 and customers such as the Lancashire MPs, given £1,000 to buy their muskets, were also looking for weapons.[30] However, their main task seems to have been amending firearms in the Committee of Safety's magazine, which at the time was the most important Parliamentarian arsenal. Armourers and pikemakers were similarly employed.[31]

This emphasis on refurbishment, which was common to the Royalists, too, appears surprising at first but it did have a rationale. In the first few months of the conflict people were being exhorted or coerced into contributing all manner of military hardware and, as a result, reasonable amounts of arms and equipment were being brought into the stores. As many of the items needed to be repaired to render them serviceable, it required a concerted effort on the part of the workforce to renovate them. It was time well spent, however, if only because it made arms and equipment available relatively quickly and cheaply.

Cutlers were the one group of arms makers who continued to manufacture new weapons through the winter. In autumn 1642 they agreed to deliver 16,127 swords to Bradley and Rowe at the Committee of Safety's magazine, and by the end of the year they had sent thousands in.[32] The gunmakers did not begin to make regular deliveries until the following spring, firstly matchlock muskets and, later, carbines and pistols. As the year progressed they were being offered large contracts again. In September the Committee of Safety set aside £5,000 to spend on arms and told Owen Rowe to deal with gunmakers and others.[33] Output rose over the course of the next few years, reflected in the downward trend in prices. Matchlock muskets halved in price between 1642 and 1645, from £1 to 10s. The cost of snaphance pistols, though more varied, fell by the same amount, from about £2 a pair to about £1. Between 1642 and 1645 the price of a long pike dropped from 4s 6d to 3s 10d and swords from 6s 8d or 7s to 4s 2d. Prices continued to fall thereafter.

In spite of expansion in the hand arms industries the pattern of production stayed the same. As before, gunmakers were the most fragmented group in terms of numbers and output. However, a small group comprising leading figures in the Gunmakers' Company, did supply firearms on a reasonably large scale. The government also employed one or two of their number in an official capacity. The brothers John and William Watson, who each made over 12,000 guns during the period, not only served as Masters of the Company but also successively acted as the Master Gunmaker in the Ordnance Office.[34] The average swordmaker continued to work in the same handicraft tradition as his gunmaking counterpart, if on a slightly larger scale, but one or two had more heavily capitalised plant. Lawrence Bromfield, a cutler and captain in the London militia, replaced Benjamin Stone as the major supplier of swords. He sold almost 3,000 swords to the Committee of Safety in the first eighteen months of the war and over a longer period 21,000 more to the Ordnance Office, field armies and local forces. Pikemakers were still few in number, though not such an exclusive group as before the war. John Edwards and Robert Thacker continued in business but shared the work with other family members and various outsiders. Anthony Webster was the most prominent of these newcomers; he first appeared in 1645 as a supplier to the New Model Army in 1645 and sent in regular consignments to the Ordnance Office, often 100 at a time, over the course of the next few years.

The warrants, from which these figures have been calculated, clearly provide estimates of the scale of output by individual craftsmen (gaps in the record notwithstanding) and also give a rough indication of delivery dates, as well as the interval before payment. They do not reveal details of the original bargain, however, and therefore cannot be used to see how well the manufacturers fulfilled the terms of their agreement. Surviving contracts to supply the New Model Army between April 1645 and April 1646, used in conjunction with the warrants and a list of delivery dates for 1646–7, help shed light on this issue.[35] The data reveal a changing pattern over the year but do show that throughout the period the contractors generally brought their goods in on time or with only a slight delay. Indeed, in 1645 the contractors delivered their ware within days or weeks, suggesting that they could draw upon existing stocks and fulfil large-scale orders with relative ease. In 1646, with fewer reserves, contractors took longer to dispatch their goods and were more likely to deliver them in instalments. Nevertheless, they did adhere to delivery dates. To fulfil some of these contracts the craftsmen still shared the workload between themselves, either in an informal way or through the auspices of their livery company.

Partnerships were particularly prevalent at times of high demand, notably in the first few months of the war, in 1645, when the New Model Army was being supplied, and during the Irish and Scottish campaigns of 1649–52. Although the groups tended to be loose associations, brought together for a particular job and then dissolved, certain individuals regularly consorted with each other. The gunmakers, George Day, William Greaves, William Watson and Thomas Smith often formed partnerships, as did Robert Murden, Miles Knight and William Judge. Among the cutlers, the pre-war collaborators, William Cave and Robert South, delivered two consignments of swords to the Parliamentarian Committee of Safety but then disappear from the records. In 1649–51 Alexander Normanton and Stephen Heard jointly sent in several loads. Not surprisingly, gunmakers formed the biggest consortia; to supply the Scottish expeditionary force of 1650–1 the craftsmen organised themselves into groups of two to fifteen, the composition of which often reflected previous associations. As before, work might also be put out to more junior, non-livery craftsmen. The speed with which some of the New Model Army contracts were executed, for instance, can only be explained by the practice of subcontracting, if stock was not already available. The existence of subcontractors, not shown in the warrants, is suggested by the list of individuals who supplied holsters to the Committee of Safety's magazine in the first two years of the war.[36] Altogether, 34 people sold or repaired 5,994 pairs of holsters. They included Ambrose Sanderford and Thomas Gill, two of the leading Parliamentarian suppliers, and the gunmakers William Dawson and John and William Watson, who might have bought in holsters, but most of the names are otherwise unknown.

Groupings were based on the need to spread the load rather than to pool individual skills. Among the gunmakers, one or two individuals might have a specific emphasis in their work – Robert Murden, for instance, specialised in pistols – but they generally dealt in all types of firearms. Naturally, they supplied the simple matchlock musket, which remained the standard product throughout the period and provided them with the bulk of their income. Most of them sold the more complex snaphance and wheel-lock pistols and carbines, too, for if they did not make the locks themselves, they could obtain them from a locksmith. Snaphances were made in some number during the period but wheel-locks remained comparatively rare and more expensive. Similarly, when repairing firearms, gunmakers might refurbish worn-out parts themselves or merely obtain a replacement. Regimental gunsmiths, of course, had to possess the requisite skills if they were to maintain the firearms in good working order while on the march.

Repairing arms was a routine job but it was a profitable one for the craftsmen and, as noted above, it made a significant contribution to the war effort. Many refurbished weapons were returned to the magazines and thence sent to the armed forces. On 20 June 1651, for instance, four gunmakers received a warrant for £425 for 1,000 old matchlock and snaphance muskets, newly repaired and proved.[37] Nevertheless, the system was open to abuse, especially as the same people sold new as well as reconditioned weapons. Between 1649 and 1651 a number of London gunmakers were found guilty of sharp practice. The worst offender, William Gardiner, was accused of false accounting, selling weapon parts belonging to the State as his own and passing off old arms that he had bought as refurbished government stock. In the light of such malpractice one might wonder what Christopher Fell, another London gunmaker, did with the old caliver barrels and parts of fowling pieces he had bought off Commissary Bowles of Kent in 1644.[38]

In the provinces Parliament controlled the important industrial and commercial centre of Bristol for the vital first few months of the war. Elsewhere, Birmingham stood out as a centre of manufacture. In 1643 Robert Porter was said to have supplied 15,000 swords to Essex and other commanders. The Royalists later burned down his blade mill, which had cost £100 to build, because of his refusal to make swords for them. In the same year the town's gunmakers supplied firearms to Parliament.[39]

In the north-west, Manchester emerged as an important manufacturing area for weapons and munitions, a position that strengthened in the late 1640s with the intensification of the struggle in Ireland. In February 1649 the Army Committee contracted with one Brown for 1,000 muskets with some bandoliers and swords, which were to be shipped to that country.[40] In general, however, the output of local enterprises was modest; not only was demand lower but productive capacity was restricted by a lack of specialist workers. Of course, there did exist a pool of craftsmen and artisans like blacksmiths, turners, metalworkers and edgesmiths, who could adapt their skills to the task, and all that might be needed was an example for use as a template. According to Parliamentarian accounts, gunsmiths, adept at dealing with the complicated firing mechanisms of snaphance and wheel-lock weapons, as well as with the simpler matchlocks, could be found in a number of counties. In March 1645, for instance, Rowland Hawse, a Northamptonshire gunsmith, earned £3 8s 4d for making eight snaphance locks, which he affixed to muskets, and for three carbines.[41] Repair work was the mainstay of local craftsmen and this business increased as magazines multiplied and as the war took its toll on weapons. At times after an engagement, campaign or the return of a body of soldiers the small but steady stream of arms being brought in for refurbishment increased dramatically. On 24 March 1645 Gilbert Clement of Arundel Castle was paid £8 3s for repairing and refurbishing arms that had come from Sir William Waller's army, then in the West Country.[42]

Local craftsmen might operate as independent contractors, selling weapons to order. At Gloucester, Richard Till, a cutler, sold thirty swords and belts in the summer of 1642 as the city sought to improve its defences in the face of the impending Royalist attack. At the same time the Earl of Denbigh, the Midland Association commander, bought eighty firearms from the gunmakers of Coventry.[43] In some places individual craftsmen and artisans were paid a retainer by the authorities to do work as and when required. At Norwich Samuel Calthorne did the job, whereas in Warwickshire they included men like John Farr and John Guy, gunsmiths, and Nicholas Jackson, a pikemaker. It is often possible to identify those 'on the staff'; apart from the wages, they did many of the repairs and sold goods with greater regularity than others. Many artificers were employed to work by the day or the piece. At Nottingham, gunsmiths earned between 1s and 1s 6d a day and the pike header 1s 2d. The general level of production was quite modest. In Cumberland, for instance, John Cotforth was the most prominent person among a group of gunmakers who delivered muskets, carbines and pistols to the county committee in 1648–9 and he only sent in a few at a time. Extant accounts for such counties as Gloucestershire, Staffordshire, Warwickshire and Worcestershire indicate that weapons tended to trickle into the magazine in small lots, though this pattern might occasionally be disrupted by the receipt of a larger consignment.[44]

Centralisation might increase output. In 1643 a smithy for the gunsmiths was set up at Nottingham Castle and equipped with a pair of bellows, two vices and a turning frame. Accounts of expenditure list the tools and equipment of the trade: chains and axletrees for the pistols, steel to make springs and chains, plate, files, cutting files, oil and borax (for solder). In December 1644 the governor purchased two grindstones, probably for the cutler to edge blades and rehone swords. To a certain extent the workforce adopted an assembly-line system. The gunsmiths, for example, fitted together weapons from parts made by specialist locksmiths, stockmakers and barrellers. Gunlocks were purchased at up to twenty-four at a time, barrels in average lots of twenty and gunsticks at 1s a dozen. Pikes, too, were assembled in the castle. Some pike heads were made on site but most were bought in. Timber for the staves was obtained from wood found in the locality; on 10 January 1647, one labourer was paid 1s 2d for a day's work choosing suitable timber and another the same amount for felling it. Between 14 December 1644 and 28 March 1647, 726 pike heads and 340 round heads were obtained, though the task of assembling the parts seems to have been a seasonal one.[45]

ROYALIST

In developing weapons and equipment manufactures at Oxford the Royalists encountered the problem of a shortage of skilled workers. This was an issue that a committee, set up to find means to improve the stock of arms, looked at early in 1643. It recommended that an effort should be made to attract able men from London and other parts of the country. As an inducement, the king offered a pardon to all gunners and artificers still at the Tower.[46] A few people did respond: according to Stern, Jonadab Holloway, with fourteen other gunsmiths, went to Oxford in 1644 and remained in the city until its capture in June 1646. Holloway was certainly there on 26 April 1645, delivering to the king's stores 100 muskets he had repaired. He had returned to London by 17 July 1651 when he received warrants for payment for 46 muskets and (with fourteen other gunsmiths) for 235 pairs of pistols.[47] Most people, however, put commercial (and possibly political) considerations first and stayed put. In Royalist areas, skilled workers might be required locally. Lord Herbert, commenting on the situation in the Forest of Dean, said that he could not send any gunmakers or workmen to Oxford and that to increase output he needed some himself.[48] To make best use of available personnel, artificers were gathered together in the Schools' Tower and set to work making and repairing weapons. The Schools' Tower housed the armoury of the Ordnance Commissioners and, in practice, this meant that Sir George Strode and John Wandesford were put in charge. They also contracted with craftsmen working outside to make weapons and equipment for them.[49]

The provision of firearms was a matter of immediate concern. In December 1642 the Council of War ordered Sir John Heydon to work with the Committee of the Ordnance to find gunmakers as quickly as possible and get them to make muskets for dragoons.[50] One such person was Michael Bastin, the king's master smith, who did general blacksmith's work as well as assembled and repaired firearms. He received the locks he needed from the stores. In this respect, he was probably typical of the gunsmiths employed at Oxford, although little is known of the level of production they achieved. Indeed, according to the accounts, gunsmiths delivered only 18 new muskets to the stores, and 12 of those had been made at Bicester or Blewbury, a village south of Didcot.[51] Five more muskets, together with 9 pairs of pistols (one French), 4 carbines, 1 caliver, 3 pistol barrels and 1 pistol lock were found at the workshop of Richard Weller, a gunsmith, and sent to the stores on 11 February 1643.[52] Weller contined to work in Oxford, so why did he not send in the firearms himself?

The gunsmiths must have made more than a handful of weapons, but from the evidence it appears as though they were kept busy repairing firearms. William Standinnought, the master gunsmith at Oxford, spent the bulk of his recorded time doing such work. Between 12 January and 23 October 1643 he repaired, fixed or stocked 505 muskets and only definitely made 4 new ones. Repair work was a particularly important service at Oxford, which housed the central magazine; from here weapons were distributed to the army and later returned after use for storage and refurbishment. The Council of War recognised the value of the work. On 20 June 1643 Strode and Wandesford were ordered to get the gunmakers in their charge to fix all the muskets delivered by the army as soon as possible, pay for the work and take special care to return the arms again.[53] With limited supplies it was important to bring weapons quickly back into use. Thus, when 140 'broken' muskets from Lord Wentworth's regiment were distributed among the gunsmiths in February 1643, ten of the men were given 3 days to refurbish 80 muskets and 3 others were allowed a fortnight to repair 56 muskets that needed new locks and/or stocks. Other garrisons took similar care of their weapons. At Skipton Castle local gunsmiths were being paid to mend the muskets, carbines and pistols there.[54]

Strode and Wandesford were also involved in assembling pikes and bills in the Schools' Tower, sending 499 to the king's stores on 6 April 1644 and 900 more thirteen months later. Many of the heads and staves used were produced locally or in the towns and villages around Oxford by craftsmen and artificers whose skills could be adapted to make weapons. For staves, Thomas Hill, a pikestaff maker from Chieveley was a major supplier. On 18 January 1643 he fulfilled a contract made with the commissioners for 202 pikestaves 15 ft 6 in long and by the end of July he had dispatched a further 1,160, together with 232 long- and 50 halfpikes.[55] Several blacksmiths, mostly from Oxford and its suburbs, provided heads. One of those listed, Robert Fuse, came from Blewbury, a village in which a number of Royalist contractors lived. In March 1643 Fuse delivered eighty-four bill heads.[56] Although the accounts record no further consignments from the village, it remained a valuable source of supply. In February 1645, for instance, the treasurer ordered 1,500 pike heads from Blewbury.[57] Other heads were obtained from the ironworks of Shropshire and the West Midlands operated by ironmasters such as Richard Foley of Stourbridge. They were sent to Oxford via Worcester; 1,798 pike heads were among the items included in three shipments dispatched by Sir William Russell, the governor of Worcester, between February and May 1643. This link persisted, for in February 1645 Foley, then in arrears with 1,900 heads, was asked to provide 2,000 more to be delivered at Worcester.[58]

Strode and Wandesford put out some of the work to blacksmiths and joiners. Thomas Hill and Robert Fuse were among those who made pikes and bills, as were blacksmiths such as William Bromingham and Richard Spencer of Oxford, John Stroud of Cowley and Robert Wallis of Blewbury. They also provided the heads. James Bull, an Oxford locksmith, specialised in poleaxes, sending 916 to the stores in the first half of 1643. David Woodfield, a local joiner, concentrated on halberds, although he did make one or two pikes and the occasional javelin (a light lance). These people seem to have fashioned at least some of the parts themselves, whereas others received their materials from the commissioners. On 25 February 1643 Martin Goldbourne, a joiner resident in Catte Street, Oxford, was given seventy heads and long pike staves and a fortnight to do the job. In the event, he took nine days.[59] Two further batches, 70 pikes apiece, were delivered on 13 and 18 March. Another outworker, George Eaton, a stockmaker, returned 1,274 pikes he had headed in the months from March to June 1643. On 26 April 1645 he delivered 391 more. Stray references from a later date, like this one, which can be repeated for numerous suppliers, suggest that consignments continued to come in regularly in the intervening period and that the accounts greatly under-record actual production levels.

For swords, the Royalists initially relied upon the traditional handicraft skills of cutlers such as Jeremy Poole, who on 11 February 1643 sent fourteen swords to the New College magazine.[60] However, the Council of War soon realised that output had to be increased; on 20 June, therefore, it authorised Strode and Wandesford to fit grindstones and wheels to the cannon-boring equipment in Christ Church College to enable it to glaze and grind sword blades. The following month 400 swords were sent to the stores from the Schools' Tower.[61] Even more capacity was created when on 20 November William Legge, the Master of the Armoury, was voted £100 to build forges and a grinding mill and to furnish them with the essential tools and equipment. Forging the blades was undertaken at Gloucester Hall, Oxford, but edging them was carried out at a new mill erected on a bank of the Thames at Wolvercote, $2\frac{1}{2}$ miles to the north-west of the city. In February 1644 £2,000 was allocated to Legge to make swords and belts which, if made at the contemporary Parliamentarian price of 8s, represents 5,000 weapons (though Royalist unit costs were probably higher).[62]

At the same time, the commissioners were still manufacturing blades at their forge and on 7 April 1644 dispatched 126 swords.[63] Clearly, the productive capacity of the Royalists was quite reasonable, if below Parliamentarian levels, but this is not reflected in the records. Moreover, the evidence does no more than hint at the intriguing possibility that Benjamin Stone, the king's old blademaker, supervised the transformation of the industry at Oxford, providing the Royalists with the expertise necessary to develop a large-scale concern. He was theoretically available, for after delivering a consignment of swords to the Parliamentarian forces in the winter of 1642/3 he disappears from sight. However, the identification rests on linking him with the Mr Stone, blademaker, who on 19 May 1643 repaired nine swords and put them in scabbards.[64] This seems an underuse of a man of his talents!

A report appearing in the Parliamentarian newsheet, *Mercurius Civicus*, suggests that the manufacture of 'archaic' weapons was not neglected either. On 28 September 1643 the writer informed his readers that the Royalists had set up a new magazine outside the Northgate at Oxford exclusively for making, maintaining and storing bows and arrows. He warned them that they were busily gathering together all the bowyers, fletchers and arrowhead makers they could find and putting them to work there. Wood and metalworkers, adapting their skills to the task, could have augmented numbers. As a result, the writer thought no arrowheads should be moved from London towards Newbury or to any place accessible to the Cavaliers.[65] As Parliamentarians were making arrows, it would not be surprising to discover that the Royalists were doing the same. However, there is no record of anyone supplying bows or arrows to either the soldiers or to the various stores, nor is there any reference to any being issued from the magazines.

Other sources of supply were needed to supplement production at Oxford, especially as the wastage in weapons was considerable. In September 1643 Lord Hopton complained about the lack of care that the soldiers took of their weapons, which 'appear to be expended as fast as their ammunition'.[66] The capture of Bristol in July 1643 transformed the situation, even if the benefits were slow to emerge. A month after the victory Hopton noted in a letter to Prince Rupert that 'arms here . . . rise very slowly', mainly because the garrison had to be rearmed and many of the existing firearms repaired. Once this short-term difficulty had been overcome – and he suggested that he be granted a share of the arms brought in by a Dunkirker – he claimed that the gunmakers in Bristol could send 200 muskets and 30 pairs of pistols to the stores each week. By January Richard March, then in charge of the Ordnance Office there, could report that the target was being met.[67] In order for the gunsmiths to concentrate upon their vital work the king sent a warrant to exempt them from the duties of watch and ward. The manufacture of pikes was not so advanced, however. March suggested that Percy might try Reading, as previously he had received consignments from there.[68] A year later March was even more ambitious. In March 1645 he promised that if the artificers were paid promptly (and they were already owed £1,200), he would deliver 15,000 muskets and 5,000 pikes to the king annually.[69] In the following month the Royalists, building up their resources for the Naseby campaign, sent an urgent request to March for 2,000 pikes and a great quantity of muskets.[70]

Weapons manufacture was also developed in the Royalist bases on the Welsh Border. At the beginning of the war the Earl of Bristol suggested that all gunsmiths in Shropshire should be brought together at Shrewsbury. Production had begun by the end of the year, for a consignment of muskets and carbines was sent to Oxford at the beginning of 1643. On 19 January Edward Hyde reported to Sir Francis Ottley, the governor of Shrewsbury, the king's pleasure at receiving them and his hope that he could supply some more. As he stressed, 'the king infinitely depends on you'. Unfortunately, another letter three weeks later reveals that Ottley had found difficulty in putting together a second batch so quickly.[71] At nearby Chester, there were enough gun- and pikemakers to fulfil an order for 800 muskets and 200 pikes in spring 1644.[72] In the north, firearms could be obtained at York. On one occasion Colonel Neville bought 400 muskets there on behalf of Lord Loughborough, the Royalist commander in the East Midlands. The garrison at Skipton Castle obtained muskets, pistols and snaphance locks for their pistols there, too.[73] Outside such centres, stray references indicate that small-scale production of arms was carried on in a number of places. In north Worcestershire a Kidderminster joiner, John Brancill, seems to have been employed by Edward Broad of Dunclent to make stocks for muskets.[74]

SCOTLAND

When relations between Charles I and the Scottish Covenanters deteriorated during the course of 1638 and 1639, the latter prepared for war by importing shipments of arms from abroad.[75] They also obtained what they could from individuals and institutions at home, supplemented by contracts with local manufacturers. Although small by comparison to its English counterpart, the Scottish arms industry was of some significance, having had to supply the military requirements of an independent kingdom until 1603. Nevertheless, as in England, the industry was in decay by 1638. The Union of the Crowns had facilitated the movement of *matériel* from England to Scotland in the early seventeenth century and years of peace had reduced demand. In May 1634 Colonel Monro, the future Covenanter, asked Charles I for a three-year lease to make arms in Scotland to remedy the shortage of weapons there.[76] Map 2 gives some indication of the location of arms manufacture during the first half of the seventeenth century and the number of people involved, though because of gaps in the records it provides only a minimum figure. Of course, at any given time numbers actually working would have been fewer. On 6 August 1652, for instance, Patrick Cunningham, an Edinburgh cutler, was admitted burgess free of charge because 'ther is none of that trade in the Towne'.[77]

As noted in a previous chapter, the Tables placed the burden of providing soldiers and weapons on the shires, working through local committees of war.[78] By making use of the weapons already in the hands of the population, the authorities hoped to build up and then to replenish their stock of military hardware quickly and cheaply. At Monimail, Fife, in 1639 there were (probably) 167 men in the parish able to bear arms, of whom 49 possessed muskets and 29 had pikes. Thirty more agreed to buy muskets, with 2 undecided, while 18 others said they would obtain pikes and 7 were non-committal. Thirty-two men either refused to obtain a weapon or, more commonly, lacked the means to do so. The inhabitants also possessed 78 swords and 2 pistols. The following year there were 196 able men in the parish and some of those without weapons now had acquired them. If there were 3 fewer pikemen, there were an additional 38 musketeers; 5 were still unwilling to contribute and a further 46 could not afford to buy arms. The number of swords had risen to 97 and pistols to 8. On the Balcarres estate in Fife the barony of Ardross and town of Elie had 154 able men, 23 of whom had muskets (21) or hackbuts (2) and a further 86 who could furnish themselves with either a musket (40) or a pike (46). Most of the men had swords. At St Monans 24 of the 95 men possessed muskets and swords, while 5 more could do so, and a further 27 could provide themselves with pikes and swords. In the two baronies, those unable to obtain a weapon amounted to 45 and 39 respectively. In the barony of Kinnocher none of the able men were provided for.[79]

How were the men without weapons armed? Those who had the means bought arms, perhaps under a certain amount of pressure from the authorities. At Stirling in July 1638 the brethren of the guild were given fifteen days to

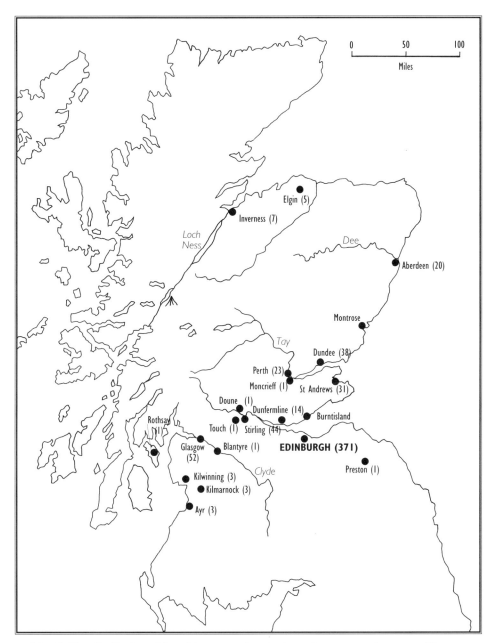

Map 2: The distribution of Scottish arms makers in the early seventeenth century. The figures indicate the number of recorded apprentices and craftsmen in the years 1600–52.

acquire the appropriate arms of a musketeer or pikeman. When in the following February the council at Glasgow learned that a large number of people did not possess weapons, it ordered the inhabitants to obtain them or face a fine of £20 Scots.[80] A rotational system, in which service in the army was divided among three or four people, also helped since it spread the cost.[81] Those with insufficient income were given weapons. Ordinances stipulated that masters and heritors should provide arms for their servants and tenants. In 1638 the Laird of Ardross had in readiness 30 muskets with furniture, match and gunpowder; 4 pairs of pistols (2 with wheel-locks); 4 sets of foot armour and 2 further sets; 2 dozen lances and 6 bundles of staves; and 3 steel bonnets. He also intended to procure 20 pikes. Individuals who raised their own units might, like the master of Forbes, compel heritors to give arms.[82]

In the burghs the town council took the lead. In February 1639, Edinburgh's council loaned 80 muskets, rests and bandoliers and 40 pikes to the large number of the able and fencible men in the crafts who did not possess arms. The following summer the burgh of Peebles provided 41 muskets and the same number of pikes to its soldiers. In December Glasgow's council ordered the borough treasurer to buy 100 muskets (with furniture), 30 pikes, and 400 lb each of gunpowder and match, which eventually cost £1,888 8s 8d Scots.[83] The townspeople might have had to contribute to their purchase. At Peebles in August 1639 the provost and bailies were told to exact the cost of the muskets and pikes delivered to the inhabitants. As public property, arms loaned out had to be returned. At Edinburgh in 1639 the dean of guild received bonds from the commanders of the companies of the city's regiment for the return of the arms and armour provided.

Without careful oversight, many pieces disappeared. Peebles tried to keep a check on its weapons; within months of handing them out in 1639 officials were trying to find out who had received the arms left in the camp. Two years later the council summoned recipients to a borough court held on 8 December to account for the weapons they had received.[84] As in England, the authorities had to deal with soldiers in the standing army who had sold their weapons and horses. To compound their offence the troops were pocketing money when recruited again in the new levies. In an attempt to stop this abuse an act was passed on 12 May 1648 which forbade the practice and imposed a death penalty on soldiers who left their colours. Inevitably, some of them flouted the law. In April 1651 the Committee of Estates heard that the soldiers and officers at Stirling were selling the muskets they had been supplied with by the shires. The committee decided that the officers should be answerable for the arms they had received, though it conceded that those lost in service would be replaced from the magazine.[85]

Clearly, weapons had to be bought to supplement those available in private hands and in town magazines. Arms shipments from abroad supplied weapons in bulk but smaller numbers could be obtained at home. Edinburgh possessed the greatest number of arms manufacturers, attracted to the capital, as in England, because it was the seat of government and at its port of Leith the site of the central magazine. The keeper of the magazine at Leith distributed weapons to units of the army in various parts of the country but local authorities also bought arms from the city's manufacturers to top up their own stocks. At the beginning of 1639 the provost of Glasgow travelled to Edinburgh to purchase arms. In 1644 its council bought muskets there and in 1646, pikes. In January 1644 the bailies of North Berwick procured muskets and pikes worth £73 6s 8d Scots from two Edinburgh merchants, Sir William Braid and his son, Andrew.[86] Edinburgh's arms manufacturers, however, were not able to do more than provide a proportion of the arms needed, especially in an emergency. Thus, as preparations for the war gathered pace in early 1639 supplies began to run out and the arms makers found themselves unable to cope with demand. At the end of May Archibald Campbell could find no pikes, muskets or swords in the city but noted that some were expected nightly, that is, from abroad.[87]

Burgh and shire magazines, albeit smaller than the one at Leith, would have sustained a handful of artificers, especially as the men could augment their income through general sales. Map 2 indicates that it was possible to buy arms at a number of centres and, given the county basis of the forces, local commanders undoubtedly made use of them. Lord Dalhousie bought pistols and possibly pike and lance heads at Edinburgh for the levies on his Panmure estate in Forfar but made greater use of nearby Dundee, where he purchased swords, muskets and perhaps pike heads. He also obtained deals from which three members of the Lyall family made lances. In 1639 the Royalist, Gilbert Blackhall, a priest and former soldier, asked Alistair Smith, a smith and a tenant of Lady Aboyne, to make him four Highland axes. At Glasgow, John Colquoun fulfilled a contract with the burgh for 600 lances in September 1650.[88]

From the burgh lists certain types of weapon makers stand out. Armourers, cutlers and dagmakers comprise two-thirds of the craftsmen (66.1 per cent), emphasising the country's specialisms, as well as hiding one or two basic crafts. Scottish pistols or dags, characteristically made completely out of metal, were widely used. Lord Balcarres's brother, Robert, had some Scottish pistols in his house in 1638. In the same year a regiment of Welsh and Cumbrian dragoons were to be armed with 'Scotch' pistols, as well as with a musket and sword.[89] Edinburgh dominated the trade but several other towns, notably Dundee and Glasgow, had several manufacturers of firearms. The reference to Thomas Caddell, a gunsmith at Doune in 1646, is significant for he was the first of a dynasty of pistol makers in this Perthshire village who made 'Highland' pistols there.[90] The inventories of two Edinburgh dagmakers at work in this period suggest that, like many handicraft workers, their output was not large. David Clerk died in 1645, leaving six pairs of pistols, valued at £100 Scots, and equipment ('warklumes in his buith') worth £20 Scots. In 1651 Richard Hamilton of Calton merely had 'certain pistols' in stock. As in England, such men might combine to fulfil large-scale contracts. In a later example from 1669, Alex Wilson contracted with other gunsmiths from the Canongate in Edinburgh to supply the magazine at Edinburgh Castle with 3,000 muskets.[91] Wilson had been apprenticed to a dagmaker in 1635, and if others pursued a similar career,

TABLE 1

SCOTTISH ARMOURERS' PROBATE INVENTORIES, 1646–50

	John Hislop, armourer, burgess of Edinburgh died 1646		*James Park, armourer, burgess of Glasgow, died August 1649*		*William Burrell, armourer, burgess of Glasgow, died January 1650*	
swords	1 cutlass sword belonging to Lord Balcarres					
blades	9 braid sword blades	£24	45 sword blades @ 57s each; 11 sword blades @ 42s each	£128 5s 0d £23 2s 0d	7 score of sword blades @ £55 per score	£385
hilts	rapier hilts; 3 pairs of gilded shell hilts	£30 £20				
guards	3 pairs of close guards	£4 10s 0d	51 pairs of sword guards @£18 per score	£45 18s 0d	50 pairs of guards @ £18 per score	£45
muskets	1 musket rest and bandoliers	£12				
partizans	1 gilded partizan	£12				
cloth					in working 3 pairs of plaids and 3 score ells of linen cloth	£80

Source: Whitelaw, p. 296.

it helps to account for the paucity of gunmakers in the records. In 1644 an Edinburgh dagmaker, John Twedie, sold sixty muskets to the corporation at £9 Scots each. Many armourers manufactured firearms too; at Edinburgh a number of them specialised in making muskets and hackbuts.[92]

Cutlers, who mainly made knives and daggers, were the leading edge tool manufacturers. Soldiers carried daggers but, of course, the number of cutlers reflected the domestic use of their products too. One or two cutlers probably made swords, as did the swordslippers, though strictly speaking the latter ground and sharpened the blades rather than forged them.[93] Armourers were the craftsmen who normally put together the swords and at Dundee, Edinburgh and Glasgow the term was interchangeable with that of swordslipper. Armourers might fashion the parts themselves but often obtained them from specialists. At Edinburgh they bought guards from guardmakers, a job which some lorimers did. The inventories of one Edinburgh and two Glasgow armourers that survive for the period suggests that they, too, assembled swords from parts made elsewhere (see Table 1). Many of the blades were imported from the Low Countries. In October 1644, for instance, Glasgow's council ordered the Master of Work to obtain 120 blades in Holland.[94]

The number of bowyers still at work in Scotland in the first half of the seventeenth century, especially at Edinburgh, is a reminder that there was no abrupt transition from bows and arrows to firearms. To maintain custom they might have adapted by diversifying, becoming pike- or lancemakers, for instance. These crafts do not appear in the burgh lists for the period but they did exist, especially at Edinburgh where they could readily obtain work from the military establishment. When the widow of Donald Bain, an Edinburgh bowyer, died in 1635 her appraisers not only listed 300 bows and £20 Scots worth of arrows made and unmade but also 1,000 clubheads and shafts made and unmade, certain pike heads and shafts and 60 spears made and unmade. Other Edinburgh bowyers supplied pikes and lances to the Covenanting armies. Thomas Trustrie, apprenticed as a bowyer in 1618, was paid £71 10s Scots when he delivered 33 pikes to Captain John McCullous in September 1643.[95] The following year he received £176 Scots for 240 lances. In December 1644 John Forrest was given £3,666 0s 8d Scots for pikes and lances.[96] The versatility of bowyers is perhaps reflected in the appointment of William McCulloch, an Edinburgh bowmaker, as the king's armourer in October 1649.[97] If bowyers continued to ply their trade, so should have fletchers and arrowhead makers. Lack of reference to them suggests that, like Bain, they were classed with bowyers. Smiths also made arrowheads, though in April 1639 Archibald Primrose could not find one to make forked heads. They were probably all fully occupied. By the end of the month he had received three dozen from Sir Colin Campbell of Glenorchy.[98]

Because the authorities asked for individuals to contribute arms as part of burgh or shire quotas, many of the weapons must have been in need of repair. As in England, the workforce had to spend much time refurbishing arms. John McKen, a Glasgow dagmaker, for instance, repaired muskets and rests in 1639 and 1640.[99] On 5 June 1639 the dean of guild at Edinburgh was ordered to make arrangements with 'expert artificers' to mend all the muskets and pikes in the magazine. Royalists gave them custom too, especially if, as in spring 1639, they were being palmed off with substandard weapons. On 29 April the Marquess of Hamilton informed Sir Henry Vane, the king's Secretary of State, that many of the arms were defective and that the worst of them would be given to their Scottish allies![100] Because the task of repairing the weapons was a recurring one, it brought a steady income to many artificers, especially to those employed in maintaining arms in the central magazine at Leith. In August 1645 Michael

Acheson, an Edinburgh musket stockmaker, returned to the stores 130 muskets that he had either dressed or stocked. In the same month three men received a total of £27 18s 8d Scots for refurbishing thirty-eight muskets. Elsewhere, David Logan of Glasgow earned £24 Scots in August 1646 for fixing muskets belonging to the city's regiment. In 1648 James Jaffrey was carrying out similar work. In the same year Sir William Scott of Harden had to pay £4 Scots each for dressing, cleaning and adding new stocks and locks to sixteen muskets.[101] Particularly large amounts were laid out at the beginning and end of a campaigning season. In 1644 the Earl of Balcarres's regiment of horse received £4,800 Scots to repair arms and other accoutrements damaged on account of hard service. Four years later, in May 1648, as the Engagers were preparing for the forthcoming campaign, they issued a warrant for 5,000 merks, to be used in fixing arms in the magazine.[102]

IRELAND

Like the Royalists in England, the Irish of whatever party had to start virtually from scratch. Indeed, their plight was worse. There certainly were people with relevant skills – and plant that could be adapted – but they were too few to create an arms industry quickly and easily. The Ordnance Office at Dublin employed craftsmen and artificers and although they made some weapons, they were mainly involved in maintaining and refurbishing arms kept in store. Smiths could fashion basic weapons and mills could be converted to the manufacture of arms, but their output was not large. One way in which the Confederates tried to increase production, as well as to improve the quality of their ware, was by bringing in artificers from abroad. Although the native arms industry was undoubtedly rudimentary, this can only be deduced in a negative way, for the assumption rests on contemporary accounts of shortages and the high price of war material. Naturally, evidence of this nature has to be treated with caution because of the element of special pleading often present in it. The Royalists constantly complained about the lack of arms from England, painting a gloomy picture of the situation in order to stimulate action at Westminster. The Catholic rebels used similar tactics to encourage foreign powers to supply arms and later to improve their bargaining position at home with the Royalists.[103]

According to their comments, the Irish Royalists experienced problems shortly after the insurrection had broken out. On 13 November 1641 William St Ledger, the President of Munster, informed Ormond that he had neither cannon, pikes nor swords. A week later Viscount Clandeboye, in a letter to Hugh Cunningham, expressed a wish that the king would send men and munitions, especially muskets. Shortages continued the following year. On 20 July William Stewart, surrounded by rebels at Letterkenny, Donegal, told Ormond that the situation there was 'deplorable'. He had tried to get some muskets from Scotland and elsewhere but 'wee are marvelous destitute of Pykes swords and Ammunition'.[104] By the end of the summer the stock of arms in the magazine at Dublin Castle, on which the Royalists had been relying, was virtually empty.[105] On 1 September the

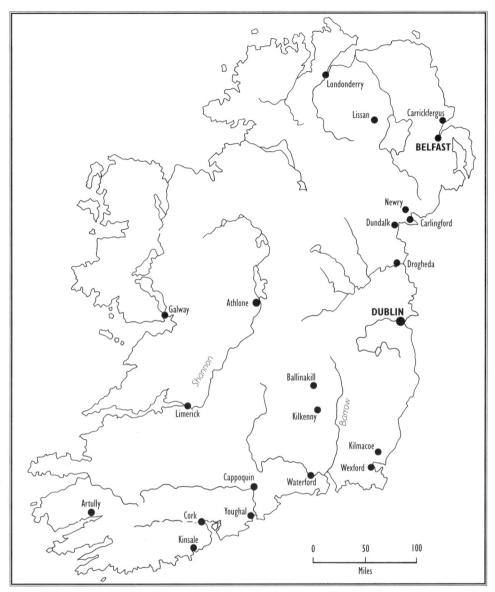

Map 3: Ireland, location of places mentioned in the text, including ports and sites of magazines and arms industries.

Lords Justices wrote to the Irish Committee in London for arms, pointing out that 'our arms are much broken, decayed and grown unserviceable, insomuch as we have not sufficient now in any degree to arm our men fully'.[106] Unfortunately, not only were their pleas largely ignored but they were also unable to replace many of their weapons from home sources.

The Catholics were short of weapons, too, especially in the early stages when all they possessed were those they had seized from Royalists as they advanced through the country. On 8 March Hugh Bourke observed that had the insurgents not lacked arms, artillery and munitions, they would have taken Dublin in six days. On 10 May he claimed that Drogheda and Dublin were only able to hold out because the Catholics possessed few arms and experienced soldiers. Three days later Geoffrey Barron, writing from Nantes, declared that 'We do extremely want gunpowder and muskets and money to pay an army for six months.' After this, he predicted (putting his faith in help from abroad), 'we would be able to maintain ourselves'.[107] To a certain extent this is what did happen and the rebels seem to have been adequately supplied, if from overseas sources. Lenihan considers that the shortage of firearms was a reason for the employment of 'Celtic' tactics. He also argues that the small number of musketeers that the Confederates initially had in their ranks was a response to the lack of gunpowder in Ireland.[108]

The country did have some manufacturing capacity but output was small and the weapons dear. When Lord Byron, the governor of Chester, asked Ormond for help in summer 1644 he was told that good-quality arms were being produced but because of the scarcity of coal and iron, they were expensive. Muskets, somewhat shorter than the ones made in London, cost 17s each. Those of the same size with Spanish locks and described as 'very handsome and useful arms' could be obtained for 21s. A pair of cased pistols with the same locks fetched £2. In London the Parliamentarians probably paid 2s to 3s less. Ormond told Byron that if he sent over iron or coal he could have any of these types of firearm in a short space of time.[109] This seems to indicate that the Royalists could draw on the services of some gunmakers, even if they did not have ready access to raw materials.

Conversely, the Catholics, who controlled most of Ireland, could exploit the country's raw materials. In about 1624 two ironmasters, Blacknall and Wright, had found iron ore in a mountain in Co. Cork and proceeded to extract it. They discovered further deposits near Bandonbridge, Co. Cork, and in the lands of Balligarran and Ballyregan, Co. Waterford. Charcoalling wood was also readily available.[110] A lease granted by the Earl of Cork in 1626 gave them liberty to dig mines and to operate the plant on the sites. They included a furnace and forges at Kilmacoe, Co. Wexford, two furnaces at Cappoquin, Co. Waterford, and a forge, nail house and slitting mill at Liffinen. In the war the Confederates could make use of facilities like these. In 1641 they seized an ironworks at Lissan, Co. Tyrone, and subsequently forged pike heads there. In 1645 they were operating the works at Artully, Co. Kerry.[111] To run these concerns they sought, through their agents abroad, to persuade foreign arms makers to come to Ireland. Some arrived early in 1642 and, to encourage others to come, in June the Confederacy offered them free bed and board until they could support themselves, immediate naturalisation, licence to name their own price for their products and lifelong exemption from taxation. In December the Supreme Council asked Hugh Bourke, its agent in the Spanish Netherlands, to invite men working in any trade relating to war to come to Ireland 'where all warlicke accomodacions are so necessarye and soe coveted'.[112] It still sought men the following year. On 28 June 1643 it asked the Franciscan, Luke Wadding, and Father James Talbot if they could find two or three smiths who could 'make and temper sword blades, muskets, petronell barrailles and locks'. Single men were preferred. In January 1645 a special request was made for musket makers.[113]

CONCLUSION

By the time that the Ordnance Office in the Tower fitted out the expeditionary forces for Ireland and Scotland in the years 1649–51, the soldiers were largely armed and equipped with home-produced hardware, a situation that contrasted sharply with that of their opponents. Of course, it helped that the officers had sufficient money to buy *matériel* and access to an arms industry that had developed over the course of ten years of fighting and which could now draw on the resources of the whole country. In the earlier years the situation had been different and deficiencies in supply had to be met by ransacking private and public magazines and, more importantly, by importing goods from the continent.

The inability of the native arms industry quickly to adapt to the demands of war in the years from 1638 was largely institutional. Craft based and fragmented into numerous small units, output per person was comparatively small. Moreover, demand fluctuated wildly between times of war and peace and made the business a particularly risky one to enter, even if there were profits to be made when soldiers needed arming and equipping. In the peaceful years of the 1630s numbers in the arms industry dwindled and new recruits were not encouraged. There was a market for arms on the continent among the combatants in the Thirty Years' War but the government was reluctant to allow the export of strategic materials. Moreover, possible customers were more likely to favour continental manufacturers, whose skills and techniques had been honed and improved in the crucible of war. English, Scottish and Irish arms makers, divorced from the conflict, had not kept up with weapons technology and were perceived as being backward and inefficient. Irish Confederates attempted to overcome this problem by bringing in experts from abroad. Scotland did have its own specialisms, as, for example, dags and broadswords, but, even so, many weapon parts, notably sword blades, had to be imported.

The Ordnance Office experienced difficulties in obtaining enough arms and equipment from home producers when called upon to fit out the soldiers for the Bishops' Wars in 1638–40. Its problem was compounded by the suppliers' reluctance to deal with a body chronically underfunded and from which they had great difficulty in obtaining their money. Nonetheless, the arms makers did make an effort, and from the warrants we can see that they did produce thousands of weapons. In addition, they often delivered them in the amounts stipulated in the contracts and roughly on time. To do so, they combined together in an informal way, or through their livery companies, and divided up the contracts among themselves. Parliament inherited both these contractors and a more favourable climate to arms manufacture and should, therefore, have been able to supply their forces with arms and equipment relatively easily. In practice, the number of consignments coming into the central stores between autumn 1642 and spring 1643 was remarkably small and great reliance had to be placed on imports. The workforce seems to have spent much of its time refurbishing arms, much of it brought in on the Propositions, taken from magazines or seized from opponents. The situation gradually improved and by the time that the New Model Army was being equipped in 1645–6 home producers were capable of supplying a significant proportion of the *matériel* required.

The Royalists had to start afresh but, nonetheless, developed Oxford as a centre for arms manufacture with commendable energy. However, it did not dominate production to the same extent as London did for Parliament, and other centres, notably Bristol in the West Country and York in the north, were promoted as alternative sources of supply. Over time, however, output declined as it lost territory to the Parliamentarians and therefore the king was forced to an ever greater extent to rely upon imports. The Scottish Covenanters were in some respects better placed than the English Royalists because they inherited a functioning arms industry. It provided them with some of their weapons, and parish and county quotas would have been at least partly met with home-produced arms. Ireland, in contrast, had virtually no arms industry at the start of the insurrection in 1641 and only a modest one developed during the course of the conflict. Both Royalists and Confederates continued to rely upon imports.

5

HOME SUPPLIES: ORDNANCE AND MUNITIONS

Before the Civil Wars the ordnance and munitions industries were concentrated in south-eastern England and were dominated by a handful of large-scale producers. In this respect, their organisation was different from that of the weapons and equipment industries. The manufacture of ordnance required comparatively expensive fixed plant, and munitions were more effectively made in the same way. Manufacturers could (and did) make munitions by hand but they essentially refined and mixed ingredients and these were processes best done in bulk, using mechanisation and powerful energy sources. Inevitably, the relatively high level of fixed and working capital required, limited entry into the business. Moreover, it was easier for prominent ordnance and munitions manufacturers to obtain raw materials, some of which were in short supply in the country and had to be imported. The government encouraged the monopolistic tendency in these industries. By dealing with a few large-scale producers it could regulate the business more efficiently, channelling essential raw materials to where they could be best employed, and minimising the crises of shortage and over-production inherent in an industry where demand was subject to considerable fluctuation. On the eve of the Civil War Charles I made gunpowder manufacture, cannon founding and shot casting actual monopolies.[1] For these reasons it was difficult for those parties that did not have access to existing facilities quickly to create their own industries (even though the gunpowder monopoly was abolished in 1641).

To secure an adequate and regular supply of munitions was a matter of particular concern to all sides. With the exception of cannonballs, which could be salvaged, all other types of munitions could only be used once. War used up *matériel* at an alarming rate and not just on the field of battle. Gunpowder decayed over time and a good deal of match was wasted because it had to be kept lit as a precaution whenever near the enemy. Munitions were also required for training soldiers and sailors and to test ordnance and firearms. On 14 November 1640 Astley, the army's commander, ordered that 1 lb of gunpowder and a proportional amount of match be issued to each musketeer for thirty-eight days of exercises that had begun on 6 November.[2] Stocks had to be constantly replenished and it is, therefore, not surprising to note that a shortage of munitions was one of the most frequently recurring themes of the conflict. To help meet rising demand output was increased. Parliament, controlling the main centres of production, stepped up its activities and the other parties developed their own facilities, normally by adapting existing plant. The Royalists did the best, creating a full range of forges, foundries and mills at Oxford and at other sites, and achieving a reasonable level of production. The Scottish Covenanters established a gun foundry at Edinburgh and also produced some munitions, but output was not particularly high. In Ireland, production was far lower. Even if the success rate varied, none of the operations achieved self-sufficiency and imports remained essential.

An indication of the large amount of munitions used is revealed in a notional inventory of the ordnance and munitions required for a field army of 10,000 men, drawn up on 28 March 1642. The foot regiments were allocated 7½ tons of gunpowder, 7½ tons of musket shot and 10 tons of match, and the artillery train, comprising ten large field pieces and sixty galloping guns, 10 tons of gunpowder and cannonballs.[3] It is easy to see how the tonnage mounted up. Typically, an individual musketeer had twelve ½-oz charges in his bandolier, twelve bullets (1 lb) in his pouch and a ½–1lb coil of match around his arm.[4] Each cannon, whether in an artillery train or on a town wall, might have 100 or more cannonballs and perhaps a number of rounds of case shot as well.[5] Artillery pieces needed gunpowder and match too, perhaps ½ cwt of gunpowder and ¼ cwt of match apiece.[6] Actual fighting cut deeply into stocks. When Newcastle fought Fairfax at Tadcaster on 6 December 1642 the battle only ended at dusk when both sides had exhausted themselves and their ammunition. Fairfax calculated that 40,000 bullets (about 1½ tons) had been fired, using up, one might add, similar amounts of gunpowder and match. At the First Battle of Newbury, on 20 September 1643, the exchange of fire was so heavy that the Royalist artillery ran short of cannonballs and the foot lacked gunpowder. A long siege, as the Royalists found at Gloucester, took a heavy toll on resources. The Parliamentarian, Sir William Brereton, experienced the same problem while investing Chester in 1645, calculating that between 20 September and 16 December 1645 he had expended 7 tons of gunpowder (140 barrels), a proportional amount of shot and 20 tons of match. Asking for more gunpowder on 18 December, he protested that 'no one could have been more frugal than he had been, but it is incredible how much is spent'.[7] Defenders' reserves, often more limited, were run down too, especially on days when they had to repulse an assault. At Lyme in June 1644 the garrison, 1500 strong, were said to have spent fifteen barrels of gunpowder and nearly a quarter ton of match on such occasions.[8]

ORDNANCE

In the period leading up to and including the Civil Wars the iron ordnance industry was concentrated in the Weald of south-eastern England with its plentiful water power and abundant supplies of iron ore and charcoalling wood. It was also located close to its most important customer, the Ordnance Office. Although the region maintained its prominence in the early seventeenth century, other areas, notably South Wales and the Forest of Dean emerged and increased their output.[9] The manufacture of brass ordnance was not so closely tied to its raw materials and developed in London; foundries being established at

Houndsditch, Lambeth, Vauxhall and Southwark. [10] As founders of iron cannon had the necessary equipment to make 'brass' pieces (made of a mixture of tin and copper), that branch of the industry was often carried on at the same sites. Brass ordnance was deemed to be superior and was certainly more expensive: in 1650 iron guns cost £20 a ton and brass ones £27 6s.[11] Cannon were cast in one piece in a loam mould and imperfections in the cylinder bored out with a drill, processes introduced into England in 1543.[12]

A number of families were engaged in the business but the group was a restricted one. Keeping production in the family enhanced exclusivity; several generations of the Brownes of Kent, for instance, were involved in making cannon (see Table 2). Iron founders, in general, tended to work on a larger scale than the norm and ordnance manufacturers certainly had bigger than average concerns. When John Browne, the king's founder, built a new foundry at Brenchley in 1637 the estimated cost was £1,700. Apart from the costs inherent in the industry, founders also had to have the means to withstand the problems of fluctuating demand caused by conditions of war and peace, restrictions on free trade and the difficulty in getting the main customer, the government, to pay.[13]

In the late sixteenth and early seventeenth centuries English iron cannon enjoyed a Europeanwide reputation and a thriving export market. The Crown tried to regulate the sale of such a strategically important commodity by instituting a licensing system but with only partial success. Gunfounders needed this market to remain in business. In 1619 over half of Browne's output was bought by the Dutch, by men like Elias Trip, who between 1612 and 1622 exported 200–300 cannon from England every year.[14] The Trips, one of the leading mercantile families in Europe, had wide-ranging connections in the international arms trade. The family became involved in the Swedish gunfounding industry – developed with Dutch capital and expertise – in the 1620s and 1630s. Elias and Pieter Trip, related by marriage to Louis de Geer, the pioneer of the Swedish industry, invested heavily in the venture and profited from it. Swedish cannon were just as good as English ones and because they were cheaper, were preferred. By the time of the Irish insurrection England was a net importer of cannon and among those willing to supply them were the Trips.[15]

Ironmasters and gun founders cast cannonballs in moulds, mostly in large quantities. On 30 June 1639, John Browne received a debenture, valued at £272 0s 8d, for 1,265 saker balls, 6,686 drake balls, 845 saker grenades and 12½ cwt of burr shot that had delivered.[16] Some cannonballs were made on the march in portable moulds like the ones Captain Phipps, a commissary officer for the New Model Army, acquired. In April 1645 he obtained a mould for demi-culverin cannonballs and two for sakers, while two weeks later he received six moulds for 1-lb shot and twelve for ½-lb shot.[17] Gunfounders also made the casings of mortar shells. Incendiary bombs, however, were the preserve of the specialist 'fireworker', who made up a combustible mixture of oils and resins, added sulphur and saltpetre, and wrapped up the device in canvas daubed with pitch.[18] Because fireworkers were highly skilled they were well looked after. On the Royalist side considerable effort was made to keep Monsieur La Roche supplied

TABLE 2

BROWNE AND FOLEY CANNON-FOUNDING PARTNERSHIP
INVENTORY OF STOCK AT THEIR FURNACES IN THE SOUTH-EAST, 26 JUNE 1655

Ref: Herefordshire Record Office, Foley Papers E 12/VI/2/4967

Commodity	Rate	Value (£s)	Totals
Horsemonden furnace			
1,600 loads of mine (ore)	5s a load	400	
20 loads of brass	15s a load	15	
6 loads of stones for the hearth: at the furnace	10s a load	3	
1 broken gun, gun heads & cast iron: 2½ tons	£5 a ton	12.5	
1 new gutt & penstocks & timber & workmanship		2.5	
8 vault stands	1s each	0.4	
500 foot of planks	16s a cwt	4	
350 foot of coal wain boards	6s a cwt	1.05	
9 loads 10 foot of hewed timber	£1 a load	9.2	447.65
Bedgebury furnace			
1,700 loads of mine	5s a load	425	
3 tons of gun heads & cast iron	£5 a ton	15	
2 forge hammers pieces: 10 cwt		3	
5 cwt of wrought iron	18s a cwt	4.5	447.5
Barden furnace			
750 loads of mine	5s a load	187.5	
5 loads of brass	15s a load	3.75	
4 cords of wood	8s a cord	1.6	
30 tons of unhewed timber at the furnace	16s a ton	24	
10 cwt of wrought iron	18s a cwt	9	
5 cwt wrought of gun heads and cast iron	5s a cwt	1.25	
16 loads of stones for the hearth & not brought in	5s a load	4	231.1
Scarlett furnace			
240 loads of mine	5s a load	60	
4 gun heads pieces: 3 cwt	5s a cwt	0.75	60.75
Cowden furnace			
150 loads of mine	5s a load	37.5	
100 loads of coals	30s a load	150	
15 cords of wood	8s a cord	6	
1 gun head: 1 cwt	5s a cwt	0.25	
10 cwt of flat and square iron	18s a cwt	9	202.75

with money and materials necessary for his work (though not always successfully).[19] Apothecaries, known as drugsters, provided many of the ingredients. For the Scottish and Irish campaigns of 1638–42 the Ordnance Office dealt with Robert Hill, a London drugster.[20]

In the Bishops' Wars two people, carrying on their families' tradition of gunfounding, were largely responsible for supplying the king with home-produced ordnance. John Browne had the monopoly to make and sell iron ordnance and shot, having purchased it from the king in October 1635 for £12,000. He also encroached on the preserve of Thomas Pitt, designated the King's Founder of Brass Ordnance.[21] Browne possessed a number of furnaces and forges in Kent and Sussex, notably at Brenchley and Horsemonden in Kent and at Brede in Sussex. He also had a three-quarter share in a partnership with Henry Cruttenden, gent, at the furnaces at Barden and Cowden in Kent.[22] Pitt's family was associated with the manufacture of 'brass' cannon at the Houndsditch foundry.[23] Both supplied ordnance when the artillery train was being assembled for the First Bishops' War in 1638 but thereafter Pitt seems to have concentrated on providing ordnance for the East India Company.[24] He did, however, carry out those mundane jobs that formed part of his official duties; in December 1640, for instance, he screwed touch-holes onto three brass pieces lying at Chatham.[25] Browne supplied ordnance to the army and to garrisons but the bulk of his trade was with the navy. In one contract he made 102 brass cannon of various sizes for the *Sovereign of the Seas* at the new workshops specially erected for the purpose at Brenchley. The cannon weighed 156 tons and cost £25,217 5s 0d including incidentals.[26]

Parliament

In the Long Parliament there was considerable feeling against surviving monopolists like John Browne, but when the conflict began there was no one else who could do the job. Walsingham later commented that 'the rebels have no guns or bullets but from him . . . there being none in the Tower which is forced to provide else they would put others into his works'.[27] In 1643 he dispatched 36 pieces of brass ordnance, 17,314 cannonballs and 4,120 hand-grenades to the Ordnance Office.[28] His indispensability even enabled him to survive serious accusations of treachery in 1645, when it was alleged that he was a Royalist sympathiser in touch with dissident elements in Kent. Among other charges it was said that he had sent some of his men to Oxford to assist the king and that he had deliberately 'gone slow' in his work with Parliament. While under investigation, Browne's business was run by his associates, Samuel Ferrers, a London ironmonger, and Thomas Foley, his son-in-law and an ironmaster. On 30 December 1645 the House of Commons decided that it was in the best interests of the State to allow Browne to regain control of his business.[29] Perhaps significantly, references to the Pitt family begin again. In January 1646 a Mr Pitt cast seven brass guns destined for Northampton.[30] In March 1650 Richard Pitt and John Browne jointly contracted to cast new brass pieces out of 22 tons of unserviceable cannon and in the same month they shared 3 tons of brass to make two mortars.[31]

Because of his dominant position Browne was able to extend his operations during the war, acquiring additional capacity at other foundries.[32] At some point in the 1640s he involved his son-in-law, Thomas Foley, in the business. Foley had provided him with 80 tons of pig iron by 1649–50 and a further 61¼ tons the following year. In 1651 he was casting ordnance at Barden.[33] As before, most of the ordnance and shot made was earmarked for the navy. In 1645 he was due to make an estimated £2,507 19s ½d worth of cannon, shot and grenades for the summer fleet and in 1650 he contracted to cast 180 guns for six new frigates. Nonetheless, he did provide some ordnance for the army, notably helping to restock Essex's artillery train after the disaster at Lostwithiel on 1 September 1644 when forty-two pieces were lost. On 12 September he received an order to make a number of brass drakes of 3-lb ball for the army.[34] Browne continued to supply tons of cannonballs and grenades to the Parliamentarian forces via the Ordnance Office and, on occasion, direct to them. He also maintained a retail outlet. Ordnance intended for sale on the open market was sent to his London agent, Richard Pearson, at his house in Philpot Street, for delivery to Samuel Ferrers at the Half Moon in Thames Street. At his examination on 24 June 1645 John Browne deposed that Ferrers had 'bespoken' 300 small pieces for the market.[35]

Parliament made some use of leather guns, producing them mainly in London. James Wemyss, the ex-Master Gunner of England and a nephew of Robert Scott, made a set for Waller, and they did good service until captured by the Royalists at Cropredy Bridge on 29 June 1644. As part of his arms procurement drive in the capital in the winter of 1642/3 Lord Brooke obtained three frames, containing four brass pieces in each. In spite of their apparent fragility, they survived the proof. Sir Thomas Myddleton purchased others there in May 1644.[36] Waller's guns were possibly made at Lambeth;[37] others were cast at Vauxhall. According to an inventory of stock, taken on 20 May 1644, there were ninety frames in the workshops, ready to serve as mounts for the cannon, and about sixty imperfect ones.[38]

One or two provincial founders manufactured ordnance; for example, a gunfounder named William began working for the Warwickshire Committee in spring 1643.[39] Such men mostly made cannonballs because they could easily be cast in moulds and required less specialised plant. John Arundel delivered 9 cwt of cannonballs and assorted artillery ware to Sir Thomas Myddleton in 1644. The garrison at Gloucester obtained cannonballs, grenades and petards from the furnace at Newent in 1643 and the one at Nantwich received shot and mortar shells from Hough furnace in Cheshire a year later. In Staffordshire the committee dealt with the Royalist founder, Sir Walter Chetwynd of Rugeley, working on Cannock Chase.[40] At Nottingham, the garrison made some of the cannonballs on the spot; on one occasion Richard Hall earned £2 5s for casting 6 cwt of cannonballs and dressing 3 tons in weight. Most, however, came from outside and Hall was employed in bringing them in. In 1644 the garrison obtained cannonballs from Ecclesfield furnace near Sheffield but thereafter received regular consignments from the furnace at North Wingfield in Derbyshire. In July 1647 the arms and ammunition brought from there required fifty to sixty carts to move them. At Sheffield itself the forges turned out cannonballs for the Parliamentarian forces when they besieged the castle in the aftermath of the Battle of Marston Moor.[41]

Because foundries supplying ordnance and munitions were located close to deposits of ironstone, iron guns and cannonballs could be made with local materials. For its own stock, the Ordnance Office might deal with an ironfounder or with a merchant. In August 1649, for instance, Edward Barker, an arms and metal merchant from Coldharbour in London delivered 40 tons of iron and 10¾ cwt of steel for the Irish campaign.[42] It was more difficult to obtain tin and copper in this country for deposits were mainly to be found in Cornwall and in the fells of north-west England respectively.[43] The government, therefore, tended to purchase stock and supply its founder of brass ordnance with it. In the 1630s Thomas Pitt worked exclusively with metal given to him. John Browne, however, often bought his own material, though increasingly during the 1640s he worked with Ordnance Office supplies. Wherever possible, metal was reused, hence the recasting of 25 tons of unserviceable ordnance in March 1650.[44] In desperation pots, pans and kettles were melted down; in March 1645 a party of four men from the garrison at Nottingham were sent out to look for brassware.[45] Imports helped to improve the situation and were especially welcome in an emergency. The cannon that Browne made to restock Essex's army in 1644 were made partly with Dutch metal.[46]

Royalists

Although the king lost his gunfounder and plant, his plight was not as desperate as it might appear. The accident of geography provided the Royalists with a more than adequate supply of raw materials and a number of ironworking sites that could be geared up to produce ordnance and munitions. These were located in South Wales, the Welsh Border, the West Midlands and the north-east. Forest of Dean ore was of a particularly high grade, ideal for the armaments industry and, as a result, pig iron from the Forest was sent up the River Severn to the forges in Shropshire and the West Midlands.[47] Iron ore from the Clee Hills of Shropshire was also distributed around the region.[48] Like the Parliamentarians, the Royalists had greater difficulty finding the raw materials to make brass ordnance. Donations of brass and copper goods helped but this was obviously a diminishing resource. More encouraging was an individual offer of a ton of brass in April 1644 and the promise of regular deliveries of 5 cwt a week in return for ready cash.[49]

At Oxford a gun foundry, complete with boring equipment, was set up Christ Church and a second foundry was built in Frewin Hall. Workshops and forges were established in the artillery park in Magdalen College grove.[50] Mr Lanyon, possibly a pre-war proof master in the Ordnance Office, was put in charge. To assist him he probably had several of John Browne's workforce, including Hugh Richardson, described as a founder.[51] To obtain some of the metal the authorities ordered the inhabitants of Oxford to contribute their household brass; in March 1643 Anthony Carter, a brazier, went round the city, house by house, collecting pots and pans.[52] Initially, the results were poor: the first pieces cast (two small brass cannon) proved to be unserviceable and had to be melted down.[53] The Ordnance Commissioners, Strode and Wandesford, also began to cast ordnance and in March 1643 Sir John Heydon was ordered to deliver to them a large copper furnace for the purpose. When the city was captured in 1646 there were thirty-eight pieces in the works.[54]

A far more important source of ordnance and shot for the Royalists were the foundries of Shropshire and the West Midlands, notably those at Leighton, Bridgnorth and Bouldon in Shropshire and at Dudley and Stourbridge in Worcestershire.[55] Production began with commendable speed, for at Stourbridge Richard Foley was casting cannonballs by August 1642. Later, he made cannon there as well. Payments made by Sir William Russell, the governor of Worcester, for ordnance and shot delivered commenced in December 1642.[56] In Shropshire Matthias Gervase dispatched consignments of cannonballs to Chester and grenades to Oxford from the forge at Leighton near Shrewsbury early in 1643. At Bouldon Francis Walker had earned nearly £1,000 by September 1643 for casting 3 tons of cannonball and forty-four iron cannon for various garrisons. Some of the cannon went to Bristol, where Lord Hopton, the governor, was so pleased with them that in August he ordered thirty more. In August 1643 four cannon, manufactured in Shropshire, were assigned to a warship at Chester.[57]

Although West Midlands ironmasters dispatched their ware far and wide, a key task of theirs was to augment and replenish the stocks in the central magazine at Oxford. Consignments were shipped by river to Worcester, thence by cart for the final stage of the journey. Between February and May 1643 Russell sent monthly cargoes to Oxford, providing the hard-pressed ordnance officers there with welcome supplies. These included 20 cannon, 1,053 hand grenades, 144 mortar shells, nearly 7,000 cannonballs and 9½ tons of iron. A convoy of 95 carts that arrived on 22 April, carrying 5,378 cannonballs, 130 mortar shells, 821 hand grenades and 1,046 pike heads, caused a particular stir on account of its size.[58] When that part of Walker's consignment of 1643, earmarked for Oxford, was held up at Worcester until the following spring, it created problems there. To ensure that the city was adequately defended, the army had to loan brass field ordnance, which led to shortages in the artillery train. At the same time Digby asked Prince Rupert to send to Oxford as quickly as possible the cannonballs and mortar shells cast at Leighton, 'for there is great want of them here'. The high command wanted to be ready for the campaigning season.[59]

Ordnance and shot from the ironworks of south Wales and the Forest of Dean were generally employed locally. In 1643 Lord Herbert's forces in south-east Wales obtained cannon from sites in Glamorgan, Breconshire and the Forest of Dean, capable of producing 20 tons of iron a week.[60] When the Royalists invested Gloucester in August 1643 they had a readily available source of *matériel* in the Forest; the army received 527 cannonballs from Sowdley furnace alone.[61] Sir John Wintour was an important figure; although he leased Sowdley and other sites to Sir Baynham Throckmorton, he retained several forges and furnaces in his own hands, notably at Lydney. According to John Corbet, the personal chaplain of Colonel Massey, the governor of Gloucester, Wintour's iron mills and furnaces 'were the main strength of his estate and garrison'.[62] In 1644 Massey attacked Wintour at Lydney but, failing to take the house, burned three of his iron mills.[63] The north, with its separate Ordnance Office, also tended to deploy its resources within the region, though it did send occasional consignments to Oxford. In August 1642 the authorities assembled a convoy, comprising native and foreign ordnance, at York for forwarding to the king at Nottingham. Included in the train were mortar pieces made at York.[64] The ironworks of the north-east must have been a major source of supply for the Royalists, judging from the large quantities of cannonballs that the Scots obtained from Sunderland from 1644 onwards. The capture of Sheffield in May 1643 added extra capacity.[65]

The activities of ironmasters like Foley and Walker ensured that the Royalists had a regular supply of ordnance. In the first few months of the conflict in England they seem to have produced a sufficient quantity of cannonballs to meet their needs. Early in 1643 Orlando Bridgeman reported that he had an adequate stock at Chester and that there were enough at the furnace at Leighton to provide for the four cannon he was sending to Shrewsbury. By April 1643 Lord Capel, the Royalist commander in Cheshire, Shropshire and north Wales, had obtained so much ordnance that he could give Prince Rupert, then at Lichfield, three spare cannon and numerous cannonballs.[66] Some shortages did occur during 1643 and 1644 but they could be made good from existing facilities. Thus, when a delay in providing the requisite amount of mortar shells, hand grenades and cannonballs, ordered for royal garrisons in 1643, came to light Matthias Gervase of Leighton was asked to exhort his fellow founders in Shropshire and Staffordshire to provide them.[67] Prices charged were comparable to the ones Parliament paid. In September 1643 Francis Walker received £40 for casting 3 tons of round shot, a lower rate than the £6 6s Sir Thomas Myddleton paid for 9 cwt of cannonballs in April 1644, though more than the £12 a ton that John Browne charged. In 1645 Richard Foley was selling bar iron to Lord Loughborough for £18 a ton, whereas a consignment of flat iron for the New Model Army in August cost £19 2s 8d a ton.[68]

Scotland and Ireland

Influenced by their experience in the Swedish army, Scottish commanders took pains to create an effective artillery train when they prepared to fight Charles I. Apart from acquiring ordnance abroad, the Covenanters made use of Alexander Hamilton, the veteran of the Swedish service, to cast cannon in Scotland.[69] In 1635 he returned to his native country and when the conflict with Charles loomed, set to work casting cannon at Potters Row in Edinburgh. Here he made the leather guns for which he was renowned, as well as heavier ordnance.[70] A report on the state of preparedness of the Covenanters, written on 22 April 1640, noted that they were well provided with siege artillery and field pieces (including leather guns) and that they were busily making them at home.[71] Hamilton supplied ordnance to the Army of the Solemn League and Covenant, too.[72] His successor in the late 1640s was James Wemyss, who had also gained experience on the continent. He continued to make leather guns at the Potters Row foundry until defeat at Dunbar in September 1650 led to the loss of Edinburgh.[73] To re-create an artillery train Wemyss had to take ordnance from various castles and attempt to purchase others abroad. In 1651 he also obtained two brass cannon from James Menteith, an Edinburgh pewterer, who cast them at Stirling.[74]

Apart from the guns themselves, other work was involved. Leather guns were easy to move but larger field pieces had to be mounted on carriages. When required, carpenters, joiners and wheelwrights were employed to do the work. In August 1649, for instance, Sir Charles Erskine, the governor of Dumbarton Castle, received £800 Scots to pay for the mounting of eight cannon. Two years later John Scott was ordered to construct carriages for the two cannon that Menteith had made at Stirling.[75] Cannonballs had to be cast too. In early 1639 Archibald Campbell of Glencarradale, Argyll, was in Edinburgh ordering them for his uncle, Sir Colin Campbell of Glenorchy. Unfortunately, the caster could not use the mould sent so Archibald had to have another one made. The delay meant that when the mould was ready Sir Colin had to take his place in the queue, for demand had increased as preparations for war accelerated. The man, Archibald noted, 'hes so mutche work in hand for the Nobilitie and he can not weill overtak.'[76] James Menteith was later involved in this work. In August 1646 he delivered thirty cannonballs weighing 90 lb to the council at Edinburgh. As he was similarly engaged in providing lead shot to the army, Menteith was a key figure in the supply of ordnance and munitions.[77] When casting cannonballs, care had to be taken to ensure that they were of the right dimensions. In February 1651 the Duke of Hamilton sent drawings to indicate the size required when he asked John Hamilton of Bangour, West Lothian, to buy cannonballs (probably at nearby Edinburgh) or have one Mather make them. Altogether, he wanted 120 cannonballs of $2\frac{1}{2}$-in diameter for falcons, 160 of 3-in for minions and sixty of $3\frac{1}{3}$-in for sacres.[78]

Some of the raw materials could be obtained at home, though at the time the country possessed few deposits of exploitable weapons grade iron ore.[79] As in England, domestic utensils were melted down for their metal. For example, in May 1639 James Cocheran, dean of the guild at Edinburgh, was given four old copper kettles, weighing 93 lb, to be cast into field pieces.[80] The Covenanters also received large consignments from abroad. The report of 22 April 1640 noted that they had obtained 'good store' of copper and brass from Holland and the Sound. The Swedes gave copper to Field Marshal Leslie as part of their 'decommissioning gift' to him in 1638 and in August 1640 the Covenanters' envoy, Colonel John Cochrane, asked for cannon, and copper to make more ordnance in Scotland.[81] They also sent iron, a continuation of a trade that pre-dated the wars but which now had strategic importance.[82] In 1638 John Maclean, a wealthy Scottish expatriate merchant based at Gothenburg, shipped 6,746 lasts of iron to Scotland (1 last = either 4,000 lb or 2 tons). He also dispatched 16,640 lasts to Amsterdam, some of which probably continued on to Scotland in Dutch bottoms.[83] Iron certainly came from Zeeland ports; surviving admiralty licences record that between October 1639 and August 1640 four shipments of iron, totalling nearly $9\frac{1}{2}$ tons, left for Scotland.[84]

Cannon played an important role in the Irish campaigns. Sieges were common, while a number of towns incorporated elements of the *trace italienne* in their defences. Limerick and Galway are the best examples.[85] Some capacity for making ordnance already existed in the country before the war, based on local mineral deposits. The iron ore that Blacknall and Wright mined in Co. Cork in the 1620s was ideal for casting ordnance and in 1626 they set up a gun foundry at the site at Cappoquin, leased from the Earl of Cork.[86] Elsewhere, cannon were produced at a foundry belonging to Sir Thomas Ridgeway at Ballinakill, Co. Leix; ten 3-lb minions were cast there in 1633. Wentworth had a financial stake in this foundry and ordnance from it may have been sent to the central magazine at Dublin Castle.[87]

One or two gun foundries sprang up in the initial stages of the war but they appear to have been small-scale enterprises. At Athboy, Co. Meath, in 1641 a smith cast a brass cannon out of pots and pans, which blew up when fired at the walls of Geashill, Co. Offaly. Another one, used against Castle Coote, Co. Roscommon, was more successful. At Ballyally, Co. Clare, the besiegers constructed a leather gun. The following year Colonel Richard Plunkett was reputedly making gunpowder and cannon at the Earl of Fingall's house, probably at Killeen, Co. Meath. It is likely that the iron works at Artully, Co. Kerry, and Lissan, Co. Tyrone, were making cannonballs, if not guns.[88] In 1646 the Leinster provincial council employed Richard Cantwell, a Kilkenny smith, to make ironwork for the cannon and a year later it contracted with Tirlogh Duff, a carpenter, for cannon- and wagon wheels and yokes for the oxen that pulled them. The timber was found in the woods of Leix.[89]

To overcome the shortage of skilled workers in Ireland, foreign artisans were brought in. A number of them had arrived in the country by the end of February 1642. Specialists from Liège, for instance, ran the foundry at Ballinakill. In response to the Supreme Council's request for arms manufacturers from abroad, General Preston induced the Fleming, Nicholas Lallo, to come to work for the Confederacy as chief engineer. According to his petition of August 1646 he had been variously involved in making ordnance, cannon ware and gunpowder in Flanders and since coming to Ireland had been at considerable charge building workshops for a similar purpose at Kilkenny. His comments suggest that he was mainly engaged in manufacturing gunpowder and cannon ware rather than casting guns.[90] In October 1644 he seems to have been 'on loan' to Ormond, who described him as a man skilled in casting brass and iron cannon and making saltpetre and gunpowder. Interestingly, the information is revealed in a letter Ormond sent to Lord Byron, the governor of Chester, who was being asked if he could give him employment. Ormond observed, 'such are our wantes heare that I am not able to set him a worke', suggesting that the Irish Royalists had neither the plant nor the raw materials to cast ordnance. Lallo did not go to Chester, for the petition indicates that he was still working for the Confederates. In early 1645 he seems to have been directing engineering operations for the insurgents at their siege of Duncannon, Co. Wexford.[91]

To augment home supplies the Confederates imported raw materials. In June 1643 Luke Wadding and Father James Talbot, then at the Spanish Court, were instructed to obtain copper, iron and steel, as well as arms, munitions and workmen. In January 1645, in an attempt to achieve greater self-sufficiency, the Supreme Council sought the services of a person to prospect for minerals and to direct their processing and manufacture. They asked Hugh Bourke as a matter of urgency to scour Flanders and Spain for 'one of the most skilful in the discovery of mines of silver, lead, copper, brass and iron, and that will know how to dispose of and direct those works'.[92]

AMMUNITION

Unlike the iron ordnance industry, the manufacture of lead bullets was not carried on in close proximity to its raw material. Ore was smelted in furnaces erected in lead-producing areas such as the Derbyshire Peak District, the Mendips, Durham, Northumberland and the Yorkshire Dales, and sold as pigs or sheets to merchants or manufacturers. Before the Civil Wars, much of the lead to make bullets was taken to London, where the Ordnance Office and the shot casters, who provided it with bullets, were major customers. The casting of bullets for firearms was a relatively straightforward process and could be done by a competent plumber using basic equipment. All that one needed was a source of heat, a pot in which to melt the lead, ladles for pouring out the molten metal and moulds of different sizes, according to bore. The type of equipment required is revealed in the probate inventory of Hugh Canter, a Coventry plumber and glazier, who made bullets for the Warwickshire forces. The appraisers of his goods in 1678 listed a wooden mould to cast lead in the cellar (10s), a vice, glass and lead in the shop (£2), a little furnace and a warming pan (10s), and a little beam and scales (3s 4d) in the hall.[93]

Production could be carried on in the field and armies were routinely issued with the necessary equipment. In April 1645 John Phipps ordered 2 cwt of lead for ordnance, 3 iron pots to melt lead in, 12 great melting ladles and 24 small dipping ladles for the New Model Army. He also obtained 5 dozen bastard musket moulds. The Royalists did the same. While at Kingston upon Thames in November 1642, they made 8 cwt of musket shot. In 1643 the garrison at Skipton Castle, West Riding of Yorkshire, bought an iron pot in which to melt lead for bullets.[94] Nonetheless, in keeping with the typical pattern in the munitions industry, the manufacture of bullets was best carried out in comparatively large units where it could benefit from the economies of scale. Thus, while many plumbers could – and during the war, did – make small quantities of bullets, the leading manufacturers worked in casting shops, fitted with furnaces, crucibles and moulds. There, output was measured in tons.

Before the English Civil Wars, government contracts were dominated by Joseph Day, the master plumber in the Ordnance Office. Although paid a retainer, he supplied bullets as a contractor rather than as a mere employee using materials given to him. Indeed, he sold lead to the Ordnance Office. Throughout the Scottish and Irish campaigns he sent in regular consignments of lead, generally in sheets, several hundredweights at a time. His largest single delivery was of 5 tons of lead in pigs in August 1638.[95] Presumably, the Ordnance Office wanted to keep stocks of lead, some of which would be made into bullets in the Tower but which could also be given to the armed forces for conversion into bullets on the march or in garrisons. Day alone supplied home-produced bullets for the land and naval forces during this period. He was particularly active in the build-up to the First Bishops' War, delivering tons of musket shot throughout 1638 and early 1639 with peaks of 20 tons in March and September 1638 and May 1639.[96] He seems to have supplied sufficient bullets to meet the needs of the armed forces for there is little evidence of imported ware, though the ambiguous use of the word 'shot' obscures the issue.

Parliament

Joseph Day did not supply Parliament with any bullets, a service initially carried out by assorted London merchants and shot casters. Some of the biggest consignments were imports delivered by the merchants; in September 1642, for instance, Mr Edward Hooker sold 8.9 tons of bullets to the London militia. Among the shot casters John Montgomery stands out. Between March and July 1643 he delivered 17 tons of bullets to the Committee of Safety's magazine. These were the people to whom Essex turned at the beginning of the war; in August 1642 Robert Smith delivered 30 cwt of musket shot and in September Thomas Fryer sent in 5½ tons.[97] Over the next few months others shipped tons of shot downriver to the garrison at Windsor. Some of these manufacturers continued to supply Parliament with bullets. Thomas Madlock delivered forty-six barrels of musket shot to Bradley and Rowe in September 1643, 20 tons to the Ordnance Office in March 1647 and a further 30 tons in June 1651.[98] The most important figure, however, was Daniel Judd, who succeeded Day as the Ordnance Office's plumber and eventually as the main source of its bullets. He dealt directly with the field armies; in 1644 he was purveyor-commissary to Sir William Waller's army[99] and in the winter of 1644/5 he sent 6 tons 13 cwt of musket and pistol shot to Essex's army. Nevertheless, the bulk of his business lay with the Ordnance Office. The first recorded delivery occurred in March 1643 and by the time of the Worcester campaign in 1651 Judd had delivered about 430 tons of shot, mostly for muskets but for carbines and pistols too.[100]

Provincial shot casters, scattered around the country, might sell ammunition to a field army: in May 1643 an Exeter plumber delivered £70 worth of bullets to the Earl of Stamford and in East Anglia the Eastern Association obtained supplies locally.[101] However, as most of them operated at a fairly modest level, they mainly dealt with their local forces. In this respect, the war offered opportunities for plumbers to earn extra money and one might have expected a number of them to switch to the production of bullets. In reality, though, there was no free-for-all because many local committees or garrison commanders came to an arrangement with a particular plumber and provided him with available lead. In Staffordshire William Stone was specifically hired to make bullets.

In Warwickshire, where the county committee dealt with Hugh Canter of Coventry, the accounts enable us to see the entire process in operation. In April 1643 a carrier brought him 2 tons 9 cwt. of lead which, together with a further 3 tons 18½ cwt, he cast into bullets. On 7 August 1644 he presented a bill of £17 10s for the job.[102] Canter was being paid 4s a cwt, whereas the shot caster at Nottingham Castle only earned 1s. For work done during the siege of Gloucester in August–September 1643 John Barnard received about 3d a lb for the 601 lb of musket, carbine and pistol bullets he made out of his own lead and about 2d a lb for the 694 lb of bullets cast with the city's lead.[103] Figures for Gloucester, Nottingham, Warwickshire and Worcestershire, coupled with other stray references, suggest that an average monthly output ranged from a few hundredweight to half a ton. Nonetheless, local forces still suffered shortages and had to ask for help from central stores. Sir Samuel Luke, the governor of Newport Pagnell, regularly had to send an officer to London to beg for supplies.[104]

Output depended upon the availability of lead and Parliament only had intermittent control over those areas where deposits were located. In the Peak District they faced serious Royalist competition. In 1643–4, 564 lead pigs worth about £1,100 were sent to London and, probably in autumn 1644, a ton of lead was dispatched to Brereton in Cheshire. However, a load of 57 fodders (about 57 tons), destined for Bristol in summer 1643, was acquired by a Royalist supporter.[105] Because the enemy was taking so much lead, on 3 August 1644 the Earl of Manchester forbade anyone from buying it and insisted that it be taken to Gainsborough for distribution. This decision caused consternation among the founders and merchants and was counter-productive as it disrupted the normal trading pattern.[106] Merchants were essential links in the trade and on a national scale they were the ones who supplied lead to Ordnance Office contractors such as Joseph Day and Daniel Judd, or direct to the army. In December 1642, for example, John Mould sold 7 pigs of lead weighing 18 cwt 3 qr 18 lb to Captain Cannon, commander of the Earl of Essex's artillery.[107] As the armed forces made increasing use of commissary officers to obtain supplies, they tended to bypass traditional institutions. The most obvious manifestation of the emerging command economy occurred at times of shortage, when lead had to be obtained in a hurry. Roofs and guttering were prime targets: during the siege of Gloucester in August–September 1643 the 'Vineyard' at Over was stripped of lead to make bullets. The search for lead might be organised, as in Rutland, where Ambrose Ruddill supervised a team of lead gatherers, who brought it to a central storage point.[108]

Royalists

At Oxford James Fletcher, a plumber, and Charles Greene, a conductor to the artillery train, became the Royalist shot casters at the beginning of the war. They delivered their first consignments in January 1643: Fletcher sent in 2¾ tons and Green 2 cwt. In spite of the intrusion of the two ordnance commissioners, Strode and Wandesford, in mid-1643 both men continued to cast bullets for a considerable time. Fletcher's last recorded delivery took place on 27 April 1644, at the end of a month in which he dispatched 3 tons 19 cwt of musket shot to the stores. By this date he had made at least 20 tons 13½ cwt. Green carried on until 20 May 1646, having produced 11¼ tons of bullets. By May 1645 Strode and Wandesford had cast 10½ tons. Normally, the lead was supplied to the manufacturers, often for a specific casting. Most bullets that Fletcher made in April 1644 were cast from 3 tons 16 cwt 31 lb of lead delivered to him from the stores on the 4th and 15th. In spite of the shortcomings of the documentation it is clear that production at Oxford lagged behind that at London. During the same period Daniel Judd cast 94 tons of shot, three times the quantity.[109]

Fortunately, because of the Royalists' more decentralised structure, they were not entirely dependent upon the output of their arms industries at Oxford. Bullets, like other munitions, were made elsewhere, especially at Bristol. The capture of the city on 26 July 1643 greatly improved the supply of arms and munitions to the Royalists. Several plumber/shot casters, capable of producing hundredweights of bullets at a time, were already working in the city and the Royalists could make use of their services.[110] In October 1643 Richard March was dealing with a plumber who for £16 in cash promised to make a ton of musket shot a week. This was a reasonable price, even if Parliament was paying about £15 a ton, and Lord Percy's delay in responding to March's request for authorisation is puzzling. Eventually, the order came through at the end of March and the plumber started work.[111] In the north, Newcastle's army must have received supplies from Sunderland, but, again, we can only make this assumption because of the amount of ammunition that the Scots acquired there after they captured the town in March 1644. Other centres were involved, notably York. The garrison at Skipton Castle seems to have obtained most of its supplies from the city, though in April 1643 it received a load of bullets from Ripon. In January 1643 Thomas Sawer, a York shot caster, received £1 2s 6d for 2 cwt of lead bullets he had sold to the local garrison. At £11 5s a ton this was very cheap.[112] Elsewhere, we learn of shot casting from stray references. Presumably, the Exeter plumber who had supplied the Earl of Stamford with £70 worth of bullets in May 1643 subsequently worked for the king, when the city became a Royalist stronghold.[113]

The Royalists had the same problems as the Parliamentarians in obtaining an adequate supply of raw material. They competed for Peak District lead and, especially after Newcastle had regained the ascendancy in the area in December 1643, had some success. Skipton Castle received consignments from nearby Grassington.[114] The magazine at Oxford obtained lead from different parts of the country. In January 1643 the Earl of Northampton sent 79 pigs of lead (4 tons 7 cwt 48 lb) from Banbury, which Fletcher had cast into bullets by 11 March. On 13 April 1644 a consignment of 16¾ cwt of lead arrived from Bristol.[115] The last load may have come from the Mendips or from abroad but some of the others were 'salvage' stock. At Worcester, the cathedral roof was stripped of lead, as was that of St Mary's Church at Cardiff.[116]

Scotland and Ireland

In Scotland, initial orders to the shires for arms did not stipulate lead bullets, though, presumably, the authorities expected the soldiers to be given shot and gunpowder as well as weapons.[117] In his return of arms made in 1638, the Laird of Kincraig said that he would provide gunpowder, lead and match. The following year Perth sent 100 men to join Montrose's expedition against Huntly, providing a barrel of gunpowder and giving each man a fortnight's provisions, together with 1 lb of gunpowder and match and 1½ lb of bullets. According to a letter sent by Mungo Campbell to Sir Colin Campbell of Glenorchy in March, soldiers in the Campbell contingent were to receive 3 lb of gunpowder, 5 fathoms of match and a proportional amount of lead bullets.[118] In 1643 the Act of 18 August specifically asked each local war committee to provide munitions at the rate of 2 lb of gunpowder and 4 lb each of match and shot for every fencible person in the county.[119]

As any plumber could readily make lead shot in moulds, quotas must have been met by employing local men to do the work. Further supplies could be obtained from the burghs, especially from Edinburgh. While in the city in February 1639, Archibald Campbell told his uncle, Sir Colin Campbell, that he would arrange to have bullets cast for the muskets he was ordering there.[120] In August 1646 James Menteith, the Edinburgh pewterer who cast ordnance, delivered 3 cwt of musket ball to the city's magazine.[121] As the government's principal contractor for lead shot, he also supplied much larger consignments than this one. In some respects his career was very much like that of Daniel Judd in London. Their position in the trade indicates that although shot casting was amenable to small-scale production, the business was best conducted on a large scale. Menteith delivered 17,500 lb in February 1644 at the beginning of the campaign in England and further instalments of 18,400 lb and 6,500 lb in April and June respectively, a total of almost 19 tons.[122] At the time, he was based at Berwick. In 1651 he was at Stirling with the artillery train. On 11 April the Committee of Estates contracted with him for 30,000 lb of lead shot (26,000 lb of musket ball and 4,000 lb of pistol shot) at the rate of £20 Scots per 100 lb. He was to receive £4,000 immediately and the balance of £2,000 on delivery. He agreed to supply 20,000 lb within fifteen days and the final 10,000 lb a fortnight later.[123]

Lead could be mined at a number of sites in the country, though mostly, as at Islay and Lismore, on a small scale. Leadhills in Lanarkshire was the principal site and when Sir James Hope took possession of the mines in 1638, he stepped up production. Output reached 300–400 tons of ore a year.[124] However, the authorities also had to resort to the expedient of stripping roofs and guttering. This is suggested by an order of 1 February 1639, given to the treasurer of Edinburgh, to come to an agreement with 'some honest neighbours' for a ton of lead for bullets, as well as gunpowder and match. Indeed, on 25 January 1643 the city's authorities allowed Sir John Smyth and Henry Rollock to bring in 500 fodder of lead from England, custom free, for roofing.[125] In 1651 the burghs were ordered to assist Menteith in fulfilling his contract by supplying him with lead at a reasonable price and in cash. If they refused, their lead would be seized.[126] It is not surprising to note that there were shortages of lead in 1651. For some time imports had been needed to supplement home supplies. Between January 1644 and March 1645 enough English lead was obtained to make 14¼ tons of bullets for the Covenanters' army, three-quarters of the amount Menteith supplied.[127] The Scottish Royalists had to look further afield. In his mission to the Duke of Courland in 1645–6 one of the items on Sir John Cochrane's shopping list was 150 lasts of lead.[128]

There is little evidence of casting bullets in Ireland but it was being carried on. Lenihan asserts that the supply of bullets and match was less of a problem than the provision of gunpowder[129] and, undoubtedly, plumbers in the country were busy casting bullets for one party or the other. The problem of oversize bullets that Lord Broghill encountered in one engagement may reflect the employment of non-specialists to do the job.[130] In 1647 the Confederates engaged Thomas Clinton as a bullet maker; in June they paid him £17 15s 0d, representing about ¾ ton or more of lead shot.[131] They also brought in artificers from abroad. Some of the raw material they used could be found in the country; in 1647, for instance, the Confederates were mining lead and supplying Clinton with it.[132] Moreover, they adopted the same expedients as were employed in England and Scotland. In July 1644 the Earl of Kildare wrote to his kinsman, Ormond, that he had taken down the spouts of his house and as a result had obtained 'great store' of lead.[133] Home production, nonetheless, was small-scale and insufficient to meet the needs of the armies. Both Royalists and insurgents complained about the shortage of munitions and at times specifically referred to a lack of bullets. At Letterkenny in July 1642 William Steward told Ormond that he had to pay 6d a lb for ball because of the shortage of munitions. In September 1643 William Cole wrote to Ormond from Enniskillen to ask for arms and ammunition 'which is extreamely wanting with me at this tyme'. Without gunpowder, match and lead, he averred, he would not be able to repel the expected rebel attack the coming winter.[134] Earlier that year the Confederate, William Browne, had had to send an urgent request to his father for arms since most of his firearms, gunpowder, match and bullets 'are spent and wasted'.[135]

GUNPOWDER

The constituent ingredients of gunpowder are saltpetre, charcoal and brimstone (sulphur), the first to provide the oxygen for combustion, the second to furnish the essential carbon and the third to promote ignition and rapid burning. Charcoal, preferably from willow, alder, alder buckthorn or hazel, was readily available in Britain but the other ingredients were harder to obtain. All of the brimstone had to be imported, largely from the volcanic regions of Italy and Sicily.[136] Until 1561, when the German, Gerrard Honrick, was contracted to instruct Englishmen in the art of making it, most of the saltpetre came from abroad, too. Home-produced saltpetre was obtained from decaying nitrogen-rich material found in privies, stables, dovecotes and the like. Nonetheless, saltpetre continued to be imported, partly because of inadequate home supply and partly because of the superiority of the foreign product. In the 1570s consignments came from Morocco and in the early seventeenth century the East India Company emerged as a major supplier, drawing on natural deposits located in north India.[137] To make saltpetre, the 'black' earth was dug up and laid in beds to expose it to the air. Lime and urine were added and the heaps constantly turned until calcium nitrate was formed. To reduce the calcium content and to increase that of potassium, wood ash was applied. The nitrous material in solution, leached out by this process, was known as saltpetre liquor. It was then boiled and run off into vats. As the liquid cooled, crystals of potassium nitrate formed. These were skimmed off and the process repeated.[138] The operation consumed large quantities of fuel.[139]

Gunpowder makers combined the ingredients in varying proportions but by the mid-seventeenth century a ratio of 75:15:10 for saltpetre, charcoal and sulphur respectively had become the norm.[140] Initially, gunpowder makers ground (incorporated) the ingredients together by hand, using a pestle and mortar. The resultant 'cake' was then dried on trays and, finally, glazed. However, the 'serpentine' powder, as it was known, did not bind together well and tended to separate out. The process of corning – that is, forcing the cake through a sieve to create a more cohesive, granulated product – overcame the problem.[141] For pistols, a finer powder was needed and a sieve with a smaller mesh was employed. Mechanisation improved the incorporating process, mixing the ingredients more thoroughly than before. In the fifteenth century hand-operated stampers, installed in mills, were being used and later the machinery was harnessed to horse, wind and water-power. By the mid-seventeenth century the largest gunpowder mills in England were driven by water.[142] After drying and glazing, the finished product was put in barrels and dispatched, though this might not be the last that the gunpowder maker saw of his handiwork. If kept too long or badly stored, gunpowder decayed and it would have to be brought back for 'amending'.

In 1589 the government restricted production to patentees, who agreed to supply a certain quantity of gunpowder to the Crown for a set number of years at a fixed price. In 1624 the amount was raised to 240 lasts a year (1 last = 24 cwt) Surpluses could be sold on the open market.[143] The patentees enjoyed a virtual monopoly but did face some competition, notably from the East India Company, which built a gunpowder mill at Chilworth, Surrey, in the mid-1620s, and from illicit gunpowder makers. Bristol was a notorious centre of illegal activity, in which the Baber and Coslett families were prominent.[144] At first, the patentees had to find their own saltpetre but in 1620 the government appointed a special group of saltpetre men, who had to supply a certain quantity of saltpetre a week from their allocated part of the country. In 1630 amounts varied from 1–10 cwt.[145] The population at large hated saltpetre men because of the aggressive way they went about their business. According to their terms of employment, they had the right to enter premises where saltpetre might be found – even empty cellars in inhabited houses. Afterwards, they were supposed to make good any damage committed, leave a gap of a few years before returning and take care about the times when they worked. The flood of protests suggests that they did not always comply.[146] Nonetheless, in spite of their oppressive behaviour they could not supply the gunpowder maker with sufficient material and the government had to import it.

Charles I himself cynically abused the system, especially in his manipulation of the terms of a new contract signed on 1 November 1636 with Samuel Cordwell and George Collins. Cordwell, a gentleman from Higham in Kent, provided the capital and Collins, whose father, Edward, had made gunpowder for the East India Company, the technical skill.[147] They agreed to produce the set amount of 240 lasts but required a loan of £2,000 to develop and extend the site at Chilworth. The king saved money by negotiating a price of 7½d a lb rather than the 8d that the previous patentee, Sir John Evelyn, had received. The contractors, moreover, were obliged to sell their entire product to the king.[148] In the following year Charles banned imports and forced all private customers to buy gunpowder from government stores.[149] He then raised the retail price from 1s to 1s 6d a lb. This, naturally, caused an outcry and drove customers into the arms of the illicit gunpowder makers, who responded by stepping up production. For his part, the king ordered the authorities to make more strenuous attempts to suppress them.[150] Once Parliament was recalled in 1640 it was inevitable that the gunpowder industry would be on the agenda. In a debate on the issue on 5 March 1641, opposition to the monopoly was widespread, Mr Whistler and Sir John Hotham calling the practice 'a grievance and a monopoly and against the liberty of the subjects'. In spite of a speech in favour of it by Evelyn and a later petition by Samuel Cordwell, the system was doomed and on 10 August 1641 the trade in gunpowder and saltpetre was opened up to all-comers.[151]

The king's intrigues had strategic consequences, too, contributing in no small measure to a shortfall in the amount of home-produced gunpowder delivered to the Ordnance Office. The performance of the two contractors in the first four accounting years (beginning on 1 November) was patchy. In 1636–7 and 1638–9 they met their annual target of 240 lasts but failed to do so in the years 1637–8 (by 40 lasts) and 1639–40 (by 24 lasts).[152] The main reason, as Cordwell observed in December 1638, was insufficient saltpetre delivered to him.[153] More serious was the king's unwillingness or inability to pay Cordwell for the gunpowder sent to the Ordnance Office. In July 1640 Cordwell complained that as he was owed £4,000 for powder, he could not pay the saltpetre men. The consequence, he warned, was that his works were in danger of coming to a halt.[154] Promises were made but it seems as though the experience taught Cordwell to dispose of his stock elsewhere. He began to buy East India Company saltpetre in bulk and to sell much of his gunpowder privately.[155]

The impact on the Ordnance Office magazine was dramatic. In July 1641 it was reported that 'of late no Powder hath been brought into the Kings store'. By the following February it seems as though the Ordnance Office had received no gunpowder for thirteen months.[156] In that month it was calculated that after all the allocated gunpowder had been distributed, there would only be four lasts left in the Tower.[157] Clearly, the freeing of the trade in gunpowder and saltpetre did not improve the situation. No new contractors came forward to offer a serious challenge to Cordwell, who nonetheless claimed that the ending of the monopoly had damaged his business. Not only did he find it difficult to gauge his requirements but because the saltpetre men were withholding supplies in order to raise prices he also had trouble obtaining saltpetre. These problems occurred at a critical time, in the years covering the Scottish and Irish insurrections. Ironically, the political crisis forced the king to abandon a potentially lucrative overseas market, for in December 1638 he had to stop granting export licences for gunpowder.[158] While, as noted above, the Ordnance Office did issue large quantities of gunpowder,[159] it took months to produce, especially as native saltpetre was in short supply. The deficiency had to be bridged by greater quantities of saltpetre and gunpowder from abroad.

Parliament

When the Civil War began in England in August 1642 there were a mere 10 lasts of gunpowder in the Tower.[160] Parliament did gain the Chilworth site and the services of Samuel Cordwell but it also inherited his problems. In the short term, too, the mills were made inoperable by the ebb and flow of battle. As the king advanced on London in Autumn 1642 Sir Richard Onslow was ordered to pull down the buildings and take away the powder-making materials. He evidently did not do the job thoroughly for when the Royalist army retreated in November, Sir John Heydon was told to complete the task.[161] Cordwell seems to have been back in operation by mid-March 1643, though the first recorded deliveries were made in July.[162] A Royalist raiding party under Lord Percy may have returned that month but, if it did, it did little damage. Parliament continued to worry about the safety of its supplies; in January 1645 it ordered Cordwell to dispatch his gunpowder to the Tower as soon as it had been made 'for fear of the enemy coming into those parts' and never to keep more than a week's supply of saltpetre at Chilworth.[163] Perhaps it suspected him of Royalist sympathies.

Cordwell did not have to sustain the war effort on his own. By the end of 1642 John Berisford, a London grocer, was developing the lower Lea valley as a centre of gunpowder making and one that during the course of the war was to surpass Chilworth in output. Moreover, as the area was firmly under Parliamentarian control, it was more secure than the Chilworth mills. Even so, when on 7 December 1642 Berisford declared that he was willing to supply the Parliamentarian forces with gunpowder, the Commons, mindful of the trouble at Chilworth, ordered him to demolish the bridges leading from his gunpowder works at Temple Mills to the Leyton highway.[164] By 9 February 1643 he had sent a consignment to the London militia's magazine at Leadenhall. Existing warrants for payment reveal that in June and July he was making regular deliveries of forty barrels a week.[165] Some of the gunpowder may have been made at Sewardstone Mills further upstream for Berisford had been admitted as a copyhold tenant in the manor in 1640. However, there is no direct evidence of production there before 1646.[166]

TABLE 3

PARLIAMENTARY GUNPOWDER RECEIPTS, OCTOBER 1642–JULY 1643:
HOME PRODUCTION AND IMPORTS (IN BARRELS)

Date	Home	Imports
1642:		
October		18
November		–
December		44
1643:		
January		739
February	144	168.7
March	160	273.52
April	1,078	380.5
May	99.83	197.24
June	160	12.25
July	480	

Sources: PRO, WO 55/1660; SP 28/261–4

By mid-1643, therefore, both Cordwell and Berisford were fully operational and supplying tons of gunpowder to the Parliamentarian forces (see Table 3). Cordwell continued to produce gunpowder until his death in the winter of 1647/8 when his brother, Robert, who had long been associated with him, took over.[167] It was he who supplied the Chilworth powder used in the Irish campaign; in July 1649, 300 out of the 400 barrels he delivered to the Tower were earmarked for Ireland.[168] Robert died between 5 June and 11 July 1650, when the administration of his estate was granted to his widow, Mary.[169] She maintained production at Chilworth and in the three months between August and October 1650, delivered 890 barrels, which Cromwell's army employed in the reconquest of Scotland.[170] In spite of performing this crucial service, her involvement in the business did not last long. As Vincent Randyll, the owner of the site, observed, 'she being unable to manage so great a work, sold her stock to merchants'.[171] John Berisford, in contrast, continued to operate throughout the whole period, though at a lower level from 1650. His last consignment was dispatched in mid-1651 and thereafter he focused on the saltpetre end of the market.[172] Apart from producing new gunpowder, Cordwell and Berisford also made good old and decayed stock and references to this practice occur regularly in the records. On 18 March 1644, for instance, a warrant was issued to pay Berisford £57 10s for repairing forty-six barrels of gunpowder.[173]

During the course of the 1640s a handful of people from the London area also supplied powder to the Ordnance Office. John Samyne, a grocer like Berisford, further developed gunpowder making along the River Lea, converting Walthamstow mill for the purpose. Although contracted in October 1644 to supply 14 barrels of gunpowder to the navy, a warrant to pay for it was not issued until November 1645.[174] Between 1648 and 1651 he produced 250–450 barrels per annum. In 1646 Thomas Fossan, a ship's chandler, produced over 600 barrels of powder, though his normal output amounted to less than 50 barrels a year.[175] More powdermen entered the business at the end of the 1640s, partly because new opportunities presented themselves as gaps in the industry appeared. They included Daniel Judd, the Ordnance Office plumber, who, although he mainly dealt in shot, also supplied gunpowder and match. He worked the gunpowder mills at Faversham in Kent.[176] John Freeman and William Pennoyer were two merchants who, having imported gunpowder (and other war materials) throughout the 1640s, began to involve themselves in the manufacturing process at the end of the period. John Freeman took over Sewardstone mill from Berisford, probably in 1650, but was not a major provider of gunpowder until after the Battle of Worcester.[177] Conversely, during the course of 1650, Pennoyer's warrants refer to 3,130 barrels.[178] At the same time Josias Dewey acquired the Chilworth mills from Mary Cordwell and quickly made his mark. In the three months from April to June 1651, he received warrants for 1,535 barrels.[179] George Bowerman was the one significant supplier of gunpowder to the Ordnance Office who did not live in the London area. He resided at Stockwood in Dorset and sent most of his consignments to magazines located in southern and south-western ports.[180] These were the men who provided the government with gunpowder during the First Dutch War of 1652–4. In July 1652 Dewey, Freeman, Judd, Samyne and Steventon contracted to deliver 2,200 barrels at the rate of 300 a week, beginning on 8 August.[181]

Berisford was the more important of the two major suppliers, especially the longer the war continued, suggesting that at some point in the mid-1640s Sewardstone mill became operational. Interestingly, the figures indicate that production rarely reached pre-war levels of 20 lasts a month (537.6 barrels at 100 lb a barrel), partly owing to a shortage of raw materials but on occasion due to the gunpowder makers' reluctance to continue production when owed money for goods already delivered. At critical moments they had added leverage. Thus, in July 1649 the Council of State, fully occupied putting together supplies of arms and armaments for the imminent expedition to Ireland, complained to the Army Committee that several of the gunpowder contractors had forborne bringing in their consignments. Some gunpowder was sent; Berisford delivered 1,200 barrels early in the year and Robert Cordwell had just completed a contract for 600 barrels.[182] In general, recorded figures for receipts are minimum ones, as direct deliveries to armies or local forces were not always noted. Similarly, the retail trade is under-represented; for example, one has to look in the minutes of the East India Company to find that on 17 January 1644 it wanted to buy 100 barrels from Cordwell.[183] Even so, it is clear that home production was insufficient to meet demand and that gunpowder had to be brought in from abroad to make good this deficiency.

Shortages in the supply of home-produced saltpetre were magnified by the war, which increased demand but limited the area from which resources could be obtained. In addition, supplies to Ordnance Office contractors were affected by the diversion of material to local works. An ordinance of May 1643, the first of several to deal with the issue, recognised the need to improve production, and reconstituted the old system of regional saltpetre men. Another of 7 February 1646 envisaged the delivery of £12,000 worth of saltpetre each year (about 150 tons at £4 a cwt) to Cordwell and Berisford, seemingly in the proportion of two to one. Inevitably, output fell far short of what was required and as no formal arrangement was made to pay the saltpetre men, the system was abandoned in 1648.[184] By then, it had long been evident that saltpetre had to be brought in from abroad. Initially, Parliament did much business with William Courteen; one delivery of 78¼ tons to Cordwell and Berisford enabled them to fulfil a contract negotiated with the Committee of the Navy on 8 October 1644.[185] Shortly afterwards, Courteen ceased to trade, putting the East India Company in a much better bargaining position. It insisted on competitive bidding and the Parliamentarian contractors were not always successful. For example, in September 1648 the company, intent on getting £3 10s a cwt, rejected Berisford's offer of £3 5s. A month later it was sold to Richard Clutterbuck at £3 12s a cwt. It was perhaps due to a desire to maintain its independence of commercial supplies, that the Council of State resurrected the notion of home production in the critical month of July 1649.[186]

County forces and garrisons bid for gunpowder from the central stores but also received supplies from more local sources. The mills at Manchester had a regional importance. In early 1649 they were producing large quantities of gunpowder and match and there is indirect evidence to suggest that by then manufacturers and merchants had already established trading links throughout the north-west and West Midlands.[187] The Manchester dealer, William Sunderland, was a leading distributor; from 1644 he sold considerable amounts of munitions to the Cheshire, Lancashire, Staffordshire and Shropshire forces.[188] Brereton certainly used his gunpowder and match at the sieges of Chester. One consignment in 1645 was worth £849 6s 6d.[189] Sunderland's goods were more expensive than those delivered by London's munitions manufacturers, however; in April 1645 he was demanding £6 for a barrel of gunpowder and 6d for 1 lb of match compared to the £4 10s 0d and 3d that they charged. The higher price probably reflects local shortages at a time when resources were being diverted to London to help provision the New Model Army.

Parliament also built or made use of gunpowder mills at Gainsborough, Gloucester, Leicester, Northampton, Nottingham, Stafford and Coventry and no doubt elsewhere too.[190] These works operated at a more modest level than the one at Manchester and often utilised existing buildings. At Stafford a gunpowder mill was established in a house by the churchyard in December 1643 which, though deemed suitable by the gunpowder maker, was hardly in an isolated position. A year later, after what must have been a nervous time for the local churchgoers, it was decided to move it 'into such convenient place within the garrison as it may stand without danger of Fier unto it . . .'.[191] At Gloucester a gunpowder works was set up in a part of the bishop's palace in June 1643. At the same time a second saltpetre furnace was built, probably in the same place, supplementing the one in the college.[192] Gunpowder making, if hand operated – as many of these provincial works must have been – required little capital. At Gloucester costs for equipment mostly comprised payments for pestles, trays, barrels and sieves. At this level, the most expensive process was that of making saltpetre. Among the items required were tubs to steep the impregnated earth and furnaces and copper containers to boil the liquid. In January 1644 it cost George Bainbridge, the gunpowder man at Stafford, £2 10s to acquire two furnace pans.[193]

Access to essential raw materials, especially saltpetre, might pose a problem. Much time and effort, therefore, was spent locating deposits and extracting the earth. In Warwick several labourers were employed in digging saltpetre out of a pit at Grey Friars Steeple, from where it was sent to the works by the Bishopsgate in Coventry. At Bardwell in Suffolk house-to-house collections were made of saltpetre and ashes and the filled tubs taken to the furnaces at Westley or Hepworth.[194] Gloucester's gunpowder industry provides a good example of the importance of local supplies. Even during the siege of 10 August–5 September 1643, essential ingredients were getting through to the defenders. Most of the city's supply of saltpetre solution, ashes and charcoalling wood came from the city, its suburbs and from places lying within a five-mile radius. The bulk of the coal was brought in from elsewhere, probably from the Forest of Dean via the river Severn. Brimstone had to be obtained from abroad or from stocks already in the country. Fortunately, the stock had been replenished before the siege and as further consignments arrived during the course of it, production continued.[195]

Gunpowder making was a skilled craft and could only be undertaken by specialists. At Gloucester, Robert Hill, a local goldsmith, might have been in charge of production but in practice a saltpetre man, Thomas Barnes, and a gunpowder maker, Thomas Davies, carried out the work. When Matthew Silleby established gunpowder works at Northampton in about October 1643 a London saltpetre maker was brought in to help him.[196] Because of the pre-war monopoly such people were in short supply and attempts were made to poach them. In November 1643 Sir John Gell, Parliament's commander in Derbyshire, tried to entice Richard Wilson away from his work at Nottingham Castle but the authorities there protested vigorously that 'we have not sufficient [gunpowder] for our own defence And to have our maker of it secretly invited hence now, we cannot take it well'. Gell had already approached George Bainbridge, a Derby man, to do the job but Bainbridge had had to turn him down because Sir William Brereton had asked him to make gunpowder at Stafford. In a fit of pique at his rejection Gell had ransacked Bainbridge's home, taking away malt and clothing, and had quartered soldiers in the house.[197]

The output of these gunpowder works, though small in comparison by the standards of Cordwell and Berisford, was significant, especially if their activities were replicated across the country. By relieving pressure on the Ordnance Office, they gave the officers greater flexibility in the disposal of strategic supplies. At Gloucester stocks were quickly topped up after the siege, and production was maintained through the early months of 1644, the period when a large convoy was making its way to the city with supplies. As Captain Backhouse wrote in February 1644, 'they make powder and match every week much or more than they spend'.[198] Unfortunately, local production did not always meet demand and even counties like Warwickshire, Staffordshire and Northamptonshire, and garrisons such as Nottingham, which had developed their own industries, had to be supplied from outside. At Coventry, in spite of all the efforts of Thomas Greene, the gunpowder maker, extra stock had to be brought up from London. Between May 1643 and July 1645 at least eight consignments of gunpowder arrived from the capital, though the prices, which included transport costs, were higher than his.[199]

Royalists

The Royalists quickly established gunpowder-making facilities at Oxford. There are references to a powder mill between December 1642 and June 1643 and to a saltpetre house in April 1643. The mills, powered by water, were situated along the river at Osney, just within the city's defences and away from the mass of the population. Old mills were adapted – including a fulling mill – and new ones built.[200] The cost was considerable; William Baber, the gunpowder maker, later claimed that the works and equipment were worth £532 3s 6d and that in total he had spent £3,000 providing gunpowder for the king.[201] In early 1643 the flow of water to the mills was affected by the flooding of the meadows on the south-western side of the city. As a result, Colonel Lloyd, the resident military engineer, embarked on a scheme to widen the channels to the mills.[202] Baber delivered his first consignment of four barrels into the stores on 8 January 1643 and over the next few months his output steadily increased to peak at fifty-five barrels in May. After that he made no more recorded deliveries; perhaps he went back to Bristol (captured in July) for he later claimed to have worked there. He still retained his official position at Oxford, however, and was only forced to relinquish it in February 1644 when the king gave Strode and Wandesford the sole right to manufacture saltpetre and gunpowder in the country. Baber was not happy about this turn of events, especially as he felt inadequately compensated for his outlay. In February he refused to hand over his equipment and was put in gaol. He may even have sabotaged the mills.[203]

The commissioners first became involved in production in mid-1643; in a letter of 21 June sent by Charles I to Lord Percy he referred to their appointment 'to make prouision of Match and powder to Furnish our Magazine withall'.[204] They made their first delivery on 13 July, six weeks after Baber's last recorded consignment. Production should have leapt after February 1644 when they could use their patent to corner supplies. It may have done. Recorded deliveries in April 1644 amounted to 135 barrels. Thereafter, monthly totals, which never reach treble figures, are affected by gaps in the record. An undated letter, possibly of January or February 1644, states that thirty-five barrels a week were being made there.[205] Strode and Wandesford seem to have been motivated by the prospect of financial gain, justified by the undoubted expenditure they had already incurred in supporting the king.[206] Their action bred resentment in Oxford, recalling as it did the king's exploitation of the pre-war monopoly, and allegations of profiteering were made against them. They hoped to sell the gunpowder at 1s a lb, that is, £5 a barrel, at a time when Parliamentarian contractors were asking £4. Trevor, probably making calculations based on the rate given to the pre-war contractors, thought that they would clear £100 a week. This never happened for they could not produce enough barrels of powder nor effectively police their monopoly throughout the country.[207]

Because the output of Oxford's mills was insufficient to meet their needs, the Royalists established other important centres of gunpowder production. Among the earliest ones built were those located in their western strongholds of Chester, Shrewsbury and Worcester. Gunpowder was being produced at Shrewsbury before the end of 1642 and at Chester in spring 1643.[208] At Worcester the commissioners of array were a little more dilatory, but a reminder from the king on 8 March did the trick. Between 1 May and 23 October 1643, £227 was paid for processing saltpetre and £155 1s 9d for making gunpowder.[209] In summer 1643 Robert Dolben of Denbigh was given the task of manufacturing gunpowder in north Wales, while in November Captain John Young and his partners were appointed as gunpowder makers in Glamorgan. At Reading Jacob Astley reported on 16 October 1643 that he had found a person who would make gunpowder 'vpon Reasonabell termes & a good proportion.'[210]

The most significant event, however, was the capture of Bristol, with its industrial and commercial facilities and its tradition of gunpowder making. In January and February 1644 Richard March was negotiating with gunpowder makers in the city and at Wells. At the same time the commissioners of array for Devon ordered Colonel Edward Seymour to erect a gunpowder mill near Totnes 'and to employ skilful men for the making of powder'.[211] The problem, as Colonel Seymour might have said, was to find skilled powder men. Why else did the king appoint William Baber as the person to establish a gunpowder works at Oxford? Baber and other members of his family also developed gunpowder-making facilities at Worcester, Bristol, Taunton and Exeter. At Chester, Orlando Bridgeman hoped to attract a Bristol man, a further indication of the value of the ex-pirates to the Royalist cause. In turn, Chester supplied three of their best workmen to help Robert Dolben in north Wales. Ex-saltpetre men, like Tobias Atkins at Wells, were among those pressed into service because of the skills they had acquired.[212]

In the north the accounts of Skipton Castle suggest that York was an important centre. During the course of 1643 local carriers made regular journeys to the city, bringing back with them one or two packs of gunpowder at a time. At £5 a barrel the price was high by London standards, where the cost ranged from £4 3s a barrel for imported powder to £4 10s for home-produced ware. However, in early 1643 the Parliamentarian forces in Lincolnshire and the north were having to pay £5 10s a barrel for their stock. One consignment of 120 lb of the finer pistol powder, bought at York and delivered to Skipton Castle in the autumn, certainly was expensive. At £10 it was almost as dear as the hard-pressed Royalist troops in Ireland were paying. It is possible that some of the gunpowder sold at York had been imported through north-eastern ports. When the queen returned to the city from Holland in February 1643 she brought with her arms and munitions purchased abroad. Similarly, Captain Carr of the Skipton Castle garrison probably had the choice of home-made and imported powder when he went to Newcastle to buy arms in the winter of 1642/3.[213]

Like the Parliamentarians, the Royalists were concerned about the supply of raw materials. References to shortages appear regularly in the records. At Shrewsbury in September 1644 gunpowder was scarce, but little could be done to remedy the situation because of a lack of brimstone and other materials. A year later the gunpowder mills at Oxford were at a standstill for the same reason and, as a result, Secretary Nicholas asked the king to order the removal of brimstone from Worcester to these works. In Glamorgan Captain Young and his partners were unable to sell gunpowder at the projected 14d a lb because a survey found that the saltpetre grounds had been depleted by earlier workings. In consequence, they had to raise the price of gunpowder to 18d a lb.[214] Whenever a good source was found, officials were keen to exploit it. In 1645 deposits of saltpetre were discovered in the Banbury district and a gunpowder manufactory was hastily built nearby.[215] Many consignments of raw materials came from abroad. Brimstone was a regular item in shipments of arms; in May 1645 a cargo brought in on a frigate belonging to van Haesdonck, the Royalist gunrunner, included 50,000 lb of brimstone.[216] Saltpetre also had to be imported; on 17 February 1644, for example, Sir George Strode contracted with the king to bring in £4,000 worth, to be landed at Bristol or Weymouth.[217]

It is difficult to compare the level of Royalist production with that of Parliamentarian suppliers because the data are not really amenable to statistical analysis. Output was certainly lower and there were more noticeable shortages. The Venetian ambassador reported a scarcity of powder in May 1643, and in September Lord Hopton, then governor of Bristol, informed Prince Rupert that 'gunpowder is an irreparable want at present'.[218] Nonetheless, production levels were probably more substantial than historians have assumed. From late 1643 to early 1644, the period in which production peaked, several sites were manufacturing a significant amount of gunpowder. Apart from Oxford with its thirty-five barrels a week, Bristol, Chester, Shrewsbury and Worcester were major producers. At Bristol Richard March thought fifteen barrels a week could be made – for cash – and more could be obtained from Wells. The other three centres probably produced slightly fewer barrels, perhaps ten a week. In April 1643 Lord Capel believed that the mills at Chester and Shrewsbury could supply sufficient powder for the region. Robert Dolben at Denbigh and John Young in Glamorgan added their output to the stockpile. In the north gunpowder was being produced at the regional centres of York and Newcastle, perhaps as much as at Shrewsbury. It is therefore likely that in some months in 1643–4 Royalist production may have been nearly 100 barrels a week, but at a higher price than Parliamentary contractors charged and with greater fluctuations over the year. In early 1644 south Wales gunpowder cost £7 10s a barrel and even at Bristol and Wells it sold at £4 10s–£5. Parliament paid between £4 and £4 2s 6d.

Scotland and Ireland

Before the Union of the Crowns there must have been a native gunpowder industry in Scotland but it would have declined after 1603, since the king could obtain what he needed from English patentees. To remedy this defect, on 29 July 1626 the Scottish Privy Council told Sir James Baillie to go to England to find 'strangers or natives' skilled in making gunpowder and to induce them to go to work in Scotland.[219] It is not known if this initiative was followed up but gunpowder was certainly available in the country. In August of the following year twelve Aberdonians were recorded as having 900 lb of gunpowder and 500 fathoms plus 100 lb of match in their possession. Two others had unknown quantities of gunpowder and a further six are listed but have no figure entered after their name.[220]

When war approached in 1638 it was possible to obtain gunpowder, at least in Edinburgh. On 18 July the treasurer was told to buy 10 cwt each of gunpowder and match and put them in the city's magazine. The following February he had to obtain 13 cwt of gunpowder, 8 cwt of match and 20 cwt of lead shot. Of course, he may have dealt with merchants importing munitions but some gunpowder was undoubtedly being produced locally. Included in the February order was a commission for him to contract with local artificers to make a further ton of gunpowder, 12 cwt of match and a ton of lead ball. In April 1639 Archibald Campbell told his uncle that he could obtain gunpowder there.[221] Nonetheless, output at best was low and in September the commissioners of the shires ordered that measures should be taken to establish gunpowder making in the country. Some action was taken, though not necessarily in response to this exhortation. In December 1643, for instance, the Marquess of Argyll, preparing to face MacColla, obtained ten barrels of gunpowder from the newly built powderhouse at Irvine. The following November, Ayr and Irvine were asked to supply him with a further twenty barrels as a matter of urgency.[222]

To aid the process, shipments of raw materials were brought in from abroad, especially from the Baltic. The cost was high because Christian IV of Denmark added a 78 per cent tax on saltpetre (and other war materials) passing through the Sound, quadrupling its net price. As a result, saltpetre began to pile up at Danzig and on the River Weser because it was assumed that Christian's action was designed to prevent it going through the Sound. However, the Danish king made it known to Francis Gordon – his (and Charles I's) agent in Danzig and a man suspected of Covenanting sympathies – that as long as merchants there paid the enhanced price, they could send saltpetre wherever they liked. Christian's main aim, it seems, was to blockade the Sound against imports to Sweden.[223] Although Christian promised Charles I that he would stop arms ships travelling to Scotland through the Sound, some got through, apparently with the connivance of the Danish authorities. A proportion of the saltpetre was first of all taken to the United Provinces before transhipment to Scotland. It is likely that the 15,416 lb of refined saltpetre that Thomas Cuningham sent from Veere in 1640 had come through the Sound.[224]

This saltpetre must have been made into gunpowder and used by the army in the Second Bishops' War but there is no record of the gunpowder makers who manufactured it. The continuing lack of home capacity is suggested by the decision of Edinburgh's council in June 1644 to send decayed gunpowder over to Holland to be amended. When the Scots army entered England in January 1644 it took 45,000 lb of gunpowder with it but there is no indication where it had come from. Most of it was probably imported. Certainly the magazine at Leith was replenished during the course of the year by consignments brought in by local merchants or by expatriates like Thomas Cuningham. At Glasgow, too, merchants were involved in supplying the local forces with gunpowder. On 24 October 1645 the provost was given a warrant, allowing him to take 50 lb of pistol powder from any merchant in the city for the Lanarkshire regiment.[225]

Very little is known about native gunpowder makers. Only two possible people appear in the accounts of Sir Adam Hepburn, the army treasurer. On 25 December 1644 he paid £28 4s 5d sterling to James Carstairs for 521 lb of gunpowder at 13d a lb, and at some time after 24 December the following year £4 5s 6d sterling to Peter Naisfield.[226] The Scots, while in England, were often short of powder, and tended to be restocked from English sources rather than Scottish ones.[227] The evidence, though negative, suggests that the Scottish gunpowder industry was not very large.

Before the Civil Wars the Irish authorities obtained their gunpowder from England. Because of the ban on private trading in the commodity, they monopolised the market and profited by selling it to those who needed it. In May 1627 they recommended that the system should continue. At the end of that year, however, Hugh Grove, a saltpetre man and a powder maker, petitioned the king for permission to transfer his operation from England to Ireland. Apart from allowing the saltpetre beds in England to recuperate, the scheme would save money, reduce the hazards of transportation and provide employment. The matter was referred to the Commissioners for Irish Causes who consulted John Evelyn, the gunpowder patentee. The commissioners were clearly in favour but, claiming that they did not have the power to make a decision, they returned the proposal to the Privy Council.[228] It appears as though nothing was done. Consequently, the Irish were no better placed than the Scots when rebellion broke out, and complaints by both the Royalists and Confederates about the lack of gunpowder were among the most frequent and most strident.

The gunpowder monopoly prevented manufacturers openly producing and selling their ware, while Wentworth's policy of restricting the amount individuals could buy, reduced demand and therefore the stock in private hands.[229] The Royalists were particularly affected by the shortage of capacity at home. In a letter to the Lords Justices on 10 January 1642 the mayor of Londonderry wrote that his troops dared not fire on the enemy because they had to preserve what little gunpowder they possessed to repel an assault. He asserted that for want of powder and arms the country was being lost. Most of what gunpowder the Royalists could use had to come out of existing stocks. On 20 February 1643 the Lords Justices complained to the Irish Committee that because of their own needs and those of the garrisons, they had spent most of the gunpowder and match in store at Dublin Castle and that, apart from the little sent from England, the stores had not been replenished. In October, Ormond, replying to a request for gunpowder from the archbishop of York at Beaumaris, commented that 'this is except money the scarcest Commodity with vs'.[230] The lack of gunpowder is reflected in the prices charged. William Stewart's precarious position at Letterkenny, Co. Donegal, might account for the £8 a barrel he paid in July 1642 (and £10 for fine gunpowder), but prices were consistently high. In February 1644 Ormond charged Lord Byron at Chester £7 7s 11d each for forty-two barrels of powder.[231] At the time a barrel of powder could be bought for £4 in London and £5 in Oxford.

The Confederates were also short of gunpowder in the initial stages of the insurrection. They decided against besieging Lismore, Co. Waterford, in the winter of 1641/2, for example, because they scarcely had enough gunpowder for the few firearms they possessed, let alone the ordnance they could have brought from Dungarvan, Co. Waterford.[232] In September 1642 Hugh Bourke reported that at the siege of the strategically important fort of Duncannon, Co. Wexford, in the summer gunpowder had cost 4–5s a lb. This was an outrageous price and, if correct, was clearly due to special local circumstances. By September, Flemish powder was commanded a price of about 1s a lb at source and 19d, all expenses paid, in Ireland.[233] This was still not cheap but at least it encouraged merchants to ship over supplies.

To reduce costs and to make themselves more self-sufficient, the Confederates sought to produce gunpowder at home. In June 1642 Dr Daniel Higgins of Limerick was making gunpowder of excellent quality. According to a deposition, it 'gives but a small report but drives a bullet with extraordinary force'. At Kilkenny the Confederates reputedly made gunpowder at St Patrick's Church and dug up graves (especially Protestant ones) for nitrogenous material.[234] The Supreme Council was particularly concerned to bring in foreign specialists, emphasising the need for gunpowder makers when asking their agents to find workmen abroad. When Owen Roe O'Neill landed at Castle Doe in July 1642 he brought with him some workers to make gunpowder and match. In December General Preston's wife contracted with Anthony Le Fevre and William Goure, two Flemings from Namur, to work for the Confederacy at 6s a day. Asking Hugh Bourke to hasten their journey, the Supreme Council stressed that 'we shall be in great want of men of their profession'.[235] It was at about this time that General Preston persuaded Nicholas Lallo to come to Ireland.[236] At Kilkenny, Lallo built a saltpetre house and two powder mills, apart from two forges where he cast cannon ware.[237] In January 1645 the council was still asking Bourke for more gunpowder and saltpetre makers.[238] Raw materials were also imported. O'Neill brought a considerable amount of brimstone with him in July 1642 and supplies continued to be shipped to Ireland. In July 1647 Lallo asked for six barrels of brimstone, stored at Waterford, for his powder works at Kilkenny.[239] The output of these works is not known but it was unlikely to have reduced the dependency on imports by a significant amount. Nonetheless, they did give the Confederates a degree of independence, which the Royalists did not possess.

MATCH

To make match, a length of tow or hempen cord was first soaked in saltpetre and lime water, although as alternatives vinegar, the lees of wine or even brandy seem to have been used. It was then dipped in melted sulphur.[240] Finally, it was bundled into skeins and stored in vats. Costs varied according the quality of the cord; in May 1649 John Freeman and Thomas Steventon sold to Parliament match made out of fine hempdresser's tow at £26 a ton and match made out of coarse tow at £22 a ton.[241] In an emergency any kind of cord would do. When besieged at Devizes in June 1643, Hopton ordered his officers to collect together all the bedcords they could find to make match, and the expedient worked![242] Match making was essentially a summer pursuit because of the need for warm, sunny conditions to dry out the product in the open. George Fletcher, the leading supplier to the pre-war Ordnance Office, emphasised this point when negotiating a contract with the government in November 1639. Deliveries, he said, would only start in April the following year for 'it cannot be made but in the summer'. His anxiety to come to an agreement stemmed from the seasonality of purchasing materials and manufacturing the product. As he stated, 'if there not be order taken within these 14 days or a month at furthest, it cannot be done in that time 12 months, this being the season for buying the stuff whereof it is made'.[243]

Match makers were dependent to a certain extent upon imports; in November 1639 Fletcher commented that the materials to make match could not be found in the country.[244] This was certainly true for sulphur and partially so for saltpetre but flax and hemp were grown in many parts of the British Isles. At Gloucester, the city's match maker during the Civil War obtained some hemp and flax from patches of ground just beyond the city walls, and other supplies from the surrounding district. Recorded consignments came from Over (2 miles away), Tirley (7 miles), Arlingham (11 miles) and Tewkesbury (11 miles).[245] Often grown in small plots and processed by people of humble means, the hemp and flax industry was one of those projects advocated by contemporaries as a means of providing work for the poor. Such a pool of labour could be put to good use in the war. At Weymouth John Strachan, the Royalist agent, noted in March 1644 that output could go up by some 250 per cent if money were made available to obtain more raw materials and employ the poor.[246] At Nottingham, the garrison supervised the entire process. There, William Porter, the match maker, had under him one or two boys (or, occasionally, a girl) to open the hurds, one or two labourers to beat the fibres and a person to spin the hurden yarn.[247]

In the late 1630s government match-making contracts were not controlled by a patentee but were, nonetheless, channelled through a single person – George Fletcher. A London merchant with diverse interests, he dealt in match as well as arranging for the manufacture himself. The business fitted in well with his other activities, notably the provision of saltpetre, 'firework' materials (sulphur and resin) and naval stores, such as rope, tar and pitch.[248] As he traded on the Barbary coast, albeit as an interloper, he could obtain stocks of saltpetre there.[249] In January 1639 he received a debenture for 24¾ tons of match he had delivered to the stores, as preparations were being made for the Scottish campaign. In November 1639 he signed a contract to provide 100 tons of English match for the Second Bishops' War. In it he agreed to deliver 15 tons a month at £45 a ton, beginning in March. He did insist on an advance of £1,500 in order to buy materials: like other suppliers he was aware of the problems of getting the government to pay for the ware it received![250] In January 1640 the Council of War, impatient with the delay, resolved to ask Fletcher to provide 50 tons of foreign match and to get him to make as much match as he could.[251]

Parliament

George Fletcher disappears from the records at the opening of the Civil War in England, and in the first year or so of the conflict merchants shipping in match from abroad took his place.[252] By 1644 a handful of entrepreneurs provided the bulk of the material. Like George Fletcher, they were manufacturers as well as merchants. In the period up to September 1651, four men delivered over 100 tons of match to Parliament, often much more. Daniel Judd brought in well over 370 tons. Their dealings in match can be seen as a natural part of their business activities. David Davidson, a rope merchant, traded in 'firework' ware and rope, while John Freeman, a grocer, was involved in gunpowder manufacture and imported naval stores (among other items) from northern Europe. Thomas Steventon was a partner of Freeman's. Daniel Judd, the plumber and shot caster, seems to have been a commercial opportunist, first developing a separate interest in match and then extending his range into gunpowder and other ware. Unfortunately, it is difficult to disaggregate the totals for each individual to discern the proportion of match that they made themselves or obtained from other manufacturers at home and abroad. Large consignments of match certainly were imported through Amsterdam. The amounts delivered did fluctuate, high points coinciding with the provisioning of the New Model Army in 1645–6 and the expeditionary force to Scotland in 1650–1. Perversely, there were reports of serious shortages of match in mid-1645, reflected in peak prices at the time when deliveries were increasing. On occasion, both the New Model and the Scots armies lacked adequate stocks of munitions.[253]

There were many other people who delivered consignments of match to the Parliamentarian forces around the country. Some, like George Margetts, a London rope merchant, supplied the Ordnance Office.[254] Others, notably those living in the provinces, provisioned local forces. At Plymouth the matchmaker was Thomas Boyes and the material he produced locally was of great value to such a strategically important but beleaguered Parliamentarian base. In August 1644 he was owed £200 for deliveries made, representing some seven tons of match.[255] At Coventry, several people dealt with the county committee, though James Pinley supplied the bulk of the ware. At Gloucester, two ropers, John Williams and later Thomas Portnell, sold some match to the garrison and made more from the raw materials given to them. At Nottingham, the match maker and his staff were supplied with all their materials. They were continuously employed between November 1644 and February 1647, the period covered by the records, but there is no indication of the amount produced.[256]

Royalists

As part of the initial flurry of activity to develop Oxford as an industrial centre, a match house was set up in the city, though its location is unknown. Roger Daide was installed as the match maker and on 25 January 1643 sent his first consignment, 10 cwt 17 lb, to the magazine. Production levels steadily increased over the next few months and by the end of May he had dispatched over 21 tons. In spite of this impressive performance he, too, found his position undermined by the ordnance commissioners, Strode and Wandesford. In the second half of the year they produced almost 19 tons of match and he under 3 tons. Perhaps they employed Daide; they certainly were using the match house by November 1643. Under their direction, recorded monthly production figures were no better than those of Daide, peaking at 7½ tons in October 1643 and April 1644. This suggests that Daide's highest monthly total (8¾ tons in May 1643) might represent the limit attainable with the resources to hand. The recorded, though imperfect, data reveal that in 1644 they delivered over 13 tons and in April–May 1645, 2 tons 13 cwt.[257] In comparison with Parliament the Royalists did surprisingly well in the initial stages and thereafter might match the output of one of the leading Parliamentarian suppliers in a single month. However, even allowing for *lacunae* in the record, it is clear that Royalist output fluctuated more wildly than did theirs and steadily diminished over time.

The extant receipts reveal that the amount of match in the magazine was augmented by ware included in the occasional convoy from the north, from individual contributions and by unused material returned from a garrison or an army detachment. Consignments must also have come in from some of the provincial match makers, too, but they do not feature strongly in the list. It is known that match was sent. In March 1644 John Strachan at Weymouth reckoned that match could be made there for 25s a cwt, delivered to Oxford for 30s. At the time 8 or 9 cwt were being made in the town but Strachan felt that with extra material 30 cwt a week might be produced.[258] There was a certain amount of traffic downstream with the magazine at Reading, where Nicholas Ashmore, 'the king's matchmaker' was in charge of production. In October 1643 he sent 239 lb of match to Oxford.[259]

Match making was established in other centres, notably in the south-west. In September 1643 match from Bristol was sent to the Royalist army, then besieging Gloucester. Charles Lloyd, the governor of Devizes, was trying to produce match in January 1645 but was having difficulty because 'the time of ye yeare [was] ill to make any'. Shortly afterwards, however, production of match in the West Country was stepped up when a licence was given to one Morgan to establish a factory in Wells, aided by a grant of £100 from Hyde, the Chancellor of the

Exchequer. In the north the garrison at Skipton Castle obtained regular consignments of match from York.[260]

Strachan's estimate of 30s for a cwt of match compares favourably with Parliamentarian prices but the Royalists certainly found greater difficulty in securing adequate supplies in the country. An important consideration was the lack of raw materials. As the king observed in a letter to Sir Francis Ottley, the governor of Shrewsbury, on 20 April 1643, 'our affairs here require a far greater proportion of Match than all the Tow, Flax and Hemp to be had in these parts'. Ottley was asked to obtain supplies from the surrounding area.[261] Shortages continued to occur from time to time. In March 1646 Lord Byron, then at Caernarvon, told Sir John Owen at Conway that he could not spare any match until the country folk brought in the ingredients to make more of it.[262] Much-needed material might come in from abroad. Strachan looked to France for his additional stocks, reckoning that he could get tow shipped in daily for 14s a hundredweight.[263]

Scotland and Ireland

The instructions to the shires in 1639 to develop gunpowder making in Scotland did not encompass the manufacture of match but the measure did have an effect on its supply because it increased the amount of essential ingredients available. Moreover, there were artificers in the country with appropriate skills and who could adapt their work to the production of match during the war, even if they had not already done so beforehand. One of the main suppliers of match to the magazine at Leith, for instance, was Lawrence Johnston, a tow maker. Undoubtedly, some of the 44,200 lb of match that the Army of the Solemn League and Covenant took with it to England in January 1644 was produced in Scotland.[264] Local match makers were certainly topping up the stocks at Leith shortly afterwards. On 17 July Johnston delivered a consignment of 1,450 lb of match, produced in the English fashion. In the same month John Denholme of nearby Newhaven sent to the magazine three loads of match, totalling 7,640 lb. The only other recorded delivery occurred on 11 September when Johnston supplied a further 700 lb. Johnston, like Denholme, must have worked in the Edinburgh area for he brought in a load that Denholme had made. Denholme may have doubled as a commissary officer of the army, though a reference to John Denholme the elder as a match maker, could indicate that the role was filled by his son, John junior.[265]

In Ireland negative evidence suggests that little match was made in the country, especially by the Royalists. In terms of the volume of complaints, references to match were the most numerous. On 23 April 1642 the Lords Justices asked the Lord Lieutenant for all kinds of arms and armaments but stressed, above all, the need for match, without which 'we shall be in very great extremity'. On 12 October they asked the king's secretary, Nicholas, to hasten over the match 'of which we have extraordinary want'.[266] At Letterkenny in July match cost £3 14s 8d a cwt. By May 1644 the price had gone down to £2 6s 0d at Mayo, but in London it cost £1 6s and even at Coventry £1 10s. In February 1645 Prince Maurice, then at Chester, was ordering Irish match at £3 a cwt, indicating how little there was in that country and incidentally how desperate the English Royalists were for it.[267] There is little evidence that the Royalists developed match making capabilities, though *ad hoc* arrangements were resorted to in an emergency. In October 1642 Lady Dowdall recounted that when all the match had been used up at Kilfinny Castle, Co. Limerick, the defenders were able to hold out because they replenished the stock out of materials to hand.[268] The Confederates suffered from a lack of match too. They were short of match, as well as gunpowder and weapons, in February 1643[269], for instance, and at other times reports commented on their lack of unspecified munitions. Even so, in spite of their problems, they were better supplied with match than were the Royalists. Apart from imports, Lallo and other foreign artificers helped to increase output at home.

CONCLUSION

At either end of the period the resources of the whole country could be utilised to provide the munitions needed to deal with the Scottish and Irish rebels. That Cromwell made better use of them is due as much to political considerations as to economic ones. In between, in the English Civil War, these resources were divided, albeit unequally, between the Royalists and Parliamentarians. Parliament, with its control of London and the south-east – the centre of the armaments industry – undoubtedly gained the advantage, both in terms of facilities and a skilled workforce. Under the circumstances, the Royalists did remarkably well. They quickly developed Oxford as an arms manufacturing centre and within a few months its mills, workshops, forges and furnaces were producing all kinds of ordnance and munitions. They also fostered the armaments industry at York, Sunderland and Newcastle in the north and at Bristol in the West Country. In addition, the Royalists were helped by access to vital raw materials such as hemp, iron, lead, tin, saltpetre and charcoalling wood, which, if insufficient to meet needs, were just as good as the resources found in the Parliamentarian zone. Moreover, they possessed plant, notably in the iron industry, that could be easily adapted to produce munitions. In Scotland production of ordnance and munitions increased in response to the need to equip the army. Indeed, cannon made at Potters Row helped to defeat Charles I's forces. In Ireland, the munitions industries were far more rudimentary but the Confederates, at least, did attempt to develop them by encouraging foreign specialists to come to work for them.

Thus, while Parliamentarian production was superior to that achieved by the Royalists, the difference, especially in the first two years of the war, was not as great as might have been thought. Unfortunately, gaps in the record do not allow calculation of output levels with a great deal of precision, especially on the Royalist side; to a certain extent this is due to the greater decentralisation of their system. It is not enough merely to know the figures for production at Oxford. These are imprecise enough but there are no accounts of output at Bristol or at any other centre. All that we have are odd literary references. Parliament, in contrast, had a much more centralised system of production and administration and the records deal with a greater proportion of the business being conducted. For both sides, the figures, when totalled up, are impressive. Tons of ordnance and munitions were produced. Nonetheless, as participants noted with some surprise, war used up resources at an amazing rate. Even Parliament's armaments makers could not cope. Both sides, therefore, had to augment their stock from elsewhere, trying to obtain from abroad what could not be made at home. In Ireland and Scotland the evidence of home production is even more anecdotal and the most that one can say is that all types of munitions were being produced. The Scottish Covenanters probably fared the best but even they were largely reliant upon imports. The Irish Confederates, starting from a low base, achieved some success but could do no more than supply a small proportion of their needs from home. The Royalists seem to have done little to develop their own industries but because they controlled a number of ports were able to bring in munitions from outside, that is, if they could evade the blockade.[270]

6

HOME SUPPLIES: CLOTHING
AND EQUIPMENT

To fight effectively, soldiers had to be properly clothed and equipped. Failure to do so not only weakened them but also affected their morale and loyalty. Moreover, the problem of provisioning was a recurring one, for uniforms and footwear quickly wore out. To supply the soldiers' needs, a range of craftsmen and artificers were employed. Apart from uniforms and shoes soldiers wore a variety of belting and accessories: powder bags, bandolier collars and chargers for the gunpowder; girdles, hangers and belts for swords and carbines; and knapsacks for food and spare clothing. Some troops also donned protective armour. A certain amount of specialisation occurred, especially among equipment makers, because of the variety of materials involved. Armourers had always made weapons and continued to do so, though individuals might focus on the production of armour. In London, the establishment of the Gunmakers' Company in 1636 did have an impact on their work but the dispute took many years to resolve and armourers carried on producing firearms and pikes throughout the Civil Wars. In terms of organisation, the two branches of the business were run in completely different ways. Whereas the manufacture of armour and equipment was organised by craftsmen working within the handicraft tradition, the clothing industry was dominated by merchants. Although not as pronounced, the same distinction can be discerned in Scotland and Ireland too.

CLOTHING

The demand for uniforms, as for all military equipment, fluctuated wildly between times of peace and war. However, production during the Civil Wars could be increased relatively easily because the commodities being made were items of everyday wear. The transition from making civilian garb to military dress was further facilitated by the lack of specifically designed uniforms.[1] Only the coat and facings in a distinctive colour distinguished the soldier from the civilian. In England, at least, the size of the consignments and the speed with which they could be put together were made possible by two key developments in the clothing industry in London in the early seventeenth century. Firstly, the business became increasingly dominated by a handful of capitalist drapers, whose methods can be observed in the reaction of those affected by their actions. In the mid-seventeenth century poorer freemen of the Merchant Tailors' Company were complaining about 'Rich men . . . taking over great multitudes of Apprentices' and employing a 'multitude of Forreyne Taylors . . . within the walls

& liberties . . . & likewise out of the liberties'. Secondly, there emerged out of the ranks of the tailors of Elizabethan London a set of retailers, known as salesmen, who dealt in ready-made garments. Their number grew in the early seventeenth century, also to the annoyance of traditional tailors, whom they undercut and whose livelihoods they threatened. The salesmen often employed non-apprenticed labour, drawn from the ever-growing population of the capital and its suburbs, thereby challenging the authority of the company and its monopoly and undermining quality control.[2]

The original impulse for these developments may well have been the rapid growth in the population of the capital in the late sixteenth and early seventeenth centuries, particularly in the number of inhabitants of humble means. Traditionally, such people obtained second-hand the clothes they could not make at home,[3] but as their numbers grew, entrepreneurs took the opportunity to exploit the potential market that they represented, by promoting the sale of cheap, mass-produced, ready-made clothing and footware. The business brought in by fulfilling military contracts reinforced the process. Between 1585 and 1604 England was almost constantly at war and to clothe its forces the government placed large orders with London suppliers. The army needed clothing and footwear in standard sizes and in bulk, and was an ideal customer for those used to dealing in large quantities of clothing, especially ready-made garments.

The two London clothing merchants, Uriah Babington and Robert Bromley, who supplied the uniforms to the forces that conquered Ireland in the last years of Elizabeth's reign, were men of this sort. Robert Swann, a linen draper, given the task of 'prouiding and making' shirts for the soldiers and sailors in the 1620s, acted in a similar way. Although he made most of the shirts on contract, he worked on a large scale, employing 300 men and women at a time.[4] Even if the clothing and footwear supplied did have to conform to certain criteria set out in the agreement, the contractors generally could influence the outcome by taking patterns with them when negotiating a deal. In this way, they could supply ware 'off the shelf' or set their employees to work, making standard items.

By the time of the Civil Wars the continuing growth of the population provided opportunities for provincial manufacturers to sell ready-made ware too. They were certainly active in Oxford in the 1630s, which, incidentally, was to prove a boon to the Royalists when they established their Civil War headquarters there. At the petty sessions held in the city in 1638 seven men were accused of being salesmen, infringing the 1563 Statute of Artificers by selling clothes ready-made. In their defence, they pointed out that their trade, being about thirty years old, post-dated the statute and that 'they doe not make the coates or things they sell, but only buy them ready made, of the Taylors whose Trade it is to make garments; and buying them ready made and soe selling them againe'.[5] To date, no lists of salesmen's stock in the pre-Civil Wars period have come to light but a late seventeenth-century inventory, in which the goods of Richard Cartridge of St Botolphs, Aldersgate in London, are appraised, reveals the scale of business in London at least. When he died in 1688 he had 1,174 items of men's and women's clothing, comprising suits, coats, cloaks, gowns, waistcoats, breeches and petticoats, in his two shops and warehouses.[6]

The Wool and Cloth Trades

According to the Civil Wars' contracts, coats were to be made of broadcloth, a heavyweight material fashioned out of good-quality carded wool, and therefore an ideal cloth for an outer garment. Sometimes, the type of broadcloth to be used was stipulated. One contract signed in March 1648 stated that the coats were to be made of Coventry, Gloucester or Suffolk cloth or some other cloth as good. Coats were often faced with bayes or cotton.[7] Breeches might be made of broadcloth, too, but more commonly were cut out of kersey, a cheaper woollen material. For lining, one reference mentions East Country linen, though manufacturers used whatever they had to hand. Shirt fabric was normally lockram but there are references to Osnabrucks, dowlas and Lubeck cloth. Most stockings were made out of cotton or frieze – Welsh and Irish cottons are referred to – but some were knitted. Headgear comprised either felted monteros or knitted woollen Monmouth caps. For shoes, neat's-leather was used.[8]

Suitable materials were not always available. In the hundred years before the British Civil Wars, various changes occurred in the native textile industry and these had a bearing on the supply of cloth during the conflict. In particular, the traditional woollen industry, based upon fine, carded wool, declined and growth was restricted to the so-called 'new draperies', using long-stapled coarser wool. The broadcloth industry was affected the most and by the late 1630s production of fine, undyed cloths was confined to the West Country and parts of Suffolk and Essex. Coloured broadcloths were also produced in the same area of East Anglia, while other, newer dyed cloths of a high quality could be found in Dorset, Kent and Berkshire. Kerseys were made in the south-west and in parts of Wiltshire, in the West Riding, and in some areas in southern England. Cheaper cloths, such as friezes and cottons, were produced in Wales and Lancashire.[9]

In England, therefore, both sides could procure suitable cloth, though the quantities available did not always meet demand. For their coats, the Royalists, with access to the foremost broadcloth-producing area in the country, were better placed and they did obtain the bulk of their material from Gloucestershire. The Parliamentarians acquired most of their broadcloth from East Anglia. Inevitably, the war hampered long-distance trafficking. Before the conflict, a large proportion of the cloth had been taken down to Blackwell Hall in London, either for export or for redistribution round the country. The trade with London never stopped completely but the West Country and Welsh clothiers, in particular, had difficulty in getting through. Scotland and Ireland produced considerable quantities of wool, too, but it was not of the same quality. Scottish wool and flax made particularly coarse yarn, though in contrast Irish wool did improve during the course of the seventeenth century.[10] The various parties in the two countries made some of their clothes out of local materials but they also obtained cloth from England and abroad.[11]

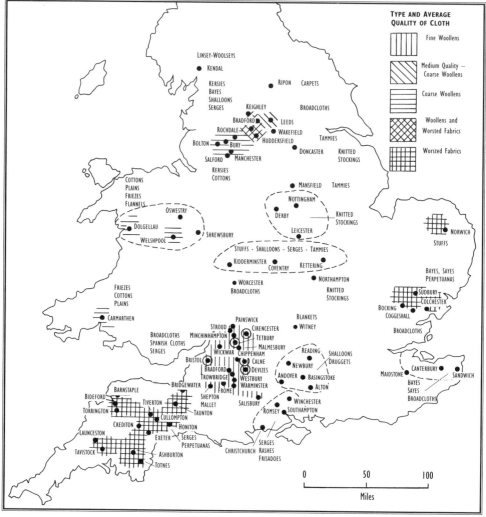

Map 4: Main centres of the wool-textile industry and their principal products, in the late seventeenth century. (from P.J. Bowden, *The Wool Trade in Tudor and Stuart England*, London, Frank Cass, 1972)

One of the reasons why the character of the industry changed in the preceding period was a deterioration in the quality of the wool, brought about (at least partly) by the progress of enclosure. This process was most notable in Midland and eastern pastures, which traditionally had supplied the surrounding textile areas with good-quality wool. Because the coarsening of the wool affected the broadcloth industry to the greatest extent, surviving centres had to look further afield for their supply. One source was the fine wool of Herefordshire and Shropshire, employed by clothiers as far apart as the south-west and East

Anglia.[12] When the war broke out it severed this west–east link. West Riding clothiers also suffered. Traditionally, they had used Midlands and Lincolnshire wool for their broadcloths and kerseys but as its quality declined, they experienced shortages in supplies and difficulties in finding adequate replacement stocks. The situation was made worse by the competition for the better-quality wool from clothiers in East Anglia. As a result, they had to draw on supplies of poorer wool from the northern counties, as well as from Scotland, Ireland and elsewhere. They made particular use of Irish wool.[13]

THE SCOTTISH AND IRISH REBELLIONS 1638–42

Developments in the clothing industry, especially in London, eased the task of kitting out the troops. When war broke out with the Scots in 1638, however, the government did not place large-scale orders on the London market because of Charles's reliance upon the militia. This means that the king passed on the task of finding uniforms and footwear for the recruits to the county authorities, and the expense onto the local population, who had to pay for them through coat and conduct money. Absence of any evidence of contracts being given to London merchants suggests that sufficient money was raised by the levy to provide clothing for the county militias. Local tailors and seamstresses must have done much of the work and, if so, the recycling of the money in the area would have helped to dampen down opposition. Conversely, later experience during the English Civil Wars, indicates that purchasing agents from counties in a wide arc around London made shopping trips to the capital to buy goods they could not readily acquire at home.

The response to the Irish rebellion was completely different; traditionally the militia were exempted from service in Ireland and, therefore, contracts were made with London merchants for clothing. Little was done for some time, however, perhaps because of the struggle between Charles and Parliament over control of military supplies. Bulk orders did not really start arriving from England until spring 1642 when reinforcements were being sent to the country. On 31 March George Wood, the Commissary for the Clothing, dispatched a consignment of stockings and Monmouth caps. The next day the House of Commons voted to bring certain loyalist garrisons into their pay and to provide money for clothing and footwear.[14] Thereafter, leading London merchants tendered for more of the business. On 6 May Richard Turner and other London woollen drapers agreed to furnish 10,000 coats (in three sizes) at 8s 6d each and 10,000 pairs of cotton stockings at 12d a pair, promising delivery at the rate of 2,000 a week. A fortnight later, two London cappers, Henry Paman and Edmund Hunt, contracted for 20,000 Monmouth caps at 23s a dozen. In June Richard Aldworth (a Bristol merchant) and Richard Wollaston offered to supply 4,000 fine Osnabruck shirts at 2s 9d each and Christopher Fisher, a London seamster, a further 1,800 (without wristbands) at the slightly higher price of 34s a dozen.[15]

Even before the first consignments of clothing had arrived, the Irish Council complained to the Lord Lieutenant, the Earl of Leicester, that no breeches were being sent. It pointed out that the suits had to be complete so that they would keep the soldiers warm in winter. Later consignments did include breeches and doublets. In August six London woollen drapers – Maurice Gethin, Tempest Milner, Richard Turner senior and junior, Samuel Turner and Richard Wollaston – contracted with the Irish Committee for 7,500 suits, comprising a cap, doublet, cassock, a pair of breeches, two shirts and two pairs of shoes and stockings, for the army in Ulster.[16] The committee also discussed the establishment of clothing storehouses at Dublin and Cork, stocked with a total of 13,000 suits (cassock, doublet and breeches), 3,000 cassocks, 30,000 shirts and 26,000 pairs of shoes and stockings.[17]

Consignments of boots and shoes were put together in the same way. Between the latter part of May and August two sets of London shoemakers delivered 27,500 pairs of shoes to the commissioners.[18] Both groups were called companies, suggesting a more permanent arrangement than a temporary or informal association to meet specific orders. When necessary, the main contractors brought in others or put out some of the work. James Greaves and Lawrence Stanley, for instance, formed the core of one company, but a third person, Jeffrey Badger, also signed a contract for 8,000 pairs of shoes on 27 May 1642. The two men agreed to supply a further 10,000 pairs of shoes later in the year and when sold, the phrase 'bought off us and our partners' suggests a distinction within the group.[19]

The Londoners had to share the trade with men from Northampton, a town with an established reputation in the industry. Its shoemakers seem to have responded more quickly to the crisis in Ireland than had their counterparts in the capital; at the end of February they arranged to make 7,000 pairs of shoes at 2s 4d a pair and had completed the order by the beginning of May. On the 13th a party of shoemakers from the town, led by John Herbert and John Scoven, were reported to be coming to London to negotiate a further contract. The 8,000 pairs of shoes agreed upon were ready by 24 June when George Wood was ordered to Northampton not only to organise their carriage to Chester but also to obtain more footwear in the town. On 30 June he made a deal with the Johnson group, who promised to provide 4,000 pairs of shoes at 2s 4d a pair and 600 pairs of boots at 7s on or before 13 August.[20]

The merchants supplied thousands of items of clothing in a remarkably short space of time. By 17 June 7,000 of the 10,000 coats and pairs of stockings that Richard Turner and his partners had contracted for on 6 May had already arrived at Dublin.[21] To do so, they may have had to 'cut corners', being economical with materials, taking and perhaps altering goods already in store, and employing numbers of semi-skilled workers. Some of the clothing was of poor quality. In the summer the soldiers refused to accept one batch of 3,000 coats; according to the Lords Justices, the cloth was bad, the coats too short and scant and had no lining. Another consignment of 6,000 suits, unloaded at Dublin in mid-September, was even worse.[22] Nonetheless, shortages persisted, to the extent that they prejudiced military activity. Plans to besiege Wexford and Ross had to be abandoned because of a desperate lack of money, clothes and shoes.[23]

It seems as though cargoes of clothing were the goods most commonly held up in England. In September the Lords Justices complained that the 'coats, caps, stockings, and shoes which were coming over thither from the Parliament . . . were stayed in their way . . . by the king's warrant.' Charles claimed that they had been stolen at Coventry by Parliamentarians.[24] Similarly, consignments were diverted to the Parliamentarian forces in England. On 19 August the Committee for Safety ordered the Irish Committee to deliver up the coats, shirts, shoes and knapsacks in their possession to three London merchants, Stephen Estwick, Francis Peck and Thomas Player, who had been contracted to fit out twelve of the Earl of Essex's regiments with these items.[25]

Parliament

Throughout the Civil Wars Parliament continued to make use of the same merchants, whose prominence in the clothing trades was matched by their political radicalism.[26] They were particularly active at times when armies had to be kitted out *en masse* and were therefore responsible for clothing the New Model Army in 1645–6 and the expeditionary forces to Ireland and Scotland in 1649–51, as well as offering to provide all the arms and equipment for the projected (but aborted) offensive in Ireland in 1647.[27] Some of the middlemen were specialists, notably the cappers, hosiers, linen drapers and buff coat makers, but in general they supplied a range of clothing. To do so, they must have subcontracted the work to others or bought goods in, using their contacts in the mercantile community.

This was the course of action adopted by John Davies, a Carrickfergus merchant, when he obtained the contract to supply the anti-Confederation forces in Ireland with arms, munitions and equipment in 1644. The names of the people with whom he dealt have a familiar ring, including Richard Downes, who supplied most of the clothes for the soldiers and cloth for the officers; Humphrey Primate, who provided the buff coats; and Thomas Andrews, Richard Thorogood and William Smith, who sold him most of the linen.[28] A single consortium, comprising ten leading London merchants, tendered for the Irish contract of 1647.[29] For the Irish and Scottish forces of 1649–51, however, the authorities treated with specific contractors and seem to have singled out the leading individual in a particular trade, with whom to do business. Richard Downes, the woollen draper, stands out. In turn, he and the others like him, must have dealt with others.[30]

The reference to Hugh Primate, a haberdasher who lived outside the Newgate, helps to resolve one of the mysteries of Parliamentarian supply, namely, the source of buff coats. Although generally only worn by officers and the cavalry, and rather expensive,[31] they should appear more regularly in the accounts. Primate sold buff coats to Davies in 1644–5 and he later supplied £40 10s worth of 'buff coats and the like' (perhaps twenty to twenty-five coats) to Colonel Audley Mervin in August 1646, as subcontractor to Maurice Gething and others. Joseph Vaughan, a leather seller, supplied the bulk of the coats for Colonel

Mervin's regiment, his bill of £272 1s 0d for 'buff and the like' representing 135–150 garments. In August 1642 Vaughan had supplied 53 buff coats at £1 18s 0d. each to the troop of horse raised in Watford for Essex's army. At the same time Primate and a Mr Blackbrough sold buff coats valued at £58 15s. 0d. to the Buckinghamshire troop. The only other supplier found is a William Hunter, who in January 1646 acknowledged receipt of £4 10s for three buff coats delivered to three of Lieutenant-Colonel Thorp's soldiers.[32]

Although merchants controlled the business, humble craftsmen and artisans did the actual work, as is revealed in a case heard in December 1645 concerning the 1644 contractors, John Davies and his partners.[33] Richard Downes, the woollen draper, deposed that he had agreed to supply 9,500 suits, comprising cassock and breeches, at 15s 3d each. In addition, Davies's partners furnished 1,500 suits, and the partners, Arthur Dew and Edward Harris, a further quantity. Downes delivered the finished garments principally to William Dobbins, a commissary officer for Ireland, and two tailors, Messrs Dellingham and Perkins, viewed them. Downes paid the tailors and seamstresses he employed 10d for each suit made, giving them the cloth to do the work. According to other depositions the numbers they made varied from 15 to 200.[34] He recouped his expenses from money collected in several south-eastern counties on the ordinance to raise £80,000 for Ireland. Two cutters, Chandler and Grimes, also acted as intermediaries, distributing the cut-out pieces of cloth to various people themselves.[35]

The size of these contracts provided the merchants with the opportunity to profit from the war and for the unscrupulous with the means of earning more through sharp practice. The clothes trade was particularly susceptible to fraudulent activities. The contractors of the 1590s and 1642, for instance, were accused of the same abuses that John Davies allegedly perpetrated in 1644–5.[36] Deponents in the 1645 case commented on the poor quality of the cloth, the skimping on the material used and the inferior workmanship. Typically, Thomas Watkinson said that the coats and breeches were made of very bad cloth and the shirts of the coarsest linen and that they were so badly cut and sewn that the suits could not be worth more than 9–10s. Furthermore, the linings of the breeches were only half the depth of the garment and the pockets so small and shallow that the wearer could hardly put his hands in them. Finally, he claimed that the shirts 'were so shorte as thatt they did not Cover their pryvy parts'.[37] The language is reminiscent of the complaints made by freemen of the Merchant Taylors' Company about the use of non-time served tailors and the quality of their work. Indeed, one deponent alleged that some of the people employed by Chandler and Grimes were 'Apple women & diuerse others thatt were nott taylors' and so would do the job cheaply. They were given no more than 4½d for sewing up a suit.[38]

The evidence is damning, but apart from the on-going battle between guild and non-guild tailors, it is possible that Davies fell foul of a plot hatched among a city faction, allied to the Irish Adventurers, who were political opponents of Sir John Clotworthy.[39] If he were so corrupt, why was he given another contract in 1646? Moreover, Richard Downes, described as Davies's partner in 1647, became the government's chief supplier of clothing by the end of the decade.[40] Nonetheless, the action of George Wood, one of the deponents in the suit, does suggest that there was some truth in the allegation. As Commissary for the Clothing for Ireland, he was clearly an interested party and seems to have been genuinely shocked at the fraud. Scandalised by the prices demanded for such shoddy goods and the profit margins enjoyed by the contractors, he claimed that he could provide decent clothes at a much lower rate. From a completely different source, we learn that he did follow up his assertion. Looking at samples of ware, he calculated that a coat and a pair of breeches should cost 9s 9½d, that is, 9s ½d in materials and a further 9d for the workmanship (1d per 1s) As the State allowed 17s a suit, the profit to be made when clothing an army of 10,000 amounted to £3,604 3s 4d! In practice, the poor soldier suffered, as the cost traditionally was taken out of his wages. If 17s were to be the accepted price – and it was still the one charged in 1649 – he pointed out the improvements that could be made in quality. He also thought that the 1s. included for the job should be paid by the State and not by the soldier.[41]

In a carefully controlled system such abuses should not have occurred. Just as arms makers had to supply ware according to certain specifications and subject their goods to being proved, clothing contractors had to keep to a particular pattern and allow inspectors to view and, if necessary, turn down, their garments. When on 4 May 1642 Turner and other London woollen drapers offered to make thousands of suits for Ireland and presented their patterns and prices to the Irish Committee, the committee kept the patterns and deputed several people to find out the true cost of fashioning the clothes. Terms were drawn up two days later and include reference to quality, price and delivery dates and also to the need for inspection.[42] In a contract for 2,000 coats, breeches and pairs of stockings for the New Model Army made by Richard Downes on 14 February 1646 the type and colour of cloth to be used and the length of the coats were stipulated. To maintain the shape and size of the suits, they were to be pre-shrunk in cold water. Downes pointed out that, while it was impossible for anyone exactly to match the provisions every time, he promised to do his best and that 'as neere as he can none of ye said provisions of Coates, Breeches & Stockins shall be worse than ye patternes presented'. To ensure quality, the purchasing committee could appoint their own inspectors, who had the power instantly to reject substandard ware.[43]

Problems occurred when inadequate supervision was made. Thus, although provision was made in the contract to examine Turner's coats and stockings in May 1642, in the haste to send them to Ireland the committee ordered their immediate dispatch, unseen. When they arrived, they were found to be defective. In 1645 Davies not surprisingly tried to restrict the number of clothes viewed but those that were seen, both at Southampton House and on the backs of soldiers, were universally condemned. As a result, they seem to have been scrapped but, because the deception bought the partners time, a good deal of money had been paid out. Downes, for instance, had delivered suits to the value of £6,000 and had received all but £300–£400 of it.[44]

The boot and shoe industry continued to function in a similar but largely independent way. One or two clothing contracts did include footwear but in general they were provided separately. Several partnerships can be identified among the London shoemakers. The number, composition and scale of activity of these groupings did fluctuate over time but, as in the case of Jenkin Ellis's company, core and peripheral members can often be distinguished.[45] To a certain extent, changes were inevitable as individual circumstances altered; people died or retired and gaps had to be filled. At the end of the decade James Greaves was the sole survivor from among those who had contributed footwear to the soldiers in Ireland in 1642. He seems to have died early in 1651, still supplying shoes.[46]

Some shoemakers took the lead in negotiating contracts for a wider group. In a bargain for 8,000 shoes made between the Committee for the Army and thirteen shoemakers on 24 February 1646 Jenkin Ellis and Lawrence Stanley were prominent.[47] By the time that the Irish and Scottish expeditionary forces were being shod, the system had been refined, with 90 per cent of the business seemingly going to the partnership of James Greaves, Jenkin Ellis, Francis Marriott and Theodore Reynolds. Between January 1650 and August 1651 they were paid £10,166 for 57,550 pairs of shoes and 14,880 pairs of boots.[48] It seems unlikely that these four men could dominate the industry to this extent and, as in the clothing trade, they must have put out much of the work to others.

Northampton shoemakers continued to supply footwear. At the end of May 1643 4,000 pairs of shoes were dispatched to London for shipment to Ireland.[49] Later in the year, however, the industry there seems to have suffered from a shortage of manpower, many of the apprentices having enlisted in the Parliamentarian army. The master shoemakers, worried about the possible economic consequences, petitioned the county committee for their release, but to no avail.[50] There certainly are fewer references to Northampton shoes but business did go on. In June 1644 Sir William Brereton, while on the march from London to Cheshire, bought thirty pairs of boots for his troopers from Thomas Pendleton at Northampton 'where bootes are Cheape'.[51] In 1648 Pendleton, who was mayor that year, delivered 2,500 pairs of shoes to the Army Committee and shared in a further consignment of 550 pairs of shoes and stockings.[52] If these rather meagre figures seem to justify the dire warning of 1643, the fault may lie with the documentation rather than with the level of activity in the town. Indeed, there is indirect evidence to suggest that London's shoemakers were subcontracting out some of their work to their counterparts in Northampton, whose endeavours are therefore hidden from sight. On 12 August 1648, for instance, a warrant was issued to pay two of the capital's shoemakers, William Blissett and Ben Harris, £375 for 3,000 pairs of leather shoes. They also were to receive £2 10s towards the expense of going to Northampton to collect their money, which was to be raised on that county's assessment. As it was customary for counties to pay for work done within their borders, the entry implies that the shoes had been made there. Indeed, Pendleton's bill for his 2,500 pairs of shoes had been paid from the same source.[53]

The example of Northampton, though an exceptional case, is a reminder that there were many people making clothing and footwear outside London.

Hoskins's argument that a significant proportion of the workforce in the early modern town was engaged in supplying the basic human needs of food and drink, clothing and shelter, is borne out by the evidence of records containing occupational information. In particular, they incorporate many references to people working in the clothing and footwear trades and crafts.[54] Most county forces seem to have been provisioned locally and even regional armies like that of the Eastern Association obtained much of their ware from within their borders. The Earl of Manchester, for instance, had the coats of his lifeguards made by John Burton, a Cambridge tailor.[55] As forces were assembled in each locality, drapers, tailors, shoemakers and the like found themselves being asked to step up production and to concentrate on furnishing goods for the soldiers.

As an example of the productive capacity of an area, the accounts of John Cory of Norwich, merchant and collector of the weekly assessment, give some indication of the output of local craftsmen, who were being organised to supply goods to the army. In the seven months from 29 April to 20 November 1644, Cory paid £480 to 20 people for supplying 150 canvas waistcoats, 62 shirts, 8 pairs of breeches, about 750 pairs of stockings and 635 pairs of shoes, as well as cloth worth £313 10s 0d.[56] In this respect, the contrast between the Eastern Association and the Earl of Essex's army, which was supplied by London merchants, is pronounced. Even a county as close to the capital as Hertfordshire made some use of local suppliers. In 1644 William Gardiner, a Hertford draper, fitted out the county troop with 53 coats at 10s, 25 pairs of grey hose at 2s 6d, 105 shirts at 3s 4d and 60 pairs of shoes at 3s 4d and 40 pairs at 2s 8d.[57]

If convenient or necessary, goods were brought from London. In 1643 Sir Thomas Barrington, a leading member of the Essex Committee, contracted with Willam Grey, a merchant tailor from London, to supply 1,000 coats for the county infantry regiment. As an MP it was easy for him to deal with the capital's merchants.[58] To keep the vital outpost of Plymouth open, local supplies of clothing and shoes, as well as of arms and munitions, were hugely augmented by imports from London. In the period from May 1644 to January 1646, 13 capes, 100 waistcoats, 433 shirts, 533 pairs of stockings, 1,029 pairs of shoes and 3 pairs of boots were made locally, but 800 suits, 1,800 shirts, 2,891 pairs of stockings, 2,520 pairs of shoes, 42 pairs of boots and 800 knapsacks were shipped in.[59] In the Eastern Association the development of a centralised commissariat during the course of 1644 led not only to tighter organisation of the local workforce but also to bulk buying of war materials in London. Between August and December two London shoemakers, Richard Crofts and Edward Poole, sold 2,264 pairs of shoes and 1,000 pairs of boots. One consignment of 1,000 pairs of boots was handed over to the association's agent at St Albans.[60] Ironically, the merging of the regional forces into the New Model Army led to the return of some of the arms, equipment and clothing to the capital. In November 1646, for example, a warrant was issued to pay Thomas Russell, the high collector for Cambridgeshire, £21 19s 6d spent in transporting coats, breeches, shirts and knapsacks to the Tower.[61]

In many ways the organisation of the provincial industries mirrored that of the capital. Individual craftsmen continued to carry out small-scale tasks, as and when required. In Warwickshire a shoemaker named Hodges was involved in four separate transactions between April and May 1645, in which he sold boots to four of Captain Potter's troopers for £2 15s 6d and made five more pairs, as well as three pairs of breeches, for 7s. In Rutland, two local shoemakers sold a few shoes to soldiers in Captain Torey's troop on their way to besiege Belvoir Castle in April 1646.[62] However, this was hardly the way to clothe and shoe an army and during the wars many men like Hodges became cogs in a much larger machine. They might, like those paid by John Cory, fulfil contracts, either individually or in a group. In Cheshire, four Nantwich tailors, Peter, John and William Burstow and Thomas Greenall, made 344 infantry coats and 55 troopers' coats during the winter of 1643/4 and delivered them to Sir William Brereton's commissary officer on 22 February 1644.[63] The largest consignments were those assembled by merchant-capitalists, who put out the work to individual craftsmen. William Gardiner, mentioned above, must have operated in this way. For the Eastern Association, the major suppliers of clothing were Thomas Buckley, a Cambridge tailor, and Samuel Moody, a Bury St Edmunds clothier and local treasurer for the association. In spring 1644 Buckley delivered 2,396 coats, in red or green with red or blue facings, 100 shirts and 13 pairs of breeches, at a total cost of £1,407 0s 2d. In November he was paid a further £1,025 10s 2d for 698 coats, 1,167 pairs of breeches and 500 doublets. A month earlier Moody was asked to make 1,000 coats for the garrison at King's Lynn and the order had been completed within two months.[64]

Consideration had to be given to the supply of cloth. In East Anglia, the Suffolk clothiers were prominent, making broadcloths and kerseys for army coats and breeches, though they were dependent to some extent on more distant stocks of wool.[65] Lancashire clothiers, especially those from Manchester, supplied Cheshire and Staffordshire forces, as well as their own troops, with cloth. In Bristol, the governor, Colonel Fiennes, dealt with local drapers.[66] Traditionally, cloth had moved by road and this practice continued; in 1644, for instance, horses and carts brought cloth from Lancashire and Yorkshire to Staffordshire.[67] During the Civil Wars, however, for the sake of speed and ease of access, a much greater proportion of cloth was dispatched round the coast (in spite of the danger posed by privateers). In Samuel Moody's accounts for Suffolk there is a reference to a consignment of fifty-five yards of cloth being shipped out through King's Lynn. Plymouth received its cloth by ship from London. Between April 1644 and October 1645, 3,577 yd of woollen cloth, mainly kerseys and broadcloths, and 4,651 yd of linen cloth, were brought in.[68]

How did provincial prices compare with those at London? Problems in obtaining sufficient cloth, and perhaps an adequate workforce, might raise prices. Moreover, as George Wood noted, much depended on the quality of the material used (and the integrity of the supplier!). In 1644 Buckley at Cambridge made clothing at a range of prices: coats cost from 10s 0d to £2 3s 6d, and breeches 7s 2d to 16s 6d. Twenty-eight suits, comprising long coats with bayes buttons and silk, and lined breeches, were valued at £3 each. Where the goods are comparable, Buckley's prices are similar. His standard suit (coat and breeches) cost only 2*d* more than was being paid in London. His lockram shirts, at 3*s* 8*d*, were appreciably more expensive than the 2*s* 10*d* Christopher Nicholson charged the New Model Army eleven months later, but they were probably of a better quality. In October 1644 the Eastern Association obtained other shirts from an unknown source for 2*s* 9*d* each. Moody's coats at 9*s* 6*d*, the 'usual rate', were even cheaper than Buckley's.[69]

The prices the two men charged were comparable probably because of the scale in which they worked. In contrast, a few months later, the craftsmen on Cory's list produced stockings, shirts and shoes that were more expensive than those cited in the initial contracts for the New Model Army. This is borne out in a direct comparison between shoe prices in the last few months of 1644. A local shoemaker, Richard Carter, charged the Eastern Association 3*s* 3*d* for his shoes, whereas the two Londoners, Richard Crofts and Edward Poole, asked for 2*s* 6*d*, 2*s* 7*d* or 3*s* 0*d* for the shoes they delivered, including transport costs. Again, one should be aware of differences in quality and the added charge for waxing shoes. In October 1644 the bill of William Gardiner, the Hertford draper, included shoes at 2*s* 8*d* and 3*s* 4*d* a pair. His coats were the same price as Buckley's basic garment and shirts 4*d* less.[70] Some of the additional cost seems to have been due to higher labour charges, perhaps because properly skilled tailors were used to a greater extent. In London Downes paid 10*d* a suit, whereas the four Nantwich tailors, referred to above, earned 1*s* 2*d* for a foot soldier's coat and 1*s* 6*d* for a trooper's coat. In Warwickshire a coat and a pair of breeches, with linings, cost 3*s* to make in 1643 and a coat in Lancashire a year later, 1*s* 0*d*.[71]

Royalists

When the Civil War started in England in August 1642, the king had been away from London for several months and therefore unable to make use of the capital's merchants for uniforms and footwear. Unlike Essex, he could not expect to have a whole army kitted out in a matter of weeks. Charles I was not without resources, however; he had ready access to suitable cloth and thousands of craftsmen who could be organised to supply the needs of his armies. Within his zone of influence, moreover, there were towns which specialised in the manufacture of items of clothing or footwear. The chief industry of Bewdley, Worcestershire, was the making of Monmouth caps. According to Richard Symonds, who passed through the town with the royalist army in 1644, the caps, which poor people knitted for 2*d* each, were sold for between 2*s* and 4*s*.[72] Shoemaking was a feature of a number of towns, including Evesham, Shrewsbury and Wells.[73] As the situation deteriorated, the king and his supporters began to prepare for the coming conflict, ordering clothing and shoes for potential recruits, as well as stockpiling arms and armaments. Thomas Bushell, for instance, clothed the king's Lifeguard and three other regiments with suits, stockings, shoes and hats. In the north, Newcastle supplied his infantry, the 'Whitecoats', with uniforms of that colour.[74] Given the circumstances, it naturally took time for the Royalist war effort to gather momentum but the evidence, though rather anecdotal, suggests that the king's troops were adequately supplied with uniforms. This was achieved by adopting similar principles to the ones governing the Parliamentarian system of supply.

The Royalists quickly moved to make Oxford a centre for the manufacture of clothes. In January 1643 they established a clothing magazine in the Schools of Music and Astronomy and pressed tailors and seamstresses from the whole area to work there. Anthony Wood reported that he had heard that 4,000–5,000 people were being employed in cutting out the material, which was then made up into uniforms.[75] Oxford lay on the fringe of the West Country clothmaking region and in the war drew most of its material from clothiers there.[76] Although the trade was subject to disruption, the Royalists gradually extended their control of the area – their failure to take Gloucester notwithstanding – and this did improve the situation. Production continued throughout the war. When, early in 1644, Charles I heard a report that large stocks of cloth, canvas and lockram were piled up at a number of Gloucestershire cloth towns, he ordered Prince Rupert to dispatch a party of horse to bring the material back to Oxford. The owners were to be given a voucher, for which security could be obtained when they presented it at the Royalist capital. In March the following year a convoy took eighty horseloads of Gloucestershire cloth, earmarked for soldiers' uniforms, to Banbury.[77]

Nonetheless, the business did have its problems: apart from the threat from Parliamentarian attack, many of the clothiers in the West Country seem to have possessed Parliamentarian sympathies and were reluctant suppliers. Geography dictated that they deal with the Royalists but many of them were determined to run the gauntlet of Royalist garrisons and continue to trade with London. They were not always successful. On one occasion, in June 1643, soldiers from the Wallingford garrison plundered a convoy of Wiltshire carriers of their cloth, acquiring enough, it was said, to 'make new clothes for all their soldiers'. As a result, a large number of soldiers from Wallingford descended on Oxford to have the cloth worked up into uniforms for themselves.[78]

In the procurement of clothing for the Royalist forces, Thomas Bushell is a key figure, if a rather quixotic and restless one. A Worcestershire man and an ex-monopolist, lessee of the silver mines in Wales and mint master, he supplied the king with money, as well as arms, equipment and clothing. On 6 March 1643 he offered to fit out the king's soldiers with suits – consisting of cassocks, breeches, stockings and caps – at a reasonable rate and to deliver them to Oxford. When one load had been brought in and paid for, he promised to send a second one, and so on until the whole army had been clothed. The source of Bushell's supply is uncertain but he had good contacts, presumably among the woollen and linen drapers of Wales and the west of England. Like the Parliamentarian contractors, he acted as a middleman and put out the work to others. That they were men of means themselves, employing tailors and seamstresses to do the actual work, is made clear by Bushell. Those who provided the clothes were to decide on the mode of payment, either in cash or as a bill of exchange to be paid at London.[79] The enterprise was a success and in January 1644 the king ordered that Bushell be paid £2,000 on account for his sterling work 'in which he has done us acceptable service and disbursed great sums of money'.[80] Because of the efforts of Bushell and the workforce in the Schools, Anthony Wood could later recall that in July 1643 'all the common soldiers then at Oxford were newe apparrelled, some all in red, coates, breeches, & mounteers; & some all in blewe'.[81]

Bushell's initiative is indicative of the level of capacity in the Royalist zone, and manufacturing activity outside Oxford significantly boosted output. In fact, despite the creation of a central manufactory at Oxford, the process of making clothing and footwear was decentralised. The Royalists exploited these resources as much as they could, but unfortunately we only learn about their activities through a series of snapshots, which is all that the documents available provide. When required, reasonably large orders for clothing and footwear could be put together in a comparatively short space of time. This suggests an element of organisation but the details are only occasionally discernible. Reference to Sir William Waller's seizure of wool and kersey going to Exeter to be made into uniforms in December 1645, reveals the continuing importance of the city as a clothing centre.[82] However, the records give the impression that in their relations with clothing and footwear manufacturers the Royalists were more inconsistent and arbitrary than the Parliamentarians were. Regional commanders undoubtedly made commercial arrangements with local suppliers and as a result the industries developed. However, the king and his council sometimes appeared to be reacting to events, asking for supplies when needed and obtaining goods by exerting pressure, rather than through contracts. Of course, this judgement might reflect a bias in the records that have survived. It could also be pointed out that if the sets of contracts and accounts collected together in the Commonwealth Papers were taken away, the Parliamentarian achievement would not seem as impressive.

The Royalists' rather capricious approach is illustrated by their tendency to put the onus on the localities to do the work of organising supplies. County commissioners and other local authorities were asked for contributions and left to find the items themselves. During the course of the war Totnes in Devon by itself contributed £3,000 to buy clothes and other provisions. When in September 1644 it was decided to fit out all the Royalist soldiers with new uniforms, which were to be made in the south-west, the commissioners in the region were ordered to raise money and provide the clothes. Cornwall's quota was fixed at 2,000 pairs of shoes and an unknown number of stockings; Devon's at 3,000 uniforms and accompanying shoes and stockings; and Somerset's at either 3,000 or 3,500 uniforms, together with pairs of shoes and stockings. The task of making the shoes and garments was divided up among the textile centres, according to ability. A list of places that supplied shoes and stockings reveals the range: whereas Bristol had to send 150 pairs, Nether Stowey's contribution was 50. The uniforms appear to have been made at towns such as Chard, Exeter, Totnes and Wells. While the 5 October deadline was not met, consignments from Somerset and Exeter and the western parts had arrived at the collecting point at Wells by 13 November, for forwarding to Bath. A year later the commissioners of Devon were asked for further supplies of clothing and provisions for the army.[83]

On other occasions, the Royalist army demanded clothing and shoes while on the march. Its passage through Worcestershire in 1643 cost the county £1,813 and at Droitwich alone the inhabitants were forced to pay £312 to clothe the soldiers. On 16 June 1644 Charles I paused long enough at Evesham merely to fine the townspeople £1,000 for a transgression and to demand 1,000 pairs of shoes. These he paid for at rates of between 1s 4d and 2s 0d.[84] That the citizens could immediately lay their hands on so many shoes is an indication of the resources that the king had at his disposal.

A good example of the way in which the Royalists operated can be seen in the clothing of English troops shipped home from Ireland in autumn 1643. Ormond had already warned the English Royalists that the soldiers, hungry, poorly clothed and badly paid, could easily be induced to desert if these defects were not remedied.[85] The response was immediate. On 8 November, Secretary Nicholas reported to the Irish Justices that three regiments from Munster had disembarked at Bristol and that 'clothes are making for them as fast as may be'. To the north, similar arrangements were being made for those due to land at Chester. The commissioners of Anglesey, Caernarvonshire and Merionethshire were ordered to provide sufficient clothing and footwear for 1,300 men, and food or money to maintain them for fifteen days.[86] At Chester Orlando Bridgeman coordinated the effort with commendable vigour, touring north Wales to cajole suppliers and raise money. To assist him, he enlisted the support of Viscount Bulkeley of Baron Hill, Anglesey, and John Williams, the Archbishop of York, at Conway Castle, Caernarvonshire. The first troops came ashore in Flintshire on 16 November and marched on to Chester. By the 29th Bridgeman could write to Ormond to say that he had provided shoes and stockings for 1,000–1,200 of them and that more were being made. He also thought that he had acquired enough cloth and frieze to clothe them and that he expected that the job would be done by the end of the following week.[87] Surviving documentation shows Bridgeman at work, dealing with merchants, craftsmen and tradesmen and arranging for the transport of raw materials and finished goods to Chester. Some of the suppliers were working for themselves and others seem to have acted as middlemen. Of the latter group, John Hilton supplied 494 pairs of shoes, 136 pairs of stockings and 100 pairs of hose, and Samuel Ince at least 756 pairs of stockings. The Shoemakers' Company of Chester also provided some 320 pairs of shoes. Others were set to work at Chester to make clothing and stockings. Richard Haswell and John Prentice dyed the cloth, Hugh Dodd, John Maddock and William Pimlow did the tailoring and Richard Haswell put in the linings. Fifteen individuals, seven of whom were women, provided the canvas to wrap up the merchandise.[88]

Scotland and Ireland

Initially, the Covenanter army had a kaleidoscopic appearance for there was no official attempt to clothe the soldiers. Lairds and clan chieftains might kit out their retinues and contingents; in 1640 the Master of Forbes armed and equipped his own regiment and fined heritors refusing to outfit his men £10 13s 4d Scots. Only with the raising of the Ulster army in 1641 were the soldiers issued with specific clothing.[89] In practice, throughout the period the cost of fitting out the soldiers appears to have been borne by both the local and national authorities. First of all, shires and burghs were asked to make 'voluntary' contributions. In January 1641 Stirling's inhabitants were 'invited' to contribute at least 900 merks to buy clothes. Three years later, on 10 April 1644, the treasurer at Edinburgh gave the commissioners, Archibald Sydserff and Robert Micklejohn, money to procure 800 pairs of shoes for the city's regiment, then in England. At the end of the year the Committee of Estates asked the parishes in the presbyteries of Linlithgow and Stirlingshire to provide enough money to pay for 600 suits, and pairs of shoes and socks for the Earl of Callender's regiment of foot. In 1651 Dundee stinted its inhabitants £13,332 13s 4d Scots to pay for outfitting its company of soldiers.[90] At the same time, the central Treasury supplemented local contributions by providing money to commanders or commissary officers who requested help. The relationship between the two can be illustrated in the experience of Callender's regiment. As the contribution did not cover costs, Captain Livingston, the captain of Callender's own company, petitioned the Committee of Estates for a supply of clothing (among other things). The committee agreed to release the money. Of course, the shires and burghs had to pay for this facility through loans and taxes. On 7 July 1648, for instance, the Earl of Panmure was asked for a loan of £1,000 Scots to outfit the army.[91]

To obtain uniforms the authorities could draw upon the native leather, textile and clothing industries. In the early seventeenth century more and more of the hides that had hitherto been exported were tanned at home.[92] In wartime they could be made into buff coats, as well as into boots and shoes.[93] Coarse linen and woollen cloths, using local materials, were woven extensively in the countryside and were taken to towns to be finished and sold.[94] Aberdeen was an important centre for woollen plaids and stockings and Glasgow and Dundee were noted for linen. By 1639 merchants were exporting 121,000 ells of plaid from Aberdeen. Presumably cloth was diverted to the home market during the war years, though the need for revenue ensured that the export trade had to be maintained. Stocks were certainly available in the country. In September 1644, when Montrose entered Perth after the Battle of Tippermuir, the corporation had to provide him with 4,000 merks worth of cloth.[95] Because Scottish products were of inferior quality, however, much material was imported. In March 1644, an Edinburgh merchant, Alexander Johnstone, sold 1,058¼ ells of frieze and 53 ells of broadcloth to the Committee of Estates for £2,359 17s 0d Scots.[96] Large consignments were sent from England. In July and August two Leeds clothiers received £8,000 sterling for 19,455½ yd of kersey and 26,418¼ yd of broadcloth. A year later the Scots paid out £7,661 15s 7d sterling for 54 packs of cloth and 28 fardels of lining.[97]

Making the clothes and footwear was less of a problem: villages and towns had their tailors and shoemakers, who could be put to work on war production. When on 4 February 1646 the Earl of Balcarres asked the Committee of Estates for 3 yd of cloth a man (*inter alia*) he presumably knew of tailors who would stitch the material up into clothes.[98] In August 1650 the glovers' guild at Perth kitted out their trooper and gave £2 Scots to a local tailor to make his riding coat, socks and under clothes. The coat needed 2 ells of English cloth at £5 Scots an ell and the socks an ell of frieze at 11s Scots. Buttons and silk cost £1 Scots. James Drummond charged £9 Scots for the trooper's boots, while a pair of spurs and a hat with a ribbon cost a further £3 12s. A pair of gloves added 36s Scots to the bill. An ell of hodding at £1 Scots was needed for the saddlecloth.[99] Some probate inventories list stocks of material; thus, William Burrell, a Glasgow armourer, left three pairs of plaids and 60 ells of linen cloth when he died in January 1650.[100]

In May 1640 Aberdeen's corporation agreed to the 'Bon Accord', whereby to avoid being sacked the town had to provide the Covenanting forces with 1,200 pairs of shoes and 3,000 ells of harden cloth, ticking or sail canvas to make tents. At a second visitation, made in October, the shoemakers were forced to reveal how much leather they possessed, and told to complete their proportion of the 2,000 pairs of shoes (sizes ten and eleven) for the army before the 11th. The shoemakers made eighty-four pairs but they had to do the work by themselves because, as at Northampton, their servants and apprentices had joined the army. Moreover, as they were only given the price of the leather and not the cost of workmanship, they received a mere 17s for a pair worth 30s. The city's merchants were not only ordered to deliver their quota of clothing, namely 2,000 suits and 2,000 sarks (shirts), but also had to allow a specially convened committee to take account of how much grey cloth (bleached and unbleached harden cloth) they had.[101]

Aberdeen was particularly targeted because of its anti-Covenanting sympathies and reluctance to fulfil its obligations. Nonetheless, the incident does show the level of output that could be achieved, especially if pressure were applied. In general, too, the examples reveal that Scottish craftsmen were able to supply clothing and footwear in reasonable quantities. However, they were not working at the same level as the woollen drapers of London, and costs were higher. The glovers' company of Perth paid £1 5s 8½d sterling for clothes (not including hat and gloves) and 15s for boots, whereas in London they would have cost 17s and 14s 6d respectively. The relative prices suggest that supplies of leather were more readily available in Scotland (or at least in the Perth area) than suitable textiles, a point which is also reflected in the use of English cloth for the coat. The scale of the Scottish commitments must have overstretched the workforce, too. Apart from the demands of the various armies operating within the country, they had to clothe the Scots army in Ulster. The soldiers there were initially supplied with clothing and footwear from England but thereafter very little was shipped out to them. As a result, the troops suffered great hardship and money and clothing had to be sent from Scotland. Sir James Melville of Hallhill, Lanarkshire, was one of those who contributed to the 'voluntary' loan of 1 March 1643, giving 4,000 merks for victuals and clothing on 20 June. More was dispatched in March 1645 after the commissioners had despaired of getting the English Parliament to honour its promises. The Committee of Estates sent money, clothes and victuals but it was hard-pressed to do so.[102]

In Ireland, the problem of clothing the soldiers in the initial stages of the insurrection was a desperate one. Many of them were dispossessed settlers who had fled from the rebels with little more than the clothes they stood up in – 'stript and almost naked' according to the Lords Justices. On 23 April the Council members begged the Lord Lieutenant for clothing as well as arms and armaments. 'Such is our want of money, victuals, clothes and shoes for the soldier', they wrote, 'that our soldiers are no longer able to march abroad til those supplies arrive from England.'[103] Initially, very little clothing came so it had to be provided at home. On 14 March the wife of the mayor of Waterford proposed to buy £60 worth of broadcloth, probably for soldiers' coats, as a means of relieving dispossessed English settlers from Counties Kilkenny and Ross and elsewhere.[104] At Dublin, Sir William Anderson and a local merchant, Tobias Norris, were appointed to furnish uniforms and by the end of August 1642 the two men had spent thousands of pounds on clothes, £3,336 1s 0d of which was still owing to them. They, too, had a willing workforce to hand and were able to give employment to 800 families of displaced persons, mainly the destitute wives and children of those in the king's service. The work created by the order was found to be 'a very great comfort and relief' to the refugees. Although they may not have had formal training, the women would have possessed basic seamstress skills. Indeed, they made better clothes than the ones brought from England.[105] A workforce of this size could make a reasonable number of garments but in most garrison towns there would have been a group of tailors and seamstresses who could put together uniforms for the soldiers. Thus, in September 1644 the Scots at Dungannon asked for 200 suits of clothes or the cloth and canvas to make them.[106]

Local supplies of wool and flax could be used to make clothing, especially breeches, shirts and stockings. Some clothmaking capacity existed in Ireland, for bundles of cloth, especially friezes and cottons, were exported,[107] However, the industry mainly focused on producing yarn, much of it for the outside market. In the period from 1632 to 1640, 192,768½ stones of wool were exported, while between 1635 and 1640 6,276½ packs 62 lb of yarn were sent from Ireland, earning £60,915 1s 1d in customs and licences.[108] As a result, there may have been too few weavers in the country to raise production of cloth to cope with demand in the initial stages of the conflict. Moreover, as the income derived from exports was so valuable, overseas trade had to be maintained. Cloth, therefore, had to be shipped from England. On 17 May 1642 Richard Wollaston and Richard Aldworth contracted to send 16,000 ells of lockram to Dublin, 8,000 ells to Munster and 6,000 ells to Carrickfergus, enough to make 6,000, 3,000 and 2,250 shirts respectively.[109] Even after clothing began to arrive from England, the Lords Justices wanted to maintain the local industry, which had proved its worth both as a source of supply and as a means of providing jobs. Therefore, they requested cloth, bayes and linen to make more clothes. Consignments were still coming in the following year. In late 1642 Sir William Anderson, by then Commissary of the Clothing, contracted with Robert Stafford for supplies and by the end of January 1643 had received 5,722½ ells of dowlas at a cost of

£309 17*s* 8*d*.[110] For footwear the armies could draw on supplies of Irish leather. Hides were a major export item; in the years 1640–1, 59,269 units were sent overseas. As in the textile industry, the country's emphasis on raw materials probably meant that there were insufficient craftsmen to process the hides quickly, if diverted to home use. Similarly, consideration had to be given to customs revenue, worth £2,963 9*s* 0*d* in 1640–1.[111] Although little is known about the leather industry in the country, many shoemakers would have been at work in towns and villages. In July 1643 Ormond intended to procure shoes from either Drogheda or Dundalk.[112] In one sense, shoemakers were more valuable to the forces than tailors for they possessed special skills and equipment not normally accommodated within the household.

When the Civil War broke out in England the supply of clothing and footwear to Ireland virtually dried up, as did the money to pay for consignments of cloth.[113] The Irish Royalists, therefore, had to fend for themselves with what they could make at home or import from abroad. The pitiful requests they made for help indicate that they did not manage. On 8 June 1643 the Lords Justices had to ask Sir Michael Ernley and Colonel Richard Gibson to assure their soldiers that as far as possible they would make good their lack of stockings, shoes and other necessities. A month later the situation was no better, as they admitted in a letter to the Speaker of the English House of Commons: 'The soldiers' wants of clothes and shoes are also very grievous, which of necessity must be speedily supplied, they being now so bare even to rags as doth much dishearten them, and is indeed besides the grief to them and us a shame and dishonour to behold.'[114] In March 1646 Inchiquin, then supporting Parliament, even claimed that a lack of clothing over winter had either killed most of his soldiers or had rendered them unfit for service. He informed William Lenthall, the Speaker, that Lord Broghill wanted 4,000 complete suits of clothes sent to him. In 1648 John Ashurst insisted on being given an adequate supply of coats, hose and shoes when asked to raise a regiment for Ireland, 'a wett and rawe countrie'.[115] Although little is known of the condition of the Confederates, it appears as though they were better clothed and fed than the Royalists.[116] After all, they had greater access to essential raw materials.

ARMOUR AND EQUIPMENT

Scottish and Irish Campaigns, 1638–42

For armour the Ordnance Office could call on the staff of its own armoury, housed at Greenwich, though naturally they could only make a few suits. Their main task was to examine armour brought in and to maintain and repair those suits in store. In wartime the armoury dealt privately with a number of artificers, individually or in small groups, or placed larger orders with the Company of Armourers to which they belonged. Even the royal armourers had their own workshops where they carried out their private business. The probate inventory of Henry Keene, taken in 1665, provides us with a glimpse of what went on in such a shop. As is shown in Table 4, Keene left a number of suits of armour, many individual pieces, and some hand arms. He also had a variety of tools and equipment. He was owed £267 9s 4d in good and desperate debts and his salary as one of the king's armourers was £97 in arrears.[117] From the information we can learn about the processes involved in making armour from beginning to end, from the forging of the plates to the final polishing of the finished items. The inventory reveals that making armour was a complicated and multifaceted process, including the affixing of leather straps and padding as well as the shaping and joining together of pieces of metal. While any competent blacksmith could repair a back, breast or pot, only a specialist could fashion new pieces. It took skill, patience and time, and therefore it was difficult for the industry quickly to respond to increased wartime demand.

When Charles I called out the militia to fight the Scots, he expected the soldiers to turn out fully armed and their horses completely furnished. Most of the troopers would have worn the pot and corslet of the light horseman but some would have been dressed as cuirassiers. To supplement this personal supply and to provide a stock from which those deficient in armour could buy items needed, the king at first looked abroad. This was a reasonable decision, given the amount required and the lack of capacity at home. However, it caused an outcry among native armourers who thought that they ought to have had the business. Thomas Stevens, a master armourer at Greenwich, claimed that as the king's servant and trained in the craft, he could do the job as well and as cheaply as strangers. In November 1638 the ordnance officers, having discussed with the armourers the number of foot or horse armour they could make monthly, did seal a contract with them. However, shortly afterwards the armourers tried to renegotiate the deal, claiming that since the agreement had been concluded not only had the price of iron gone up by 50 per cent (from 20 marks a ton to £20) but also that the material was not as good as before. To answer this objection, the committee agreed to provide the armourers with plate iron at reasonable rates.[118]

In the event, the armourers did some business with the Ordnance Office and Thomas Stevens got his wish. In December 1639 members of the Company of Armourers, including Stevens and his partner, Nicholas Marshall, supplied 1,000 headpieces at 7s 6d each, 100 suits of light harquebusiers' armour at £1 15s and 20 suits of heavier armour at £2.[119] In the same month, the Company of Armourers was again approached to find out how many suits of armour their members could supply monthly. This time, its estimates were lower than the previous year's totals. William Legge, the Master of the Armoury, who made the contact, also reported that the some of the leading armourers were evasive. The reason for their reluctance to deal with the government, he noted, was because they had been busily supplying the nobility and the gentry with armour at inflated prices and were loathe to forego this profitable business. Legge's suggested remedy was to order all the armour made in London to be sent to the Tower and, as an inducement, to pay the armourers in ready cash.[120] Inevitably, most of the business went abroad.

Equipment was provided by groups of suppliers, who specialised in making bandoliers or belting. John Gace and William Beacham, two London turners, jointly provided the bulk of the bandoliers directly contracted for. They delivered

TABLE 4
PROBATE INVENTORY OF HENRY KEENE OF ST SEPULCHRE'S PARISH, LONDON, ARMOURER, 1665

	£	s	d
New Armor plate	13	18	00
Old Armor plate	02	03	06
29 horsemans brestes forged	04	16	08
5 gross of candlestick panes	00	18	00
5 polony Capes 1 not made up	00	16	00
1 paire of bellowes for a Armorer	00	10	00
2 Anvills	05	00	00
8 Forgeing hammers great & small	00	12	00
15 Trampeing hammers	00	05	00
19 Swageing & riveting hammers	00	04	00
6 paire of Sheares great & small	02	10	00
5 hamering stakes	01	05	00
6 Swageing & Cresting stakes with 3 rings	00	12	00
2 small Bickirons	00	04	00
3 pound of wire	00	01	06
4 paire of compasses & 6 punches	00	01	00
4 paire of Forgeing tongs	00	04	00
3 Vices	01	13	04
14 Ruff files small & great	00	09	02
10 smooth Files	00	10	00
8 paire of Nipers	00	06	00
2 paire of hand vices	00	04	00
5 Burnishing Stones	00	10	00
3 Hollow hamers	00	01	00
193 horsemen brests with 190 backs 193 horsemen head pieces all at	76	12	00
4 stronge head pieces 3 Fine Stronge backes & brests with 3 Gantletts	05	08	00
7 old short Gantletts	00	02	04
2 paire of Fine Joyntes for horsemens armes	00	04	00
4 paire of brass Joyntes for Footemens armes	00	16	00
4 paire of brass Joyntes for headpeeces	00	02	00
3 paire of guilt Joyntes for headpeeces	00	03	00
1 paire of silvered Joyntes for headpeeces	00	01	00
200 guilt nayles	00	01	04
3,000 brass nayles	00	09	00
3,000 Tined nayles	00	04	00
1,000 Flatt nayles	00	01	00
2 Fine white Footemens armes ready sett	04	00	00
9 Fine white Gorgetts one of iron ready sett up	02	14	00
1 horesemans Armour white & Light	00	18	00
8 white polony headpeeces with guilt nayles & Joyntes	04	16	00
1 Guilt Gorgett	00	10	00
12 pike heads 9 Fine & 3 ordinary	00	16	00
1 scull couered with cloth	00	06	00
1 Footemans headpeece	00	02	00
8 pikes 3 with Fine heads	01	04	00
4 new iron Ladells 1 iron kettle	00	05	00
2 white Footemens Armes at second hand	03	15	00
29 Footemens Armour Ready sett	17	08	00
13 Footemens Armour lacking Gorgetts	06	16	06

14 Footemens Armour old lacking Gorgetts ready sett	05	19	00
7 odd headpeeces for Footemen	00	14	00
1 old headpeece for a horseman with cheekes	00	04	00
12 old quirsyear headpeeces	00	18	00
2 old horsemans Backes & brests	00	05	00
2 old pistolls & 1 carbine	00	08	00
4 old swords	00	01	04
old Lumber in ye Shop	00	06	00
Summa	174	03	08
Ready Money	54	00	00
Good Debts	19	17	06
In Hosier Lane at the Legg . . .			
Sperate Debts			
by the kings Majesty for ye Testators Sallory for Armour	97	00	00
Desperate	144	05	06
Debts owed (by Henry Keene)	125	03	10

Transcript kindly supplied by Dr David Mitchell

---

thousands of bandoliers to the magazine during the First Bishops' War, including old ones renovated by affixing new pouches to them. In November 1639 they were asked to contract for bandoliers for the second war and on the 30th agreed to furnish the Ordnance Office with bandoliers made of well-dressed ox hide with bullet bag and priming wire in two sizes, at 3s and 2s 6d. Like the weapons makers, they asked for money on account, promising on receipt to make 1,500 bandoliers in the first month and 2,000 a month thereafter. They seem to have performed creditably. On 31 January 1640 an imprest of £200 was authorised to help defray the cost of manufacturing 1,500 bandoliers and by 2 March they had sent in a consignment of 4,000. Toby Bury, a girdler, provided most of the belts. He dispatched 1,000 belts in August 1638 and 5,000 more two months later. On 30 November 1639 he agreed to make 4,000 girdles, hangers and belts a month, provided that he received £200 in hand and the rest on delivery.[121] However, he seems to have died or retired shortly afterwards as his place was taken by a consortium of four other girdlers: John Dickinson, Leonard Hickford, Thomas Jones and James Lawrence. In September 1640, having already delivered 'a great quantity' of belts and swivels for carbines, they received an imprest of £50 and an exhortation to bring in the rest of the ware as soon as possible. In May 1642 Thomas Jones individually delivered 728 girdles and hangers for use in Ireland.[122]

Parliament

In the first year of the war most armour continued to be imported as Parliament sought quickly to build up its stocks. By the end of 1643 at least 3,788 suits of armour and 6,054 corslets had been shipped over from Amsterdam, whereas London armourers had only provided 275 suits (see Table 8).[123] Like the gunmakers, they had spent the winter refurbishing armour in the Committee of Safety's magazine. In the provinces, maintenance of armour (and weapons) remained the mainstay of the armourers' work. At Gloucester, several people were employed in scouring armour, the men being paid 1s 6d a day and the women 1s 0d. John Welstead, the smith, repaired and replated old armour at the rate of 1s 2d or 2s a day.[124] In London, the first recorded bulk delivery of English armour occurred in June 1643 when Thomas Stevens, Nicholas Marshall and William Harrison dispatched 265 suits of harquebusiers' armour.

The situation only started to improve in 1644. In that year small groups of armourers, including Thomas Stevens and Nicholas Marshall, combined to supply Brereton with 540 suits of armour and 350 spare helmets, and the Eastern Association with 800 complete suits. Edward Anslow individually furnished the Kent forces with hundreds of suits.[125] By the time that the New Model Army was being equipped, the native industry had finally developed to the extent that it could supply a large proportion of the armour required. In spring and summer 1645 contracts were given to a number of leading members of the craft such as Thomas Stevens, Nicholas Marshall, Anthony and Peter Newman, Richard Wellman and Silvester Keene. To prepare for the campaigning season of 1646 the circle was widened to include several other practitioners, including Edward Anslow. Between April and December 1645 the armourers delivered 2,140 suits of armour and 1,100 additional headpieces and in first four months of 1646 a further 3,482 suits.[126] According to price, twice as much body armour was made for the foot regiments as for the horse and very few cuirassier suits were sent in. By 1650 Edward Anslow had become the leading figure, heading the group of armourers who delivered 1,500 suits early in the year. Edward Barker, an arms dealer who supplied a further 1,000 suits later in 1650, obtained his stock from the armourers, either by subcontract or direct purchase.[127]

Familiar names crop up among the equipment makers, too. Although Thomas Jones, the girdler, decamped to Oxford, two of his erstwhile partners, Leonard Hickford and James Lawrence, supplied belts to the Parliamentary forces. John Gace remained the leading producer of bandoliers, delivering at least 13,000 complete pairs of bandoliers and 4,000 collars in the period 1642–50. Moreover, by the end of the 1640s his son, John Gace junior, was involved in the business. Others came forward during the course of the war to fill the gaps and to help meet increased war demand. Even so, the group of contractors remained quite a small one. Fewer than ten people made all of Parliament's knapsacks and, of these, two individuals stand out: Michael Rayner as a supplier for the New Model Army and James Gough for the Irish expeditionary forces of 1649–51.[128]

There was a degree of overlap among the belting manufacturers, especially in the fashioning of leather bandoliers, belts and girdles. Apart from supplying over 15,000 carbine- and 20,000 sword belts, Henry Thrall and Thomas Bostock, the two leading girdlers, sold over 10,000 pairs of bandoliers apiece. Holster and knapsack makers, in contrast, tended to be specialists. In addition, some bandolier makers, depending upon their craft background, might focus on a particular type of pouch. John Gace, a turner, made more wooden chargers than any other sort, whereas Nathaniel Humphreys, Thomas Jupe and Thomas Roach produced plated ones. Some provincial manufacture was carried on, too. At Nottingham Castle powder containers were a speciality. Bandoliers were bought at the rate of twelve a week, many of them from John Francis. Twice that number of powder bags, an alternative to bandoliers, were obtained.[129]

Royalist

To establish an armoury the king employed Nicholas Sherman, a master armourer in the royal service who, like Jones, had moved to Oxford to help the Royalist war effort. Although he died in August 1643, he had time to put his expert knowledge to good use, setting up the facilities needed to produce suits of armour and to get their manufacture under way.[130] Surviving records suggest that he was mainly involved in refurbishing armour that had been brought in. Between 18 February and 29 July 1643, he returned to the New College magazine 83 backs and breasts, 90 headpieces, 21 pots, and 30 gorgets that he had mended and cleaned.[131] It was work that needed to be done. Well over one-quarter of the 491 backs and breasts and nearly one-fifth of the 383 helmets brought into the stores between 30 December 1642 and 22 May 1644 were classed as old or defective. In this respect, Sherman's actions conformed to a pattern of activity that was common among the artificers who worked for Royalists and Parliamentarians alike.

It is not known if Sherman made new suits of armour at the same time but one or two others did. Michael Bastin, the master smith, William Standinnought, the master gunmaker, and Richard Spencer of Bicester, an armourer and cutler, were mainly employed on other work but they did put together a few suits. They only appear in the documents in spring 1643, a time of intense activity at Oxford, but they may have continued to produce armour thereafter. Their output was not high. Richard Spencer seems to have made two suits of armour or the equivalent a month, delivering one back, two breasts and four headpieces on 29 March, two backs, two breasts, two headpieces and gorgets on 19 April and two backs, two breasts, three headpieces and one gorget on 29 May. The records are patchy but the regularity in the numbers and intervals suggest that in this case they might reflect the limit of this particular person's capacity. The one entry for Michael Bastin refers to the delivery of eight headpieces and six backs, breasts and gorgets on 11 April.[132] Even allowing for gaps in the documentation, it is clear that Oxford did not supply all the armour that the Royalist troops needed. From where then did they get their armour? Some suits may have been produced at towns such as York and Bristol but there is little hard evidence. York had been developed as an arms manufacturing centre during the Bishops' Wars, partly with skilled workmen from the south, and presumably they would still have been there to help the Royalists.[133] Home production, nonetheless, provided only a small proportion of the armour required and the Royalists continued to be dependent upon imports, especially from the Low Countries and Denmark.[134]

The Royalists also developed facilities for making the essential accoutrements for the weapons and in one area at least, namely belting, they had the services of a pre-war contractor. Thomas Jones made the belts for the powder bags and probably those for swords and carbines too. Others employed include John Blackgrave of Cropredy who provided musket rests; William Standinnought, the gunsticks; George Cole, the gunners' horns; and various Oxford glovers the powder bags. William Riley, the ladle maker, dealt in cannon ware, as expected, but also made and repaired bandoliers. Mostly, he affixed new sets of chargers to the collars. The accounts reveal the details of manufacture, listing priming wire, basills (tanned sheep skins) for the pouches, glue to stick the pieces together and tape for lacing and binding. Recorded output varied between individuals and crafts but might be at a reasonable level. Jones, for instance, sent in 2,000 girdles and hangers in just over five weeks in June and July 1643.[135] This compares quite favourably with the consignments he made to the Ordnance Office before the breach with Parliament.[136] William Riley's monthly output of bandoliers might have reached sixty to eighty. Production levels at Bristol seem to have been higher. In January 1644 March reported that 200 pairs of bandoliers were being made a month, a level which, when he wrote a year later in March 1645, he said could be raised to 15,000 a year if money were readily available.[137]

Scotland and Ireland

In Scotland, county levies would have mustered with the appropriate equipment and armour, as well as with their weapons. On 10 June 1639, for instance, the Committee of Estates, working through the local committees, ordered the 'third' men in each parish to assemble at Burntisland with their bandoliers fully filled and with twelve lead shot and sufficient match.[138] The Act of 18 August 1643 that raised local forces for the Army of the Solemn League and Covenant ordered the cavalry to present themselves at the rendezvous on the Links of Leith wearing steel caps or bonnets and secrets.[139] Landowners and burgh officials helped make up for deficiencies. In 1638 the thirty muskets the Laird of Ardross had in his armoury were furnished with bandoliers and rests. He also possessed four suits of footmen's armour and three steel bonnets. The Laird of St Monans had one set of cavalry and three sets of infantry armour, one secret and three pikemen's corslets. In June 1648 Lord Innerpeffer supplied his quota of seven musketeers with bandoliers and rests as well as with their muskets.[140] Such items could be purchased, especially at Edinburgh. Archibald Campbell bought them there for his uncle, the Laird of Glenorchy, in April 1639, as did Lord Dalhousie at a later date. The latter also obtained some at nearby Dundee, where he also purchased belts, as well as swords.[141]

Evidently there were artificers and craftsmen in the country who could make equipment, though Whitelaw's list of arms makers does not provide a single example. An Edinburgh armourer, John Hislop, left a pair of bandoliers and a rest, as well as a musket, a partizan and a number of sword parts when he died in 1646, but he probably bought them from someone else.[142] As in England, many of the equipment manufacturers were involved in non-military trades that required similar skills. Bandolier makers were probably turners or metalworkers, according to material, and strap- and web makers and girdlers made belts. For Ireland we have no information at all.

CONCLUSION

People who made armour and military equipment were skilled craftsmen and it was therefore difficult to step up production quickly in wartime. To fight the Scots Charles I did place orders with the leading London manufacturers but he also had to obtain most of his supplies from abroad. The Civil Wars placed an even greater burden on the manufacturing capacity of the three kingdoms and although an assortment of craftsmen, working in wood, metal, leather and textiles, were pressed into service, especially outside London, shortages did occur. As a result, for many years home supplies still had to be massively supplemented by imports.

Like the trade in hand arms, self-sufficiency was only achieved when Cromwell's troops were being fitted out for the conquests of Ireland and Scotland in the years 1649–52, and for the same reasons. The Royalists, divorced from the London market, faced the greater problem but managed to achieve a creditable level of output. Production at Bristol augmented that at Oxford and by 1644 it had probably become the more important centre of the two, at least for bandoliers. Nonetheless, hardly had the Royalists reached a peak in output when military reverses and loss of territory brought about a decline. They were always more dependent upon imports than were the Parliamentarians but this reliance became more pronounced in the latter stages of the conflict. For Scotland and Ireland there is very little information on the manufacture of armour and equipment. Some work was undertaken but the lack of evidence suggests that output was not large, a conclusion that is reinforced by the amount of ware imported into those countries.

It was easier for all sides to obtain supplies of clothing and footwear because they were items of everyday wear and because manufacturers did not have to switch from one distinct form of clothing to another. Even local forces could obtain some of its clothing and footwear ready-made. At Northampton, moreover, there was a shoemaking industry that was of national importance and even supplied boots and shoes to Londoners. In the command economy of the war, priority was given to the needs of the army and by focusing the attention of the workforce on military production, the authorities were able to outfit their soldiers with home-produced goods. There is little evidence of imports, even in Scotland and Ireland. Tailors, seamstresses and shoemakers could be found in all parts of the country and this must have reduced the level of dependence on the London market. It probably did, for many county and regional forces were fitted out with locally made clothing and footwear. The Royalists particularly benefited from the existence of a skilled workforce in the area it controlled. Not only did they bring local tailors into the Schools of Music and Astronomy to produce garments *en masse*, but also placed large orders in other clothing towns.

London remained an important centre, firstly for the kitting out of soldiers for Ireland and then for the Parliamentarian forces. Commissary officers, with access to London and limited time to obtain the goods they needed, went to the capital or, in the case of footwear, to Northampton. Developments in the organisation of the industry, whereby capitalistic merchants controlled large numbers of workers, which allowed armies to purchase stocks of clothing ready-made, ensured that substantial orders could be fulfilled relatively quickly. Even the Royalists and the Scots, stuck out in the provinces or in the north, could adopt these practices. Of course, shortages did occur and the soldiers affected complained bitterly about their lack of suitable clothing and footwear, especially in Ireland. Given the scale of the demand and the need constantly to provide replacements, this is hardly surprising.

7

HOME SUPPLIES: HORSE AND TACK

All sides paid great attention to the securing of an adequate supply of horses, especially as demand soared during the war years.[1] Various approaches were adopted, ranging from requests to supporters to outright theft from the horse-owning population at large. Many horses had to be bought, though a considerable proportion of draught animals were hired. In some theatres of war oxen were viable alternatives for the draught. Because the turnover rate in horses was so high, stocks had constantly to be replenished. In action, horse casualties were higher than those of soldiers. If an enemy bullet (or arrow) did not wound or kill an animal, the rigours of campaigning often wore it out. In the aftermath of the Battle of Marston Moor, for example, the Royalist cavalry was in a very weakened condition and the horses exhausted by forced marches.[2] Replacements, however, could not be 'knocked up' in a workshop in an afternoon. Horses were living creatures; they had to be bred, reared and allowed to mature. A colt ideally could not serve as a cavalry mount before the age of four and a draught horse took longer. Further consideration had to be given to their keep, especially to stabling and fodder, and it was a foolish commander who ignored such concerns. Oliver Cromwell was particularly attentive to the well-being of his mounts.[3]

A few horses were imported from abroad but overwhelmingly the armies made use of home-bred and reared animals, reflecting the strength of horse breeding in England and Wales. In the hundred years before the conflict, quality had improved greatly, due to the admixture of foreign blood and a more careful approach to breeding. Monarchs from Henry VIII onwards took the lead, importing horses and maintaining a number of studs, notably at Hampton Court (Middlesex), Tutbury (Staffordshire) and Malmesbury (Wiltshire). Danish, German and Low Countries blood increased the strength of the draught animals and (initially) Neapolitan coursers the quality of the warhorses. As changing cavalry tactics placed greater emphasis on mobility, coursers gave way to lighter foreign breeds such as the Spanish ginete, Turk, Arab and barb. The Crown encouraged the landed classes to take an active interest in horse breeding and studs were established on a number of estates in the three kingdoms.[4] Some individuals, like Sir George Reresby of Thrybergh Hall, West Riding of Yorkshire, became enthusiasts. His descendant, Sir John Reresby, noted that Sir George's pastime 'was sometimes haukes, but the cheefest was his breed of horses, in which he was very exact'.[5] By the mid-seventeenth century horses with eastern or ginete blood in them could be found in the studs and stables of a number of gentle and noble families. Sir John Fenwick of Hexham, for instance, had a famous stud of Arab horses.[6] Sir Thomas Fairfax and Prince Rupert both owned barbs. The blood of these animals was also beginning to circulate more

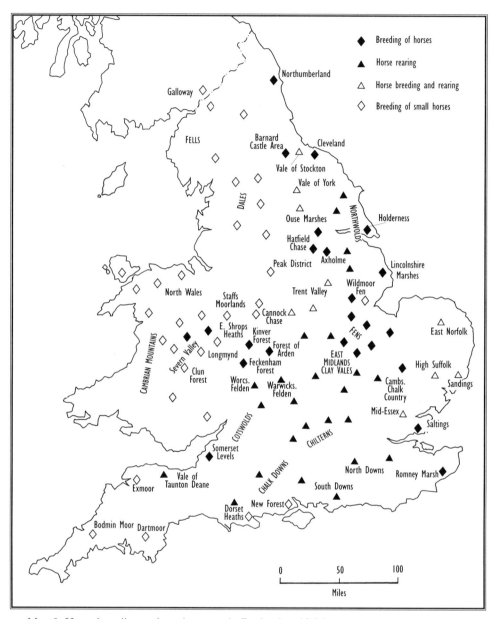

Map 5: Horse breeding and rearing areas in England and Wales.

widely throughout the equine population as a whole and could be found in some of the troop horses of the time.[7]

The dictates of fashion and recreation aided the process. Good horsemanship was a mark of a gentleman, highlighted by the vogue for the *manège* in the late sixteenth and early seventeenth centuries. The upper classes also hunted on horseback, raced horses and employed them between the shafts of their coaches. For whatever purpose, they wanted the best and in fashionable colours, with the correct action and a pleasing shape. If they could not meet all their needs at home, they could buy required horses from others of their class. They might even obtain what they wanted at a fair. By the mid-seventeenth century a handful of places had acquired a reputation for the sale of good-quality horses and were patronised by the élite. According to Newcastle, a fine judge of horseflesh, Lenton (Nottinghamshire), Penkridge (Staffordshire), Malton (North Riding of Yorkshire) and Ripon (West Riding of Yorkshire) were the best for saddle horses and the East Midlands fairs of Market Harborough, Melton Mowbray, Northampton and Rothwell the leading outlets for coach and carthorses.[8]

To meet their militia obligations the upper classes kept cavalry mounts but they also possessed other horses that in wartime could readily be pressed into service. Of course, some animals might be unusable. In summer 1643 Charles Staynings offered to exchange a horse he had sent in for another one, on account of its fiery temperament. He thought that it might ride 'very hot' in a troop of cavalry and therefore disrupt the others.[9]

Suitable horses could also be found on farms, and in towns throughout the country, too. This, in itself, partly reflected upper-class interest in horse breeding. They sold off surplus or superannuated stock and sometimes allowed a stallion of theirs to service a tenant's mare.[10] Moreover, by paying high prices for top-quality animals they encouraged good practice among non-gentlemen breeders and rearers. Some transactions, especially between tenant and landlord, were conducted privately but horse fairs provided the customary venue for the sale. Fairs also played a vital role in integrating the equine resources of the entire country, acting as staging points in the movement of horses from one region to another.[11] The pattern created by the flow of the traffic in horses was undoubtedly complex, with numerous cross-currents, but in general horses moved from breeding areas, mainly located in the north and west, to the rearing areas of lowland England, concentrated in the Midlands and south. The best saddle horses came from the north-east, especially from Yorkshire.

ENGLISH HORSES AND THE BISHOPS' WARS, 1638–40

For the Scottish campaigns Charles I did not buy horses from the prominent Smithfield dealers with whom his Masters of the Horse had hitherto done business and who were to provide so many animals to the Parliamentarian armies.[12] By calling out the militia he placed the burden on his subjects and they should have been in a position to help him. Surviving sets of estate records from the 1630s indicate that there were well-stocked stables in the north and elsewhere in the country. In Yorkshire Lord Bayning's farrier's accounts for 1637 refer to sixty-five horses, including brood mares, a Neapolitan and a barb. In Westmorland in the 1630s Sir John Lowther of Lowther maintained a comparatively small but well-organised stud, producing several foals each year. The stable account, taken on 29 October 1636, lists five entire horses and colts, eight saddle geldings, and five mares for riding and for breeding and two immature mares. The young horses comprised a barb foal, three yearling foals, two two-year-old colts and a two-year-old filly. Elsewhere, Sir Thomas Pelham of Halland, Sussex, noted on 7 May 1639 that the Earl of Northumberland's barb stallion horsed his bay mare 'Howard'.[13]

Charles's army, therefore, had access to good-quality mounts, though as the Scots were surreptitiously buying stock at local fairs, there were fewer available in the north than normal.[14] A number of people did obtain horses for the army. On 6 March 1639, the Earl of Holland, General of the Horse, promised to supply 100 horses at his own expense and to bring them to the rendezvous at York by 1 April. Sir Edmund Verney provided both saddle and draught horses. At Skipton Castle the Earl of Cumberland obtained ninety-eight horses in spring 1639, mainly from the stables of northern gentlemen, including the noted Fenwick stud. He also spent £50 on horses in London.[15] Some county troops were adequately supplied. According to Captain Anthony Thelwall, writing to Secretary Windebank on 17 January 1639, the horses raised for the Lancashire and Cheshire cavalry, 180 strong, were of good quality, even if the riders and arms were faulty.[16]

Unfortunately for the king, the response was not as good as he might have expected. In February 1639, when summoned to the rendezvous at York, noblemen lined up to make their apologies to Secretary Windebank. On the 12th the Earl of Bridgwater informed him that, 'I find it extreme hard to get horses and I believe it will be impossible to have arms ready.' Two days later the Earl of Peterborough claimed that because of the short notice he was ill-equipped with horses and arms. On the 15th the Earl of Thanet wrote, 'For what number of horses I shall send, I find the scarceness both of horses and arms such that I shall not be able to send either such number or in such good equipage as is answerable to my desire.'[17] In a few cases there may have been a genuine problem. Concern about the supply of horses is also reflected in the imposition of tighter controls on exports in January 1639, even if requests for licences were still being considered at the end of the year.[18] Nonetheless, it is evident that many members of the landed classes chose not to honour their militia commitments for reasons other than a lack of animals: apathy, special pleading and political opposition to the king also played a part.[19] Peter Heylin, the chaplain of the Order of the Garter, later remarked on the number of serviceable horses that were sent, but like the arms, they probably did not all arrive in time.[20]

The English forces could also obtain draught horses from the Yorkshire wolds and vales but many had to be brought in from further afield, notably from the Midlands and the East Anglian fens. On 24 June 1638 the Marquess of Hamilton, writing to Charles I from the north, concluded that horses strong enough to pull the heavy cannon would have to be obtained in the south 'for ther are non to be had ther that will be abill to draw them ther'.[21] In fact, most of the carts and draught horses required were obtained by imposing quotas on the counties. On 29 March 1639 the Lord Lieutenant of Northampton was told to provide fifty strong and able horses and seventeen able carters and to have them ready at Newcastle by 20 April. Payment was to be at the rate of 1s a day for a horse and 8d a day for a carter. A year later Staffordshire had to find fifty horses and Lincolnshire sixty, and then pay to send them to the artillery train in the north.[22] Like coat and conduct money, those who had to contribute resented this imposition.[23] Failure to return the horses compounded the offence. In September 1641, almost a year after the signing of the Treaty of Ripon, the Lord Lieutenants of Huntingdonshire and Lincolnshire were still awaiting the return of their horses and wrote to the authorities to ask what had become of them.[24]

HORSES AND THE ENGLISH CIVIL WARS

The conflict between Parliament and the king created problems in England by disrupting the long-distance traffic in horses. While there was a reasonable pool of horses in the country as a whole, the creation of rival zones of influence caused local shortages in one kind of horse or another. The Royalists, for example, had access to an adequate supply of saddle mounts for the cavalry, plenty of packhorses but fewer for the draught. To provide adequate facilities for his artillery train, in autumn 1642 the king requisitioned horses and carts at Chester in transit for Ireland.[25] The situation in the area controlled by Parliament was the mirror image of the Royalist one. Draught horses were readily available. Large horses were bred in the fens of East Anglia and suitable animals could be acquired from the mixed farms of the East Midlands and elsewhere. Of course, the supply of colts for training, emanating from the vales of northern and western England in Royalist hands, dried up. Fewer saddle horses were bred in the region but Parliament could obtain stock from towns, notably London, and from landed estates. Overall, geography was likely to have a greater impact over time, as replacement horses were needed. However, wartime demand did stimulate production and encourage greater self-sufficiency.[26]

Horses were being collected months before the formal declaration of war, especially under the terms of the Propositions. The response was patchy, especially in the provinces, reflecting the degree of localism and neutralism that existed, as much as scepticism about repayment. In Cheshire the gentry would not subscribe anything until assured that the money, horses and arms raised would be used for local defence.[27] London and the Home Counties proved to be the most enthusiastic for the cause. Lists drawn up between 21 June 1642 and 6 July 1643 reveal that the inhabitants of London and several south-eastern and eastern counties gave in 6,704 horses for the defence of the capital.[28] In the same month, the Royalists, through the Engagement, instigated a similar scheme. Forty-four lords and officials signed the agreement, whereby they promised to maintain 2,015 horses for three months.[29] In July the Lincolnshire gentry subscribed 168 horses and in August the Worcestershire gentry a further 92. These figures, in general, represented real horses and not merely empty promises.[30]

Lists of horses brought in upon the Propositions reveal that many non-gentry possessed animals of a suitable standard. Nonetheless, the gentry stand out from the rest on account of the quality of the horses and the numbers presented. Some large donations were made. In Staffordshire Henry Jackson of Stanshope brought in eighty horses, which with tack and arms, were worth £850.[31] Trained horses, which the gentry kept for the militia, were a particular bonus. Several were brought in to the Hertfordshire commissaries in 1642. On 9 November Sir John Wittewrong, whose estate accounts show him to have had a keen interest in horse flesh, sent a trained horse and arms worth £14.[32] Partisans among the landed classes often took the initiative, opening up their stables to help the cause. Many officers supplied their own mounts and if they raised a troop, might fit it out with horses. Captain Greathead equipped his cavalry troop with arms and horses, each one being worth £10. For the Royalists, Colonel Borlay raised a regiment at his own expense and Sir William Pennyman recruited and maintained a regiment of horse and one of foot. Naturally, the king drew on the stock in his studs; in 1643, for instance, Prince Rupert obtained colts from Tutbury.[33]

Horses continued to come in upon the Propositions for some time. However, the need to make good shortages and to find replacements did increase the degree of compulsion in the process. On 10 May 1643 Parliament added clauses to the Propositions legislation to enable it to enforce a quota system; the Parliamentarian county committee of Staffordshire regularly acquired horses in this way.[34] The Royalists followed suit; in May 1644 Lord Wilmot, the Lieutenant-General of Horse, was ordered to collect 600 horses due from Berkshire (120), Gloucestershire (80), Hampshire (50), Oxfordshire (120), Wiltshire (150) and Worcestershire (80).[35] Inevitably, the response of individuals to requests for money, arms and horses was widely seen as a test of loyalty or malignancy and those who did not subscribe were viewed as enemies. In Shropshire the Royalists told recalcitrant gentry to come to Shrewsbury Castle on 15 December 1642 with their horses, arms and equipment or be reported to the king as ill-affected.[36] It was not long before both sides resorted to sequestrating the goods of their enemies, by force if necessary.[37]

Not surprisingly, the pressing need for horses and the use of soldiers to get them led to abuses. Examples of plunder abound. The distinction was not always made between friend and foe, let alone between neutral and enemy. In June 1645 the admittedly biased Parliamentarian newsheet, *Perfect Passages*, reported that where the Royalists 'finde better horses then their own they take them, be it friend or foe: they stand not to expostulate the matter, and by this means the Kings horse are all well mounted'.[38] In consequence, commanders, governors and county committee-men had to deal with a number of irate requests for restitution, even from supporters. Owners regularly had to resort to offering money to buy their own horses back. Petitions concerning the theft of horses formed the largest group of cases heard by the Parliamentarian indemnity committee, established in 1647 to protect soldiers from acts committed on behalf of the army during the war. Some needed it. In 1647 the inhabitants of Bishopton, Warwickshire, gave warning that they were going to prosecute Captain Potter 'both for plunder & takeing & sellinge of horses, & in respect he hath left his Comand. It would be requisite that he were enjoyned to put in securety'.[39]

All kinds of horses were seized but draught animals were particularly targeted. This was largely due to the different responses armies made to the fluctuating levels of saddle and draught horses required. Horses were valuable capital assets but were expensive to maintain. It therefore made sense to buy or sell them according to demand or to hire them when needed. This could not be done for saddle horses, especially cavalry mounts, which not only had to be trained but which also had to be readily available. They were a vital resource and possession of an adequate number could not be left to chance. It should be noted that the cavalry was used in a variety of ways for, apart from its battlefield role, it also served as an instrument of control and a means of rapid deployment. It also undertook such jobs as foraging and convoy protection. As a result, troopers were responsible for their own horses. Some draught horses were kept, especially in the artillery train, but they were not treated in the same individual way as saddle mounts. Because they were much more readily available on the roads and farms of the country, typically they were hired, with or without carters, to perform specific tasks.

In spite of acquiring thousands of horses through a mixture of appeal, threat and arbitrary action, armies still had to obtain many more in the normal way of business, through private purchase, by contract, or at markets and fairs. Some were procured by supporters, who bought in what they could not provide themselves. In October 1642 the Royalist Earl of Cumberland spent £7 10s on a horse at York, probably for use as a cavalry mount for his garrison at Skipton Castle. He also paid £10 6s 8d for two wagon horses. Three months later he bought a remount for one of the soldiers who had lost his horse in service at Broughton. On the Parliamentarian side details appear in the later accounts of pay due to individual officers. On 17 October 1645, for instance, Captain Thomas Warren claimed £300 for twenty-five horses that he had obtained for his troop.[40] Many more were bought directly by commissary officers, acting for the various armies. In 1644 Lieutenant Russell spent several thousand pounds on horses for the Eastern Association.[41]

People like Russell often bought in large lots and at particular places. Among other sources of stock, they might patronise those markets and fairs, which continued to be held during the course of the conflict. The Smithfield, the great livestock market in London, remained a very important outlet for horses for the Parliamentarian forces. Sir Thomas Myddleton, commander of the North Wales army, and Sir Arthur Hesilrige bought horses there, as did the Eastern Association and the New Model Army, as well as the county forces of Essex, Kent and Surrey.[42] The Eastern Association also obtained horses at Bedford, Bury St Edmunds, Huntingdon, Northampton and Stamford.[43] County forces tended to buy locally (except those with access to London), either privately or at nearby markets and fairs. Stray references among the surviving horse toll books of the war years reveal the presence of individual soldiers there. Robert Machin, a soldier in the garrison at Bridgnorth, Shropshire, exchanged a horse with half an ear shot off for a nag at the local fair on 22 July 1644.[44] Soldiers also made casual purchases or exchanges on the road.

The Smithfield flourished because the most prominent horse dealers in the country served it and because it was immune to Royalist attack. Many market centres, however, were vulnerable, if only to a lightning raid, and were obvious targets for enemy action. Traders were stopped on the road, too. In general, therefore, trade conducted at markets and fairs languished as participants developed more secure means of doing business.[45] With the exception of Northampton, it is not even certain that the officials of the Eastern Association who bought horses at the East Midlands and eastern towns, noted above, acquired them at the fair. Indeed, the evidence suggests that they were dealing privately with individuals and merely using known centres as collecting points. Significantly, on 4 April 1644, 6*d* was paid to Gilbert Riches, the town crier at Ely, for displaying a notice ordering people to bring in 'the State's horses' on a certain date. Presumably, sellers and purchasing agents would come along to the town that day to do deals. In effect, commissary officers and the dealers with whom they traded, forestalled the market and developed their own informal system.[46] Even at the Smithfield market some private dealing went on, mainly in nearby inns and stables. Some of the horses that lieutenant Vaughan obtained at the Smithfield for the Surrey troop were bought in a stable there.[47] Armies, clearly, were able to reshape the market to their own liking and they did so not only because they had the power but also because the arrangements met the particular problems of the time. They were good customers, too, buying in bulk and (on the Parliamentarian side at least) paying promptly.

The Parliamentarian armies obtained many of their horses from dealers, mainly by contract. In this way, they passed on the problem of finding sufficient horses to specialists, who could tap their own sources of supply and bypass the market-place. For Parliament, the business was dominated by a handful of large-scale horse dealers, who lived in and around the Smithfield in London and who had extensive experience in long-distance trafficking in horses. The most prominent ones were Richard Clough, Harvey Conway, Peter Everett and John Styles, although Thomas Benion, William Booth, Thomas Crosman and Percival Stanley were associated with them in fulfilling some contracts. It is not known if their counterparts in Royalist areas operated in a similar way but the system worked so well for Parliament that it would have recommended itself to the other side, too.

The Smithfield dealers supplied horses to a number of forces, including county and field armies and the expeditionary forces to Ireland and Scotland.[48] The authorities naturally turned to them when the New Model Army was being fitted out during the course of 1645. Parliament gave the four leading dealers contracts to supply 1,200 troop- and 120 dragoon horses to the army on 1 April and three days later it granted them a monopoly of the trade. All other dealers were forbidden from buying horses for a month, ensuring that they had a free hand to acquire the horses needed.[49] Percival Stanley contributed to some of the consignments, and between them, either singly or in combination with one or more of the others, these dealers delivered 7,801 horses in the following seventeen months.[50]

The size of the New Model Army's cavalry was set at 6,600[51] but mounts did not have to be found for the troopers at once. Cavalry detachments from the old field armies brought many horses with them and thousands more were seized from the Royalists.[52] Nonetheless, a supply of horses had to be maintained, especially when preparing for a campaign, and the dealers made regular deliveries over the months, with numbers fluctuating according to demand.[53] That they could obtain so many suitable horses after several years of fighting is testimony to their knowledge of the trade and to the underlying strength of horse breeding in the country. They were helped by the expansion of the area under Parliamentary control, giving them access to additional breeding grounds and stocks of horses. Furthermore, estate accounts reveal that among the gentry horse breeding continued unabated throughout the 1640s. Among the breeders were Parliamentarian supporters like the Brookes of Warwick Castle.[54] The Royalists, in contrast, suffered as the area from which they could draw their animals shrank.

Once obtained, horses were branded for ease of identification and to indicate ownership. For Parliament, thousands were duly marked in the months after the Propositions were first issued. In January 1643 Thomas Fairclough and Clement Grymes, keepers of Moorfields in London, were paid £5 each for their work, valuing and enrolling horses and arms at various times since June 1642. Noted down were the parties' names, number of horses given, and the animals' colours and marks.[55] The system continued through the war. In November 1645, for instance, Sir Thomas Fairfax ordered the Committee for the Army to pay for the fifteen remounts of Captain Groves and to have them branded. If the horses were bought from dealers, their servants might do the job.[56]

The measure helped the army to recover horses illegally sold to civilians, either by deserters or merely by soldiers hoping to earn a little money. To cover up the sale it was not uncommon for troops to claim that they had lost their mounts. This practice was expressly forbidden but, with pay often in arrears and a horse to feed as well, it is not surprising they resorted to such an action. The authorities viewed the matter seriously. In July 1644 the Staffordshire Committee railed against soldiers who defrauded the State and the inhabitants of the county by selling off their horses to countrymen at a cheap rate. Those caught were to be imprisoned and to receive further punishment, while the buyers were to forfeit their purchases without recompense.[57] The Royalists were also concerned about this practice and legislated against it. A proclamation issued on 5 January 1643 ordered that all horses illegally bought from soldiers were to be returned to Winter Graunt, the Wagon-Master-General, or his deputies.[58]

In spite of the effort taken to secure supplies of horses, shortages did occur, some of them serious enough to hamper operations. In March 1644 Prince Rupert, then at Shrewsbury, asked Lord Loughborough for 700 dragoon horses, without which he could not move.[59] In September that year, the Parliamentarian commander, Sir William Waller, found himself in a similar position of forced inactivity. With the threat of a possible Royalist advance on London looming, he warned the Committee of Both Kingdoms that with few troops and a lack of horses to mount them, he could do nothing to prevent it. Major-General Browne, in another letter to the committee, confirmed this bleak picture, reporting that the Abingdon area was 'so emptied of horses that I much fear I shall not be able to perform your commands'.[60] Whereas the situation became comparatively easier for Parliament, the problems of the Royalists grew correspondingly worse: the effect of losses such as the defeat at Naseby or Hopton's surrender in Cornwall were compounded by the death of so many horses and the capture of thousands of others by the enemy.[61] Shortages of draught horses, whenever they occurred, proved a further handicap. As a result of an earlier raid by Cromwell to the west of Oxford, Prince Maurice could not move his ordnance out of the city in June 1643 for want of horses and this delayed the opening of the western campaign.[62]

SCOTTISH AND IRISH HORSES

There was a plentiful supply of indigenous saddle horses in both Scotland and Ireland but as most were under fourteen hands, there were few that could be classed as 'serviceable'. Draught horses were also in short supply. Transport in Scotland, with its rugged terrain, was more suited to pack carriage and the native breeds were ideal for the job. The situation was worse in Ireland; partly due to the nature of its agriculture and economy, draught horses were scarce and oxen performed much of the work.[63] Shortage of serviceable horses did have an impact on tactics. Even in Scotland, where many Covenanting officers had served under Gustavus Adolphus of Sweden, uncertainty of supply tended to depress the cavalry's importance. Separate regiments of horse were only established after the return from Sweden of David Leslie in 1640.[64] When Montrose began his campaign against the Covenanters in 1644 he did acquire a few cavalrymen, mostly English and poorly mounted. In March, the Earl of Newcastle contributed 100 troopers, riding 'lean, ill-appointed horses'. As the main strength of his forces lay in his Highland and Irish infantry, however, he was not really affected by the shortage of serviceable mounts in the country. At the battle of Tippemuir on 1 September he fielded three horses. The adherence of the Gordons and their lowland cavalry early in 1645 somewhat altered the make-up of his army and enabled him to fight more conventional actions. The Gordon horsemen did Montrose good service and, as at Auldearn (9 May) and Alford (2 July), they played a crucial role in his success.[65] The Irish Confederates also had few suitable horses and thus they focused on sieges and skirmishes rather than on pitched battles.[66] When forced into a formal fight, they were generally defeated. Undoubtedly, an inadequate supply of good quality troop horses was a factor but it is also clear that their commanders lacked experience of mounted warfare and that the cavalry units they did possess were largely ineffectual.[67]

Saddle Horses

In Scotland the galloways of the south-west were hardy and indefatigable and although excellent for skirmishing and foraging, were too small for use in pitched battle. Bishop Leslie had observed in 1578 that they were not fit to carry an armoured man.[68] The traditional solution to the problem was to seek suitable saddle and draught horses elsewhere, especially from England. In the days before the Union of the Crowns in 1603, however, Scotland was a hostile country and English law forbade trade in such a strategic commodity.[69] The situation eased in the early seventeenth century but the Covenanters still found it necessary to obtain horses clandestinely from across the border. On 21 September 1638 it was reported that they had bought up a great number of horses in Cumberland and had taken them back to Scotland. In response, Charles I ordered that the traffic should be stopped and the horses impounded. Some animals were netted, for a week later the Covenanting lords complained to Hamilton that their horses had been seized.[70]

The wars exacerbated the shortage of serviceable horses, a problem which the Committee of Estates sought to alleviate by imposing quotas on counties.[71] Unfortunately, not all of the horses were suitable. When the Covenanting army entered England in 1644 many of the cavalry were poorly horsed on 'the verriest nags'. A year later a muster roll of Lord Dalhousie's regiment of horse reveals that there were only 84 serviceable mounts for 274 horsemen. In autumn 1648, following the defeat of the Engagers' army in England, cavalry horses were particularly hard to find. On 11 September the council at Glasgow agreed to send thirty well-mounted troopers to Lieutenant-Colonel Menzies, but two months later still had not obtained the horses. In 1650 an enquiry in the town found that there were only enough horses to furnish one troop.[72] It was possible to purchase reasonable quality mounts but they appear to have been expensive. In 1644–5 troop horses, bought from various gentlemen for service in England, were valued at between £140 and £160 Scots. On 20 October 1648 Lord Innerpeffer gave £20 sterling to Captain William Scott for a horse and arms, complete with rider, clad in back, breast and headpiece. In August 1650 the glovers' guild at Perth spent £100 Scots on an ordinary troop horse, at least £1 and probably £2–£3 more than would have been asked for in England. In October, in the aftermath of the Battle of Dunbar, Sir Thomas Nairn's quartermaster paid the Earl of Airlie 800 merks for two horses.

The scarcity of horses and the high prices they fetched led to an upsurge of horse stealing in the late 1640s and induced the authorities at Edinburgh to introduce a toll-book system on similar lines to the one practised in England and Wales. Details of horses sold at the market were to be recorded, together with the names of the buyers and sellers, and the rolls sent weekly to the clerks of the burgh.[73] Because of their difficulties, the Committee of Estates exhorted its supporters to provide themselves with serviceable horses. In

April 1651, for instance, letters were sent to all the nobles, gentlemen and heritors in the counties of Angus, Clackmannan, Dumbarton, Kincardineshire, Perth and Stirling, ordering them to be in readiness with their best horses and arms.[74] By then, there must have been very few left in the country.

In Ireland irregular cavalry had long used hobbies, which, though only pony-sized, were renowned as easy-going, tractable saddle horses. As Thomas Blundeville observed in the late sixteenth century, 'the Irish men both with dart, and with light spears, do use to skirmish with them in the field. And manie of them do proue to that use verie well by meanes they be so light and swift.'[75] By the 1630s, however, the breed had declined; in January 1634, Charles I expressed his concern to Wentworth, the Lord Deputy, on hearing that 'the breed and race of those Irish hobbies . . . is now wasted and utterly worn out'. The remedy, according to the king, was to send back the progeny of those hobbies, 'which heretofore were brought over in great numbers', to reinvigorate the breed. The crisis was compounded by the shortage of serviceable horses in Ireland, which left the cavalry unmounted. The Master of the Horse, the Marquess of Hamilton, therefore had the double duty of finding suitable horses of both types and sending them to that country.[76] For their part, the Confederates strove to make best use of the stock they had at their disposal. On 15 June 1642 the Supreme Council ordered that all the horses presented by the county councils as suitable for war should be sold to the army at a reasonable price.[77] Furthermore, in the initial stages of the uprising the insurgents had specifically targeted serviceable horses, as well as arms and armaments, when they plundered the homes of their enemies. At Kinard, Co. Tyrone, on 22 October 1641 an eyewitness observed that they only took arms and the best horses, the ones fit to mount cavalry.[78]

The conflict had the same adverse effect on the supply of cavalry horses in Ireland as it had had in Scotland. By the end of summer 1642 even the Royalists, with initial access to existing stock and English supplies, were concerned about a lack of suitable animals. On 1 September the Lords Justices complained to the Irish Committee in London that the troopers did not have enough money or credit to shoe a horse, buy a girth or crupper or repair their arms. Moreover, many of their horses had been lost in service and, as a result, the men were forced to serve on poor weak jades altogether unserviceable.[79] The situation did not improve; the following May the Lords Justices told the king that they had 'no strength of serviceable horse'. As time wore on the situation deteriorated further and musters reveal an assortment of animals. Lord Dunsany's troop in May 1646 contained five horses that could be categorised as good, nine as average and six as substandard.[80] Parliamentarian troops brought over their own horses and did so from an early stage of the conflict. On 22 June 1642, for instance, the Committee for Irish Affairs authorised the payment of £120 to Sir William Balfour to transport the sixty horses in his company. When the tide of battle in England turned in their favour in the mid-1640s, numbers increased, as troop deployment built up.[81]

Draught Horses

As noted above, there were few draught horses in Scotland.[82] In 1639 Baillie reported that there were insufficient horses to mount an invasion of England, though when it did occur the following year enough animals had been obtained to do the job. Three-thousand horses were found (mainly through county quotas) to move the baggage and conveyances provided for the heavy cannon.[83] Localities continued to supply teams; in January 1644 the barony of Saltoun contributed a close cart with three horses and furniture, for the march into England. Even so, shortages persisted and the problem was never satisfactorily resolved.[84] Their concern about the precariousness of their supply is perhaps reflected in the vigour with which the authorities tried to maintain the scheme and punish individuals who did not contribute. During Cromwell's campaign in Scotland in 1650–2, pressure was brought to bear by quartering troops on non-contributors.[85] As in England, many draught horses were requisitioned. On 8 November 1645, the Committee of Estates issued a general order for horses to carry provisions to Edinburgh Castle. Four years later, on 23 August 1650, the authorities at Edinburgh, needing horses for the train of artillery, ordered Robert Walwood to appropriate as many 'country' horses as he could find in the city and its suburbs, telling him to make a special search of all stables. The horses of ministers and of those bringing provisions to the town were the only ones exempted.[86]

In Ireland, the situation was more serious and the Royalists soon ran into trouble. On 27 February 1642 the Lords Justices wrote to the Lord Lieutenant in England to ask for 100 draught horses, explaining that as almost the entire country was in rebellion, it was impossible to obtain horses to pull the ordnance.[87] Matters only grew worse and Ormond, as Deputy Lieutenant, received numerous reports detailing the difficulties the shortage created. On 1 August 1643 Viscount Montgomery blamed his failure to march, as ordered, on 'the extreame scarcetye of baggage horses, and wants of my officers'. Colonel Jones, the Parliamentarian commander, had a similar experience when at Dublin. In 1647 he noted the lack of carts and carriages in the city, a complaint that probably encompassed a shortage of horses, too.[88] Cromwell's attention to detail is revealed in the provision he made to remedy this defect when he invaded Ireland in 1649. Regiments were provided with carts, wagons and draught horses and the artillery train with 900 horses.[89] Oxen offered an alternative form of power and were extensively used in the country, especially by the Confederates.[90]

TACK

Some of the saddlery ware that the armies required was obtained along with the horses raised. Light horsemen in the English militia or in the Scottish levies were supposed to come completely armed and accoutred and the horses fully furnished. Many did, though not all. Similarly, horses brought in on the Parliamentarian Propositions, the Royalist Engagement, or part of a parish quota, were often fitted out with the necessary saddlery ware. Most of the Hertfordshire horses, raised on the Propositions, for example, were fully equipped.[91] Unfortunately, the amount proved insufficient and most of the tack had to be bought. At Oxford the king had to start anew, but because makers of saddlery ware could be found all around the country, he did have people he could employ. Blacksmiths were even more common. For Parliament, Londoners predominated, though local forces made use of provincial craftsmen. The armies in Scotland and Ireland similarly drew on the local workforce. To a certain extent craftsmen, accustomed to dealing with the civilian population, had to adapt their skills to meet the soldiers' requirements. In particular, the cavalry needed specialist saddles and metalware, though dragoons could manage with civilian items. The manufacture of horse tack was craft based and, as in other handicraft industries, the workforce often accommodated wartime demand by cooperation with one another and with shared contracts.

The Ordnance Office had its own smith, Thomas Hodgskins, who was responsible for the ironwork. All cavalry troops had a farrier and a saddler on the roster, who did essential work looking after the horses and maintaining the equipment. In the Covenanting army each regiment had a smith and several saddlers.[92] Such men were also employed in the artillery train. According to a contemporary assessment, a notional artillery train of thirty pieces needed 1,038 horses for the draught and 16 smiths and farriers to look after them. The author of the report insisted that this was a minimum number, commenting on the seven farriers that 'fewer there cannot be, these hardly able to the worke required of them, hauing 150 horse to a man to shooe'.[93] In January 1646 the Irish Confederate army employed a master smith and three other smiths in its ranks.[94] Much casual work was also given to local blacksmiths, as and when the need arose. This might entail the shoeing of one or two horses or the provision of some horseshoes, but it might be a more substantial job. The war increased the movement of horses around the country, especially to and from army detachments, and some, if not all, of them had to be shod.

The Bishop's Wars and the Irish Insurrection, 1638–42

Like the riders, militia horses in the king's army should have mustered for the Scottish campaign fully furnished. Deficiencies could similarly be made good from government stores.[95] To improve its supply the Council of War treated with the leading saddlers in January 1639, inviting them to look at a pattern of a saddle brought from the Low Countries and to state how many of that design they could make a month, and at what price.[96] In just over a month three saddlers, Thomas Harrison, Thomas Kite and Daniel Potter, sent in 300 saddles and dispatched further lots throughout the year. Harrison, the king's master saddler, also repaired over 100 saddles.[97] The following year the Master of the Ordnance was asked to deal with the Saddlers' Company.[98] For the Irish campaign in 1641–2 the militia could not be used and the government supplied the saddlery ware sent out with the horses. Thomas Harrison was again involved, as was Daniel Potter, working with three other saddlers, Benjamin Potter, Daniel Holdenby and Ellis Parry. In one contract, sealed on 22 June 1642, they agreed to provide 400 troop saddles and furniture – made to a pattern given to them four days earlier – at the rate of £2 5s each. They were to deliver the saddles in weekly batches of 100, beginning on 27 June.[99]

In general, the saddles were sold fully furnished, but the finished item was the product of more than one person's handiwork; in particular, there was a division between those who made leather and metal parts. In 1639 Harrison sold some of his saddles with bits, and even bits alone, but shared the business with the bitmaker, George Vickars. In 1642 three lorimers and bitmakers, John Savage, Nicholas Holton and John Milborne, supplied the 400 bits that accompanied the saddles noted above, in lots of 100 at 5s each. On 16 July Daniel Potter provided saddles for 160 horses and John Milborne the bits.[100] Harness making was another specialisation and its practitioners made separate arrangements with the Ordnance Office. John Munnings, in partnership with Thomas Harrison II, a harness maker, supplied the harness for the Bishops' Wars and some untanned hides, as well.[101]

English Civil Wars

From the onset of the war in England London saddlers supplied the Parliamentarians with the bulk of their saddlery ware. Because of the shortage of saddles in store they dealt directly with purchasing officers, who were provided with money by the Committee of Safety to buy their own ware. On 10 September 1642 Captain Oliver Cromwell was given £32 10s for saddles 'because the stoares cannott afford them'.[102] A year later a warrant was given to Owen Rowe to deliver twenty saddles to Captain Fountain, but as there were none in store, Fountain received £42 and was told to find them himself.[103] These saddlers sold saddles to the Earl of Essex and to a number of local forces. Naturally, they were on hand when a regiment of dragoons was being raised in London in October 1642 to protect the capital. They were also available when Lord Brooke's agent was in town in the winter of 1642/3 on a shopping trip for arms and equipment. In 1644 the Eastern Association did business with them.[104]

London's saddlers really proved their worth in 1645–6 when engaged in fitting out and then re-equipping the New Model Army. Between April 1645 and December 1646, 29 saddlers sold 10,569 saddles. Not surprisingly, the greatest number (2,500) were delivered in April 1645 but a further 1,650 were sent to the Ordnance Office in July, the month after the Battle of Naseby. In February and March the following year 2,290 were handed over in preparation for the campaigning season. Individuals signed most of the 114 contracts, though there seems to have been a general sharing out of the work among them, probably under the auspices of the Saddlers' Company. Several of the contractors were known members, including William Pease, the leading supplier; indeed, his first contract (for 600 saddles) was made with the company. The orders were dealt with quickly; in the year beginning April 1645 saddles were delivered on average within a week of the signing of the contract (where known) and payments made within another three days.[105]

In the Scottish campaign of 1650–1, the largest orders (1,000 saddles) were carried out by a group of eight saddlers, including leading figures such as Daniel Holdenby, William Pease and Thomas Webb. A group of three saddlers, Humphrey Gaywood, William Stoarer and Nathaniel Walters, provided some troop saddles but were mainly responsible for supplying the associated tack such as bridles, bits, stirrups, girths, leathers and headstalls. They also delivered packsaddles and crooks for packhorses. At the same time they supplied troop saddles and furniture for Ireland, including a batch of 1,000 in spring 1651.[106] The price of saddles, like those of weapons, came down during the 1640s as production expanded and as purchasing officers negotiated discounts on bulk orders. The key period was 1645–6, when the New Model Army was being equipped. In 1642 a troop saddle with furniture cost about £1 10s but in 1645 it had fallen to 16s 6d and in 1646 to 15s.

Many saddles and furniture were obtained from provincial saddlers, and local forces often made use of them. In Warwickshire the county committee did business with several saddlers, notably John Holloway, Robert Lunn and Thomas Stratford, buying one or two items at a time. Much of the work done by these saddlers, as elsewhere, involved refurbishing worn saddles and their accoutrements. In May 1645, John Holloway received £8 in part payment of his bill for repairs.[107] The Warwickshire example reflects the typical level of transaction conducted and reveals the army's 'corner shop' attitude to local saddlers, who were patronised when it needed the odd saddle or some running repairs. In May 1644 William Reeves put in a bill to the treasurer of the Eastern Association for payments made to five people for saddlery ware, three straps, two bridles and a bit, a breast plate and a stirrup, as well as for work done plating and repairing his saddle.[108] Occasionally, they supplied larger numbers. In 1645 Thomas Stratford helped to equip the Worcestershire troop with saddles, twenty or thirty at a time.[109]

During the English Civil Wars the saddlers increased their hold on the business, often reducing the bitmakers to the status of subcontractors. Occasionally, regimental accounts reveal direct contact between purchaser and the actual producer. In September 1644, for example, Lieutenant-Colonel Thorp bought saddles from Mr Francis, a saddler in the Strand, some of which had been imported from France and which he had furnished. Thorp, however, did buy his bits from a nearby bitmaker.[110] Unlike most bitmakers, the collar and harness makers maintained their independent position, as can be seen in the contracts they fulfilled for the New Model Army in 1645–6. John Munnings of Whitechapel was still a leading member of the group and remained so until the end of the period. The New Model Army contracts were often quite specific, not only stipulating the proportion of trace to thill harness, prices and delivery dates, but also the weight of the individual pairs of harness.[111] Like the saddlers, they generally made individual contracts but one or two partnerships were formed. John Pitchford always worked with Thomas Skinner, and Richard Blissett senior associated his son, Richard junior, with him. In the years 1649–51 the Blissetts, either working together or in combination with other harness makers, provided most of the harness for the Irish and Scottish expeditionary forces.

The Ordnance Office's smith, Thomas Hodgskins, not only provided and maintained metalware but also sold blacksmith's stock. One contract he made with the Army Committee in February 1646 included the delivery of 3,000 horseshoes at 4d each and 30,000 horseshoe nails at 9d a lb. He also kept a supply of horseshoes in the Tower for distribution to army units.[112] On the march, regimental smiths and farriers did the work, supplemented, if necessary, by hiring local blacksmiths for specific tasks. In 1644 Northampton's blacksmiths earned £1 3s 7d for shoeing eighty horses being taken to Hertford for the Eastern Association army.[113] Moving horses involved other expenditure, too. In an account detailing the cost of driving eighty draught horses from London to Essex's army in Worcestershire at the end of September 1642, expenses include money spent on hiring help to catch horses that had broken loose and on a farrier for treating sick animals. A guide who took the party from Wheatley to Worcester received 3s. The total bill came to £44 13s 0d.[114]

As ever, evidence for the other parties is very patchy. Nothing is known about the manufacture of saddles at Oxford, for instance, though harness making is well documented. It is likely that a more formal record was kept of harness because of the existence of a permanent pool of draught horses there and the need to purchase tack for them. Several collar makers are recorded in the accounts; one or two worked at Oxford but others came from Brackley, Buckingham and Witney.[115] Robert Herring, designated the King's Master Collar Maker, lived at Buckingham. The collar makers, as a group, were specifically used in spring 1643 to build up supplies as the army prepared for the campaigning season. Thereafter, only Herring was employed. Though surviving data suggest that output was inferior to that of Parliament, Herring's personal contribution is comparable and there are undoubted gaps in the record. Where given, prices are very similar. Stray references show the Royalists paid 10s–11s for thill harness in 1643 and 1644, whereas in 1645–6 Parliamentarians gave 10–14s for theirs. These men also seem to have had their own sources of leather, for on several occasions they delivered hides to the New College stores. In this way, they supplemented the stocks brought in by George Cole, the Commissary to the Artillery Train.

Where did the Royalists, as well as the Scots and Irish, get their saddles from? The answer is that we do not really know, except to note that they seem to have exploited existing centres of production and to have developed them wherever possible. In the north, York was an important source. Early in November 1642, the Earl of Newcastle, then preparing to enter Yorkshire, asked for saddles for light horsemen to be made there and kept until his arrival; he would pay in cash. The Earl of Cumberland at Skipton Castle was another Royalist who patronised the city's craftsmen. In September 1642 he bought ten horse harnesses from Henry Leeds, a Petergate saddler. Leeds, who must have sold saddles too, was still active in 1644 as he features prominently in assessment lists.[116] In the Midlands the Worcestershire towns of Evesham and Pershore seem to have specialised in saddlery ware and harness making.[117] In neighbouring Warwickshire Parliamentarian forces under Captain Bridges seized a consignment of saddles being taken from Warwick to Stratford-upon-Avon in January 1643.[118] As with clothing, there is a feeling that at times the Royalists were operating in a rather hand-to-mouth way and that their sources of supply were neither secure nor abundant. Shortages did occur. In April 1644 Colonel Mynne at Newent, Gloucestershire, had to send an urgent request to Prince Rupert for saddles and bridles to mount dragoons. Because of an imminent Parliamentarian counter-attack they were desperately needed.[119]

FODDER

Warhorses could not merely be put out to graze and be expected to operate effectively; they also required more nutritious feed such as oats, pulses and barley.[120] Thus after the horses belonging to the Edgbaston garrison in Warwickshire had eaten all the hard corn and barley in the grounds, they had to subsist mostly on grass and hay and, as a result, 'were very vnfit for seruice'.[121] Supplementing the diet with suitable fodder added to the cost of keeping horses and increased the difficulty of finding sufficient supplies. It has been calculated that the normal daily requirement for a serviceable horse was 14 lb of hay, 7 lb of straw, 1 peck of oats and ½ peck of peas. Though somewhat generous in peas, this is approximately the rate applied in the Civil Wars.[122] In July 1643, the daily ration of some of the Earl of Denbigh's horses was 6d worth of hay, a peck of oats and a little peas or beans.[123] Other accounts suggest that horses were given 6d worth of hay and a peck of oats (6d) a day. Costs began as soon as the horses were bought. Innkeepers in and around the Smithfield earned a regular income in livery charges for horses awaiting collection, after being purchased in the market. In January 1644 the Surrey Committee bought forty-one horses from three dealers – Richard Clough, Thomas Crosman and Peter Everett – and they were put up at three inns on the Strand (the White Hart, the Bull and the Swan) until Captain Jervois took them. The stay added £49 12s 6d to the bill, not counting the £2 3s 6d given to the horse coursers' men for tending to the horses and branding them. By the end of 1642 Sir Samuel Luke had spent £373 4s 8d on food for his newly mounted troop and their horses, mainly at inns in the Smithfield and at Bedford, Luton and Uxbridge.[124] Multiplied to field army scale, the costs were huge.

Commissary officers were active in requisitioning fodder when the army was on the march or in quarters. In November 1643, for instance, William Jones, Commissary of Hay and Oats under Waller, ordered the high constables of the hundreds of Brixton and Wallington, Surrey, to levy thirty loads of hay and thirty quarters of oats in their parishes and deliver them to Farnham.[125] As soldiers were supposed to maintain their horses themselves, the cost would have been deducted from their wages. If soldiers bought fodder direct from the supplier, they were expected to purchase it themselves. In 1645 Parliament laid down a scale of charges to be paid by an army on the march: 3d a night was to be given for grass, 4*d* for hay and a peck of oats, 6*d* for a peck of peas and beans and 7*d* for a peck of barley and malt. These rates were not very generous and undoubtedly made many people reluctant to supply the troops. If quartered in an area, the army might hire pasture land.[126] In practice, soldiers did not often pay on the spot for the fodder taken but merely gave the luckless hosts a voucher that could later be redeemed for cash. The system did work, if fitfully; the Eastern Association regularly paid its quartering bills.[127] In February 1644, for instance, the Earl of Manchester authorised the payment of £10 to Clifford Weedon of Cambridge for keeping horses of his troop for twenty-one days, and a further £20 to be given to Richard Marriott of Cambridge for quartering fifty horses that had come from Essex.[128]

Even if the soldiers paid for their horses' keep (then or later) the sudden descent of a large detachment of troops on an area caused problems because the animals ate up the fodder required by the inhabitants for their own animals. As Dr Tennant has so graphically described, armies on the march through the south Midlands laid waste to the countryside through which they passed and their progress can be charted in the claims for compensation which came pouring in to the authorities.[129] In the north some units of the Scots army acted in the same arbitrary manner. Between 8 and 20 January 1646 the notorious van Druschke's horse quartered at Austerfield, West Riding of Yorkshire, eating up all the fodder and leaving only a few local horses. At the hamlet of Wroofe, routmaster Taylor's troop had taken ten loads of hay and twenty-eight quarters of oats.[130]

CONCLUSION

Between 1638 and 1652 tens of thousands of horses were employed in the various conflicts in the three kingdoms. As the turnover rate was very high, the problem of maintaining a steady flow of animals was a serious one and undoubtedly it put a strain on the resources of the country. Inevitably, shortages occurred and prices rose, in England reaching levels about one-half times higher than they had been before the conflict. Nonetheless, given the scale of the demand, the horse trade is one of the success stories of the Civil Wars, at least in England and Wales. Very few horses were imported and both sides had to make do with those they could obtain in their zones of influence (by one means or another), or which they could capture from the enemy. In general, their needs were met, a reflection of the strength of horse breeding in the country and directly attributable to the lead given by English monarchs from Henry VIII onwards. The conflict itself stimulated an interest in horse breeding. While many members of the upper classes had already established studs on their estates, the insatiable demand for suitable horses both for the saddle and the draught prompted a growing number of farmers to take up horse breeding. Unfortunately, they needed to be very perceptive to take advantage of the opening presented by the Civil Wars, because of the time lag between initial action and the production of a saleable animal. At the very earliest, horses so bred would barely have been old enough for service in the Second Civil War. That they were available in some number by 1650 can be seen in the drop in prices recorded at horse fairs.[131] From 1649 onwards, moreover, licences to export horses became more freely available and in January 1657 the overseas trade was formally deregulated.[132]

In Scotland and Ireland the situation was worse, and the lack of serviceable mounts and strong draught horses was a matter of constant concern. The Scottish Covenanters wrung as many horses out of the country as possible by imposing quotas, as well as continuing the traditional practice of importing them from England, even if it proved more difficult to do so during the course of the Bishops' Wars. When they invaded England in 1644 they had access to supplies of English horses and seem to have taken a considerable number of animals for their own use.[133] In Ireland the problem was even more pronounced. The Confederates, like the Covenanters, sought to make best use of the resources at their disposal; they instructed their officials to make a survey of suitable horses and promised to buy them at reasonable prices. They also plundered them from their enemies. To overcome the shortage of serviceable mounts, they adopted guerrilla tactics. If they employed horses, they used them in hit-and-run attacks, a ploy that could be effectively performed on the animals they did possess. In pitched battle the shortcomings of their cavalry was cruelly exposed. For draught purposes the Irish could use oxen. Troops from Britain dealt with the difficulty by taking the draught and cavalry horses they needed with them or had them imported.

The war was also instrumental in bringing about changes in the trade at home. At first, participants had tried to avoid the market-place. Charles I called out the militia to fight the Scots and this placed the onus on the individual to provide the horses with which he or she was charged. In the first year of the English Civil War a significant proportion of the cavalry and dragoon mounts used were either donated by supporters on the Propositions or Engagement, seized from reputed opponents or merely appropriated from the country at large. Nonetheless, from the outset some horses had to be bought and the proportion of animals obtained in this way grew over time. Soldiers purchased horses from dealers and at markets and fairs. However, the traditional marketing institutions were not ideal venues for the purchase of large numbers of animals. They were vulnerable to attack and the prevailing insecurity of the times made people wary of doing business there. Surviving toll books record few sales and no sign of the pre-war horse dealers. It seems as though they were being employed on army business, availing themselves of their contacts to acquire stock. They still used market towns as collecting points but dealt privately with buyers who had brought along their horses to sell. Even though the records are silent on this point, it is likely that the same practice was adopted in Royalist areas, too. In this way the war hastened the decline of the traditional open market and fair. Even at the Smithfield, the great livestock mart in London, the buoyancy of its market cannot be divorced from the activities of the horse dealers who operated there, especially the small group of men who dominated the trade. Active throughout the war period, they came to real prominence when given a free hand by Parliament to equip the New Model Army with horses. Armed with this authority, they were able to shape the market to their own liking and carry further a development already under way.

8

IMPORTS

The shortcomings of the native arms industry ensured that from the outset all sides in the British Civil Wars needed imported arms to function effectively. Charles I looked abroad for weapons to meet the threat from the Scottish Covenanters and Irish Catholics and continued to rely upon foreign supplies in his struggle against Parliament. Parliament, in spite of controlling existing centres of the industry in London and the Home Counties, also had to import arms and armaments. With fewer resources at home, the Scots and, to a greater extent, the Irish, were even more reliant upon foreign supplies. In England the Royalists managed to develop their own manufacturing facilities but remained heavily dependent on imports. Parliament, however, did eventually become self-sufficient in war material but only in the late 1640s. Buying on the foreign arms market cost money, but it did give the parties at home access to a much larger and more sophisticated industry and allowed them to obtain essential supplies quickly and in bulk. The arms trade was a profitable one but for political and strategic reasons was subject to control, generally in the form of a licensing system. Of course, gunrunning had its problems; as will be shown in the following chapter, ships bringing the arms had to brave the elements and the attentions of privateers and blockading ships.

Relying on imports added an element of uncertainty to the proceedings since it placed the warring parties at the mercy of foreign suppliers, whose interests did not necessarily coincide with theirs. Charles expected to receive support from fellow-rulers, especially those in Denmark, France and the United Provinces with whom he was closely related. They, for their part, did not wish to be seen condoning rebellion, but they also had to think of their own advantage. Did the kings of France and Spain, for instance, want to supply Charles with the means to defeat his Irish Catholic rebels? Even with regard to England the situation was not straightforward; Roman Catholic rulers might not like the religious stance of Parliament but they could not afford to ignore it, especially as it grew in strength. In the United Provinces, the stadtholder, Frederick Henry, favoured Charles, whose daughter, Mary, had married his son in May 1641. Nonetheless, he had to deal with the pro-Parliament sentiment of the mercantile community, especially in Holland, as expressed through the States-General. The Thirty Years' War, then being waged in Europe, further complicated the picture because support for one or other parties in Britain had to be assessed in relation to its effect on the conduct of the war. In Sweden this was the context in which the question of supporting Charles I or the Scottish Covenanters was set. Denmark controlled shipments going through the Sound and the current state of Swedish–Danish relations affected the ease of passage through the straits. In the Low Countries arms exports were hampered by the continuing struggle between Spain and the

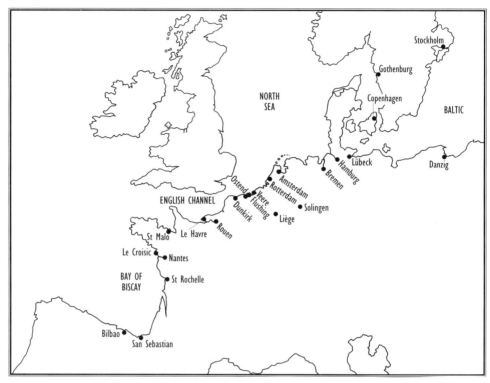

Map 6: Major foreign ports and manufacturing centres for military supplies to Britain.

United Provinces, manifested in the Dutch blockade of Flemish ports and the seizure of Dutch shipping by Flemish privateers.

FOREIGN MERCHANTS AND THE ARMS INDUSTRIES

Merchants, with commercial considerations uppermost, were more likely to provide supplies. The Dutch even traded with the enemy, Spain. Merchants might be based at home, sailing to foreign ports to obtain war materials and making use of their contacts wherever possible. Leading figures had their own representatives on the continent, who could do the detailed negotiation with suppliers and arrange for the assembly of the goods at the quayside. Other agents worked independently for one side or another, doing a similar job but acting in a more positive way to acquire supplies and to encourage others to trade with their party at home. Some, like the Royalist William Sandys at Dunkirk, were expatriates, but others were sent over to seek out military hardware. Early in 1642 Father Talbot sailed to Flanders to procure arms and munitions for the Irish insurgents.[1] Ambassadors and other officials not only tried to persuade the government to give help but also dealt with merchants. Confederate agents such as the Fransiscans, Hugh Bourke at Brussels and Luke Wadding at Rome, and the Jesuit, Matthew O'Hartegan, at Paris, were heavily involved in arms procurement.[2] Of particular value to their respective parties were supporters among the mercantile communities abroad because they were on the spot, had links with arms manufacturers and dealers and could organise the entire process. John Webster for the Royalists and Thomas Cuningham for the Scottish Covenanters stand out, but there were others. The most important group of all were foreign merchants and skippers, who traded in and shipped out most of the goods that were imported into Britain.

If merchants were more ready to sell arms indiscriminately, there was a price to pay. Apart from the partisans among them, they would only look at a venture if it appeared profitable and, therefore, had to be encouraged to do business. What they wanted was ready cash (or at least secure bills of exchange), return cargoes and trading concessions. As William Sandys noted in a letter to John Strachan at Weymouth in January 1644, 'It is the price & good payment and free permission to export all Commodityes without Restraynt will make that port thriue and the kinge well supplyed with Armes.' He also emphasised the importance of furnishing the merchants with a return cargo. He claimed that if Strachan could assure his merchant friends of the availability of saleable goods, he had £30,000 worth of arms to ship out but 'for fear of the returne ther, hinders It thither'.[3] Naturally, the goods to be sold varied according to region. The Scottish Covenanters traded coal with the Dutch and in the south-west the Royalists sold tin to France.[4] Merchants liked to be paid promptly, too. In February 1644 Lord Digby, at Oxford, informed Ormond that he was negotiating with merchants to ship arms and ammunition to Chester, Bristol or Minehead, promising them ready money if they did so. Unfortunately, some merchants were reluctant to deal with the Royalists because of their shortage of money and a casualness of approach.[5] To attract business, merchants were often allowed to trade without having to pay customs or other imposts. In June 1642, the authorities at Galway decided to allow overseas merchants to bring in arms and munitions and take away their purchases duty-free. In addition, they could sell the arms for cash at their own price.[6]

War material, bound for one or other of the combatants, came from many parts of Europe (and even further afield), but for all parties the Low Countries were the most important source of foreign supplies. By the mid-seventeenth century the region contained some of the leading arms manufacturing centres in Europe and all manner of military hardware could be obtained there. The industry, long established in the southern Netherlands, had spread to the United Provinces by about 1600 under the stimulus of war with Spain. In the south, Liège was the most important centre, its industry benefiting from plentiful local supplies of raw materials, good communications links and a skilled workforce. The Liègeois made a full range of arms and armaments but specialised in firearms, edged weapons and armour.[7] Arms production was carried on at other places, too; Mechelen was noted for cannon and hand arms, Namur for armour and muskets and Maastricht for firearms. Luxury items were made at Antwerp and Brussels.[8] The same pattern was repeated in the United Provinces as arms manufacture developed there in the late sixteenth and early seventeenth centuries. Amsterdam took the lead, producing ordnance, munitions and weapons on a considerable scale. Elsewhere, production was more restricted, both in terms of output and in the range of goods made. Delft and Dordrecht specialised in hand arms and gunpowder, Gouda in match, The Hague in bronze cannon and small arms, and Utrecht in armour and grenades. Weapons were also made at Groningen, Nijmegen and Rotterdam.[9]

Arms were dispatched to Britain from a number of ports in the Low Countries, especially Dunkirk and Ostend in Flanders and Amsterdam, Middleburg, Rotterdam and Veere in the United Provinces. Of these, Amsterdam was by far the most important. In 1643, 300 ships were said to have made the journey between Amsterdam and England (though not necessarily laden with arms), each one completing four trips a year.[10] In the months leading up to the outbreak of hostilities in England thirty-eight licences record the export of arms to England, some of the *matériel* helping to deal with the threat in Ireland, but a proportion of it going to Parliamentarians or Royalists in England, too. The list of goods sent reveals that at home there was a particular shortage in munitions. The source provides further information up to spring 1645, though the recorded figures clearly underrepresent the true extent of the traffic. Nonetheless, they do reveal that munitions continued to be imported in considerable quantity (see Table 5). Raw materials were also brought in. Sulphur is indicated in the table, but reference is made to saltpetre, too. On 23 November 1644, Lucas Schorer was allowed to export 'a lot of' saltpetre from Amsterdam.[11] In addition, weapons of all kinds were sent. Of particular value were firearms, because foreign gunmaking skills were in advance of those in England. Sword blades were imported in greater numbers than entire swords and these would have been hilted in England.

Initially, the Dutch arms trade had been import-led in order to acquire weapons to fight the Spanish, and Amsterdam came to prominence as a port through which arms and raw materials were shipped into the country. It also had good communications with arms centres such as Liège and Namur in the southern Netherlands and Solingen in Germany. The blockading of Antwerp in the late sixteenth century aided its growth, since arms made in Liège were taken up the Meuse to Dutch ports such as Rotterdam and Amsterdam.[12] After the United Provinces developed its own industry, the arms trade throve as part of the general commercial expansion of the country. The Dutch were efficient and effective traders, offering goods and services at competitive rates, and consequently established extensive commercial links with other countries. As part of this business they built up stocks of arms and military equipment and, as a result, could quickly put together large consignments and transport them to their destination. Amsterdam benefited from this development and by about 1620 had become a staple market for arms.[13] Further east, the other staple arms markets of Bremen, Hamburg and Lübeck sent some consignments direct to Britain, but many of them seem to have been taken to Amsterdam first.

TABLE 5
LICENSED EXPORTS OF ARMS TO ENGLAND: AMSTERDAM, FEBRUARY 1639–APRIL 1645

Category	Type	Quantity: 23 Feb. 1639–21 Aug. 1642	Quantity: 22 Aug. 1642–19 Apr. 1645
Ordnance	Cannon	222	12
Munitions	Gunpowder	c. 165 tons	c. 205 tons
	Match	c. 170 tons	c. 260 tons
	Sulphur	c. 100 tons	c. 15 tons
	Musket bullets	c. 12 tons	c. 12½ tons
	Cannonballs	c. 72 tons	c. 36 tons
	Grenades	600	3,700
Firearms	Muskets	3,500	c. 60,000
	Calivers		1,000
	Wheel-locks	500	
	Carbines	300	5,450
	Pistols	2,900 pairs	26,140 pairs
	Musket barrels		600
	Pistol barrels		3,070
	Locks		900
	Rests	5,000	11,120
Edged Weapons	Swords	6,650	12,000
	Sabres	1,000	
	Blades	4,303	c. 30,000
	Pikes	3,650	c. 16,000
Armour	Suits	2,390	12,230
	Helmets	2,000	2,000
Webbing & c.	Bandoliers	2,500	c. 25,000 pairs
	Carbine Belts		600
	Holsters	330	9,400
	Sword Belts	400	5,800
Ceremonial	Halberds	50	112
	Partizans	30	12
	Drums	30	31–2
	Trumpets		40
Saddlery	Saddles	330	560
Canvas	Rigging (schippond)	6,835	1,848
	Sails	1	
	Canvas (bales)	6	
	Tents	34	

Source: A.R.A. The Hague, A.C.A. inv. nrs. 1385–8, 1399–1402

Dutch enterprise was responsible for the development of the Swedish arms industry in the early seventeenth century. Louis de Geer is the key figure: he helped to modernise the industry by bringing in capital and technological expertise, providing essential entrepreneurial skills and opening up European markets to native products.[14] In association with his brothers-in-law, Elias and Jacob Trip, he first became involved through trading in Swedish copper, which the Crown offered as collateral for loans. By 1620 he was leasing ironworks, mines and factories and had begun to cast ordnance, the mainstay of the business. To ensure that his operations benefited from the most up-to-date techniques, he recruited skilled workers and supervisors from home, especially from the Liège area.[15] He expanded his activities in the 1620s, helped by the financial support of his in-laws, the Trips. In return, the Trips obtained cannon which they sold at Amsterdam.[16] By the end of the decade de Geer was involved in producing armour and firearms, also marketed through Amsterdam. Many of the Swedish arms that were sent to Britain came via that port, at times as a means of disguising their origin.

The continental arms trade was huge and run by individuals who were operating on a large scale. De Geer and the Trips may have been exceptional but there were others who maintained large stocks and who could deliver considerable quantities of arms and armaments in a short space of time. On 1 August 1642 Geoffrey Barron, then in Paris to procure arms for the Confederates, wrote that he had spoken with three men, who could in a day furnish 10,000 muskets and bandoliers out of stock in hand. Perhaps this was sales talk, and probably a more typical dealer was Arthur Aynscombe of Antwerp, who provided Sir Job Harby with arms in 1640. According to Harby, he had arms for 2,000 horse and 1,000 foot in store and could supply infantry arms at 3,000-4,000 a month or 10,000 in three months.[17] Such a person might be able to put together a larger consignment than this if he were to collect war material from various centres. This is what Daniel Fourment, an Antwerp merchant, did. On 14 February 1643 he obtained a licence to export to Newcastle 3,050 muskets, 2,400 pairs of pistols and 1,200 carbines, all with accessories, 3,000 swords, 1,000 grenades, 7½ lasts of match, 12 suits of cavalry armour and 200 saddles with furniture.[18] Details of the weapons and munitions shipped on the frigate, St Guillaume, reveal that they had come from nine different places in the north as well as the south Netherlands. The goods had mainly been sent from Antwerp, Liège and Rotterdam, but 4,823 out of the 12,745 lb of match had originated at Winocksbergen and Poperinge.[19]

Imported arms were mainly valued because they were readily available. Indeed, because of large-scale troop reductions in the United Provinces in the late 1630s and early 1640s, there was probably surplus capacity in the country.[20] Nonetheless, though the continental market might be larger and more sophisticated, foreign arms were neither necessarily better nor cheaper. In 1639 many of the weapons that the king obtained from John Quarles in the Low Countries and from Sir Thomas Roe at Hamburg were of poor quality. Sir Thomas, ambassador to Denmark, was certainly duped. Along with other arms, the weapons had been impounded as contraband by the Danish authorities and had been bought by the king. Christian IV kept the best

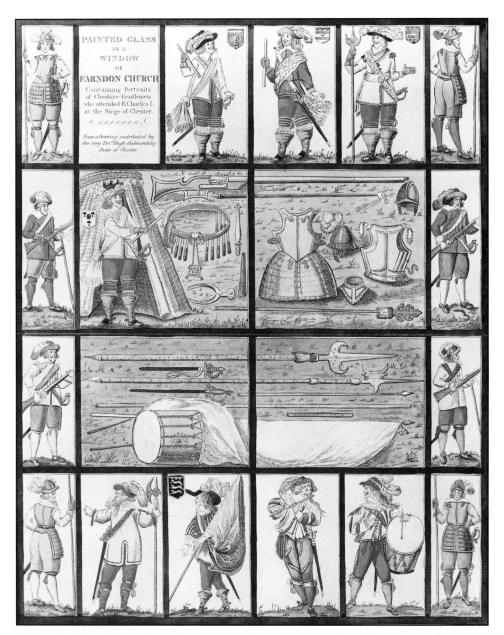

1. Farndon Church, Cheshire: stained-glass window portraying soldiers' dress, arms and equipment. The central panel depicts bandoliers, armour and staff weapons such as partizans, halberds and leading staffs. The soldiers wear marks of identification – sashes and plumes – or carry an ensign.

2. Highland troops at Stettin in the 1630s, armed with bows and arrows as well as firearms. These soldiers probably formed part of a contingent that accompanied the Marquess of Hamilton to Germany to fight for Gustavus Adophus, the King of Sweden. The battle scene in the background suggests that the archers took a position in front of the pikemen and musketeers.

3. Henrietta Maria lands at Bridlington on the Yorkshire coast under fire from the Parliamentarian navy. The queen brought with her a cargo of arms and armaments from the United Provinces which, after unloading, was dispatched to York. Part of the consignment was subsequently sent to Oxford.

Within the illustration:

His
Excellencie
Sʳ Thomas Fairefax
Generall of the forces
raised by the
Parliament.

Printed for John Partridg   Edua Bowers Pinxit   W. Marshall sculpsit

4. Sir Thomas Fairfax, the Parliamentarian commander, on horseback, dressed in cuirassier's armour. He is armed with a sword and a brace of pistols and carries his staff of office. In the background pikemen and musketeers are drawn up in squares, with squadrons of cavalry interspersed among them.

THE DESCRIPTION OF THE ARMIES OF
Sr Thomas Fairefax his Excellency, as they were a
the Fowe

Dust Hill

Prince Rupert   Prince Maurice   Sir Barnard Astley   His   Tertia

The Left Wing Commanded by
Comands Generall Treton

Coll. Butlers Regiment   Coll. Pickerings Regiment   Major Generall Skippon   Earle of Manchesters

Coll. Rossiters Regiment   Coll. Pickwicks Regiment   Major Generall

Reput Hill

Fanny Hill

The Mill Hill

Lane Lenth hill

The traine guarded with fireluckes

Needler field

NASBYE

Printed for John Patridge

5. The disposition of the Royalist and Parliamentarian armies at Naseby on 14 June 1645.
On both sides the infantry squares are drawn up in the centre with the cavalry flanking
them on the wings. Colonel Okey's dragoons line the hedges on the left and fired on

Rupert's cavalry as it advanced. The Parliamentarian baggage train with its guard of firelocks, who successfully beat off Rupert's attack, is depicted bottom left.

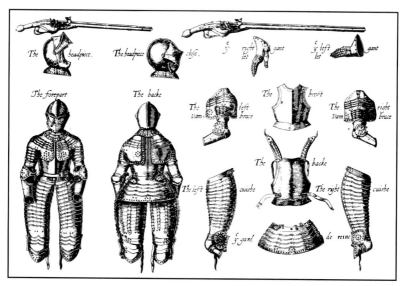

6. The armour and equipment of a cuirassier, from J. Bingham, *Tactics of Aelian*, London, 1616. Although the armour is heavy and cumbersome, the articulated pieces make it possible for the wearer to function on the battlefield, at least while on horseback. In the British Civil Wars the pistols were generally shorter than the wheel-locks depicted here.

7. A cuirassier in action, from John Cruso, *Militarie Instructions for the Cavallrie*, 1632. Very few cuirassiers fought in the British Civil Wars. Although their armour gave them considerable protection against bullets and sword thrusts, their lack of mobility told against them.

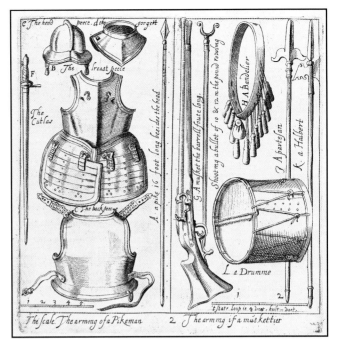

8. The arming of a pikeman and a musketeer, from Henry Hexham, *Principles of the Art Military*, 1642. Only the pikeman wore any armour and during the course of the British Civil Wars they discarded the tassets and gorget. Because of the weight and length of the matchlock musket, illustrated here, musketeers had to support it on a rest. A bandolier with its powder charges is also depicted.

9. Harquebusiers in action, from W. Dilich, *Kriegsbuch*, 1689. The trooper in the illustration is performing the manoeuvre known as the *caracole*. In the initial stages of Civil Wars the Parliamentarian cavalry employed this tactic, though the Royalists adopted the Swedish practice of charging the enemy at pace with drawn swords, only using their pistols in the ensuing mêlée.

10. Hendrik Trip's cannon foundry at Julitabroek, Sodermanland, in Sweden. By the time of the Civil Wars the Swedish arms industry, developed with Dutch finance and technical expertise (as here), had an international reputation. In particular, it had overtaken England as the leading European manufacturer of ordnance.

ones for himself and sold the worst to Roe. In September 1643 Daniel van Hecke sent a cargo of weapons to Bristol from Dunkirk, but on inspection, many of the backs and breasts and all the swords were unserviceable. Van Hecke, however, did agree to pay for the repairs.[21]

Because of the extra costs involved, foreign arms should have been more expensive. Strachan reckoned that an allowance of 20 per cent should be made for transport, customs duties and profit, though exemptions did reduce the price. In a consignment of gunpowder and match delivered to King's Lynn and paid for in May 1644 the proportion was one-sixth. Out of a total cost of £283 8s 5d, £23 16s 8d was paid for a shipping licence, customs dues, factor's fees, passport and porterage aboard and for freight to King's Lynn.[22] Moreover, not only were Dutch weapons costly but dealers never offered discounts.[23] Richard March at Bristol believed he could undercut overseas manufacturers and quoted a price of 18s 0d for his muskets.[24] Some foreign prices were certainly higher. In August 1643, Lord Percy stated that the normal rate for 1 cwt of match was 30s. Three months later, William Sandys agreed to a rate of 37s with John Shaw, an English merchant at Antwerp.[25] Worst of all, were the imports that were both shoddy and expensive, however. In March 1644, Strachan was outraged at the price demanded by French merchants at Weymouth for a cargo of arms and munitions of indifferent quality. To compound the offence they wanted to have them 'custome free, fraight free, and all the courtesy that can bee done'.[26] Imported arms were not always more expensive, however. In mid-1645, for instance, Dutch and Flemish match was sometimes cheaper than the home product.

SCOTTISH CAMPAIGNS, 1638–52

The Scottish Covenanters

Scotland did have an arms industry but because of its modest size the Covenanters had to import the bulk of their military supplies. To help them, they could make use of supporters among the mercantile community abroad, especially in North Sea and Baltic ports. On 24 June 1638 Hamilton informed Charles I that the Covenanters were not only obtaining arms and ammunition from Holland but also from Hamburg, Bremen, Lübeck, Danzig and Sweden. Hamilton advocated searching for weapons on all Scotland-bound ships of the flag at Hamburg and Veere, and in Holland, and asking the Danish king to stop others coming through the Sound. If Christian IV were to prove uncooperative, he advised Charles I to send a ship to intercept traffic sailing from Lübeck, Danzig and Sweden.[27]. Unfortunately, the king's countermeasures met with only limited success. In January 1639 it was reported that the Covenanters had recently received arms for 18,000 soldiers. The following month the Venetian ambassador in England wrote that the Scots 'have provided themselves with a sufficiency of munitions and arms from Holland and Hamburg and have fetched many guns from Sweden through Colonel Lesley'.[28] Later, when in alliance with the English Parliament, the Covenanters were able to draw on English supplies. In April 1645, for instance, four London gunmakers received £100 for firearms supplied to the Scottish army, then campaigning in the west.[29] Between 1644 and 1646 Lewis has estimated that they received some 7,717 matchlock- and 124 snaphance muskets, 993 pairs of pistols, 1,888 swords, 4,679 pikes, 1,106 barrels of gunpowder and 80.9 tons of match.[30]

In the Low Countries the radical province of Zeeland was the centre of gunrunning to Scotland. Veere, the Scottish staple port, was the main point of embarkation but supplies also went through Middleburg.[31] On 10 June 1639 Sir Patrick Drummond, the conservator at Veere, a loyalist, informed the Earl of Stirling that supporters of the Covenanters were openly shipping arms and gunpowder to Scotland and that the authorities were doing nothing to stop it.[32] A month later the *Marie* of Leith docked at its home port with six brass cannon and 50 tons of weapons and munitions from Amsterdam. More consignments arrived in September and December and the process continued the following year, even if the royal navy seized a few of the ships.[33] In June 1640 the dispatch of twenty cannon from Zeeland to Scotland led Charles I to protest to the Dutch ambassador, Joachimi, about the authorities' inactivity. Four months later Boswell, the English resident at The Hague, asked the States-General to ban the shipment of war materials to the Covenanters, but in spite of a favourable response, little was done. As the Venetian ambassador cynically observed, 'It is probable, all the same, that the results will not prove equally satisfactory, since it is not possible to bridle the career of self-interest here.'[34] Thomas Cuningham, who took over from Drummond, ousted for his Royalist sympathies in July 1640, was the leading supplier of arms. One consignment that he put together with his partners, James Weir and James Eleis, in 1640 (see Table 6), filled thirteen ships, eleven of which evaded capture.[35]

The other major source of imports was Sweden. Indeed, many of the arms and armaments shipped out of Dutch ports probably originated in that country.[36] Discussions in the Council of State reveal a great deal of support for the Covenanting cause, partly because Charles I's pro-Danish stance made him Sweden's enemy. Moreover, as Admiral Fleming pointed out, the country would make money out of the business.[37] In 1638 the Council of State released Field Marshal Alexander Leslie from Swedish service and agreed to furnish him with arms under the guise of a parting gift. To avoid political embarrassment, two wealthy expatriate Scottish merchants, James Maclean of Stockholm and his nephew, John Maclean of Gothenburg, were used as suppliers and intermediaries. Leslie was also offered copper to cast into cannon in Scotland.[38] He returned home with 200 muskets in January 1639 and in November two Swedish ships brought the rest of his consignment, comprising up to 15 brass cannons, 4,000 corslets and 1,800 muskets.[39] In February 1639 several units of Scottish soldiers (including Munro's), together with an English regiment and 30 lasts of gunpowder, 30 schipponds of match and 2,000 pairs of pistols, sailed from Sweden.[40] As part of their preparations for the Second Bishops' War, the Covenanters sent an envoy, Sir John Cochrane, to Sweden in April 1640 to ask for further stocks. By the end of August Sir John had secured supplies of munitions and copper and early in September the cargo was landed at Amsterdam for transshipment to Scotland.[41]

Shipments should have been stopped in the Sound (except for those leaving Gothenburg) and, in truth, the Danes did confiscate some cargoes. In autumn

TABLE 6

THOMAS CUNINGHAM OF CAMPVERE: ARMS SHIPMENTS TO THE SCOTS,
1640–4

1640: to Leith	*1642: to Leith*	*1644: to Leith & Newcastle*
12 brass cannon:		
18- & 24-pounders		
49,982 lb cannonballs		
95,620 lb gunpowder		7,000 lb gunpowder
123,098 lb match		130,022 lb match
15,416 lb refined saltpetre		
15,673 muskets	6,000 muskets	10,000 muskets
18,013 bandoliers	6,000 bandoliers	10,000 bandoliers
52 pair horsemens pistols		500 pair pistols &
		holsters
6,965 swords	10,000 swords	12,000 swords
	10,000 sword belts	12,000 sword belts
	4,000 pikes	4,000 pikes
32 punschions flour		
Cost R. 212,821 7 st	Cost £10,316 13s 4d	Cost R. 260,885

R = rix dollars. Source: 'Journal of Thomas Cuningham of Campvere 1640–1654', Scottish Historical Society, 3rd series, XI, (1927), pp. 54, 65, 95.

1638, a ship carrying 600 muskets, 2,000 bandoliers and 2,000 helmets from James Maclean at Stockholm, was impounded at Helsingør. The following year the *St Peter* of Leith was seized because it had 5 centner of gunpowder on board. The *George* of Leith, carrying gunpowder and lead, was similarly stayed.[42] Nonetheless, Christian IV's attitude was rather ambivalent, especially for an avowed supporter of Charles I. He specifically let the soldiers and arms pass through in February 1639. Even more surprisingly, the five Swedish warships laden with Cochrane's consignment, sailed through the Sound without being challenged. According to Admiral Fleming, this was an unprecedented event.[43] The evidence suggests that Axel Mowatt, the Rigsadmiral and a Scot, acting either under orders or on his own initiative, 'looked the other way' when the ships passed by.[44] Christian was certainly capable of subterfuge. In April 1639, for instance, James Maclean's cargo was allowed through the Sound, with the sole proviso that the Swedish resident had to guarantee that the cargo would only go to the Netherlands.[45]

How can Christian's behaviour be explained? On the face of it he should have supported his nephew, Charles, for apart from their close family relationship, the two countries were united in a confederation, renewed in April 1639.[46] It is possible that he harboured a grudge against the English king which, when coupled with Scottish diplomacy, led him to adopt a more even-handed approach than he might otherwise have done. He did offer to act as arbitrator. The Scots exerted pressure on him at home, too, through the influence wielded by those who had attained high status in the mercantile community and the military establishment.[47] They affected events, as is illustrated by Mowatt's actions. More cynically, the Danish king had his eye on the Orkneys and Shetlands, which an embattled Charles might grant him in return for support.[48] Like the Swedes, he also sought to profit from the situation. He certainly exploited his control of the Sound for his own ends, increasing toll charges, notably on saltpetre and war materials, and skimming off a proportion of the goods shipped through. His action here, like the sharp practice over the sale of arms to Sir Thomas Roe, seems to have been typical of Christian's opportunist approach to international relations. Both actions helped Charles's enemies.

Arms continued to come in from abroad, notably when troops were being equipped for service in Ulster or in England. As revealed in Table 6, Thomas Cuningham supplied *matériel* for both theatres of war, employing his own money and credit on behalf of the Covenanting cause.[49] Dutch merchants were involved, too, including members of the Trip and de Geer families. In January 1644, the month that the Covenanters, as allies of Parliament, entered England, Laurens de Geer obtained a licence to ship out a cargo that consisted of 300 muskets, bandoliers and rests, 300 swords and belts, 100 pairs of pistols with holsters, 4 iron cannon, 600 cannonballs and 400 hand grenades, 120 barrels of gunpowder and 6½ tons of match.[50] Many of these weapons accompanied the army on its march. In January 1644 it took out of Scotland 3,080 new and refurbished muskets, 3,300 pairs of bandoliers, 1,498 whole and 120 half pikes, 800 lances, 640 swords and 10,600 Swedish feathers. By the end of March 1645 numbers dispatched out of the country had risen to 6,269 muskets, 3,533 pairs of bandoliers, 113 pairs of pistols, 4,819 whole and 120 half pikes, 910 lances, 1,359 swords and 11,500 Swedish feathers.[51]

Not all of the imports went to the field army or to the central magazine, however, for one or two of the burghs restocked their stores with arms from abroad. On 8 March 1644, for instance, George Suittie, dean of the guild at Edinburgh, delivered out of the city's magazine 226 muskets and bandoliers at £9 each and 224 pikes at 4 merks, and received payment for them. Whereas he was to obtain replacement pikes at home, he was told to write to the Low Countries for 250 muskets all of one bore, for restocking the magazine.[52]

Crown, Royalists and Allies

When Charles I decided to fight the Covenanters he obtained most of his supplies abroad.[53] Initially, his military adviser, Sir Jacob Astley, dealt with John Quarles, a Merchant Adventurer resident at Rotterdam, who spent over £38,000 on arms between 22 March 1638 and 12 May 1639 (see Table 7).[54] A year later Sir Thomas Roe was instructed to buy weapons at Hamburg. There, Albert Bearnes, Christian IV's arms merchant, provided him with 2,950 muskets and bandoliers (1,450 of them with rests), 800 pairs of pistols and holsters (100 pairs with firelocks), ammunition, and armour for 700 troopers and 1,500 pikemen. Because of their poor quality they eventually had to be returned.[55] Gunpowder,

TABLE 7
CONSIGNMENTS TO THE KING FROM THE LOW COUNTRIES, 1638 AND 1640

Commodity	John Quarles, 1638	Sir John Harby's consignment from Arthur Aynscombe, March 1640	Export licence for Harby, 26 April 1640
cannon	14 brass		
mortars	*		
cannonballs	*		
hand grenades	*		
firestones	*		
match		30 tons	60,000 lb
muskets	8,221	5,000	7,500
rests	8,161		10,000
bandoliers	8,600		7,500 pairs
carbines	2,200		600
pistols	2,057 pairs	2,150 pairs	1,300 pairs
holsters			3,000 pairs
arms		650 cuirassier	
arms		1,500 harquebusier	
swords	12,323		
sword belts	10,850		
girdles & hangers	1,655		
pikes	2,599	2,500	
partizans	107		
armour		650 suits cuirassier	700 cuirassier
armour	2,010 horsemen's	1,500 harquebusier	600 harquebusier
armour			2,600 foot
corslets	2,844	2,500 Foot	
saddles	2,037	500	700 harquebusier
bits	2,117	500	
stirrups	2,010 pairs	500	
drums	104		

Sources: Quarles: PRO E351/2711; Aynscombe: CSPD, 1639–40, p. 587; Export licence: ARA, Brussels, Audiëntie, inv. nr. 1061, f. 38.

which was particularly scarce, was bought separately. In December 1638 60 lasts were shipped from an unknown port in the Low Countries and two months later Pieter Trip sent 500 barrels from Amsterdam.[56] Celio and Gabriel Marcelis, who had trading links at Amsterdam and Hamburg, and with Denmark, also provided arms in bulk. In April 1639 Celio was allowed to export from Amsterdam 25 bronze cannon and a further 50 smaller pieces, nearly 9 tons of match, 10¾ tons of musket bullets, 1,500 muskets with rests and bandoliers, 2,500 pairs of pistols, 1,000 sabres, 400 hangers and 400 shovels. On 9 June Gabriel received a licence to ship 6,000 lb of match, 600 hand grenades, 3,000 pikes and an unknown number of muskets with accoutrement, and swords.[57] The source of some of the munitions for Antrim's projected invasion of the Western Isles in

1639 is revealed in the 40,000 lb of gunpowder that was sent by the Amsterdam-based partnership of Ewout and Pieter Chardinel to Dublin in March 1639.[58]

For the Second Bishops' War, Charles I placed more contracts with native manufacturers. Stocks remained from 1639 and capacity had increased at home. Moreover, as noted above, the king had been disappointed with the quality of some of the arms imported by Quarles and Roe. Therefore, the £17,000 that Sir Job Harby was given in January 1640 to spend on weapons in Flanders was merely to supplement home-produced goods. Learning from previous experience, the Council of War instructed him to find a merchant who would supply the arms at an agreed price and according to certain specifications. To ensure conformity and good quality, John Lanyon, a proofmaster at the Ordnance Office, was sent to Flanders with templates for the firearms. There, one of the merchants with whom Harby negotiated was Arthur Aynscombe, who agreed to deliver in advance one or two specimen weapons as an indicator of what he could supply.[59] At the end of March a bargain was sealed and the arms were included in a consignment for which Harby obtained an export licence on 26 April (see Table 7).[60] Other goods were dispatched later. On 8 June the Council of War asked Harby to tell his agents in Flanders and Holland to send to London the 1,000 great saddles that had been ordered.[61] In addition, Sir James King, a Scottish officer, was sent to Denmark for troops and weapons. Unfortunately, lack of money prevented him from obtaining them, though Christian IV did allow some horses, destined for Spain, to be diverted to England.[62] A Danish offer to accept the Orkneys in lieu of cash broke down because of Charles's reluctance to cede the islands and Christian's refusal to pay for them in pawn.[63]

Because of continuing shortages at home a greater proportion of munitions had to be obtained from abroad and this is reflected in the amount of match that Aynscombe provided for Harby. Hearing that 100 tons of match were available in Flanders, the Council of War had given Harby a separate order to obtain as much of it as he could. Perhaps Aynscombe drew on this stock. It is possible that George Fletcher obtained match from the same source when asked to purchase 50 tons abroad in January 1640.[64] In August the Chardinels provided 22¼ tons through Amsterdam. That month Celio Marcelis, John Webster and the Chardinels shipped as much as 40 tons of gunpowder from there. At the same time, John Russell, buying arms in Amsterdam on behalf of Wentworth in Ireland, was granted an export licence to ship out 300 carbines, 100 pairs of pistols and 330 pairs of holsters, 2,500 musket rests, 6,000 swords, 40 suits of (cuirassier?) armour, 100 suits of cavalry armour and 900 suits of pikemen's half-armour, 30 partizans and 50 halberds, 30 drums, 34 tents and 230 saddles.[65]

Scottish Royalists and their associates had greater difficulty in obtaining supplies. Some arms came from other parts of the British Isles. During the Bishops' Wars the king hoped to promote his cause in Scotland by sending shipments of arms to Royalists like the Marquess of Huntly. On 9 March 1639 Sir Alexander Gordon returned to Aberdeen in a royal navy pinnace, escorting a merchantman, laden with 2,000 muskets with bandoliers and rests, and 1,000 pikes, as well as with armour for foot and horse, gunpowder, match and lead, carbines, pistols and lances.[66] Some shipments were captured by the Covenanters, however; in 1640 Alexander Jaffray, writing from Edinburgh, informed Patrick Leslie, the provost of Aberdeen, that 'My Lord Carnegies armes puder and ball tane cuming be sea from Kirkcaldie to Montroiss so that thair is no assurance be sea evin.'[67]

Shortages of supply affected the Royalists' military capability. On 9 June, Lord Aboyne told Hamilton that it was impossible to keep a force of any size together without money or arms. In 1644–5 Montrose received scant help from the English Royalists, who had their own problems, though he inherited the arms given to the Earl of Antrim for his expedition to the Isles.[68] To maintain Montrose's momentum the king sought further supplies from Ireland. On 4 January 1645 he ordered Ormond to negotiate with the Confederacy for soldiers, arms and ammunition. In spite of Ormond's initial optimism the Catholics proved obdurate and it was only when news of Montrose's victories filtered back to Ireland that they changed their mind. In mid-May the Supreme Council agreed to send a force of 1,000 men, supplied with a month's provisions and munitions. However, the project foundered because Ormond would not or could not accede to the council's demands. As a result, in May Ormond had to report to the king that he should not 'expect any considerable succour from hence, either into England or Scotland'.[69]

The bulk of the supplies had to come from abroad but they were difficult to acquire. In March 1645 the queen told Captain Allen to obtain arms and ammunition from the Flemish gunrunner, Jan van Haesdonck, and to convey them by frigate to Montrose, 'who we hear doth prosper miraculously'. Unfortunately, van Haesdonck refused to give Allen anything from his cargo.[70] In July Jermyn reported that £10,000 worth of arms and ammunition had been sent to Montrose from France and Holland but they did not all materialise and of that sent, some fell into enemy hands. In spring 1646 Covenanters at Teignmouth, Devon, captured a consignment from Brittany.[71] Other arms were expected from the Baltic. The Royalists hoped that Christian IV of Denmark, with peace in the offing, could be induced by the offer of the Orkneys and Shetlands to send cavalry, arms and cash to Scotland.[72] Nothing came of the negotiations. Conversely, Sir John Cochrane, now working for the Royalists, did persuade the Duke of Courland to ship gunpowder and lead to Montrose. The order took time to assemble and was then ice-bound over winter. At least the delay enabled Cochrane to add match, lead shot, muskets and bandoliers to the consignment, while the Duke offered to supply a dozen cannon. However, the ordnance was mounted on ship's carriages and almost half of the muskets were of poor quality and had to be returned.[73] The shipment finally left in July 1646 but by then it was too late: Montrose's forces surrendered on 22 July.

During 1648 the arms supply deteriorated when the Engagers assumed control, as their ascendancy split the country both at home and abroad. In particular, they lost the support of merchants at their vital supply base at Veere; Thomas Cuningham, for instance, refused to furnish them with weapons.[74] Consignments also arrived late, especially for use in the Engager invasion of England. On 4 July, the day that their army mustered on Annan Moor, they were still awaiting the promised arms from France. The leaders, therefore, looked to Holland and to their representative there, Sir William Bellenden. Sir William was already trying to put a consignment together but his efforts were being hampered by jealousy between the English Royalists and the Scots, official indifference and lack of transport.[75] Eventually, he did obtain supplies for on 18 September. He reportedly left for Scotland with 10,000 arms and ammunition. Unfortunately, they were seized by Argyll at Leith.[76] By then, the army, short of provisions and weapons, had been defeated at Preston and had retreated back to Scotland.[77]

The execution of Charles I in January 1649 transformed the situation and led to negotiations between his heir and Argyll. At the same time, Charles II made the Covenanters' enemy, Montrose, commander-in-chief of all his forces in Scotland.[78] With customary vigour he set about securing military supplies abroad, buoyed up by the wave of anti-Parliamentarian feeling engendered by the execution.[79] At The Hague he met Ulfeldt, the Danish ambassador, who thought that his brother-in-law, the new king, Frederick III, would provide him with arms for his own expedition to Orkney and further supplies for Charles II. By midsummer Montrose had received £5,400 from the Danish king, together with a donation from Ulfeldt, as well as 1,500 muskets, swords, pikes and cutlasses, 26 cannon and a proportionable amount of gunpowder and ammunition. Early in 1650 some of these weapons had to be sold to pay his soldiers, languishing at Bremen.[80] Other agents travelled to various German and Baltic states; few arms were obtained but at Danzig Sir John Cochrane was given 3,000 rixdollars and in Poland Scottish expatriates donated £10,000. The Duke of Courland loaned him six ships, manned and victualled.[81]

Sweden proved to be a valuable source of arms. In February 1649 Charles II sent as envoy, Patrick Ruthven, the Earl of Brentford, who had served as an officer in the Swedish army and who possessed estates in that country. When he arrived at Court he was given a sympathetic hearing. Queen Christina was particularly keen to provide help, and ordered weapons, munitions and ordnance to be made available.[82] The *matériel*, drawn from half a dozen locations and sent to Gothenburg, consisted of 12 3-pounders with carriages and furniture, 1,200 cannonballs, 6 lasts of gunpowder, 30 schipponds of match, 6,000 muskets and 3,000 bandoliers with 30 barrels of shot and 6 moulds, 1,800 pairs of pistols, 4,000 infantry- and 600 cavalry swords, 5,000 pikes, 2,000 suits of cavalry armour, 150 partizans and halberds and 50 drums.

To protect the Crown, John Maclean handled the business.[83] Montrose was to receive one-half of the consignment for his Orkney expedition and Ormond the other. In the event Montrose seems to have taken all of it.[84] On 10 November he travelled to Gothenburg, where he stayed with Maclean. Maclean loaned him £25,000 to purchase provisions and arms, bought weapons on his behalf and allowed him to store them in his warehouses. Local officials were told to turn a blind eye towards these activities.[85] In mid-December several ships sailed for Orkney full of troops and military hardware, the latter comprising 12 3-pounders with 1,200 cannonballs, 36 large tuns of gunpowder, 20 schipponds of match,

1,000 matchlock- and 536 flintlock muskets with 1,040 bandoliers, 20 casks of shot and 1 mould, 45 pairs of pistols and 12 pairs of holsters, 2,520 infantry- and 200 cavalry swords, 1,510 pikes, 100 suits of armour, 150 partizans, 24 drums and 1 carriage.[86] Montrose eventually left in March 1650.[87]

Montrose's task had been complicated by the actions of the Covenanters who sent out agents to promote their own cause. At Veere they enlisted the support of Thomas Cuningham to hinder the export of arms to 'malignants'. More seriously, shortly after Montrose had landed in Orkney he learned that the king was negotiating with the Covenanters.[88] When an agreement was reached in May 1650, he was, in effect, abandoned. Abroad, the shabby treatment of Montrose made it more difficult for the Royalists to obtain money, men and essential supplies. Influential figures such as Sehested and Ulfeldt in Denmark and financial backers like Maclean in Sweden and Krabbe in Denmark/Norway withdrew their support.[89] In October 1650, with an English army in the country, Sir Robert Long wrote to the king suggesting possible sources of aid. He concluded that help could only be expected from Germany, Sweden and Denmark. The following January the Earl of Lothian advocated sending someone to negotiate with the merchants in Poland and Courland and in the towns of Danzig and Koenigsberg for arms, ammunition, ships, corn and other vital materials. That person, it was stressed, should be held to greater account than Cochrane had been. Cochrane had, it seems, kept most of the money he had obtained in the Baltic States, apparently in disgust at Charles's abandonment of Montrose. Poland, with its large Scottish *émigré* population was seen as a likely source, as was Queen Christina in Sweden.[90] Shipments also continued to come from west of the Sound. In April 1651, for instance, the *Hawk* sailed from Rotterdam with 4 brass cannon and 2 petards, 1,500 grenades, 185 lb of saltpetre and 300 lb of gunpowder, and almost 4,000 assorted picks and shovels.[91]

IRISH CAMPAIGNS, 1641–52

The Irish arms industry was of modest size and, consequently, insurgents and Royalists were reliant to a great extent on imports, whether they came from Britain or the continent. At least the Royalists could draw on the stocks in the magazine at Dublin Castle, while awaiting the response in England to their urgent appeals for further supplies. The rebels, thwarted in their attempt to capture the castle and with it the arms, would not have survived for long with what they could plunder in the first flush of the rebellion. Therefore, they turned to Roman Catholic states, especially to France and Spain, for direct help or for liberty to obtain and export military hardware. The response was quite good. As a result, they seem to have acquired adequate stocks of arms and armaments, protestations to the contrary notwithstanding. Indeed, in the aftermath of the cessation and various truces, English, as well as Irish, Royalists, from time to time asked for supplies. As the Royalist cause began to decline in England, its commanders even sought arms from their supporters in Ireland.

The Catholic Confederacy

Before the rebellion had begun the Irish had made contact with foreign powers, asking for material help as well as the release of soldiers in their service. Over the winter of 1641/2, reports filtered back to England of ships being loaded with arms in French and Flemish ports, but the Spanish authorities, at least, insisted that they were not bound for Ireland. Cárdenas, the Spanish ambassador to England, further stated that he would write to officials in all parts of the Spanish Empire to ensure that they observed the terms of the articles of peace between the two countries.[92] Nonetheless, the English ambassador continued to complain about Spanish assistance to the rebels and the Venetian ambassador seemed to think that there was some truth in the allegations.[93] De Mello, the new governor of the Spanish Netherlands, certainly played a double game, neither helping nor hindering the activities of Confederate supporters. Secretly he reassured Owen Roe O'Neill, the future Irish commander in Ulster, that he would assist them in whatever way he could, and later, the Spanish king, Philip IV, told him to continue to provide undercover aid.[94]

In fact, the authorities in Spain connived at the gunrunning activities that were being carried on in that country. Thus, when in July 1642 some English sailors at San Sebastian complained to the authorities about Stephen Lynch, a Galway merchant, then loading a ship with weapons, ordnance and munitions, they found themselves imprisoned, fined and their goods confiscated. Lynch and his associates bought a second ship and moved to a nearby creek to complete their task. The following March John Creswick reported that just along the coast from San Sebastian the Irish were loading on board ship 200 pieces of ordnance and enough weapons for 20,000–25,000 troops.[95]

The English, as much as the Irish, realised the importance of foreign supplies to the rebels and before the end of 1641 demands were being made for ships to blockade the approaches to Ireland. On 16 January 1642 Richard Johnson warned that if they received ammunition, ' we are likely to have a tedious and a dangerous war'.[96] In Dublin, too, there was concern. On 31 March 1642 the Lords Justices pleaded with the Lord Lieutenant for more men, arms and equipment so that they could deal with the insurgents before the *matériel* the latter were receiving from abroad made them too strong.[97] A guard was mounted on the Irish coast, while the Dutch, responding to a Parliamentarian request, promised to police the sea off Flanders.[98] These measures had some effect but they failed to stop many of the arms from reaching their destination. The bulk of the arms from the Spanish Netherlands were channelled through Nieuport, Ostend and Dunkirk, and from Spain, San Sebastian and Bilbao. French cargoes were mainly shipped from St Malo and Nantes in Brittany and La Rochelle further south. Galway, Limerick, Waterford and Wexford were the main ports of entry into Ireland. In June 1642 the Irish Council wrote to the Earl of Leicester, stressing the need to secure Galway. It described the town as the key to the control of Connaught, possessing a harbour 'that lies open to Spain and France, forces from foreign parts may easily arrive there, and from thence annoy the kingdom and furnish all parts of the kingdom with arms and munition'.[99]

Foreign arms were available from the outset. By 13 November 1641 the Irish Council had received a report that the Catholics were expecting money and arms from Spain and the Spanish Netherlands. On 13 January 1642, 90,000 arms were said to be ready at Dunkirk.[100] Shipments seem to have begun that month, though only a proportion of them arrived safely, because the ships were either seized or forced by circumstances into an English port.[101] At this stage, the insurgents were very short of weapons and munitions, so the loss of 1,500 muskets, 'many loades' of bullets and a 'great store' of gunpowder on board a Dunkirker that had to put into Cowes, Isle of Wight, in February was a considerable blow. Nonetheless, by the end of the month the Venetian ambassador could report that they had received a large consignment of arms from Antwerp.[102]

As in Scotland, some arms were shipped back with officers and men, returning to fight for the cause.[103] Irish merchants were also active, selling goods abroad and buying arms with the proceeds. Galway merchants sold hides, tallow and butter at San Sebastian and Wexford men, herring in Flanders. Waterford merchants sailed to Nantes and le Croisic.[104] Perhaps Waterford men were the ones who sold fish at Nantes in January 1642, returning with four ships reputedly laden with 120,000 arms. Inhabitants of the town certainly bought arms and gunpowder in France the following month.[105] As the year progressed this traffic increased. The worsening situation in England distracted attention from Ireland and there was greater freedom of movement at sea. In July Gregory Finch, writing from Paris, noted that recently many ships, loaded with goods, had come to France to exchange for gunpowder and ammunition. Galway men were among those obtaining arms there.[106]

Foreign merchants were involved, too, attracted by the profits to be made, in spite of the danger. In September it was said of French merchants that they were willing to do business because it was 'as profitable a voyage . . . as unto the East or West Indies'. At the same time, Dunkirk merchants, recognising a market opportunity, were buying up great quantities of gunpowder and arms in Holland and Hamburg for resale to agents of the Irish Confederacy.[107] The business even attracted Mediterranean pirates. In November 1642 Parliamentarian ships captured two Turkish men-of-war loaded with arms for the rebels, with whom, the captain confessed, 'they have continuall traffick for those commodities'.[108] Confederate agents abroad also negotiated with merchants. In October Hugh Bourke in Flanders arranged for Nicholas Everard and Jean de la Villette, two Dunkirk-based merchants, to bear the cost of 200 barrels of gunpowder shipped out of Nieuport with some muskets and three bronze cannon[109]

Returning soldiers continued to bring in military hardware. In July 1642 Owen Roe O'Neill landed at Castle Doe with 200–300 veteran soldiers and a cargo of arms and ammunition, including 500 stands of arms and a considerable amount of gunpowder and brimstone. In the same month Robert Purcell, writing from Olmütz, offered his services and requested help in transporting the arms, munitions and men he would bring with him. In September Colonel Preston returned, along with Colonels Bourke, Cullen, Plunket and Synnot and five or six ships, laden with field pieces and siege guns and 'a vast quantity' of arms and ammunition. At the same time twelve ships full of soldiers discharged from Louis

XIII's service sailed from St Malo, Nantes and La Rochelle, taking with them a number of field and siege cannon and a 'plentiful store' of arms and ammunition.[110]

By the summer the stock of arms was beginning to improve, though the Confederates continued to complain about shortages, especially of munitions. In July Henry Plunket S.J., visiting Bourke at Brussels, commented that Ireland was being lost for want of gunpowder, but in the same letter noted that a shipload of it was just setting out for Galway. On 6 December Richard Bellings, secretary to the Supreme Council, wrote that they had plenty of provisions but very little money, arms and ammunition.[111] However, there were signs that the situation was getting better. On 9 July William Gilbert, writing to Ormond from Maryborough Castle, Queen's County, noted that in recent clashes the rebels had become much stronger. He attributed this to improved supplies of ammunition, which made them 'freer of there powder then euer they haue beene'. By September Wexford had received 'great store of arms and munitions' from abroad. When John Purcell, who had left Kilkenny two weeks earlier, was interrogated by Royalists on 15 November, he declared that the Confederates had 'great stores of arms' at Kilkenny and that ships were daily bringing in arms to Leinster and Munster.[112] The Royalists were in no doubt that the insurgents had grown immeasurably stronger during the course of the year, bitterly contrasting Catholic fortunes with their own. In a letter to the Irish Committee on 1 September the council wrote, 'thus are the rebels plentifully supplied with arms and munitions, while we want both'.[113]

Even if the situation had improved, the Confederates continued to worry about supplies, especially as they were aware of their dependence on imports. On 7 April 1643 the Supreme Council confided to Bourke that they needed money, arms and ammunition, which because the country was 'exceedinglye exhausted', could only be obtained through the good offices of their friends abroad. The same month they asked their French agent, O'Hartegan, to procure arms and ammunition and arrange for merchants to import them. They were making this request, they said, because of the possibility that one or two entrepreneurs might try to monopolise the trade by spreading false reports that they had plenty of both commodities whereas, in truth, they had not much of either.[114] To improve the flow, the Supreme Council made representations to authorities abroad to waive restrictions on arms shipments. In August 1643 it instructed Hugh Bourke at Brussels to ask de Mello if he would grant 'express' licences to Vanderkipp and some other merchants who supplied the Confederates with war materials, for religion and the nation's sake. They seem to have been given, for Vanderkipp was very active in the trade, though his motivation was rather less altruistic. He supplied arms, munitions and victuals to the highest bidder and hired out transport vessels at extortionate rates to whoever would pay him.[115]

The defection of Lord Inchiquin to Parliament in July 1644 put added pressure on the Confederates and increased their need for arms.[116] The following month de la Monnerie, the French representative at Kilkenny, relayed to Mazarin the Supreme Council's request for licence to transport war materials out of the country: 'en estant en grandissime necéssité, et spéciallement, depuis que le Milord d'Insequin s'est déclaré pour le Parlement'. According to de la Monnerie, the Dunkirkers had refused them arms and munitions in spite of their promises, while the Spanish representative had not followed up on his.[117] France, trying to increase its influence with the Confederacy, was certainly supportive, but de la Monnerie undoubtedly overstated his case. As before, arms shipments were allowed to leave Flemish and Spanish ports. In October Nicholas Everard and Jean de la Villette received permission to export from Flanders, 4,000 muskets, 1,000 pairs of pistols, 1,000 carbines, 20,000 lb of match and 600 barrels of gunpowder.[118] With both sides bidding to become Ireland's 'protector', merchants had little trouble in getting clearance to sail. The blockade and subsequent capture of Dunkirk by the French on 1 October 1646 did have an impact on the level of imports but, according to Ohlmeyer, the Confederates had by then built up reserves of munitions. In March 1646, Dumolin had reported to Mazarin that they had told him they needed money more than arms.[119]

Irish Royalists and Ulster Scots

Although the insurgents captured arms as they advanced, the Royalists still possessed the means to retaliate and resupply themselves. They retained control of a number of key ports and, crucially, the magazine at Dublin Castle. The Irish Council also sent urgent appeals to England for supplies. On 9 November 1641 the Lords Justices bluntly told the Speaker of the House of Commons that the kingdom would be lost if arms were not delivered immediately.[120] Parliament responded, but the question of authorising deliveries soon fell foul of its growing conflict with the king. During spring and summer 1642 the Ordnance Office did dispatch tons of arms, clothing and equipment to Ireland, but Ormond's forces gained little from these shipments as the troops raised by Parliament were given priority treatment. On 1 September the Lords Justices complained to the Irish Committee that since the outbreak of the rebellion they had received fewer than 100 barrels of gunpowder and less than 6½ tons of match, adding that without the initial stock of arms and munitions they would not have survived so long.[121]

Hindsight elucidates the reasons for the shortfall but members of the council were merely concerned with their predicament. They pointed out that their initial advantage in arms and munitions had been lost which, coupled with rebel superiority in numbers, made their situation dire, if not quickly resupplied from England: 'Well affected subjects . . . are now much cast down, finding our strength in men daily weakened, our munition spent, our arms defective, and our supplies not come, they on the other side daily supplied with all sorts of provision, and their men far more instructed in the actions of war.' Later in the month they drew up a long shopping list of arms and equipment they wanted to be sent from England, including infantry arms for 5,000 foot soldiers (at the rate of two to one for musketeers and pikemen) and 600 horse. They also ordered 4,000 basket-hilted swords and 4,000 long rapiers, each with belts; 300 holsters to fit pistols with barrels 18 in long; 150 partizans and 300 drums. To replenish the bandoliers they requested 90,000 chargers, 6,000 primers and 6,000 girdles. To restock damaged firearms they asked for walnut and other wooden planks, and to repair wagons, elm planking. In addition, they wanted ordnance: 10 brass sakers and 20 brass harquebuses (sic), complete with cannonware and spare carriages, and 12,000 cannonballs of various sizes, 600 assorted canisters of case shot and 500 hand grenades; and munitions: 36 tons of gunpowder, 150 barrels of pistol powder and 50 tons of match. They also required horse tack: 500 saddles, with bits and furniture and 3 barrels each of horseshoes and nails.[122]

Unfortunately, as the Civil War had just broken out in England, the Lords Justices were inevitably going to be disappointed. Some money and provisions were delivered at the end of October but far less than was required. If possible, the Irish Council's requests for arms became even more desperate, culminating in a letter to the Speaker of the House of Commons on 10 June 1643 in which it blamed Parliament for its misfortunes.[123] With the signing of the truce with the Confederacy on 15 September 1643, all hope of relief from England disappeared. As a postscript, the council wrote to Parliament on 28 October, replying to accusations of disloyalty made against it in a letter of 4 July. It pointed out that it had made repeated requests for supplies, warning of the dangers that would occur if they were not sent. It also drew up a list of the goods sent by the English Parliament in the six months 20 January to 10 June 1643. It comprised 374 barrels of gunpowder, 10¼ tons of match and 47½ tons of lead shot, as well as 500 suits of clothes, 1,000 cassocks and 818 caps, 22 tons each of butter and cheese, 447½ barrels of wheat and rye, 367 barrels of peas, and 356 barrels of oats. The council itself had contracted for 341 of the barrels of gunpowder and 7 tons of the match in Holland, but the shipment had been seized by a French man-of-war. It had only been released into Parliamentarian hands when the Irish Committee made representations to the ambassador. The clothes proved to be of poor quality, too, as had been the 6,000 suits delivered in September 1642.[124]

The Scots in Ulster had some difficulty in obtaining war materials from Parliament as well. Early in 1642, as the force was being put together, arms were being sent to the troops already there. On 18 March two ships from London docked at Carrickfergus with a great store of gunpowder and ammunition on board. Monro's regiment embarked at Largs at about the same time, but the bulk of the army followed in April and July.[125] They took with them their own arms, many of which had been dispatched from Veere by Thomas Cuningham and his partners. According to the terms of the agreement with the English Parliament, the Scots were to receive replacements from English stores, and some consignments were sent. On 1 March 1643 the London merchant, Maurice Thomson, signed for 20 lasts of gunpowder, 40 tons of lead, 12 cwt of bullets and 36 bastard musket moulds which were to be transported to Carrickfergus for the Scots army. In November the English commissioners promised to deliver 3,000 muskets, 1,500 pikes and 500 pairs of pistols, together with ammunition and cavalry equipment, as well as 10,000 suits of clothes and shoes, 10,000 bolls of meal and £10,000 in money.[126] Because little was sent, the bulk of the arms and equipment had to be shipped from Scotland. Judging from letters written by the Scottish commissioners, the plight of the army in Ulster was similar to that of Ormond's forces.[127] Inchiquin, in contrast, did receive some supplies from Parliament after he transferred his allegiance in July 1644.[128]

In spite of their dogged attempts to obtain war material from the English Parliament, the Royalists had realised by mid-1642 that it would be prudent to look elsewhere, too. On 7 June they came to an agreement with John Quarles, the Amsterdam-based merchant who had done business with the government in the Bishops' Wars, to supply £3,195 worth of arms. They arranged for the payments to be made in London and hoped that the Irish Committee would settle the bills quickly 'for the better encouragement of others to deal with us'. The compact fell through, perhaps because Parliament did not pay up, a problem that the Irish Council had to face in subsequent deals. A Dunkirker captured a second consignment, put together by Quarles and shipped out on the *Coninck Davidt* in December.[129] Earlier, in September, the council had arranged with Abraham Rickess, a Dublin merchant, to bring over a cargo of gunpowder and match from Holland – the shipment that was seized by the French. In the New Year a contract was made with Theodore Achout and Jacob Ablin, two Dutch merchants based at Dublin, who agreed to supply arms to the value of £7,893 3s 0d. Once more, the deal foundered on the refusal of Parliament to pay for them.[130]

The Royalists did obtain arms from abroad but had to foot the bill themselves. In order to encourage the trade, supplies were allowed in custom-free, though naturally merchants tried to interpret the privilege loosely. On 29 October 1643 Nicholas van Dyke wrote to ask if Viscount Taaffe's pass, allowing him to sell arms, ammunition, victuals and other war materials, could be extended to encompass all merchandise.[131] To provide the *matériel*, the Royalists made particular use of merchants from the Low Countries like van Dyke, who were operating out of Irish ports. Apart from Achout and Ablin, other Dublin merchants included Frederick Pankaert, Gerrard van Hoven, Jacob van Hoegaerden and Pieter Wybrants.[132]

Unfortunately, a lack of precise evidence makes it difficult properly to evaluate the amount of business the mercantile community conducted with the Royalists. Undoubtedly, the Parliamentarian blockade of Dublin, tightened up in 1644, did make it difficult to bring in goods and did affect supply. In June 1644 van Hoven, worried about the ships standing guard there, unloaded his cargo at Wexford and asked for an escort to convey them to Dublin.[133] In an attempt to improve the situation Ormond sent agents to France and Holland in spring 1645, but when he wrote to the Prince of Wales on 6 June he admitted that he had not heard from any of them.[134] On a brighter note, when he returned to Ireland in September 1648 to head an allied force of Royalists, moderate Confederates and Inchiquin's men, he came with arms for 4,000 foot and 1,000 horse that had been paid for by the French. Writing to the queen and Prince Charles four months later, he stressed the need to encourage French, Flemish and Dutch merchants to come to Ireland. In addition, he sought to enlist the prince's help in persuading the stadtholder to provide him with frigates, arms, armaments, armour, money and corn on the security of the customs.[135] The same year Ormond should have shared a Swedish consignment with Montrose, but the latter seems to have appropriated the entire shipment.[136]

The records, in spite of their shortcomings, make it clear that the Royalists received fewer arms from abroad than did the insurgents, and suffered in consequence. Ironically, they did best during the periods of truce with the Confederacy, when they obtained arms from them either directly or indirectly. Immediately after the cessation, John Barry was sent to Cashel with a request from Ormond for arms. On 4 October 1643 he reported that great quantities of arms and ammunition were daily expected, presumably from abroad. In the meantime, he had been told that although there was no spare gunpowder, he could buy arms at reasonable rates because stocks were plentiful. In December Inchiquin was soliciting arms through Sir John Dungan, proposing that part of the contribution money be paid in arms and ammunition, 'whereof there is good store at Kilkenny, Clonmel and Galway'.[137]

In April 1644 Barry managed to get the Supreme Council to lift the restraints placed on merchants selling arms. He informed Ormond that Bellings had contracted with a merchant for 5,000 arms and 500 barrels of gunpowder and that he could buy any surplus stock for ready money or equivalent goods. By the end of the month he had also obtained an additional 20 barrels of gunpowder.[138] The transaction had to be kept secret because the Confederacy had just refused a request from Prince Rupert for arms.[139] Further signs of cooperation were given the following year. In February 1645 the Supreme Council informed Ormond that because of their commitments they could not spare arms at present but as an inducement to stir him into action against the Scots, held out the prospect of obtaining arms from a consignment due in from abroad.[140] The Royalists also procured arms from Confederate merchants like Patrick Archer. In May 1644 he agreed to provide William Brown with £500 worth of gunpowder and match and in March 1649 he made a similar bargain with Ormond for gunpowder, match and ammunition.[141]

THE ENGLISH CIVIL WAR

The Low Countries

Royalists and Parliamentarians alike acquired the bulk of their imports from the Low Countries, although it could not be assumed that the supplies would be automatically released. Indeed, in the United Provinces the question of licensing exports came to a head at the same time as the phoney war between king and Parliament ended in August 1642. Frederick Henry, the stadtholder, undoubtedly wished to assist his new relations, but the degree to which he was committed to the Stuart cause is a matter of debate among Dutch scholars. According to Geyl, he used his son's marriage to advance his dynastic ambitions, which he hoped to strengthen further by negotiating a union between his daughter, Louise

Henrietta, and Charles, the Prince of Wales.[142] Groenveld, however, does not believe that Frederick Henry was a Stuart partisan and minimises the conflict of interest between him and the States-General. In his opinion, the stadtholder merely provided the queen with what he felt honour-bound to give as a result of the marriage alliance. Even the large consignment of arms that Henrietta Maria took with her when she set out for England in February 1643 was justified as a means of getting rid of her, 'because otherwise it appears the queen will not leave, but will continue to stay here to the noticeable disservice of the country'.[143] Moreover, Frederick Henry had to work with the States-General, and therefore did not have a completely free hand. Through political manipulation and the support of placemen he was generally able to exert his authority, but at this juncture he was threatened by a resurgent Holland.[144] Among its mercantile élite there was a good deal of sympathy for the Parliamentarian cause, based on their own republicanism and Protestant faith. In the 'Kloosterkerk' in The Hague, and elsewhere, prayers were said on behalf of Parliament and for the destruction of the king's evil councillors.[145] They certainly had little inclination to help Henrietta Maria, then buying arms locally.

The queen had, in fact, arrived at The Hague in March 1642, accompanying her young daughter, Mary, to her new home. While there, her main aim, was to secure material help for the Royalist cause. With no access to the arms industries of south-eastern England, imports were essential if the king were to defeat Parliament militarily. At the beginning of June she asked Frederick Henry for arms but, apart from his own caution, the timing was inappropriate. Nonetheless, he did what he could. By underpinning a loan to her and putting forward his own credit as security when she pawned the Crown jewels, she was able to raise money. He even sold her guns from the State magazine.[146] With the proceeds, Henrietta Maria set about acquiring war material: by 12 June she had used the proceeds to procure ordnance, gunpowder, firearms and saddles.[147]

Throughout the summer arms ships sailed to Royalist ports, mainly in north-eastern England. Reputedly, the first gunrunner successfully to land his cargo was Captain John Strachan, who early in July evaded the Parliamentarian blockade by sailing up a creek of the Humber. In the same month Prince Rupert arrived at Tynemouth with a consignment of muskets, gunpowder and arms.[148] Arms collected by Henrietta Maria in June formed the basis of a shipment sent from Amsterdam at the end of July. A note of the cargo, taken on 1 August, lists 4 siege guns, 10 field pieces, 2 mortars, 4 petards, round and case shot for the cannon, 100 barrels of gunpowder, 200 firelock- and 3,000 matchlock muskets, 1,000 carbines, 2,000 pairs of pistols, 1,000 pikes and 3,000 saddles.[149]

The United Provinces was supposed to be neutral in the dispute; indeed, a delegation from the States-General had gone to England in the summer in an attempt to mediate between the king and Parliament.[150] Nevertheless, Parliament, hearing reports of ships being loaded with arms for the Royalists, was sceptical about Dutch protestations to the contrary. On 14 July an informant reported that a customs officer at Rotterdam had admitted that export licences were being given. The writer pointed out that although the States-General had issued a warrant that such ships should be impounded, they had acted in a similar way when arms were being sent to the Scots in the Bishops' Wars.[151] Typically, while protesting about Dutch deceit, Parliament was also purchasing arms in the country. Surviving export licences reveal that a number of arms ships sailed from Amsterdam, Flushing and Middleburg to London that summer. Guilliam Momma, for example, sent 300 barrels of gunpowder from Amsterdam at the end of June and £10,000 Flemish worth of weapons a month later. On 18 August Abraham Droochbroot, a merchant from Middleburg, dispatched 130 barrels of gunpowder, 2,000 muskets, 1,000 pairs of pistols, 1,000 carbines and 2,000 pikes.[152] At the same time David Hempson, Gerard van Leeuen and Edward Petersen, merchant strangers at Dover, delivered 339 barrels of gunpowder to the fleet, then riding at anchor in the Downs.[153]

Although it obtained arms from the same source as the Royalists, Parliament continued to feel aggrieved. In September it sent over Walter Strickland to represent its interests and he immediately complained about the number of ships sailing from Dutch harbours with arms for the king.[154] Shortly afterwards, the States of Holland decided to act and ordered the detention of all ships setting out for England. By 14 September three ships had been arrested, two Parliamentarian and one Royalist, though Strickland grumbled that the authorities only made a show of stopping the queen's ship. Further investigation revealed that four other ships, laden with arms for Parliament, were ready to leave.[155] On 1 November the States-General declared a policy of strict neutrality, forbidding the export of arms to either party.[156] Strickland soon pointed out that the ban had not stopped the export of arms to the Royalists and argued that they should therefore be sent to Parliamentarians too. In spite of its shortcomings the prohibition had an obvious impact upon trade and merchants were reluctant to comply. Those at Amsterdam and Rotterdam, the ones most affected by the ban, soon broke ranks, interpreting the declaration as the right to distribute arms equally to both sides. Licences were easy to obtain from the Admiralties, given the task of policing the system in December.[157] In April 1643 David Behangel, an exporter of sword blades, deposed that Amsterdam's Admiralty officials agreed to every request to ship arms to England, adding that he had been allowed to do so many times.[158] As Groenveld has observed, 'the two largest towns connived at all kind of export of war material for Charles I as well as for Parliament'.[159]

The Royalists continued to export arms with little difficulty. Apart from the tacit support of the stadtholder they were helped by the corrupt Cornelius Musch, secretary to the States-General and friend of Heenvliet (the head of Princess Mary's household), who could be induced to overturn orders to detain arms ships.[160] When Henrietta Maria finally left for home in February 1643 she reputedly took with her 30 brass and 2 iron cannon and arms for 10,000 men.[161] Supporters among the mercantile community were heavily involved in gunrunning. Some of these merchants and arms dealers were based in England and prominent ones like Sir Nicholas Crispe and Sir George Strode employed agents abroad.[162] Most of the suppliers, however, resided on the continent. As well as natives, they included expatriates like John Webster and William Watson, men who were central to the Royalist supply network. Strickland was well aware of their value to the Royalist cause, noting on 7 July 1644, 'the great Hurt that was done by malignant Merchants, Englishmen, dwelling in the Country at Amsterdam and Rotterdam, by providing Arms and all other Things for the Assistance of those who are in Rebellion against the Country'. The previous day Parliament had outlawed Webster, Theophilus Baynham, Edward Manning, Richard Ford and James Yard.[163]

Because of his wealth, standing and range of contacts Webster was the pivotal figure. According to Strickland, he 'hath and doth furnish most of the Arms that go to those in Rebellion, whose Credit is such as makes him very fit for his Employment in that Town [Amsterdam], being allied to many in it of Note; but his Credit is likewise much in London'.[164] He supplied arms to the king during the Bishops' Wars and continued to do so throughout the 1640s. As soon as the queen had obtained money by pawning her jewels, Webster was out looking for weapons. On 11 June 1642 a Parliamentarian informant reported seeing him examining and measuring up a mortar piece, adding that he 'doth hasten exceedingly with all these things'.[165] Among others, Webster dealt with leading arms dealers such as Pieter Trip. One consignment of muskets and pikes he bought from him in early 1644 was sent to Scarborough, together with a parcel of match for Sir William Davenant, the Lieutenant-General of the northern Ordnance Office.[166] On this occasion he used a Scarborough ship, the *Charles*, but he also hired Dutch vessels. In February 1644 he chartered the *Mary* of Amsterdam to take a cargo of 1,500 muskets, with bandoliers and rests, 500 pairs of pistols and spanners, together with 537 spare pistol cases, some bullet moulds and 110 barrels of gunpowder, to either Weymouth, Dartmouth or Falmouth. He promised the sailors a bonus of 20s apiece as an inducement to undertake a second voyage with a similar cargo. Webster was still supplying match and shot in November 1648.[167]

Parliament was equally active. In the first year of the war, merchants imported the bulk of the arms and armaments used by its forces (see Table 8). Apart from remedying the shortfall in munitions, they also provided many of the weapons, allowing artificers at home to refurbish existing stocks.[168] Gunpowder, cannonware and a few weapons were sent to the Tower, but most of the supplies were stored in the Committee of Safety's magazine. In autumn 1642 the committee gave Thomas Andrews and Stephen Estwick an order for 12,000 muskets and rests, 1,200 carbines, 1,500 pairs of pistols, 6,000 pikes, 600 suits of harquebusier armour and 6,000 corslets. They, in turn, asked their factors in Holland and France to obtain the weapons and by 4 October 2,690 muskets and 3,956 rests, 246 carbines, 66 dragoons, 980 pairs of pistols with cases, 401 suits of harquebusier armour and 2,331 corslets had been received.[169]

The committee's records reveal that about three dozen other merchants supplied *matériel* between September 1642 and August 1643.[170] They seem to have been London based, although it is likely that many of them operated out of foreign ports, too. A Merchant Adventurer like Robert Gale probably had links with Rotterdam. Some of these arms came from France and the Spanish

TABLE 8

SUPPLIES TO THE COMMITTEE OF SAFETY 1642–3: HOME PRODUCTION
AND IMPORTS

Item	Home Production	Imports
gunpowder	2,121.83 barrels	1,833.21 barrels
match	6 tons	78 tons
lead shot		6 tons
harquebusier		852
muskets	600	5,663
rests	600	3,934
bandoliers		7,714
carbines	92	5,825
swivels	87	206
belts		143
pistols	478	6,058
holsters	612	1,593
cases	91	538
spanners	117	722
firearms		1,900
firestones		7,000
swords	1,200	
pikes		8,428
halberds	127	
halberd heads		40
partizans	80	
armour	275 suits	3,788 suits
corslets		6,054
other arms (value only)		£3,307.18

Sources: PRO, SP 28/261–4.

Netherlands but the United Provinces was the major supplier. Merchants also sent cargoes of arms from the United Provinces to ports along the east coast. Prominent among their number was William Sykes, a Hull merchant, who supplied the northern army and the Lincolnshire militia with arms, armaments and equipment. In the period from 23 November 1642 to 1 July 1643 he purchased goods valued at almost £8,000 and gave on the Propositions nearly £2,500 in cash and £1,000 worth of arms.[171]

Home production did improve gradually but imports remained vital to Parliament. Export licences for shipments coming out of Amsterdam, Flushing and Middleburg indicate that large quantities of arms were dispatched to England, even if it is rarely known to which side individual cargoes were going. The same mixture of merchants and arms dealers was involved in gunrunning; foreign merchants predominated but Englishmen, sailing out of home or foreign ports were quite numerous. John Freeman, the leading matchmaker, obtained additional supplies at Amsterdam. On 16 April 1644 he was given permission to export an unknown quantity of match, as well as 1,000(?) pairs of pistols and

2,000 pikes. Six months earlier he had shipped 100 barrels of gunpowder, 600 muskets, 1,000 pairs of pistols, 100 halberds and 1,000 suits of armour through the port. According to extant licences, Henry Shuttleworth was the most regular supplier, his ten consignments amounting to some 44 tons of munitions and thousands of pounds' worth of arms and armour.[172] Robert Gale continued to deal in weapons. In 1644 he sold over £1,000 worth of arms to the Eastern Association and by the end of the year Dutch pistols and armour valued at £420 11s 8d to the Kentish forces.[173] At Middleburg, the expatriate, Stephen Foster, maintained his trading links with Parliament. Between 1 August 1643 and 19 October 1645 the Zeeland Admiralty licensed five shipments of his, totalling c. 3 tons of gunpowder, 5 tons 7 cwt of match and 15 cwt of sulphur, as well as 3,100 muskets, 50 carbines, 540 pairs of pistols, 200 firelocks, 2,000–3,000 locks for firelocks and 4,100 pikes.[174] The Eastern Association obtained its arms from provinicial merchants like Thomas Toll, Maccabeus Hollis and Bartholomew Wormall. Wormall, for instance, received £8,000 for arms he had imported from the Netherlands. In autumn 1646 James Nelthorpe, MP for Beverley, procured 50 barrels of gunpowder and 6 tons of match from Holland for the garrison at Hull.[175]

Both sides had to contend with Flemish privateers, intent on disrupting the trade of the United Provinces. Arms shipments in Dutch bottoms were particularly vulnerable. Dunkirk was the main base and the headquarters of the operation. Government-sponsored, the action of the privateers formed part of a new design to defeat the rebels when war with Spain was renewed in 1621. Instead of the conventional strategy of using the army to recover lost ground, the Spanish government sought to destroy the basis of Dutch prosperity by attacking her mercantile and fishing fleets at sea.[176] There is some debate about the impact made by the Dunkirkers, but they certainly did cause damage to Dutch commercial interests and were especially disruptive of the North Sea herring industry. However, did they prevent arms from the republic reaching the British Isles? As the bulk of the prizes taken were Dutch, some arms were lost but a good deal did evade capture.

A licensing system also operated in the Spanish Netherlands, although there was no equivalent debate concerning neutrality or even-handedness. All sides obtained arms there. Naturally, the government had preferences and, as has been shown above, covertly supplied the Irish rebels with arms. In addition, the Royalists seem to have operated more freely than Parliamentarians; Flemish ports provided shelter for their ships and (especially after the cessation) privateers were less inclined to target their supplies. When Hugh Bourke asked for a licence for Nicholas Everard and Jean de la Villette to export arms to the Confederates on 21 October 1644, the Council of Finance raised no objections. Members recalled that hitherto passports had been given 'tant pour transporter armes vers l'Angleterre pour le service de ce roy que pour celuy des Catholiques d'Irlande'.[177] In February 1643 the Earl of Warwick, the Parliamentarian admiral, searching for gunrunners off the Dutch coast, noted that there were sixteen private, and eleven royal, ships ready to sail at Dunkirk.[178] The cargoes carried could be considerable. On 20 March 1644 the king's representative obtained a licence to export 10,000 muskets, with bandoliers and rests, 3,000 pistols and 3,000 carbines, all with accessories, 1,000 suits of cuirassier armour, 1,000 corslets and 1,000 saddles.[179]

Gunrunners had to evade the Dutch blockade of Flemish ports, the aim of which was similar to that of the Spanish authorities but which had been in place for much longer. On one occasion, in May 1643, the Fleming, Jan van Haesdonck, obtained safe passage by describing himself as 'an Aristocrat of her Majesty of Great Britain'.[180] For its supplies from the Spanish Netherlands Parliament was reliant to a greater extent on English merchants and, as neutrals, they should have had less trouble. Nonetheless, their ships were stopped. In spring 1643 Admiral Tromp blockaded several Royalist and Parliamentarian ships in the harbour at Dunkirk. When two of the ships, laden with arms by the London merchants, William Pennoyer and Richard Hill, eventually set sail a year later, Tromp seized the craft and took them to Flushing. Strickland eventually managed to secure their release and they returned to England in early September 1644.[181] The situation only really improved after the *St Michiel* judgement. On 9 February 1645 the *St Michiel* sailed out of Dunkirk, heading for Newcastle with a consignment of arms. When a Zeeland warship stopped it the captain, Christiaen Robijn, claimed to be a resident of England and therefore a neutral, as was his ship. Others, however, retorted that he lived at Nieuport in Flanders. Eventually, it was decided that the determining factor would be the nationality of the ship. As a result, no English-registered vessel could be confiscated for carrying prohibited goods, though searches were still made for contraband. Shortly afterwards, van Haesdonck and Allen sailed out of Dunkirk with shiploads of arms.[182]

In the first couple of years of the war William Sandys was the most prominent person engaged in gunrunning from Flanders. From his base at Dunkirk he negotiated with merchants, encouraging them to take arms to the Royalists by the promise of fair dealing and a return cargo.[183] He also carried on a correspondence with officials and commanders in the places served, badgering them to act in a way that would encourage merchants to return with further consignments. On 5 January 1644 Sandys informed Captain Strachan at Weymouth of the departure from Rotterdam of the *Fortune* in which 'a very espeteall friend', Mr Brown, was coming with a cargo of 300 barrels of gunpowder. Strachan was told to treat him well and pay him promptly. Sandys also told Strachan that as he was shortly going to send him £12,000 worth of arms, he had to exert himself and arrange for the merchant to procure a return cargo.[184]

The scale of the business Sandys generated is indicated by a contract he made with John Shaw, a wealthy London merchant, based at Antwerp, on 8 December 1643. Shaw agreed to supply 6,000 muskets (at 21s each), 1,000 pairs of pistols (51s a pair), 1,000 carbines (31s each) and 20 tons of match (£37 a ton).[185] It was later reported that in these early years Sandys had sent 40,000 arms to the north and west. By March 1645, when this assessment was made, he had left Dunkirk for France. At the time Lord Goring described him as 'a most faithful, careful and industrious servant of his Majesty', but it was later claimed that he had been involved in a fraud. He certainly left his associate, John Clarke, with a bill for 7,735 florins for arms sent to Weymouth, for which he asked Digby for repayment. Nonetheless, Clarke was still carrying on the business; he informed Digby that he had arranged with two English merchants to ship 1,500 muskets and 150 pairs of pistols, and had contracted with resident Dutch merchants for 200 pairs of pistols.[186]

Of all the Flemish merchants who supplied arms to the Royalists, van Haesdonck was the most successful.[187] Initially, he supplied Newcastle's army in the north, but by autumn 1643 he was operating between Flanders and the Channel ports. On 26 October 1643 he signed a contract to deliver to Weymouth 4,000 muskets and bandoliers at 24s each, 1,200 pairs of pistols, with holsters and spanners, at 56s a pair, 600 carbines, with bolts and swivels, at 32s each, 20 tons of match at £40 a ton and 400 barrels of gunpowder at £5 15s a barrel. The total value of the goods (which were more expensive than London manufacturers were charging Parliament) amounted to £12,200, for which he received a bond for £14,000. He had delivered the goods by 19 February. In April 1645 he sailed out of Dunkirk with four frigates bound for Pendennis Castle, with 6,040 muskets, 2,000 pairs of pistols, 1,200 carbines, 150 swords, 400 shovels, 12 tons of match and 22¼ tons of brimstone.[188] Van Haesdonck was no ordinary merchant, for he was also a mercenary soldier and a privateer. He received letters of marque on 20 December 1643 and by mid-1645 commanded ten ships.[189] Daniel van Hecke was another Fleming who assisted the royalists. In August 1643 he sent a cargo of arms and ammunition from Dunkirk to Bristol in *The Lady of Assistance*. Although some of the arms proved to be unserviceable, Sir Ralph Hopton asked for a share of them to tide him over until production in the city could be stepped up.[190]

Parliamentarian merchants also traded in the Spanish Netherlands. They bought all manner of arms and armaments there, though the evidence suggests that the country was particularly valued as a source of munitions, especially in the early stages of the war. In February 1643 five merchants, including John Freeman, sent 8 tons 8 cwt of Flemish gunpowder to the Ordnance Office stores. That month Freeman also imported 2,750 lb of Dutch gunpowder. In April and May he dispatched 80 barrels to the Committee of Safety magazine.[191] Flemish match was also imported, notably for the New Model Army in 1645–6. Freeman and his associate, Thomas Steventon, separately bought match for the Ordnance Office there, normally several hundredweight at a time but on occasion in tons. Daniel Judd, Thomas Andrews, and two partners, Richard Arnold and John Young, made single deliveries totalling 17½ tons.

Richard Hill and William Pennoyer maintained an agent at Dunkirk, a local merchant named Philipe de Pape, and must have carried on a regular business there, if not solely in arms. An anti-Parliamentarian bias is perhaps discernible in the trouble they had in sending the consignment of arms noted above.[192] They had obtained the arms at Liège early in 1643 but because of the combined actions of the Royalist resident, de Vicq, the Spanish authorities and the Dutch navy, they did not arrive in England for a year and a half. The arms were first of all stopped by de Vicq, who pointed out to the authorities that they were to be used by rebels of the king and therefore contraband. According to the law, he claimed a one-third part of the merchandise. The governor de Mello appears to have quietly shelved the case and the arms spent the winter at de Pape's house. The following spring Parliament sent a special envoy, William Spencer, to expedite the matter and by the end of April he had managed to release the cargo. However, Admiral Tromp, acting on another Royalist rumour, namely that the merchandise was bound for Spain, seized it![193]

France and Denmark

Charles I also sought help from the kings of France and Denmark, respectively his brother-in-law and uncle. However, the response was disappointing. Not only did they give less assistance than he had hoped for but they also took little action against his rebels. Indeed, Louis XIII countenanced arms shipments to the Irish rebels and Christian IV allowed ships, bound for Scotland with soldiers and arms, through the Sound. The French government may have promised support to Charles's representatives there but gave little material aid. When Montagu returned to the United Provinces in January 1643, having been sent to the French court by Henrietta Maria, he brought with him her brother's good wishes but little else.[194] Even the queen, who fled to France in July 1644, could make little impression. She was received with the honour befitting her rank, and generous provision was made for her, but she soon realised that she would receive nothing for her husband's cause.[195] Parliamentarians gained the same impression. On his return from France in April 1645, the Earl of Exeter reported that 'there is no thought of sending any supplies out of that country to the King'.[196] Unfortunately for Parliament, it was even less likely to gain French governmental support. With regard to Denmark, the Royalists did obtain supplies from Christian IV but they were infrequent and seem to have had political and commercial strings attached. Parliament fared worse, partly because its ships seized Danish vessels gunrunning to the Royalists. Such incidents soured relations between the two parties and for this reason, if for no other, Parliament received few arms from this source.

Typically, many merchants took a different view, especially if, like the French, they only had to make a short (though dangerous) sea crossing. Some of them did ship arms to England, mainly to the Royalists. In spite of Trevor's assertion in May 1645, that the Royalists had not sufficiently courted French merchants,[197] gunrunning across the Channel did develop. In 1644 Lord Digby asked Ambassador Goring to encourage merchants to bring in arms and ammunition, which he set about doing. In a letter to Nicholas on 21 June he claimed that he had personally invested in the business, backing it up with details of a contract worth £20,000, secured on his own credit, for 2,000 swords and 20,000 muskets. Moreover, French merchants responded to the king's proclamation, declaring that arms could be traded custom-free.[198] Even so, the trade was not as extensive as that with the Irish Confederacy, probably because greater profits were to be made there. As Thomas Andrews and Stephen Estwick employed agents in France as well as in Holland to fulfil the large order placed by the Committee of Safety at the beginning of the Civil War, Parliament obtained supplies from that country, too. However, there is little subsequent documentation of the trade and it probably was not that important. Occasionally, there are references to French pistols, usually because they were too large to go into standard-sized holsters and had to have special ones made. Thomas Toll, a King's Lynn merchant, delivered 120 pairs of French pistols, 60 holsters and some muskets to the Eastern Association in May 1644, the consignment being valued at £257 12s. In September of that year one Francis, a saddler on the Strand, had French saddles in stock.[199]

Initially, trade between France and the Royalists was restricted by the shortage of suitable points of entry. Only one or two Cornish ports were available, notably Falmouth and Penryn. In November 1642 Royalists at St Malo sent a consignment of weapons, ordnance and munitions to Penryn for Sir Ralph Hopton's forces in Cornwall but it was seized by Parliamentarian ships off the Scilly Isles.[200] The situation improved during the course of 1643 as the Royalists swept through the south-west; by the end of the year they controlled every port between Weymouth and Bristol, with the exception of Lyme and Plymouth. As a result, the arms trade with France picked up in the autumn and continued to grow through the winter. The arms were shipped mainly from Le Havre or upstream from Rouen, though Calais, St Malo and Morlaix in Brittany were also involved in gunrunning.[201] In the Second Civil War the same ports were used. In the summer of 1648 a shipload of arms left Le Havre for either Tenby or Pembroke, while the defenders of Colchester requested munitions from English supporters at Calais. In this respect, the geography of gunrunning to the English Royalists was different from that with Ireland. Naturally, skippers had to look out for Parliamentarian warships as they crossed the Channel, but at least they did not have to pass through the Straits of Dover. The queen, as ever, was active in obtaining supplies. If the government would not help, she could still buy arms and encourage merchants to engage in the trade. She even extended her own credit. In May 1645 she sent 400 barrels of gunpowder to Dartmouth, but merchants would not take it until she put up the security, lest they were not paid in England.[202]

The development of arms trafficking with France, especially through Le Havre, increased the importance of Weymouth; Lord Goring, for instance, promoted the trade.[203] Of course, as the nearest port to Oxford it drew in arms from further afield and, as such, was a vital asset to the Royalists. In February 1645 Lord Digby said of Weymouth that it was 'a port of high consequence in relation to all foreigne helpes of which we have great assurances'.[204] The first French merchants who landed arms at Weymouth seem to have arrived by accident on 26 November 1643. Captains Lewer and Tresaer, *en route* to Falmouth, were forced to seek shelter at Weymouth because of the westerly winds, carrying 250 barrels of gunpowder in their ships' holds. A third ship returned to France with 1,000 pistols and carbines on board. Strachan saw his opportunity to foster a valuable trading connection and wrote to Lord Percy at Oxford for a bill of credit from the treasurer to Mr Witt, the collector at Weymouth, so that he could purchase the gunpowder. Paying the captains ready money would give them a favourable impression of Weymouth, he said, and they were likely to spread the word at Le Havre.[205] Indeed, other merchants did come to Weymouth, mainly bringing munitions but a variety of weapons, too. The loss of the port in March 1645, which Nicholas declared 'a verie vnlucky blow to the Affaires of the West', seriously damaged the Royalist war effort.[206]

Charles I certainly expected his uncle, Christian IV of Denmark, to help him, even though he should have been wary after his experience during the Bishops' Wars.[207] Christian did ship arms to him but exacted his price. Arms had to be bought, money repaid and concessions given.[208] During the course of 1642 Charles sent Sir John Cochrane and Colonel John Henderson as envoys to solicit arms. Henderson asked for weapons for 2,000 horse and 10,000 foot, 24 cannon, (ranging from 4 to 12-pounders, each with 100 cannonballs) 20 tons of saltpetre and a considerable amount of match. He also requested £100,000 sterling and the use of some warships to transport the goods.[209] After some delay, Christian did release some supplies but the four ships that docked at Newcastle with 6,000 suits of armour and a considerable amount of money, also brought Cochrane, the Danish envoy, Ulfeldt, and Christian's terms. Apart from the Orkneys and Shetlands, he also wanted Newcastle in pawn. The following year, when John Poley travelled to Denmark to seek further arms, Charles had again to offer possession of the Orkneys and Shetlands as security.[210] Christian dispatched one of his ships, the *Arken*, with arms but it was captured by Parliament off Tynemouth in August. In January 1644 two Danish ships managed to evade the blockade and landed their arms at Newcastle. By then, war had broken out between Denmark and Sweden and arms were needed at home. At the same time, Christian's interest cooled, calculating that Charles had neither the money to pay for the arms nor the means to deliver the Orkneys and Shetlands as security now that the Scottish Covenanters had allied themselves to Parliament.[211] Nonetheless, Charles persisted, Henderson travelled to Denmark in April 1644 and Cochrane followed a month later. Charles specifically wanted £100,000, 6,000 muskets, 1,500 suits of cavalry armour and 20 mounted cannon, as well as detachments of cavalry. He promised to replace the arms as soon as he could, to repay the money and to meet the charges of the soldiers, offering part of the Crown jewels as collateral.[212]

Relations between Denmark and Parliament, never good, began badly with the imprisonment of Ulfeldt and Cochrane, who visited Parliament at the end of 1642 after the meeting with Charles.[213] This made it less likely that the Parliamentarian forces would obtain arms from Denmark, although indirectly they did acquire them from that source. When the Earl of Warwick captured the *Arken* he took 476 barrels of gunpowder, 990 bundles of match, 197 cannonballs, 14 lead pigs, 2,977 muskets with 3,000 bandoliers and rests, 493 pairs of pistols with 1 firkin of firestones and 1 firkin of spanners, 3,040 swords with numerous belts, hangers and girdles, 1,500 pikes, 150 belly pieces of armour and 3,000 headpieces, 50 drums, 500 Swedish feathers, 1 firkin of powder flasks and 2 kilderkins of bullet moulds.[214] Parliament returned the ship but retained the arms, immediately putting them to use. Five loads went to Cambridgeshire.[215]

The appropriation of the arms so enraged Christian that he ordered the crews of English merchantmen to be imprisoned. He also seized goods belonging to the city of London and sold them off as compensation for his loss. Imports from London were banned.[216] Moreover, his control of Hamburg meant that Parliament was cut off from a valuable source of supply; in March 1643, for instance, William Beale, Edward Boulton and John Freeman had delivered 10 tons of Hamburg gunpowder to the Tower.[217] In an attempt to restore good relations Parliament mounted several missions to Denmark between 1643 and 1645, putting added pressure on the Danes by capturing a Danish merchant ship, the *Golden Sun*, in 1644. On 26 April 1645, the two sides came to an agreement, whereby they undertook to pay compensation to each other. Financially, Christian gained the better deal but Parliament secured the lifting of the restriction on the shipment of arms from Hamburg. Further seizures of Danish ships by Parliament continued to bedevil relations,[218] though Christian was quite willing for arms ships bound for Parliamentarian ports to sail through the Sound as long as they paid the full toll.[219]

Ireland

Although the Irish Royalists were themselves short of arms, they were still asked to send supplies to England, especially to the forces in Chester, north Wales and the Isle of Man. As the king's forces retreated to the west, the importance of Irish armaments grew. Ormond did what he could, responding to requests for arms, mainly for munitions and cannon. As the Archbishop of York lamented in August 1644, 'Onleye powder we infinitelye want, & haue noe hope of supplie but from thence.'[220] The flow of arms began shortly after the cessation, which freed men and weaponry for England. With Parliamentarian forces invading north-east Wales in November, the timing was opportune. Supplies were directed to the garrisons at Beaumaris, Conway and Chester, in particular, and were essentially defensive in nature. In October Captain Thomas Bartlett transported 4 demi-culverins, 14 barrels of gunpowder, a small proportion of match and 400 cannonballs to Beaumaris for use at the new fort there. Two whole culverins should have been sent, too, but they were too heavy to put in the ship.[221]

In January 1644 Prince Rupert assumed the command of the region's army, but, finding himself short of arms, had to argue for them by proxy at Court in the face of opposition from rival factions.[222] He also turned to Ireland for supplies, on 19 February Trevor, an ally, informed Ormond that he would receive a letter from the queen asking him to furnish Rupert with arms and gunpowder. The following day Lord Digby sent a servant, Richard Shirley, to Ireland to buy arms. The letter Shirley took with him assured merchants with whom he dealt that if they were to take arms or gunpowder to Chester, Beaumaris or Bristol (especially the first two ports), they would obtain reasonable rates for their wares. In March Rupert employed Sir Edmund Butler in Ireland in a similar capacity.[223] Rupert's successful relief of Newark on 21 March transformed the political situation and opened up the doors of the magazine to him.[224]

Rupert's triumph did not alter the fundamental weakness of the Royalist logistical position, however, and they continued to look to Ireland (and elsewhere) for arms. In April Ormond, faced with requests for ordnance for Beaumaris and the Isle of Man, which he could not meet, decided on Beaumaris, reasoning that possession of north Wales was vital if the link with Ireland were to be maintained.[225] The capture of Liverpool on 9 June temporarily improved the lines of communication; five days later Digby told Rupert that he had built them a bridge with Ireland and promptly dispatched a letter to his Irish agents, asking for 200 barrels of gunpowder.[226] Liverpool was retaken on 1 November and Chester, once more, became the key to communication between north Wales and the Marches, and Ireland. Parliament had always recognised its importance and besieged it several times. Munitions in particular were in short supply; Ormond commented on 'how seasonable gunpowder will be to Lord Byron' when he sent twenty barrels with Captain Floyd on 8 October. In December a deserter from the city told the besieging force that the garrison had about forty barrels left and lacked brimstone to make any more. Significantly, on 20 February 1645, Prince Maurice asked Ormond for gunpowder and match, adding that if he could not send match, he should provide brimstone, flax, tow or hemp so that they could make it themselves.[227]

Munitions were still needed later in the year, especially when in early September Brereton invested the city for the fourth time. The failure of the relieving force on the 23rd virtually sealed Chester's fate. Piqued, Byron berated those who had ignored his pleas for supplies and pointed out that the fall of the city would render peace with the Confederates 'useless'. Further requests for supplies were sent to Ormond[228] and the city held out into the new year. However, on 2 February Byron, on hearing of the failure of the Glamorgan mission to the Confederacy, and with it all hope of Irish reinforcements, surrendered to Brereton.[229]

Ormond's resources were evidently not sufficient for the task and he was obliged to obtain arms from other sources. Some came from abroad, via the merchants with whom he arranged his own supplies. They had to be paid promptly, however. In February 1644 Ormond told Digby that he had had to settle the account for a consignment of thirty casks of gunpowder sent to him out of his own pocket. He advised him that if he wanted further supplies he would have to establish proper procedures for payment for 'the necessary conveniences and encouragement to ye marchants who are to furnish it out of Holland'.[230] He also sought the assistance of those who dealt with the Confederates. In October 1643 Ormond informed Bridgeman at Chester, the Archbishop of York at Conway, and the sheriff of Anglesey, that he had sent blank warrants to all merchants and captains at ports under Confederate control, promising them that if they took war materials to Chester or Beaumaris, they would receive safe conduct and ready money. It had some effect for the following month Nicholas wrote to Ormond to ask him to issue a free licence to Captain Bamber, who was bringing gunpowder from Wexford.[231] He also dealt directly with the Confederates for arms for the Royalists. In autumn 1643 they contributed 7½ barrels of gunpowder to a 20-barrel consignment that Ormond sent to Prince Rupert.[232] He probably also passed on some of the arms he had acquired from the Catholics himself.

At the same time, the Royalists approached the Confederacy for military supplies. In January 1644 Rupert, aware of shortages in arms in his new command, sought weapons and munitions from this source as well as the Irish Royalists. On the 18th he asked for 5,000 muskets and 300 barrels of of gunpowder from the Supreme Council.[233] Before replying, the council enquired of Ormond whether it could set off any arms it provided against arrears due under the terms of the cessation. On 8 March Ormond reported these negotiations to Digby, adding that if arms were sent to England, an equivalent value in money, victuals or cloth would have to be shipped back for the army.[234] However, in its reply to Rupert on 26 March the council wrote that it felt unable to accede to the request. It had its own shortages to contend with and this made it difficult to meet existing demands: the needs of the army, then preparing for the new campaigning season; the arms promised to Ormond; and the supplies to be given to Antrim for the expedition to the Western Isles.[235] Rupert tried again shortly afterwards, writing to Lord Taaffe for 4,000 muskets and 200 barrels of gunpowder, but to no avail. The following year a further request for 30 barrels of gunpowder was similarly rebuffed, reference being made to the scarcity of gunpowder and threats from Parliamentarians and Covenanters.[236]

While military considerations were important, the Confederates also manipulated the situation for their own political ends. By the beginning of 1645 (and probably earlier too) they seem to have been withholding supplies from the increasingly desperate Royalists, in order to induce them to conclude a peace on terms favourable to themselves. The result was the ill-fated mission undertaken by the Earl of Glamorgan, Lord Herbert, in of 1645–6 in which material support was traded for religious concessions to the Irish Catholics. In the agreement, signed on 25 August, the Confederates promised to send an army of 10,000 men to serve under Glamorgan anywhere in England, Scotland or Wales. Both sides agreed to keep the treaty secret until after the expeditionary force had set out because it would have been unacceptable to Ormond and the Protestant establishment.[237] Unfortunately, the troops were not immediately forthcoming, and the deteriorating situation at Chester made Glamorgan increasingly concerned about delays in implementing the agreement. When the news finally leaked out it caused a furore, and on New Year's Eve Ormond arrested Glamorgan for treason.[238] Publication of the terms clearly compromised the king and Ormond and they quickly repudiated Glamorgan and his treaty. Nonetheless, controversy surrounds the extent of their knowledge. Did Glamorgan act on his own initiative to establish secret contact with the Confederates, while Ormond was openly negotiating with them, or did he do it with covert official blessing?[239]

Released from prison on bail on 22 January 1646, Glamorgan returned to Kilkenny, promising Ormond that he would try to persuade the council to agree to a public treaty. At first, events went well and soldiers were mustered; 18 March was fixed as the date of sailing. Unfortunately, things then started to go badly wrong. The ships did not arrive, Glamorgan ran out of money and Chester capitulated. Stalling for time, he asked Ormond to extend the cessation. He intended to go to France, he declared, and would return with twenty ships at least, £40,000 in cash, 10,000 muskets, 2,000 cases of pistols, 800 barrels of gunpowder and 'a gallant trayne' of artillery. Glamorgan's house of cards came tumbling down when Ormond did not agree to an extension and when the king repudiated his commission to arrange a treaty.[240] Ormond, realising the need to come to an accommodation with the Confederates, if the Royalist cause were to be retrieved, negotiated his own truce on 15 September.[241]

CONCLUSION

How vital were these imports to the various parties involved in the Civil Wars? They all relied upon them to sustain their war effort at a certain level but, undoubtedly, the degree to which they depended upon them did vary and might change over time. The Scottish Covenanters, with a comparatively small manufacturing base at home, could not have waged war very effectively without the huge quantities of weapons they acquired from abroad. The Irish, using the element of surprise, initially obtained arms from their enemy but failed to capture the all-important arsenal at Dublin Castle. In spite of controlling a large portion of the country they too could not have carried on for very long if they had not received so many foreign arms.

To deal with both sets of insurgents the king had to import war material, too. Gunpowder was particularly needed because of a fall in home production, partly caused by Charles I's manipulation of the gunpowder monopoly for fiscal reasons. By the time that the Irish rebelled, virtually no gunpowder was being sent to the Tower, and little was available either. Moreover, in spite of England's tradition in gunfounding, many foreign cannon had to be imported. Initially, the bulk of the hand arms were also obtained from overseas, although according to a contemporary estimate (a somewhat optimistic one), by the time of Sir John Harby's shopping trip in Flanders in 1640, over half of the arms were either in store or being made in England.

The loss of London to the Parliamentarians during the course of 1642 made it difficult for the Royalists to secure enough arms and armaments at home to fight a war. To supplement the weapons they managed to gather in, they had to import arms on a massive scale. Even so, some of the soldiers who left Shrewsbury in September 1642 were armed with cudgels and pitchforks.[242] Arms production was developed and under the circumstances the Royalists did reasonably well. However, output was much lower than that achieved by Parliament, even when allowance is made for the poor quality of the evidence. Munitions, for instance, always seemed to be in short supply and, as a result, were prominent in overseas cargoes. In general, then, the impression given is that the arms shipments were vital to the prosecution of the war and that without them the ability of the Royalists to carry on the conflict would have been seriously impaired. The loss of their ports in 1644 and 1645, therefore, proved fatal to the king's cause.

Parliament should have been better placed to wage war. In the long term its control of the south-east and its arms industries proved an important asset, but at the opening of hostilities it had problems. Most of the leading officials of the Ordnance Office had left to join the king, and the administration was in disarray. Moreover, it had little gunpowder and none could be produced. Imports from abroad, mostly from the Low Countries, helped bridge the gap (see Table 3). Even greater reliance had to be made on foreign match. Similarly, pressing need meant that most of the weapons had to be imported. The situation gradually improved and by the end of 1643 home producers had begun to make a real contribution. By early 1645 native manufacturers were responsible for providing well over half of the arms and armaments needed. Imports were still required, of course, especially items such as gunpowder, match and self-igniting firearms, for which raw materials or the necessary skills were lacking at home. Although over half of the gunpowder was made in the country, most of the saltpetre (and all of the sulphur) had to be obtained from overseas. In addition, many of the swords had foreign blades. The equipping of the New Model Army marks a significant change, for most of the business was put out to a comparatively small group of native contractors. For the Irish and Scottish campaigns of the years 1649–52, Parliament was able to procure the bulk of its supplies at home.

9

SHIPPING, NAVAL ACTION AND INTERNAL TRANSPORT

The effort required to put weapons in the hands of the soldiers in the British Civil Wars was a considerable one, but the degree to which the task was successfully accomplished had a profound effect on the course of events. Taken as a whole, the supply network was immense, incorporating (selectively) most of Europe, and employing large numbers of people. Agents and factors abroad may have been involved in the initial stages, negotiating with manufacturers, merchants, boatmen and carters for delivery of *matériel* at the dockside, and then making arrangements with ships' masters to transport it home. It helped if foreign merchants took the initiative and organised their own carriage. The sea crossing was a time of particular danger. Apart from the natural hazards of tide and weather, there were blockades to be run and the ever-present menace of privateers to contend with. Once unloaded at a British port, consignments joined home-produced arms being taken to a magazine for storage or perhaps being sent directly to a theatre of war. Wherever possible, goods were moved by water, either along navigable rivers or around the coast, though, in practice, a good deal of traffic passed along the roads. Many consignments went partly by road and partly by water. Each side possessed its own ships but contracted for others. Internally, armies tended to hire carters and boatmen, though they also kept some carrying capacity in hand. Other essential workers included the people who made the containers or materials in which the arms were packed or the vehicles in which they were transported.

RUNNING THE GAUNTLET: SHIPPING AND NAVAL ACTION

As demonstrated in an earlier chapter, overseas trade sustained the war effort of all sides. Thousands of ships plied between the British Isles and the continent every year, many of them making more than one journey. Without the arms they brought in, the armies would not have been properly equipped, and without the merchandise they took out, Treasury officials would have had difficulty meeting military costs. Action at sea, therefore, concentrated on securing one's own trading links and trying to interrupt those of the enemy. Instead of large set-piece battles, ships were involved in small-scale skirmishes and attacks on commercial traffic, as well as in such activities as blockading or relieving ports, ferrying goods and convoying merchantmen. In this respect, Charles I's employment of ship money to build up his fleet in the 1630s appears remarkably prescient. The imposition of the tax did provoke opposition to him but the extra vessels would have proved a vital asset in the ensuing conflict. With a powerful fleet, he could have imported arms and equipment more freely, paying for them with the profits of trade, secured by naval protection. In addition, he could have mounted an effective blockade of Parliamentarian ports, strangling their trade and hampering the import of arms. In particular, pressure on London's commercial links with the outside world would seriously have impaired the economic strength of the capital, which provided the financial motor for the Parliamentarian war effort.[1] For the same reasons, the other parties in the various conflicts sought to build up their navies.

The Navies

Unfortunately for the king, the fleet went over to Parliament in July 1642 and his opponents benefited from his efforts. According to a list of ships earmarked for the summer guard, the Earl of Warwick, the Parliamentarian admiral, took over eighteen men-of-war and twenty-four armed merchantmen.[2] Although contemporary reports reveal that the navy did have some success in keeping Parliamentarian trade channels open, as well as seizing enemy shipping and blockading their ports, it had too few ships properly to fulfil each task. In addition, some of the navy's resources were switched to the army. Matters came to a head in the winter of 1644, a time when the delay in sending out the winter guard had placed merchant shipping at greater risk.[3] In February 1644 Warwick complained to Parliament that he had insufficient ships, too little money and an inadequate supply of *matériel* and provisions. In 1644 the summer guard comprised 30 warships and 38 merchantmen and the following year 32 and 25 respectively.[4] In 1645 the *Constant Warwick*, a 300-ton frigate with 26 guns and manned by 120 sailors, was built for a private consortium but hired by the navy. It was the first of eight fast frigates that had come into service by the end of 1647 and which were needed to counteract the threat of the privateers.[5] In 1646 the summer fleet had risen to 44 warships and 20 merchantmen, with a further 33 armed merchant ships held in reserve. In 1647 it consisted of 49 warships, 13 merchantmen and 29 reserves.[6] In 1648 a large part of the fleet mutinied, declared for the Royalists, and sailed for Holland. Although the revolt was eventually quelled, it left the navy temporarily in a weakened state. At least, the crisis led to reform and an improvement in the situation in 1649. Six new frigates were built that year and a further ten in 1650.[7]

The king made use of the royal navy in the Bishops' Wars and in the initial stages of the Irish rebellion, but its defection to Parliament in 1642 put him at a disadvantage in the English conflict. The loss of his prized ships was a blow to Charles; in March 1644, angling for Danish support, he complained to Christian IV of Denmark that, as he had too few warships, he would have to arm merchantmen or hire privately owned ships. He could do so because the capture of almost all the south-western ports during the course of 1643 enabled him to press into service a number of ships and to create a substitute navy. At the end of October the Venetian ambassador, commenting on the fall of Dartmouth and the capture of forty merchantmen there, thought (with some exaggeration) that these additions made the Royalist navy larger than the Parliamentarian one. The following February Warwick calculated that the Royalists could draw on 260 ships of 50–300 tons.[8] Charles I also looked abroad to augment his fleet, either by purchase or hire. In May 1644 William Sandys at Dunkirk was engaged in negotiations with a ship builder, Jacques van der Walle, for twelve small frigates, powered by oars. The deal fell through because the king would not agree to the price asked. In October the following year John Webster was making enquiries at Amsterdam about the purchase or hire or four to six ships. He informed ambassador Boswell that for £20,000 he could secure the services of four ships and two frigates for three months, fully manned, victualled and armed. Webster had also asked for information on ships at Enkhuizen and Rotterdam and in Zeeland. Nonetheless, he did think it better to buy than to hire. The Royalists continued to pursue this practice of employing foreign ships and personnel throughout the period. In 1649, for instance, Theodore Dommer, an Amsterdam merchant, offered to put himself and his six warships at the disposal of the king, Charles II, for an agreed sum, half of which was to be paid immediately.[9]

The recruitment of such men ensured that the structure and chain of command of the new Royalist fleet was far looser than before, more decentralised, and reliant on individuals working under contract or acting as privateers. In an agreement made in November 1643, one such person, Jeronimo Caesar de Caverle, obtained an independent commission, nominally as a vice-admiral under the Earl of Marlborough, in return for furnishing five 'able' ships and 500 men armed and provisioned at his own expense. He was to employ his ships against the rebels and to receive £2,000 a month to be paid out of the profits made from the prizes taken. In 1645 shipowners at Dartmouth and Falmouth were reminded that as part of their commission they had to put their frigates at the king's disposal for six weeks, but essentially they were privateers.[10] Men like Sir Nicholas Crispe and the Fleming, Jan van Haesdonck, who together provided over two dozen ships for the king, operated with a great deal of freedom.

The loss of the south-western ports during the course of 1645 and 1646 was a huge setback for the Royalists. When Falmouth surrendered in August 1646 the fleet was forced to flee to the Scilly Isles and then, shortly afterwards, to the safer harbour of Jersey.[11] Many Royalist privateers decamped to Ireland or to ports on the southern side of the Channel. For a brief period in 1648 dissent in the ranks of the Parliamentarian navy offered the Royalists the opportunity to take the initiative. With the Parliamentarians in complete disarray and many ships' crews mutinous, decisive action by the Royalists might have destroyed the remnant of Warwick's fleet. However, in the critical summer months the Prince of Wales proved irresolute and in August after a certain amount of shadow-boxing between the two sides in the Downs, he broke off, taking the fleet to Holland. Followed by Warwick, it was his turn to be trapped. A battle was averted because Tromp, the Dutch admiral, positioned his ships between the two sides. Desertion and capture reduced the size of the Royalist navy and Prince Rupert only managed to extricate the rump of his fleet in January 1649 when the Earl of

Warwick unexpectedly withdrew all his ships to the Downs. Rupert sailed to Kinsale where he joined up with Irish privateers.[12] By spring 1649 the Parliamentarians had thoroughly overhauled the organisation of the fleet and had re-established control. Rupert was blockaded at Kinsale but it was only when Cromwell's invasion force threatened him from the land that the prince felt it necessary to leave. On 20 October he escaped with seven ships and sought refuge in Portugal. Ejected from Lisbon in October, he spent some time preying on shipping in the Mediterranean, and even incorporated voyages to the West Indies. Eventually, in 1652, he ran out of ships.[13]

The Scottish Covenanters, in the build-up to the Bishops' Wars, were particularly interested in securing the advantages that a fleet of their own would bring. Not only were their supply lines extremely long but they also had to ship war material past two of the strongest navies in Europe, those of Denmark and England. In May 1639 Sir Francis Windebank, Charles's Secretary of State, was informed that twenty to thirty Dutch ships, to be manned by Scottish and Dutch crews, were being prepared to attack English ships as soon as war broke out. If merely a rumour, it had a basis in fact. The following month, Sir Patrick Drummond, at Veere, reported that a frigate, ordered by an Edinburgh merchant, David Junkin, was being built at Flushing. The ship, a 20-gunner, was to be given to the Marquess of Argyll, the Covenanters' leader.[14] In April 1640 Sir John Cochrane was sent to Sweden with a request for ships and arms. In the same year Thomas Cuningham and his partners fitted out a frigate for the Covenanters.[15] Later, the fleet seems to have been augmented by privateers operating under letters of marque, for in the Committee of Estates' minutes for 8 November 1645 there is an example of a specimen contract.[16]

Supporters of the Irish insurgents were of the same mind. In July 1642 their French agent, Matthew O'Hartegan, told his Italian counterpart, Luke Wadding, that the Confederacy could never succeed without a dozen good, strong and well-armed ships, of which they had none. In October Hugh Bourke, their agent in Flanders, wished for a number of Dunkirk-type frigates which would 'scour our coasts and damage the enemy'.[17] Although, strictly speaking, the Confederates may not have possessed any ships (Bourke was constantly counting up the cost of buying one), by the autumn the rebels had established a fleet of sorts. At the end of the year it may have been thirty strong.[18] To obtain the ships, agreements were made with privateers; apart from Irish captains, at least twenty letters of marque were issued to Flemings, mainly the infamous Dunkirkers, in the winter of 1642/3.[19] Hardly responsive to discipline, they were nonetheless very effective. By the mid-1640s the fleet may have numbered fifty to sixty warships, of which twenty-one frigates were based at Wexford.[20]

The Irish Royalists were in a similar position. At the beginning of 1642 they only possessed three ships, including two armed merchantmen, and one of these was scuttled shortly afterwards. Thomas Bartlett captained the surviving merchantman, the *Confidence*, and his brother, John, the warship, the *Swan*.[21] To make up numbers they, too, hired or pressed ships into service and gave letters of marque to privateers. In October 1643 there were twelve such ships, ranging from 16–200 tons, which, according to the terms of the agreement, were to serve the king, carry out convoy duty and perform other tasks.[22]

Naval Action

To prevent war materials getting through to the enemy, rival navies patrolled the sea lanes and blockaded ports. By extension, the ships were also used to stifle trade in general by stopping merchantmen going in and coming out. This policy involved the capture of foreign ships as well as those operating out of hostile ports. For the various parties involved in the British Civil Wars the blockade began at a distance and related to the actions of foreign powers pursuing their own policies and war aims. The Danes, for instance, could use their control of the Sound to close the straits to traffic coming from their enemy, Sweden. Of greater concern was the use of this ploy by the Spanish and the Dutch in their long-running conflict. When the Irish rebellion broke out both the king and Parliament sought to utilise the Dutch blockade for their own ends and managed to get the States-General to agree to deploy its ships against gunrunners sailing for Ireland.[23] The blockade had some effect but it was not watertight, mainly because of the cost involved and a lack of ships. For their part, the Dutch had to contend with the attacks made by Flemish privateers on their shipping.[24] From the point of view of the warring parties in Britain it meant that arms ships, plying between the United Provinces and the British Isles, had a hazardous crossing, though craft heading for Royalist or Confederate ports seem to have fared better than those going to Parliamentarian or Covenanting ones.

At home, all sides used the blockade, though there was some reluctance to extend it beyond the search for arms, for fear of alienating neutral merchants at home and abroad. Privateers had no such qualms, of course, and eventually Royalists and Parliamentarians adopted the practice. Ships carrying all manner of goods came under attack.[25] The navy was used in a policing role from the outset. As the situation in Scotland deteriorated in 1638, the royal navy was ordered to search Scottish merchant ships for arms and returning soldiers. By April 1639 twenty Scots ships had reportedly been stopped in the Thames and more had been seized in other ports around Britain. That month Hamilton was sent with a fleet of some thirty ships to blockade the mouth of the Forth. In this way, he could intercept shipping going in or out of the firth or sailing on to ports such as St Andrews, Dundee, Montrose or Aberdeen. Hamilton took three Scottish ships on his way north from Scarborough but then made the mistake of anchoring in the Leith road. From there, he could blockade Edinburgh but could not catch ships docking at other ports in the firth or going further up the coast.[26] Taken overall, the blockade did have some effect on trade, especially on Edinburgh's commerce, but seems to have made little impact on the number of men and the quantity of arms coming in.[27]

Similar attempts were made to stop arms imports reaching the Irish insurgents. On 3 November 1641 there were demands in Parliament for a blockade of the Irish coast and ten days later the Irish Council asked for extra ships to patrol the seas. The council also ordered port officials to impound incoming consignments of arms and munitions. Little was done until January 1642, when the government heard that arms and soldiers at Dunkirk were about to be shipped to Ireland. On 7 January Northumberland, the Lord Admiral, was told to keep an eye on shipping at the port and seize all men and materials bound for Ireland. The convoy slipped past and was only captured because bad weather drove it into an English port.[28] Other consignments were impounded *en route* to Ireland; in June, for instance, two Dunkirkers, laden with 'a great store' of gunpowder for Viscount Mountgarret, were driven into Southampton harbour and their cargoes seized.[29] Unfortunately, because priority was given to guarding the narrow seas, there were insufficient blockading ships in Irish waters to prevent some of the gunrunners from getting through. Sixteen royal naval ships and sixteen merchantmen were allocated to the Downs, whereas only two royal naval ships and eight merchantmen were assigned to the Irish seas.[30]

A shortage of ships similarly hampered Parliament's attempts to cut off supplies when it took over the fleet. As the situation in England worsened, most of the ships were kept in the Downs, and the Irish Sea was left with even less cover.[31] At the beginning of September the Lords Justices wrote to the Irish Committee at London, pointing out the consequences of the failure to blockade Wexford, Galway and Waterford in the spring and, subsequently, other ports. They also drew attention to the gap that had appeared in July when Kettleby and Stradling of the Irish guard, sailed off to join the king at Newcastle. The Lords Justices warned that if replacements were not quickly put on station, nothing could prevent the rebels from receiving supplies from abroad.[32]

Clearly, many arms shipments arrived at their destination, but Warwick's navy did have some success. In a tract of 24 November 1642, entitled *True Newes from our Navie*, an account is given of the capture of a number of ships bound for England, Wales and Ireland. On 5 November two Parliamentarian ships caught a French ship off the Scillies with arms for Sir Ralph Hopton in Cornwall. The following day the fleet, twelve strong, encountered two Turkish privateers on their way to Ireland to sell arms. After a fierce fight the ship and the arms were seized and sent to London. Within four days one of Parliament's smaller vessels brought in a Dutch ship going to Wales with a servant of Lord Digby, taking a request to the Earl of Bristol for money to buy munitions. The following afternoon the fleet spotted two French-built ships but because of their speed could not engage them until the next morning. The ships, which had been bought by Irish Catholics at Dunkirk, carried 12 great barrels of gunpowder, about 100 muskets and 'much' match.[33]

Undoubtedly, the Irish guard was understrength and this made it easier for the Irish Confederates to re-arm and consolidate their position. Ormond and the Irish Council certainly thought so. However, Parliament only had limited resources and it had to decide on its priorities. Naturally, it gave prime consideration to the protection of shipping going to and from its ports, especially London, since it could not afford to have its commerce disrupted and customs receipts threatened. The bulk of the fleet, therefore, had to be stationed in the

Downs. From this vantage point it could guard the approaches to the capital, monitor activity in Low Countries' harbours and intercept traffic sailing through the straits or travelling to north-eastern ports, the main points of entry for Royalist arms. Even before assuming formal command in July, Warwick had achieved a notable success, using the navy to secure the strategic port of Hull and to convoy its magazine to the safety of the Tower of London. Within a few days of taking control in July, Warwick was reporting the capture of a ship laden with gunpowder. In August the Danish ship, the *Arken*, was captured off Tynemouth and in September four coal ships, sailing to Newcastle with 400 lasts of gunpowder and a considerable amount of arms and ammunition, were seized.[34]

Some consignments did evade the net. In July Prince Rupert landed arms at Tynemouth and Captain Strachan beached his ship with its vital cargo in an inlet off the Humber. In February 1643 the queen put in at Bridlington just before a Parliamentarian squadron arrived.[35] As 1643 progressed the cordon tightened. At Newcastle upon Tyne an eyewitness alleged that the only war materials brought in during the winter of 1643/4 were 150 barrels of gunpowder, a few small pieces of ordnance and 500 muskets. In the six months before the city fell to the Scots (on 22 October 1644) the naval blockade penned the colliers in the harbour, cutting off coal exports and with them a major source of income for the king.[36] By that time, of course, the north had been lost and outposts such as Newcastle and Scarborough were irrelevant as distribution points, although they had a value as a means of tying up Parliamentarian resources and threatening their lines of communication.

As the Royalist position in the north deteriorated, the situation in the south-west improved. Military success in the region and the acquisition of a string of ports gave them a secure base; trade flourished and arms flowed in. From there, *matériel* was distributed throughout much of southern England. Parliament, with its naval resources overstretched, had difficulty in coping. As noted above, in February 1644 the Earl of Warwick complained to Parliament about the shortage of ships, sailors, provisions and money. He also claimed that operational effectiveness had been compromised because captains in port were receiving orders from local officials.[37] In spite of the element of special pleading, there was some truth in Warwick's argument. The navy did seize ships but the evidence suggests that many got through. Strachan's correspondence from Weymouth indicates a thriving, bustling port and a key centre for the reception and transmission of military hardware.

Further to the south-west the reciprocal trade in Cornish tin and continental arms continued with little disruption.[38] Even after the region's ports began to fall to the New Model Army in 1645, large consignments were still being unloaded at those that remained. Although Parliament did put pressure on trading links – and the townspeople of Dartmouth, for example, grew restless – gunrunners were still managing to bring in supplies throughout 1645.[39] In general, the performance of the Parliamentarian fleet was rather patchy and by itself did not prevent the import of arms to the Royalists in the region. In fact, the New Model Army proved itself far more capable of closing ports than the navy had been.

Success in the north-east enabled Parliament to transfer ships to Irish waters. As a consequence, the effectiveness of the Irish guard increased, although it was never able completely to sever the links with the continent. One squadron, based at Milford Haven, Pembrokeshire, covered the Bristol Channel, south Wales and southern Ireland. A second one, at Liverpool, blockaded Dublin and the north Wales coast and, as such, was aimed at Royalists as much as at the insurgents.[40] After the cessation of hostilities with the Confederacy in September 1643, which freed arms and men for the king's supporters, the Irish Royalists were targeted with greater regularity. In June 1644 Ormond wryly observed that, having vainly asked Parliament for ships to prevent arms being delivered to the rebels, they were now being used to bottle up the Royalist ports of Dublin, Cork, Kinsale and Youghal. The blockade of Dublin seems to have been quite effective, though it was still possible for a ship to slip out. In autumn 1643, for instance, the revictualling and refitting of the Irish guard allowed Ormond to dispatch shiploads of soldiers back to England to bolster the Royalist cause.[41] The temporary capture of Liverpool, and Royalist successes in Pembrokeshire during the course of 1644, offered some respite and a chance to send over arms and munitions. Trade might be encouraged, too. In September Ormond suggested to the Archbishop of York at Conway that the merchants renew their trading links and bring over coal, provisions and other commodities in demand at Dublin. Unfortunately, Parliamentarian ships blockading Liverpool prevented coal from being shipped out. [42]

The Parliamentarian blockade also hampered the Earl of Antrim's expedition to the Western Isles, led by Alistair MacColla, by making it difficult for him to obtain ships to transport the men and their arms and provisions. Flemish privateers eventually provided three frigates which, after taking the troops to Scotland, were captured by Parliamentarian ships.[43] The threat remained, especially after MacColla's force, stranded in Scotland, joined up with Montrose and won a series of stunning victories over the Covenanting armies. To add to the problem, privateers operating out of Irish and Flemish ports, stepped up their activities in Scottish waters. Vigilance, therefore, had to be maintained and the passage between Ireland and Scotland, in particular, well guarded. Apart from Parliamentarian ships the Covenanters maintained a frigate and a galley off the west coast.[44] Unfortunately, lapses did occur. In October 1644 the Scottish Committee of Estates instructed their commissioners in England to complain to Parliament that they had not maintained the two warships in the Irish Sea, nor the six ships off north-east Scotland, as required by the terms of the treaty. As a result, pirates had captured several of its ships taking victuals to its armies in Ireland and England.[45]

The Royalist fleet carried out similar operations to the ones undertaken by Parliament. It attacked ships sailing to Parliamentarian ports and mounted blockades of their harbours. In November 1643 Sir William Brereton noted that a squadron of eight ships had been hovering off the coast of north Wales for several days and that it had seized a shipment of arms destined for the Cheshire and Lancashire forces.[46] Because the fleet contained a large number of privateers, it was particularly adept at carrying out offensive action on the high seas. From their home bases in the south-western ports they inflicted serious damage on Parliamentarian shipping in the years 1643–5, while at the same time making money for themselves. By mid-December 1643 a number of captured ships had been taken to Dartmouth and this prompted the king to establish ground rules for the assessing and disposing of the prizes. On one occasion in May 1645 van Haesdonck and two other privateers put into Falmouth with a supply of ordnance and seven prize merchantmen, laden with coal, salt and other goods, and a captured Parliamentarian man-of-war of ten guns.[47]

Some Royalist privateers anchored at foreign ports, especially those in Flanders. In March 1645 the Committee of Both Kingdoms, incensed at the capture of the *Mary Anne* of London by the Ostend-based Captain Allen, protested to the governor of Flanders that Allen and his accomplices 'are harboured and countenanced at Ostend and permitted to issue in and out at their pleasure, and to make incursions and depredations upon our peaceful merchants and their friends'.[48] In Ireland, too, loyalist captains like John and Thomas Bartlett were engaged in privateering activities as well as carrying out 'official' business such as mounting guard, gathering information, relaying messages and shipping arms and provisions.

For the Confederates, privateers at ports like Wexford and Waterford proved to be an extremely potent weapon. According to Ormond, Wexford men boasted that they would make the town into a second Dunkirk. Because of their speed and mobility it was difficult for Parliamentarian squadrons to stop them, though they might chase some of them away or regain a slow-moving prize left with a skeleton crew to bring her home. During the course of 1642 Irish Catholic privateers were said to have infested all the coasts of Ireland and to have cut the route between Dublin and the mainland.[49] They never managed to do this entirely but they did disrupt its trade. The privateers continued to wreak havoc the following year. In April John Bowen reported that the harbours of Wexford and Dungarvan were full of 'Puritan' prizes, one of which (he said) was worth £50,000. Two months later privateers were daily attacking ships, even at the mouth of Dublin harbour.[50] Privateers sailed from Flemish, as well as Irish, ports and their impact on the war in Ireland increased after the capture of Dunkirk by the French on 1 October 1646. Many moved to Ireland, strengthening the anti-Parliamentarian forces at a time when the English privateers were being prised out of their strongholds in south-western England. In spite of the assignment of more ships to the Irish Sea and the western approaches, the menace grew.[51]

By 1648 the privateers posed as much a threat in the Channel as they did in the Irish Sea. Hunting in packs, they were immune from attack by Parliamentarian warships. In October, clothing and money for the troops in Ireland had to go overland to Chester because the narrow seas were infested with pirates and there was no escort ship available. Two months later, at least ten supply ships, bound for Dublin, were captured. Between February 1648 and February 1649 the *Mary* of Antrim brought in prizes valued at about £8,000, and the following July the captain of the *St John* of Waterford said that he had lost count of the number of prizes he had taken.[52] In 1649 the privateers were further strengthened by the arrival at Kinsale of Prince Rupert and the Royalist fleet. They were only dislodged from their lairs by the advance of Cromwell's army in the autumn.[53]

Over the whole period, the privateers had been a formidable foe and one which Parliament had only just begun to tame. They had affected the Parliamentarian war effort, capturing innumerable ships and doing a good deal of damage. The number of prizes (from all nations) reputedly taken in the years 1642–50 ranged from 250 to 1,900! Where evidence of the nationality of the prizes is given, it appears as though the English with 78 losses (31 per cent) suffered the most, followed by the Scots with 40 (16 per cent) and the Dutch with 32 (13 per cent). English Parliamentarians and Scottish Covenanters were obvious targets, as were the Dutch to Dunkirkers. The Dutch also paid for their commercial enterprise.[54]

Naval Protection

Although a considerable tonnage of shipping was captured and their cargoes seized, the situation would have been worse if precautionary measures had not been taken. Thus, blockading ships were not merely used to prevent goods getting in and out of enemy ports, but also to pin down their warships. On 26 February 1644 reference is made to Parliamentarian ships 'coasting up and down to scour the Seas, and a free passage for our Merchant men'.[55] This was a service that the Irish Council constantly asked the authorities in London to fulfil as a means of countering the threat posed by Confederate privateers and their associates. In August 1642 they warned that if replacement ships were not sent 'the seas will be infested beyond measure . . . and we deprived of all means of being relieved thence by sea, or of relieving from hence those places we still hold which we now usually relieve by sea'. The following June John Temple, one of the council, wrote, 'We hear of nothing of the ships sent for the guard of these coasts.' The Bartletts performed this duty but they were often absent on other errands.[56] On 10 April 1643 Captain Mugell Lucas of the *Constance* of Yarmouth signed a seven-week agreement to patrol the coast between Dublin and Wicklow. During that time he rescued several ships from the Confederates and also escorted a flotilla of merchantmen, laden with provisions, from Milford to Dublin.[57]

Of course, too few ships were allocated to the task and even when more were sent to guard the Irish coast in 1644, they could do no more than contain the privateers. Ironically, their best opportunity came after a prize had been taken. With a prize or two in tow, even frigates were vulnerable. If, as was customary, some of the crew members were put on board the captured ship, and left to find their own way home, it, too, became an easier target. This is revealed in a sortie that the Wexford-based frigate, *St Francis*, made in spring 1644. On the voyage the captain seized three ships (losing one) and rescued a fourth, bound for Dublin with rye and beans. One of the prizes, a 400-tonner, laden with a valuable cargo of arms and merchandise, was taken in the Thames estuary. A crew was put on board and the frigate sailed off, leaving the men to the mercy of four pursuing Parliamentarian ships.[58]

To protect merchantmen on the high seas a convoy system was developed. This was needed, for although merchantmen were armed, they were at a disadvantage against faster, more mobile warships, especially the frigates of the privateers. They could not provide complete security, however, for privateers often had the edge in terms of ships, gunnery, seamanship and sheer ruthlessness. Very little could be done when confronted by a superior force. In August 1643 the *Tenth Whelp* was escorting a ship with a load of 400 arms, 60 barrels of gunpowder and a number of brass cannon to the Royalist forces at Bristol when it met some Parliamentarian vessels. The merchantman was boarded and the arms taken but the *Tenth Whelp*, 'being a fast sailer', escaped and sailed to Bristol.[59]

In spite of the problem there are numerous references to requests for an armed escort to accompany merchant ships taking arms and provisions. On 2 August 1642, Mr Frost, Commissary for the Victuals, asked for some 'ships of strength' to guard six vessels ready to sail to Leinster and Ulster with corn and victuals. In March 1644 the Committee of Both Kingdoms authorised the sending of ships to look after a consignment of arms coming from Holland. A tour of duty could be quite long and complex. On 24 May 1649 John Coppin, Captain of the *Greyhound*, then at Deptford, embarked on a journey that took in a number of east coast ports, as well as Hamburg, and involved an ever-changing assortment of ships and cargoes.[60] That year, Parliament substantially increased the sum of money allocated to the navy, partly to build ships for escort duty in the Mediterranean, as well as in home waters.[61]

DISTRIBUTION OF ARMS AROUND THE BRITISH ISLES

At home, thousands of people were employed in one aspect of transportation or another. Some of them worked in an official capacity. The Ordnance Office employed a carman for 'carrying and recarrying to & from his Majesties Stoares and other places' those items kept in its magazine in the Tower.[62] The cooper at the Ordnance Office made barrels and casks for the munitions, weapons and equipment and the wheelwright built wagons and gun carriages as well as providing wheels. The smith supplied the metal bindings. During the war the Wagon-Master-General was responsible for the requisition and allocation of wagons and teams. The artillery train had its own wagonmaster, assisted by men, who maintained the wagons in good running order. Conductors supervised the carters and drivers. In 1645 it was reckoned that a train of thirty pieces needed at least ten conductors.[63] The commissary of the draught horses to the train of artillery specifically looked after the animals but dealt with other matters, too.[64] Most people were hired for a set period or to carry out a specific job but some individuals were in continuous employment for a considerable time. Agreements were made with ships' masters and their crews and even privateers might sign contracts. Lightermen transferred goods from the quayside to a ship at anchor, and bargees, keelmen and trowmen took cargoes up and down rivers. On land, carriers, conductors and drivers hired out their carts and teams. An army of labourers and porters carried out the task of loading and unloading.

For the draught, horses were preferred to oxen because of their strength, speed and agility, even if they cost more to keep. An ox could subsist on grass alone but a working horse required oats, pulses or barley as well. However, horses were particularly useful in lowland areas and on light soils where they could make their physical advantages tell.[65] In Ireland oxen were the norm; in England and Wales the Royalists made greater use of them than did the Parliamentarians, partly because of the shortage of draught horses in the north and west but also because oxen possessed certain advantages in hill country and on clayey roads. Prince Maurice, for instance, employed them in his artillery train in the Lostwithiel campaign in autumn 1644.[66] The Royalists, nonetheless, did recognise the superior qualities of horses. In March 1644 the Council of War found that the fifty-three oxen in the artillery train were 'not to bee so fitt and vsefull . . . as horses are' and authorised the Wagon-Master-General and the Commissary of the Draught Horses to sell them and buy horses with the proceeds.[67] Occasionally, depending on location, Parliament hired carters with ox teams.[68]

On the roads, carts or packhorses were used. Road vehicles comprised four-wheeled wagons and the two-wheeled carts, wains and tumbrels. Teams of horses, pulling carts, could move nearly three times as much weight as packhorses but the latter, being smaller and more nimble, were more economical and especially effective on long hauls. They were faster, could travel over rougher ground and were more flexible in their use.[69] The Royalists had more packhorses, a form of conveyance often better suited to the terrain in the areas they controlled. Parliament, on the other hand, not only had more strong draught horses but could also deploy the large Dutch four-wheeled wagons that had been introduced onto the roads and farms of lowland England in the early seventeenth century.[70] The number of vehicles and animals required was huge, especially if a field army was on the march. Carts and wagons normally had teams of four to six horses to pull them but the larger ordnance pieces needed far more. It took up to seventy horses to pull the grandest piece of all, a cannon royal.[71] Not surprisingly, they were carried by water for as much of the journey as possible.

English Traffic: The Bishops' Wars

If the militia forces raised to fight the Scottish Covenanters were expected to come to the rendezvous at York in April 1639 fully armed and equipped, the Ordnance Office still had to arrange for the bulk transportation of arms, especially ordnance and munitions. Edward Byworth, the carman at the Ordnance Office, moved supplies around the capital, taking them from the workshops to the Tower for storage or from the Tower to Tower Wharf.[72] Lighters plied to and from the shore, ferrying war materials from the quayside to hired ships anchored in the river. Hoys, based at a number of ports in the Thames estuary and the east coast, transported arms to naval ships waiting downstream at Chatham, and coasters shipped *matériel* direct to the north. Several supply bases were established, notably at Hull, Newcastle and Holy Island.

In February 1639 a shipment was sent to the Marquess of Huntly at Aberdeen to arm Royalists in the area. Weapons for the soldiers at York were brought from Hull along the River Ouse.[73] Arms moved between the magazines: northwards during the build-up and southwards after the pacification of Berwick in June. Some military hardware, including thirty-three cannon, remained in these northern arsenals, reducing the amount that had to be transported from the south in the Second Bishops' War. Nonetheless, between 20 May and 19 August 1640 29 cannon, with shot and accoutrements, 21 lasts of gunpowder, 7 tons of match and 26 tons of lead shot and thousands of weapons, were sent to ports such as Grimsby, Hull and Newcastle.[74] Unfortunately, when the decisive battle of Newburn was fought on 28 August, the ordnance and munitions were stuck at Hull. Keel boats on the Ouse, bringing arms and munitions to Selby and York for the infantry, were still delivering their cargoes in October.[75] Even after the Treaty of Ripon in October 1640 the threat remained, especially as the Scots occupied the northernmost English counties. It was, therefore, important to maintain stocks of arms and munitions in the north, and Hull was the obvious supply base.

Provision also had to be made for transporting the arms to the theatre of war once unloaded from the ships. In March 1639 it was calculated that 1,080 horses and 208 wagons and tumbrels would be needed to carry the munitions for the scheduled artillery train of 50 pieces and for 12,000 musketeers.[76] That month the Council of War asked the Master of the Ordnance to have 400 wagons made. Thomas Bateman, the master wheelwright, built some of them and Thomas Phelps, a coachmaker, others.[77] These vehicles were shipped to the north but before being put on board they were taken apart and the pieces marked for ease of storage and reassembly.[78] As noted in an earlier chapter, many of the carts and most of the draught horses were raised in the counties as part of their militia obligations and Lord Lieutenants were given quotas to meet.[79]

English Traffic: the Irish Insurrection, 1641–2

When supplies were sent to Ireland in 1641–2, geography determined that road transport would be comparatively more important than it had been in the Scottish campaign. In spite of the odd load sent across country, like one from Hull in February 1642,[80] the bulk of the *matériel* was dispatched from the Tower. One or two shipments sailed direct from the capital[81] but most of the consignments were transported overland to the western ports of Bristol, Chester or Minehead. Nicholas Cox, the messenger to the Ordnance Office, was one of those given the task of hiring the carriers. Altogether, sixty-six men were employed between 8 January and 26 August 1642. Where residence is known, it can be seen that most of the carriers lived on or near the routes taken and could, therefore, carry out these contracts as part of their ordinary business. Several of the carriers made multiple journeys. In the first half of the year they were paid at the rate of 10s a cwt and thereafter 8s. Conductors were employed to supervise carrier trains. One of those appointed, Thomas Gibson, organised a group of six conductors, who took charge of thirty cartloads of arms to Chester in the winter 1641/2. The teams were hired at the rate of 6d a mile and each conductor was given 5s a day in expenses. Because of the shortage of draught horses in Ireland, these animals were shipped over, too.[82]

Once the arms had arrived at the port of embarkation it was the Committee for Irish Affairs' responsibility to find the ships to take them to Ireland. Its task was a difficult one, not only because of the changing situation on the ground but also because of the dangers posed by privateers. Aware that ships' masters might be reluctant to deal with the government, notoriously slow settling its bills, and to sail into a war zone, the committee stressed its willingness to pay promptly.[83] Most of the merchantmen were hired in the western ports, perhaps with the help of local officials. In April John Locke, the mayor of Bristol, was asked to help find a replacement for the *Pennington*, one of two ships hired to carry soldiers and arms to Kinsale and Limerick. In the event, the *Amity*, a 60-tonner from Elmore near Gloucester, accompanied the *Ruth* on the trip.[84] The committee also sought assistance from the navy. On 15 April it requested a good ship from the fleet to carry men and ammunition to Galway. Five days later the admiral was asked if he would instruct the *Charity* of London to take arms to Carrickfergus and then to remain in the area to act as guard. When, two weeks later, the ship was found to be not large enough to carry the whole cargo, a request was made for a second ship to transport the residue.[85] Unfortunately, naval operations might clash with transport requirements. The sudden departure of the *Pennington*, ordered out of Bristol by the admiral, is a case in point. Because there were too few ships to do all the jobs required of them, none of them were carried out with complete success. Arms were delivered, just as some of the enemy's shipping was stopped, but there was a certain air of 'muddling through' and this did retard the process of resupply.

Domestic Traffic: The English Civil Wars

In the provinces a good deal of activity involved short-distance traffic. Carters, for instance, brought in raw materials to local centres of production. At Gloucester, the three main hauliers, Robert Cugley, Augustine Loggins and John Merry, busied themselves carrying loads of saltpetre liquor or wood to the gunpowder works in the city. Between 26 September 1643 and 28 January 1645 they transported a recorded total of 481 tons of materials.[86] At Skipton Castle in the winter of 1642/3, Robert Tullan alone carted 867 loads of stones to strengthen the defences there.[87] Craftsmen also sent their wares, newly made or repaired, to the county or garrison magazine where they were stored alongside goods brought in from a distance. Local magazines had their own distribution network; in 1643 and 1644 regular deliveries of gunpowder, match and lead shot were made from Stafford Castle to the troops at Stafford, and to garrisons and detachments of soldiers elsewhere in the county. For specific actions as, for example, the sieges of Chillington House or Eccleshall Castle, greater quantities were issued.[88] Bulk orders travelled longer distances since they could only be supplied from leading manufacturing or storage centres. London remained at the heart of the Parliamentarian system of supply and Oxford, too, survived as a major Royalist arms centre, though it did lose some of its pre-eminence as one or two other sites grew in importance. These centres were not self-sufficient, however, and a good deal of *matériel* passed from one place to another, according to need or specialisation.

Parliament was in a better position to move arms and equipment from the point of manufacture or collection to the place where they were needed. In particular, it possessed superior waterborne capabilities, with London as the focal point. From the capital goods made locally or imported could be sent out via the river system or round the coast. At sea, the navy offered some protection, even if it was unable fully to prevent Royalists and privateers from attacking its shipping. For the New Model Army's western campaign in 1645–6, coasters sailed down the English Channel with supplies. Parliamentarian outposts such as Plymouth and Lyme owed their preservation to the ships that brought in supplies. Rivers were highways. In 1645 the storage depot for the New Model Army was established at Reading and numerous barges, laden with munitions and weapons, worked up and down the Thames.[89] Individually, they could take as much military hardware as several wagons and at a cheaper rate. On 21 July 1645, for instance, Francis Carter sailed with a load of 3,000 muskets and bandoliers, 4,000 swords and belts, 1,000 pikes and 2 tons of gunpowder, match and bullet.[90] The Eastern Association army established its supply base at King's Lynn. As a port, situated at the head of an extensive river system, it was able to receive goods from London and abroad and redistribute them quickly and efficiently inland or round the coast. Keelboats supplied the magazine at Cambridge, while ships took arms to the Parliamentarian army besieging York in 1644. As in the Bishops' Wars, arms and equipment brought up the east coast in coasters were transferred to keelboats in the Humber for the final stage of the journey.[91]

The Royalists also transported goods by water whenever they could. In western England control of the ports enabled them to operate with a reasonable degree of freedom in spite of the attentions of parliamentarian ships and assorted privateers. The survival of Plymouth as a Parliamentarian outpost was a further obstacle, but its power to disrupt traffic was curtailed by Royalist blockades. In the Lostwithiel campaign consignments of gunpowder were sent from Dartmouth and Pendennis Castle and match from Bristol and Bridgwater.[92] Arms and equipment were also shipped along rivers. Cargoes from Oxford sailed down the Thames to garrisons like Abingdon, Reading and Wallingford. In April 1643, when Parliamentarian forces were besieging Reading, a barge brought a consignment of gunpowder to the beleaguered town. In September, after its recapture, the Royalists set up a magazine there and stocked it from Oxford by water.[93] Similarly, the Royalists used the Severn as a means of transporting supplies; munitions produced in Shropshire were sent downstream to Worcester, whence they were sent overland to Oxford.[94] The strategic importance of the river as a link between the Royalist heartland and Bristol and the outside world, however, was seriously affected by the Parliamentarian hold on Gloucester.[95]

Both sides also relied on road transport. Oxford, although a river port, was also dependent on overland communications. In this respect, the city's position in the heart of the country, straddling vital routeways, was of strategic importance. However, the attempt of its forces to control resources in, as well as movement through, the area was contested by Parliamentarian troops stationed relatively close to the city.[96] The decentralisation of manufacturing and storage facilities did help but, conversely, by establishing links between major centres, the Royalists exposed their supply lines to enemy attack. The network at its greatest extent was based on Oxford in the east, Weymouth in the south, Bristol in the west and Worcester in the north, and goods, originating or entering at any point, were passed between them.[97] In addition, the northern Royalists, who had their own source of supply, sent arms to the Oxford magazine. On one occasion the king, writing to the Earl of Newcastle, said, 'I have no greater want then of Armes nor means to supply my selfe than from you'.[98] Parliament had its own problems. Because the Irish Sea passage was so dangerous their troops in the north-west tended to be supplied overland. Sir William Brereton, commander of the Cheshire forces, obtained arms and munitions by road.[99] Gloucester, an outpost in enemy territory, was difficult to supply by land and virtually impossible by water.

Evidently it was as dangerous to send goods by road as it was to ship them by sea and, as a result, armed escorts had to be provided. Convoy duty tied up large numbers of soldiers and affected the armies' operational capabilities. Because the convoy sent to restock Gloucester early in 1644 had to pass a number of enemy garrisons, it was heavily protected. By 15 February 1644 at least twenty-eight cartloads of ammunition had arrived at the staging point at Warwick with a escort of 1,000 horse and foot, and more continued to flow in. When the convoy was ready to move out in mid-March numbers had risen to 3,150 horse and 3,500 foot. From Warwick the goods were transported by packhorse, a move designed to speed up the journey and to provide greater flexibility.[100]

The Gloucester convoy was exceptional and it is probable that, overall, the Royalists had to allocate a greater proportion of its troops for escort duty. In the early stages of the war vital imports of arms came in through north-eastern ports such as Newcastle and from there consignments were sent south to York and Oxford by road under heavy guard. As Clarendon commented, '. . . the only hope of supply was from the north; yet the passage from thence [was] so dangerous that a party little inferior in strength to an army was necessary to convey it'. Elsewhere, in May 1643, Major Craffaud detailed a regiment of soldiers to protect a convoy of ammunition *en route* to Marlborough, rather than the 150 cavalry asked for, when he heard reports of a strong enemy presence in the district.[101] The integration of the main Royalist bases added to the problem and the situation deteriorated over time. By the end of 1644 a series of reverses had had a damaging effect on supply lines, especially in the north. In spring 1645 the link with the west Midlands was lost.[102]

The armies maintained a number of draught horses and carts, primarily for use by the artillery. On 22 May 1643 there were 122 carts in the king's artillery train, and four months later – after the first Battle of Newbury – 400 draught horses and oxen. By the following February death and capture had reduced the number of animals to 260.[103] When at Oxford, they were kept with the train or sent to graze at Iffley. Vehicles were lodged near the New College magazine or in the artillery park in Magdalen College grove.[104] The Parliamentarians also had their own animals and equipment. In the months from May to July 1644 a number of draught horses were delivered to the Eastern Association.[105] Similar arrangements were made for the Earl of Essex's train. At the beginning of the campaigning season in 1644 it had 558 of its own horses, to which were added a further 55, bought on 15 May. In addition, 179 horses were hired and 50 teams requisitioned. The monthly charge of these horses and the drivers who looked after them came to £1,776 1s 0d.[106] Provision for horses for the artillery train of the New Model Army was made in an ordinance issued on 14 March 1645.[107] Under its terms committees in London and a number of counties were authorised to buy 1,056 draught horses, paying no more than £6 each for them. Many of these horses must have been bought in the Smithfield livestock market for we know that dealers there sold 1,200 draught horses to the army.

For their vehicles Parliament still made use of Thomas Bateman, who continued to supply wagons and cartware throughout the whole period. In September 1642 he sold 10 wagons to the Earl of Essex, and was one of 21 artificers (including Thomas Phelps), who delivered 120 wagons, 1 cart, 20 carriages for boats, 20 pontoon boats, 46 grapnells for the boats and 12 pairs of harness. He also did business with Sir Charles Bowles, the commissary for Kent, charging him £70 for 5 new ammunition wagons and £4 2s 0d for repairing an old one. In the spring of 1645 he was contracted to make wagons for the recently formed New Model Army and was paid £13 each for 21 closed wagons, £12 each for 6 open wagons and £5 apiece for a further 5. Bateman delivered more vehicles in 1648 and was still active in 1649–52, supplying wagons and tumbrels for the Irish and Scottish campaigns.[108] He also built gun carriages,[109] as did John Pitt, the master carpenter. Thomas Hodgskins, the master smith, made the metalwork for them.[110]

The Royalists used a number of craftsmen, living in and around Oxford, to construct road vehicles. They included the wheelwrights, Richard Walter, George Flyte of Lewknor, Thomas Allen of Wheatley and Richard and Thomas Soudley of Burford, and Peter Noway, a wagonmaker. Unfortunately, because of poor documentation they are only glimpsed briefly and their scale of activity cannot be assessed. In November 1643 Noway sent in three covered wagons, but this is the largest delivery noted.[111]

To a certain extent, therefore, the Parliamentarian and Royalist artillery trains maintained their own transport facilities and only had to supplement them by hiring carters and teams from outside. Many of them were employed for a short space of time, but in Essex's army at least, a number of people were provided with almost continuous work. Isaac Peare, for instance, was taken on at the beginning of the war and served in the train until the army was disbanded in spring 1645. Over time this trend grew more pronounced. For the Edgehill campaign Essex made use of a large number of carters, many of whom had short-term contracts. Some, like Peare, were given further work and these were the people upon whom Essex's Wagon Master-General came to rely.[112] The New Model Army's artillery train kept an even greater proportion of the business 'in house'. As a result, the number of carters and teams employed did not fluctuate during the course of the year as much as might have been expected (though the disaster at Lostwithiel in September 1644 led to a reduction in the number of horses used). What jobs were these people doing outside the campaigning season? Clearly, there was always some carriage work to be done and it is possible that these carters formed a pool of labour which the entire army could draw upon for particular tasks.

Apart from the artillery train, it was customary for the armies to hire carters as and when required to perform a specific service. Such people undertook much of the work of distributing arms to forces outside the capital. Normally the recipient was responsible for providing the vehicles. In July 1645 the Scots commissioners could not send to their army, then besieging Hereford, a consignment of 100 barrels of gunpowder, with proportional amounts of match and shot because they could not find wagons to transport them.[113] Some carters and their horses were obtained in lieu of part of local assessments[114] but most carriers were hired, along with their horses and carts. They normally received 2s 6d a horse per day, though at the opening of the war shortages of draught animals forced Essex to pay 3s 6d. The cost of a packhorse was 1s 0d to 1s 6d a day.[115]

Because of the scale of the demand, however, counties were regularly given a quota to meet. In July 1643, Lord Capel, short of carriages while preparing to attack Parliamentarian Nantwich, asked for twenty carts and teams of horses from both Denbighshire and Flintshire.[116] Compulsion might be needed and warrants issued, authorising commissary officers to impress horses and carts.[117] More arbitrary measures were taken, too. The vehicles and animals of opponents (and even of those not actively supporting a particular side) were obvious targets and likely to be seized. Casual theft was rife but from time to time a body of soldiers descended on an area and indiscriminately took everything of value they could find. Both sides issued orders against plunder but the problem was never eradicated. Indeed, at times it was carried out as an act of policy.[118]

Authorities often did pay for the carts and the animals they hired or impressed, especially in areas they controlled. Of course, much depended upon the availability of money and, if short of cash, soldiers might issue a voucher for future repayment or allow arrears to build up. It was mid-November 1642 before the Earl of Essex settled his account for carting services supplied since before the opening of the war. Some of those working for him in 1643 and 1644 were not paid until March 1645. George Greasley and his team of six horses were employed in the artillery train between 14 February and 2 September 1644, working for 201 days at 2s 6d a horse per day. At the end of the period he had only received £44 10s 0d and the residue, £106 5s 0d, remained outstanding until 6 March 1645.[119] Others never gained recompense. At Ludlow, Samuel France complained that the Royalists continually impressed his horses, losing three in the process, and leaving him with 'nothinge to maintaine me and my lame wife'. The situation in the town was so bad that the inhabitants sent a petition to the sheriff and commissioners at Shrewsbury, requesting, among other things, that the army should compensate all those who suffered losses and should make prior payment for horses and teams impressed. In contrast, local carriers at Skipton, such as Anthony Johnson and Francis and Robert Twistleton, seem to have been paid reasonably promptly for the work they did for the garrison there.[120]

Domestic Traffic: Scotland, 1638–51

The supply network of the Covenanters, based on the central magazine at Leith, was very similar to that of Parliament. Edinburgh, like London, was the centre of arms manufacture in the country and the main point of entry for imports. It had good waterborne connections to the rest of Scotland and its overland links, judged by the poor standard of the country's roads, were good. Scotland's rugged terrain encouraged the use of coastal traffic,[121] though it faced constant threat from privateers and enemy ships. In June 1646 a vessel, laden with arms, clothing and money for the Covenanters' soldiers in Ulster was stuck at Leith 'for fear of that shipping which they heare are upon the coasts'.[122] Civil war within the country also affected security on the roads but it seems to have been deemed safer. As a result, many consignments that could have been more conveniently transported by sea, were taken overland. When, on 29 April 1651, the Army Committee arranged for provisions to be brought down from the north by horse, it gave as the reason the problems of contrary winds and enemy ships lying off the coast.[123]

The army used both oxen and horses for draught and carriage purposes, but mainly the latter.[124] Most of the carriage work was performed by pack animals, though it is impossible to gauge the exact amount because the term 'baggage horse' is an imprecise one. At times, the reference suggests a pack rather than a draught animal, and this interpretation would reflect contemporary practice in Scotland. The topography of the country favoured the employment of small, sure-footed ponies and they were widely used on the farm and even in and around the major towns.[125] Units of soldiers kept them to carry their goods; in 1644 soldiers from the Panmure estate set off for the north with three baggage men in their number. In 1651 the Army Committee ordered that each foot regiment should have three packhorses and their equipment, together with two men to look after them.[126] Heavier items like cannon needed to be pulled by draught horses (or oxen) but finding them in sufficient numbers was a problem, as General Leslie discovered in 1639.[127] Horses trained in the collar certainly did exist. Many farmers possessed a cart and team for their own and their lord's haulage work and these animals could be pressed into service if necessary. In January 1645, for instance, Alexander Wood, the Wagon Master-General, took up teams for the artillery in the countryside. In a typical transaction, the barony of Saltoun provided a close cart and three horses with their furniture, for which the tenants were given recompense.[128]

Arms from the magazine at Leith (or at Burnisland, its outpost across the firth) were distributed far and wide.[129] Ships, loaded there sailed to English ports like Berwick and Sunderland in the months following the invasion of the country in January 1644. Others took consignments to forces fighting Royalists in western and north-eastern Scotland.[130] Much military hardware went overland too, notably the baggage and artillery trains that accompanied the army on its march on Berwick in September 1643 and further south the following year. On 18 November 1643 two barrels of gunpowder, destined for Berwick, were delivered to James Wilson, a sledder. Sleds were widely used on the farms and roads of Scotland to move bulky goods over short distances, in this case to the quayside. In 1650 James Henderson, sledder, moved four loads of muskets from the council house at Edinburgh to the castle in order to keep them out of the hands of the English army.[131] Land carriage was also used to supply garrisons with arms and to fit out detachments of soldiers when they were being recruited, re-equipped or were out on campaign. Thus, Baillie's movements in pursuit of Montrose in the winter of 1644/5 are reflected in the delivery of munitions and weapons to him at Dumbarton, Glasgow, Perth and Stirling. Of course, there were cross-currents in the traffic; arms were brought to Leith for storage or repair, or were dispatched from provincial magazines. In June 1645 Patrick Acheson, the keeper of the artillery at Perth, was one of those paid for transporting 1,000 lb each of gunpowder, match and lead shot from Perth to Dundee.[132]

Many of the parcels of arms issuing out of Leith were given to commissary officers or other representatives, who arranged transport to their units. In January 1645 Sir Robert Campbell sent a bond to his kinsman, Sir Archibald Campbell, at Edinburgh for 50 swords and 100 muskets, with gunpowder, ball and match. At the same time he wrote a letter to Sir Colin Campbell, asking him to take fifteen horses to Edinburgh to transport the arms and munitions to Stirling.[133] Other consignments were delivered to Alexander Forester, the wagonmaster, who was responsible for distributing them around the country. Between March 1644 and May 1647 he sent carriers overland to Dumbarton, Dumfries, Edinburgh Castle, Kelso, Glasgow and Perth and into Roxburghshire. Conductors, like William Duncan, supervised the trains in transit; in March 1647 he was put in charge of a train of munitions dispatched to Generals Leslie and Middleton at Aberdeen for use against Royalist castles in the region.[134] Carters and carriers also shuttled between the magazine, castle and quayside. Some consignments went by river to Stirling and by sea to Inverness and the north, and to Berwick and Sunderland in the south. Carriers were available for hire but, as in England, the authorities often found it necessary to requisition horses and carts.[135] Typically, the artillery train made the greatest demand on transport facilities but it did possess its own horses. In April 1645 Thomas Wemyss, General Baillie's quartermaster, spent 400 merks purchasing horses at Scone to bring the number in the artillery train up to strength.[136] Other detachments might buy their own horses, too. At the beginning of 1644 Edinburgh was busily equipping its own regiment for an expedition to Stirling and as part of the preparations John Tweedy and John Scot paid £3,838 11s 4d Scottish for baggage horses.[137]

Domestic Traffic: Ireland, 1641–9

In pre-rebellion Ireland the magazine at Dublin Castle had occupied a particularly dominant position. Most of the arms and equipment needed for the armed forces in the country had to be brought in from England and they were stored at Dublin. When the insurgents swept through the country in 1641–2, the area over which *matériel* was distributed shrank dramatically, but the rebels' failure to take Dublin meant that the magazine could supply loyalist forces in places that had not fallen. Some replacement stock was dispatched from England. The presence of enemy ships made it difficult to provision the troops from the sea but the Bartletts managed regularly to sneak out of Dublin's harbour. The Confederates distributed arms and equipment from their central arsenal at Kilkenny, as well as from provincial storehouses. Magazines set up at the ports of entry had their own networks. In summer 1642 the inhabitants of Wexford reportedly received a considerable amount of imported arms and munitions which they sent to fellow rebels in all parts of the country.[138] They, too, were affected by the naval blockade in spite of Ormond's sour assertion, made in June 1644, that Parliament had done nothing to stop traffic going in and out of Wexford, Waterford, Galway and Limerick.[139] The insurgents also suffered from extended lines of communication because they lacked a suitable port in some parts of the country. They had none in Ulster, never took Dublin and only briefly held Dundalk and Carlingford in north Leinster; they also had to contend with Inchiquin for control of Cork, Kinsale and Youghal in Munster.[140]

Within the country, water transport was used as much as possible, especially to move heavy siege pieces. In 1642 the rebels floated a demi-cannon up the River Deal and used it to secure the surrender of Askeaton Castle.[141] Bellings set out the advantages of river over road when in May 1644 he informed Ormond that the Confederacy intended to establish a general magazine at Athlone, a place 'neer for service & liinge upon the river of Shannon so as much trobill of land Carriadg may be saued'.[142] Unfortunately, a good deal of traffic had to use the roads and, owing to the shortage of draught horses, problems did occur. The Royalists soon ran into trouble. On 27 February 1642 the Lords Justices wrote to the Lord Lieutenant in England to ask for 100 draught horses for the ordnance. They explained that as virtually the entire country was in rebellion, it was impossible to obtain draught horses for the ordnance or wagon horses for the carriages.[143] The Committee for Irish Affairs responded, if a little belatedly; on 13 June it made £800 available to Lord Dungarvan to buy 100 draught and carriage horses, to be employed in Munster pulling two siege guns, four field pieces and accompanying carriages. Allowance was also made for drivers, each of whom were to be paid 8*d* a day for looking after three of the horses. At the same meeting the committee discussed the needs of the artillery train to be sent to Leinster, estimated at 16 wagons and 598 draught and carriage horses, plus 14 mounts for the six gentlemen of the ordnance and eight conductors. The horses were to be bought at the rate of £8 each.[144]

By the end of the summer such horses were needed at home and the Earl of Essex was one commander who found it difficult to obtain sufficient carts and teams for his artillery train. The king faced the same problem and in September appropriated horses and wagons at Chester *en route* to Ireland. Charles I justified his action by claiming that they had been certified useless for that service.[145] In that month the Lords Justices informed the Irish Committee that they were short of carriages and had insufficient money to repair the few they had or to make new ones.[146] Once again, distractions at home affected the prosecution of the war in Ireland. Ormond, as Deputy Lieutenant, received numerous reports detailing the difficulties created by the shortage of horses. In August 1643 Viscount Montgomery could not set out because of the scarcity of baggage horses. Parliamentarians suffered too. In January 1646 there were so few carriage horses in the vicinity of Belfast that the army could not take the field.[147] The following year, Colonel Jones could find few carts and carriages in Dublin.[148]

The situation, though bad, was not as dire as this account suggests, for in the ox Ireland possessed an alternative source of motive power. The insurgents, who obviously could not ask for additional horses to be sent from England, made great use of them. Thus, when they captured Limerick in June 1642, and with it its ordnance, they yoked up the oxen to the guns. One of the pieces, a demi-cannon that fired 32 lb balls, required twenty-five animals to remove it. Other references reveal that oxen were their customary draught animals. In 1643 16 oxen pulled one of their siege guns, in 1646 123 of them drew the wagons and the cannon of an artillery train sent to Connaught, and in 1647 64 'fair' oxen were captured with the train after the Battle of Dungan's Hill. In the 1646 convoy the largest piece travelled on a sledge.[149] The more fastidious Royalists also employed oxen. They were used in the artillery train at the Battle of Ross in March 1643, for instance, but were stolen shortly afterwards.[150] As many of these oxen were farm animals, their loss had wider economic implications. This was a problem that worried Foulk Hanks when his men set out in October that year with cannon for Lord Lambard. In his letter he asked Ormond if he could send some, if not all, of the oxen back to him 'other ways wee shall be mutch strayed for Carrages to get In the Corne'. In mid-1649 the Royalist coalition's artillery, comprising at least seven pieces, was being driven by 200 oxen.[151]

The Conquest of Ireland and Scotland, 1649–52

Because the forces sent to Ireland and Scotland were largely provisioned from England, transportation was a major logistical consideration. For the Irish campaign Cromwell assembled the army at Bristol, Chester and Milford Haven in summer 1649. War materials were brought from the Tower, from the magazines at Windsor, Hull and York, and from other parts of the country, and dispatched to the west.[152] At the same time, to protect the sea passage to Ireland action was taken to neutralise the privateers. Cromwell also secured his bridgehead by sending over reinforcements to Dublin; under the command of Colonel Jones they won the Battle of Rathmines on 2 August and with it the lifting of the siege of the city.[153] Some 130 ships were hired to move the arms and men; the artillery train left in late July and the army followed early in August.[154] Thereafter, to keep the troops supplied, at least twenty merchantmen were employed on a regular basis. Because of the threat from privateers, they went in convoy, escorted by the royal navy. The fall of Wexford and the capture of the privateers' ships there (October 1649) eased the problem, though Waterford (August 1650), Limerick (October 1651) and Galway (April 1652) held out for longer.[155]

Once in Ireland, Cromwell made good use of water transport, especially as a means of moving his artillery pieces, essential weapons in a country full of fortified towns. From Dublin he shipped his artillery down the coast to the sieges of Drogheda (taken in September) and Wexford. Significantly, he failed before Waterford, not only because he lacked undisputed control of the harbour but also because the rain had turned the ground into a quagmire and he could not move his cannon overland.[156] Ships were also employed in a supporting role, supplying the troops with arms and provisions. As he seized more ports, Cromwell was able to penetrate the interior by means of the navigable rivers. Barges were drawn upstream, moving men and supplies, as well as artillery, considerable distances.[157]

The boats could not reach every corner of Ireland, however, and provision for land transport was essential. Alerted to the shortage of draught horses and carriages by Jones's report in 1647, Cromwell took them with him. Each of the ten foot regiments that embarked for Ireland received two wagons and ten draught horses. The artillery train was given some 750 draught and carriage horses. Other horses and wagons followed later.[158] To provide these items Cromwell turned to the traditional suppliers, including Ordnance Office employees. The horses were bought in the Smithfield market from Richard Clough, Harvey Conway and William Booth, and put out to graze in Marylebone and Hyde Parks until their departure for Ireland.[159] Thomas Hodgskins supplied the horseshoes, Richard Blissett, senior and junior, John Everett, Richard Marshall and John Mullins the harness, Thomas Bateman the wagons (and some wheels), Alex Norman the barrels and John Pitt 'necessaries for the train'. All manner of tools and equipment were shipped out, including those that would be needed by the master gunsmith, blacksmith and farrier and by the armourers, carpenters and basket, collar and harness makers.[160]

Cromwell's conquest of Scotland followed the same pattern, even if the military outcome was decided by pitched battle rather than siege warfare. The regular contractors were used, and arms, equipment and provisions flooded in during summer 1650. From London, bases were established at King's Lynn, Newcastle and Berwick. The army itself gathered at Newcastle.[161] As in Ireland, Cromwell's strategy required control of the seas and the capture of ports, through which he could disembark men and war materials. The Council of State organised a naval escort for transport ships and the fleet stopped vessels bringing in soldiers and arms for the Scottish forces from abroad.[162] Twenty-three ships were contracted to take provisions north in July and during the course of the campaign at least 140 ships, hired at a cost over £11,000, transported supplies and pay for the troops. The army crossed the border on 22 July and marched up the coast, shadowed by the fleet, which kept it supplied.[163] Dunbar and Musselburgh, seized on 26 and 28 July respectively, enabled Cromwell to provision his army throughout the summer, though not without difficulty. The acquisition of Leith, made possible by the victory at Dunbar on 3 September, provided him with a sheltered port in the winter.[164] Flatboats, many built at Newcastle, were employed on the Forth in 1651 to ferry men and supplies across the firth in the attack on Fife.[165]

Logistically, Cromwell's success was due to the efficient collection and transportation of arms, equipment and provisions from one end of the country to the other, and relied on the effective use of water transport. He did not ignore the need for road-carrying facilities either. As in Ireland, the foot regiments received two wagons and ten draught horses each.[166] The artillery train, fifty pieces strong, required over 1,000 horses. The same Ordnance Office employees as before made the wagons and accessories; a warrant to pay Thomas Bateman £245 13s 4d for close wagons, tumbrels, gun carriages, wheelwrights' tools and other items was issued on 9 July 1650. The following year he built forty-eight wagons and sixteen tumbrels.[167] The Smithfield dealers – William Booth, Richard Clough, Harvey Conway, Peter Everett and Percival Stanley – provided draught horses, but other sources were used, too.[168] In February 1651 Major Jeremy Tolhurst and Commissary William Blewett were given £3,500 to buy 400 horses in the north to carry provisions to the army. Three months later draught and carriage horses were being brought to London from Essex, Surrey, Bedfordshire and Herefordshire, and sent to Scotland with wagons and drivers.[169] Awareness of the terrain is reflected in the delivery of packhorse equipment to Commissary Phipps in March 1651.[170] Apart from food for the soldiers, fodder had to be provided for the horses. Altogether, 2,800 tons of oats and about 10,700 tons of hay, mostly from East Anglia, Kent and Surrey, were shipped up to Scotland between August 1650 and September 1651.[171]

CONCLUSION

The contrast between the outcome of the Bishops' Wars and Cromwell's Scottish campaign of 1650–2 reveals the importance of transport and logistics in military planning. If arms and equipment could not be put into the hands of the soldiers, they were of little use. The task was a difficult one and made harder by the distances traversed. Centralisation of manufacture had its advantages but it did extend supply lines and made them more vulnerable to enemy action. Reliance upon imports exacerbated the problem. Securing lines of communication, whether sea lanes or roadways, was a costly affair and diverted men, money and resources from the essential business of waging war. The convoy system offered greater protection and undoubtedly ensured that some of the supplies reached their destination. If a reasonable proportion of imports had not got through, no side would have been able to sustain their war effort for as long as they did. Similarly, carriage trains distributed *matériel* around the country. The carriage train that took arms to Gloucester in the aftermath of the 1643 siege is a case in point; it provided much-needed military hardware but tied up thousands of soldiers for several months. Contrarily, convoys acted as magnets to the enemy, inviting attack and increasing the haul, if successful. Consignments were intercepted, doubly damaging the war effort by reducing one side's own resources, while increasing those of the other.

The transportation of arms had general economic consequences, too. At sea, the blockading of harbours to prevent arms shipments coming in or going out had an adverse effect on trade in general. Before long, goods of all kinds were being plundered. The same problems affected inland trade. In addition, carriers might find themselves and their teams pressed into service, carrying supplies for the army, with no certainty that they would be paid or their animals returned. Farmers' animals were also requisitioned and, if taken at a critical time of the year, the harvest would be ruined, their livelihoods threatened and the price of food raised. Even if they were paid for their horses or oxen, this did not necessarily provide adequate compensation for the time lost. Nonetheless, some people benefited from the war. The risks were high but the returns were often greater. Demand for carrying services increased enormously and ships' captains, keelmen and carriers alike were offered good rates of pay. Even farmers were glad of an opportunity to earn extra money by hiring out their teams at slack times of the year. Many profited. Of course, it did depend on being paid and on the time taken to receive the money. Parliament was better at paying up than the Royalists were, but many creditors waited months, if not years, before being recompensed.

CONCLUSION

With the advantage of hindsight the ultimate victory of the English Parliament in the wars in the three kingdoms seems inevitable. It was not as clear-cut as that at the time but logistics did favour Parliament. Its control of the country's arms industries gave it an advantage over the king and its other enemies and, if for some years they were insufficient in themselves to cater for demand, its command of the ports closest to the continent gave it ready access to the most important arms manufacturing areas of Europe. Possession of London and the support of its mercantile community, moreover, provided it with a sound financial base. The best opportunity that Charles had of winning the war was by achieving a quick victory. In the autumn of 1642 he had a chance but failed to take it for reasons that were not primarily due to deficiencies in supply. There certainly were shortcomings in this respect, but Parliament had its own problems, too. The longer the war went on, however, the more likely it was that Parliament would win, on account of its commercial and economic superiority.[1] Having vanquished the king, it could focus the full power of the English State on the suppression of the Irish and Scots, a task that Oliver Cromwell did with ruthless efficiency.

Of course, there is a political dimension to all this, just as there is to account for the failure of Charles to defeat the Scots, and then to contain the Irish insurrection. The Scots lacked the industrial base that Charles ostensibly had at his command but made up for it with massive imports from abroad. Moreover, effective military leadership and a committed army, aided by shorter lines of supply, enabled the Covenanters to sweep aside a demoralised royal army, short of arms and provisions, and with uncertain loyalty to the king. The Ordnance Office can be blamed for failing to dispatch the arms and armaments to the north in sufficient quantities early enough for them to be used against the Scots, but the officers were hamstrung by a lack of money and the unrealistic expectations of the king. In Ireland, the government was caught unawares and when (under Parliamentarian direction) it was poised to regain the initiative, events in England distracted its attention.

There were compelling reasons for the 'rebels' in all three kingdoms to fight, as there were important issues at stake. In England and Scotland a perceived threat to existing freedoms, whether political or religious, led them to take up arms. In Ireland, ironically, the Roman Catholics, who, more than any of the dissident parties, had a right to feel aggrieved about the absence of these very ideals, were more opportunist in the timing of their revolt. Released from Wentworth's grip and aware of the weakness of the government in the aftermath of its defeat at the hands of the Scottish Covenanters, they must have seen it as an ideal moment to strive once more for independence from English rule – or at least for freedom of conscience. Whether any of the groups of insurgents could have been bought off with concessions is a question that is difficult to answer, for Charles I was not a person to compromise, especially with those who protested against his policies. Over Scotland, there were many in Parliament who sympathised with the Covenanters, though they would have been at one with Charles in rejecting Irish independence and Catholic emancipation.

Historians have long argued that there was a reluctance to go to war and that, Ireland apart, resort to arms was only made when negotiations broke down. From the point of view of the arms trade, however, a different perspective can be gained. In all three kingdoms pre-planning for rebellion is apparent and in England and Scotland, at least, arms and equipment were being imported and stockpiled for months before the actual outbreak of war. The Royalists were engaged in this activity, too. Of course, such measures may have been purely precautionary but the evidence suggests that there were those on all sides who saw war coming and prepared for it in a positive way.

In England, the performance of the home arms industries during the course of the conflict is, overall, a success story. In the years 1638–40 they proved incapable of meeting Charles I's needs against the Scots and output was low in the initial stages of the English Civil War. By the end of the 1640s, however, the industries had developed to such an extent that they were able to supply almost all the ordnance, weapons and equipment to Cromwell in his conquests of Ireland and Scotland. Munitions still had to be imported but at the end of the period production was growing rapidly. The Royalist achievement was arguably as great: having to start virtually from scratch, they achieved a very creditable level of output at Oxford and later at Bristol. The Scottish Covenanters and Irish Confederates also developed their manufactories, the one expanding from an existing, if modest, base and the other with imported specialists. They never produced more than a small proportion of the arms and equipment needed but in Scotland, at least, output was not insignificant. Paradoxically, growth was achieved both by concentration and fragmentation. London, Oxford and Edinburgh continued to dominate production of arms for the party that controlled them, even if Bristol became an important industrial centre for the Royalists. At the same time, arms manufacture proliferated as centres sprang up throughout the three kingdoms in order to cater for the local demand for arms and equipment. Many of the enterprises were small but they helped increase output and allowed the ordnance officers greater flexibility in the distribution of the stores in their charge.

Rising demand undoubtedly made a career in the arms industries an attractive proposition to potential apprentices but, like the supply of horses, there was a considerable lead-in period. Thus, craftsmen and artificers with suitable skills were pressed into service manufacturing arms and equipment: blacksmiths made muskets and pike heads, cutlers fashioned swords and tailors stitched suits of clothes. Similarly, plant was converted to the production of weapons and munitions. At the same time, the Ordnance Office improved its capabilities to deliver *matériel*, indicating what it could achieve when properly funded. The Irish and Scottish campaigns of 1649–52 were as much a victory for planning and organisation as a military one in the field. Thus, Protector Cromwell was able to draw upon a greatly improved industry when embarking on his campaigns abroad in the 1650s.

Until the late 1640s the armies could only obtain all that they needed by importing arms and equipment from abroad and this put the authorities at the mercy of outsiders. In Sweden the Riksräd discussed the respective merits of supporting the Scottish Covenanters or Charles and supplying one side or the other with arms. In the Low Countries exports to Britain were complicated by the respective blockades imposed by the Dutch and the authorities in the Spanish Netherlands. The *realpolitik* of international relations can be seen in the poor response that Charles I's fellow rulers, including his close relations, made to his requests for arms. His uncle, Christian IV of Denmark, appears to have been particularly cynical. Within Britain itself arms moved between parties, though the flow changed direction as new alliances were formed and old ones broke up. In Ireland, for instance, two years after the insurrection had broken out the Royalists had agreed to a cessation of hostilities with the Confederates and immediately solicited arms and munitions from them. Before long the English Royalists were asking for supplies, as well as troops. For their part, the Catholics prevaricated, hoping to use the provision of arms as a bargaining point in negotiations to achieve their political and religious aims. In Scotland, too, arms were used against erstwhile friends. In January 1644 the Scottish Army of the Solemn League and Covenant invaded England on behalf of Parliament and, while there, received arms from its ally. Within years the alliance had broken down and the Engagers were turning their weapons on Parliament in support of the king.

The Civil Wars cost a vast sum of money and although not the greatest charge, the provision of war materials was clearly a significant item of expenditure. All sides, perhaps hoping for a quick decisive action, initially sought to raise money from traditional sources and by asking supporters for contributions. The Irish Catholics appealed to their co-religionists abroad for help. When these sources proved inadequate, as they soon did, a regular system of taxation had to be devised and one that raised far greater sums than could ever have been contemplated beforehand. In this respect, Britain achieved the fiscal revolution that enabled it to pay for the military revolution that its armies were already undergoing.[2] An important aspect of the process of fiscal change was the transformation of Parliament's attitude towards taxation. Having denounced Charles I's schemes such as ship money as arbitrary, extortionate and illegal, it found itself forced to introduce measures that squeezed the population even harder and which allowed assessors to pry even further into people's business. As a result of the experience, Parliament adopted a more responsible and positive approach to the nation's finances and this led to greater cooperation between it and the government. This meant that government could be properly funded. Wheeler concluded, 'the development of these taxes and the bureaucracies that managed them were central elements in the story of England's rise as a great power'.[3]

The wars made a considerable impact on the social and economic life of the three kingdoms as a whole. Undoubtedly many people suffered. They paid a significant proportion of their wealth in taxation, their possessions were at the mercy of the soldiers, and they risked losing their livelihoods, and even their lives, if they complained about it. Towns were besieged and property destroyed. Industry and agriculture were made subservient to the needs of the armies. Whatever they wanted, the soldiers had to have it immediately and in large amounts. Crops were wantonly trampled down, even if they were not taken, wagons were commandeered and livestock driven away. The requisitioning of draught animals at critical times of the year severely hampered farmers' efforts to cultivate the land. The energies of a host of craftsmen and artificers were diverted to the production of arms and military equipment and armies had priority in the distribution of provisions and raw materials. Suppliers of goods or services might have to wait years for full payment. Industry lost access to some of its markets; the West Country clothiers and the hostmen of Newcastle, for instance, were stopped from travelling to their main market in the capital. It also suffered from the general sense of insecurity of the times. Not only did individuals lose their jobs, but trade was disrupted as carriers were plundered of their wares, as well as their horses and carts. Even if soldiers paid for their use and returned them afterwards, there was a cost. Their demands were insistent and immediate and by withdrawing draught animals and vehicles from normal economic activity, effectively disrupted it.[4] By the end of the wars all three kingdoms were exhausted and Ireland and Scotland were especially hard hit.

There were gains, too. For all the brutality of the soldiery, it was generally in their interest to deal openly and fairly with the civilian population. This was the only way to guarantee continuity of supplies. The New Model Army, in particular, benefited from adopting such a positive attitude, especially in its western campaign. The money that the soldiers had at their disposal could stimulate the local economy and the varied requirements of the armies gave employment to a large number of people. Craftsmen and tradesmen with appropriate or transferable skills increased their earnings by making or refurbishing arms and equipment, and for many individuals this became their major source of income. Carriers and labourers also found regular employment. Farmers had a ready market for their produce and might also earn money carrying goods at slack times of the year. They benefited from the constant demand for horses and this led to a greater interest in breeding and rearing the animals. Thus, in spite of the losses during the war years, the equine population of England, at least, not only recovered quickly but was of a higher standard. Within a decade the export of horses was to prove a major source of revenue to the government.[5]

In industry, army contracts enabled some people to benefit from the war, and for some towns (like Birmingham and Northampton) to consolidate their position in specific niche markets. Much depended upon the form of organisation and the scale of production within individual industries, but at all levels there was money to be made. Wholesalers and large-scale munitions and ordnance manufacturers must have done well. In spite of possible delays in payment, money was more readily available, and in large amounts, to major suppliers of strategic materials. Arms dealers like Edward Barker of Coldharbour in London who supplied the Eastern Association, or John Davies, active in provisioning the forces in Ireland, clearly recognised the commercial opportunities offered by the wars and profited from them. Moreover, men like Thomas Andrews, Stephen Estwick and Tempest Milner, active on Parliamentarian committees in London during the Civil Wars, were able to use their contacts to acquire business. Robert and John Goodwin, who sat on the Committee for Irish Affairs, seem to have used their influence to obtain contracts for their brother, Benjamin, a London businessman.[6] Charges of corruption were made, as in the case of John Davies and his associates. Some of the accusations were personally or politically motivated but undoubtedly a number of entrepreneurs were guilty of abuse. Excessive profits seem to have been made in the clothing industries, for instance.

Not everyone profited, however. In spite of their dominant position in the manufacture of arms and armaments, including the monopoly to make gunpowder, the Royalists, Strode and Wandesford, lost heavily. Their predecessor, William Baber, claimed at the Restoration that he had lost at least £1,500 in stock and materials.[7] Like the radical merchants of London they laid out money for the cause in the form of taxes and loans, as well as earned an income from the wars. In 1642, William Dick, an Edinburgh merchant, was owed £474,126 19s 7d Scots.[8] It was important to choose the winning side and to secure payment! Even major Parliamentarian suppliers might have to wait for their money. From Veere, Thomas Cuningham, the Scottish conservator, spent years struggling to get the Covenanters to pay the Zeelanders, Adrian and Cornelius Lampsins, the money owed to them for underwriting a large consignment of arms in 1644.

The Civil Wars affected the commerce and the economy in another way. It helped bring about changes in the system of marketing, hastening the decline of the traditional institutions, the markets and fairs. The move towards private marketing had already begun in the late sixteenth and early seventeenth centuries in spite of governmental attempts to stop it. In the wars all sides dealt directly, regularly and extensively with private merchants and manufacturers. Commissary officers might still purchase goods at markets and fairs but vendors there could not provide them with the amount of arms, equipment and provisions required, or guarantee them security of supply. Such centres were vulnerable to attack and many people were reluctant to venture out onto the road. Where evidence survives, the lack of business being conducted at open markets and fairs is clearly evident. In particular, the major dealers no longer patronised them. As in the horse trade, they seem to have been fulfilling army contracts by making use of contacts to obtain ware privately. The wars increased the control exerted by middlemen in a number of other areas, too. Richard Downes, the London woollen draper, is the obvious example, but some of the weapons manufacturers seem to have also acted as merchants. The scale of production achieved by Lawrence Bromfield, the cutler, suggests that he subcontracted work to others.

Finally, the Civil Wars themselves undoubtedly increased the impact of the 'military revolution' on the management of war in the three kingdoms. Before the conflict started Britain lagged behind the developments that had occurred in Europe, but a decade and more of fighting led to advances in tactics, weaponry, fortification and siegecraft. At the outset, the sum total of military experience possessed by many of the soldiers who fought in the various theatres of war, was the training they had received with the militia. Fortunately, all sides possessed seasoned soldiers who had fought on the continent and who had come home to fight for the cause. These men imparted their knowledge to the raw recruits or at least stiffened the ranks of the soldiers fighting on the battlefield. As a result, the principles of the 'military revolution' could be applied to a series of domestic conflicts occurring in a country that had enjoyed comparative peace for a generation. At Edgehill, the Earl of Lindsey, the Royalists' Lord General, could argue with Prince Rupert, the cavalry commander, over which model to adopt: the Dutch or Swedish system.[9]

Firepower, exercised by units of musketeers or troops of horse, dominated the battlefields of Britain, though field artillery did not play as decisive a role as it might have done (with exceptions such as Newburn in 1640).[10] Furthermore, in emulation of Gustavus Adolphus, cavalry detachments attacked the enemy at pace. The lessons of the 'military revolution' were not always properly understood or fully learned, however. The inexperience of the Confederate generals in mounted warfare is reflected in the failure of their cavalry in pitched battle. Moreover, the successful use of the Highland charge by MacColla's Redshanks in Scotland was at least partly due to deficiencies among the half-trained troops they faced. MacColla, it has been said, did not employ the tactic out of a sense of conservatism but rather because he was short of firearms and gunpowder, the essential ingredients of the firepower revolution.[11]

Even if the Civil Wars are best known for their pitched battles, the characteristic actions in the various conflicts were sieges.[12] Consequently, a good deal of attention ought to have been given to those aspects of the 'military revolution' that related to siege warfare: the double circumvallation, the provision of large battering pieces to knock down walls, and the construction of new-style fortifications to prevent this happening. However, much had to be done, for in the years before the conflict, the principles of the *trace italienne* had only been spasmodically applied. Defences at a handful of strategic points on the coasts had been strengthened, as had a number of fortresses in Ireland, but in general successive governments had preferred to trust in the royal navy and the country's island position as means of protection.[13] During the wars, defences were hurriedly improved and modernised. At London a new earthen defensive line was constructed, eleven miles in extent, complete with forts, redoubts, bastions, breastworks and batteries. Defences like these, though modest by European standards, proved their worth. At Exeter, the *enceinte* created by the Royalists deterred the New Model Army in October 1645. Newark survived several sieges. In Ireland, Limerick's defences, modernised in the 1590s and improved during the 1640s, made the town impregnable to an assault.[14] Most places, of course, were not as well protected. Aberdeen was taken on a number of occasions and Belfast, in spite of possessing a circuit, studded with bastions, fell to attacks in 1644 and 1648. With regard to the besiegers, no force ever constructed a full double circumvallation.[15]

In spite of the limitations of their defences, many garrisons succumbed only after their supplies ran out. It is not that attackers did not have access to siege guns. All sides acquired heavy cannon, to a greater or lesser extent, either from home sources or from abroad. The Irish Confederates appear to have been the worst-placed at the beginning of the conflict, for when the rising began they had to rely upon acquiring cannon, as well as weapons, from the castles they captured. Initially, they lacked the skill to use them effectively, as demonstrated by an abortive attack on Lisburn, Co. Antrim, in November 1641. Veterans, returning home from the continent during the course of 1642, remedied this defect. In general, there was a lack of experts in artillery and siegecraft, especially in the early stages of the wars, and all parties had to seek out suitable personnel, often hiring foreign specialists to do the work.[16] As the conflict progressed, artillery seems to have been used in a more productive way. The New Model Army deployed its siege pieces to good effect and, as at Leicester in May 1645, so did the Royalists.[17] When Cromwell planned his reconquest of Ireland in 1649 he gave artillery a prominent role and shipped over a massive siege train. These guns proved decisive.

ABBREVIATIONS

The place of publication is London unless otherwise stated.

ACA	Amsterdam Chamber of the Admiralty
AMA	Amsterdam Municipal Archives, Amsterdam
ARA, Brussels	Belgian National Archives, Brussels
ARA, The Hague	Dutch National Archives, The Hague
BL	British Library
Bodl.	Bodleian Library, Oxford
Brereton	R.N. Dore (ed.), 'The Letter Books of Sir William Brereton', *Lancashire and Cheshire Record Society*, part I, CXXIII (1984); part II, CXXVIII (1990)
Capp	B. Capp, 'Naval Operations', in J. Kenyon and J. Ohlmeyer (eds), *The Civil Wars: A Military History of England, Scotland and Ireland* (Oxford University Press, Oxford, 1998)
Carte	Carte Manuscripts, Bodleian Library, Oxford
Carte, *Ormond*	Thomas Carte, *The Life of James Duke of Ormond*, II–III (Oxford University Press, Oxford, 1851)
CIA, I and II	I: Minute Book of the Commissioners for Irish Affairs (4 April–1 June 1642), in V.F. Snow and A.S. Young (eds), *Private Journals of the Long Parliament, 7 March–1 June 1642* (Yale University Press, New Haven, 1987); II: Minute Book of the Commissioners for Irish Affairs (7 June–12 October 1642), in Snow and Young (eds), *Private Journals of the Long Parliament, 2 June–17 September 1642* (Yale University Press, New Haven, 1992)
CJ	*Journals of the House of Commons*
CSPD	*Calendar of State Papers Domestic*
CSPI	*Calendar of State Papers Ireland*
CSPV	*Calendar of State Papers Venetian*
Cuningham	E.J. Courthope, 'The Journal of Thomas Cuningham of Campvere 1640–1654', *Scottish Historical Society*, 3rd series, XI (1928)
DRA	Danish Rigsarkivet, Copenhagen
Fissel	M.C. Fissel, *The Bishops' Wars* (Cambridge University Press, Cambridge, 1994)
Fransiscan MSS	Historical Manuscripts Commission, *Report on the Fransiscan Manuscripts Preserved at the Convent, Merchants' Quay, Dublin* (Dublin, 1906)
Furgol	E. Furgol, *A Regimental History of the Covenanting Armies 1639–1651* (John Donald, Edinburgh, 1990)
HMC	Historical Manuscripts Commission
Hogan	J. Hogan (ed.), *Letters and Papers Relating to the Irish Rebellion 1642–1646* (Stationery Office, Dublin, 1936)
Hutton	R. Hutton, *The Royalist War Effort 1642–1646* (Longman, 1984)
Gilbert	J.T. Gilbert (ed.), *History of the Irish Confederation and the War in Ireland 1641–53* (7 vols, Dublin, 1882–91)
Grosjean, thesis	A. Grosjean, 'Scots and the Swedish State: Diplomacy, Military Service and Ennoblement 1611–1660', unpublished PhD thesis, Aberdeen University (1998)
KB	E. Marquard (ed.), *Kancelliets Brevbøger, vedrorende Danmarks indre forhold, 1637–1639* (Copenhagen, 1944); *1640–1641* (Copenhagen, 1950); *1642–1643*, G. Olsen (ed.) (Copenhagen, 1957); *1644–5*, J. Jorgensen (ed.) (Copenhagen, 1968); *1646*, J. Holmgaard (ed.) (Copenhagen, 1987); *1647* (Copenhagen, 1989); *1648* (Copenhagen, 1991); *1649* (Copenhagen, 1993); *1650* (Copenhagen, 1950)

KCFB	C.F. Bricka and J.A. Fridericia (eds), *Kong Christian den Fjerdes Egenhaendige Breve*, 4, *1636–40*; 5, *1641–44* (Copenhagen, 1969); C.F. Bricka and J.A.F. Udgave (eds.), *Ibid.*, *8, 1584–1648* (Copenhagen, 1970)
Lewis	D.E. Lewis, 'The Office of Ordnance and the Parliamentarian land forces 1642–1648', unpublished PhD thesis, Loughborough University (1976)
LJ	*Journals of the House of Lords*
LJRO	Lichfield Joint Record Office
Murdoch, thesis	S.W. Murdoch, 'Scotland, Denmark–Norway and the House of Stuart 1603–1660: a Diplomatic and Military Analysis', unpublished PhD thesis, Aberdeen University (1998)
NA	Notarial Records, Amsterdam
NAS	National Archives of Scotland, Edinburgh
NLS	National Library of Scotland, Edinburgh
NLW	National Library of Wales, Aberystwyth
Ohlmeyer, *Antrim*	J. Ohlmeyer, *Civil War and Restoration in the Three Stuart Kingdoms: the Career of Randal MacDonnell, Marquess of Antrim* (Cambridge University Press, Cambridge, 1993)
Ohlmeyer, *Ireland*	J. Ohlmeyer (ed.), *Ireland from Independence to Occupation 1641–1660* (Cambridge University Press, Cambridge, 1995)
Ohlmeyer, Wars	J. Ohlmeyer, 'The Wars of Religion, 1603–1660', in T. Bartlett and K. Jeffery (eds), *A Military History of Ireland* (Cambridge University Press, Cambridge, 1996)
Ormond	Historical Manuscripts Commission, *Manuscripts of the Marquess of Ormonde Preserved at Kilkenny Castle*, new series, I (1902), new series, 2 (1903)
PRO	Public Record Office, Kew
ROP, I and II	I. Roy, 'The Royalist Ordnance Papers', part I, *Oxford Record Society*, 43 (1965); part II, 49 (1975)
Reid	S. Reid, *The Campaigns of Montrose* (The Mercat Press, Edinburgh, 1990)
SRP	S. Bergh (ed.), *Svenska Riksrådets Protokoll*, VII, 1637–9 (Stockholm, 1895); VIII, 1640, 1641 (Stockholm, 1898); XIII, 1649 (Stockholm, 1912)
Stevenson, Finances	D. Stevenson, 'The Financing the Cause of the Covenants, 1638–51', *Scottish History Review*, 51 (1972)
Stevenson, *Government*	D. Stevenson, *The Government of Scotland under the Covenanters 1637–1651* (Edinburgh, 1982)
Tanner Letters	C. McNeill (ed.), *Tanner Letters* (Stationery Office, Dublin, 1943)
Terry	C.S. Terry (ed.), 'Papers relating to the Army of the Solemn League and Covenant 1643–1647', *Scottish Historical Society*, 2nd series, 16 (2 vols, 1917).
TRHS	*Transactions of the Royal Historical Society*
TT	Thomason Tracts
VCH	*Victoria County History*
Wheeler, Four Armies	S. Wheeler, 'Four Armies in Ireland', in (ed.), *Ireland from Independence to Occupation 1641–1660* (Cambridge University Press, Cambridge, 1995)
Wheeler, Ireland	J.S. Wheeler, 'Logistics and Supply in Cromwell's Conquest of Ireland', in M.C. Fissel (ed.), *War and Government in Britain, 1598–1650* (Manchester University Press, Manchester, 1991)
Wheeler, Scotland	J.S. Wheeler, 'The Logistics of the Cromwellian Conquest of Scotland 1650–1651', *War and Society*, 10 (1992)
Wheeler, *World Power*	J.S. Wheeler, *The Making of a World Power: War and the Military Revolution in Seventeenth-Century England* (Sutton Publishing, Stroud, 1999)
Wheeler, *Cromwell*	J.S. Wheeler, *Cromwell in Ireland* (Gill & Macmillan, Dublin, 1999)
Young and Holmes	P. Young and R. Holmes, *The English Civil War: a Military History of the Three Civil Wars 1642–1651* (Eyre Methuen, 1974)
ZCA	Zeeland Chamber of the Admiralty

NOTES

The place of publication is London unless otherwise stated.

Introduction

1. ROP, II, p. 468, n. 74; R. Brenner, *Merchants and Revolution* (Cambridge University Press, Cambridge, 1993) p. 163–4.

2. Brenner, *Merchants*, pp. 114, 320–4, 343–4, 359–60, 364–5, 371–4.

3. PRO, SP 28, *passim*.

4. PRO, PROB 11/281/520.

5. P. Edwards, 'The Low Countries, the Arms Trade and the British Civil Wars', *Journal of European Economic History*, forthcoming; Cuningham, pp. xii–xiii; ibid., pp. 93–7, 152; for Webster's marriage: AMA, Nieuwe Kerk, Amsterdam, registers, no. 421/f. 210. For his career: AMA, NA 142/26v–28, 129v, 109, 93; 144/1, 212; 145/79, 85v, 142; 146/84–84v; 147/128; 151/17, 65v; 218v; 152/8v, 17v; 201/39–40, 120v; 351/157v; 662/2/44; 694B/60, 64; 669/2/24v; 739/3; 1113/330; 1132/37.

6. C.J. Rogers (ed.), *The Military Revolution Debate* (Westview Press, Boulder, 1995), pp. 2–6; G. Parker, *The Military Revolution* (Cambridge University Press, Cambridge, 1989).

1. Arms and Equipment: A Survey

1. J.L. Malcolm, *Caesar's Due: Loyalty and King Charles 1642–1646*, Studies in History, 38 (Royal Historical Society, 1983), pp. 99, 101–2.

2. Ibid., pp. 100–3.

3. C.H. Firth, *Cromwell's Army* (Methuen, 1962), pp. 69–70; Parker, *Military Revolution*, p.18, says 3–4 to 1. Firth indicates that this is the trend on pp. 76–7.

4. Parker, *Military Revolution*, p. 18.

5. *CSPD, 1639–40*, p. 166; W.M. Stern, 'Gunmaking in Seventeenth-century London', *Journal of the Arms and Armour Society*, I, v (March 1954).

6. C. Ffoulkes, *The Gun-Founders of England* (Cambridge University Press, Cambridge, 1937), p. 36.

7. *CSPD, 1639–40*, p. 316.

8. PRO, WO 49/7.

9. Firth, *Cromwell's Army*, p. 88.

10. PRO, SP 28/11, i, f.19.

11. PRO, SP 28/29–41, *passim*.

12. NAS, GD 112/39/90/25.

13. Firth, *Cromwell's Army*, p. 89.

14. PRO, SP 28/4, f.107; ROP, I, pp. 76, 91; J.C. Hodgson (ed.), *The Journal of John Aston, 1639* (Pallas Armata, Tonbridge, 1999), p. 29.

15. Young and Holmes, p. 41.

16. *CSPD, 1639–40*, p. 369.

17. BL, Fairfax Papers, Add. MS 18,979, f.113.

18. Firth, *Cromwell's Army*, p. 82, n. 2.

19. PRO, SP 28/176, f.1v; SP 28/240, ii, *passim*.

20. Young and Holmes, p. 38.

21. Firth, *Cromwell's Army*, p. 79; PRO, SP 28/60, i, f.74 and *passim*.

22. Firth, *Cromwell's Army*, pp. 79–80.

23. PRO, SP 28/28, iv, f. 367.

24. Firth, *Cromwell's Army*, pp. 92, 114.

25. Ibid., p. 123.

26. Ibid., pp. 125–8.

27. Infra, p. 13.

28. Firth, *Cromwell's Army*, pp. 70–1; J. Kenyon, *The Civil Wars of England* (Weidenfeld & Nicolson, 1988), p. 54.

29. ROP, I, p. 66; PRO, SP 28/352.

30. Firth, *Cromwell's Army*, pp. 73–4.

31. ROP, I, p. 108.

32. Firth, *Cromwell's Army*, p. 74; Young and Holmes, p. 39.

33. PRO, SP 28/130, iii, f. 41v–42.

34. Firth, *Cromwell's Army*, p. 74.

35. Parker, *Military Revolution*, p. 50.

36. Lewis, p. 267; *infra*, p. 17.

37. TT, 12 E.69 (8), *Mercurius Civicus*, 28 September 1643, p. 6; University of Sheffield Library, Hartlib Papers, 57/1/5A.

38. NAS, GD 112/39/69/17.

39. Hartlib Papers, 26/3/1b.

40. TT, 12 E.69 (8), *Mercurius Civicus*, 28 September 1643, p. 6.

41. PRO, SP 28/262, i, f. 99; BL, Add. MS 34315, ff. 37v, 47, 48.

42. Hartlib Papers, Ephemerides 1643, 30/4/86a–93b; Lewis, p. 251, quoting Cal. Proc. for Advance of Money, vol. I, p. 7.

43. Hodgson, p. 28; *His Maiesties Passing Through the Scots Armie* (1641), p. 4.

44. NAS, GD 406/1/1153.

45. NAS, GD 406/1/412.

46. NAS, GD 112/70/18; GD 112/39/90/17.

47. *His Maiesties Passing Through the Scots Armie*, p. 4; NAS, GD 406/1/8335.

48. P. Lenihan, 'Celtic Warfare in the 1640s', in J.R. Young (ed.), *Celtic Dimensions of the British Civil Wars* (John Donald, Edinburgh, 1997), p. 129.

49. Grosjean, thesis, pp. 175–6.

50. Lenihan, 'Celtic Warfare', p. 129.

51. Parker, *Military Revolution*, pp. 17–18.

52. Ibid., p. 23.

53. Firth, *Cromwell's Army*, pp. 112–16.

54. ROP, I, p. 71; II, p. 434.

55. Furgol, p. 8.

56. BL, Add. MS 34315, f. 18.

57. Furgol, p. 8; Firth, *Cromwell's Army*, pp.113–14; Kenyon, *Civil Wars*, p. 56.

58. Firth, *Cromwell's Army*, pp. 116–17.

59. PRO, SP 28/32, i, f. 116.

60. Firth, *Cromwell's Army*, p. 11; C.H. Firth, 'The Raising of the Ironsides', in I.R. Christie (ed.), *Essays in Modern History* (Macmillan, 1968), pp. 139.

61. PRO, SP 28/162.

62. Firth, *Cromwell's Army*, p. 87.

63. C. Carlton, *Going to the Wars* (Routledge, 1992), p. 100.

64. PRO, SP 28/41, v, ff. 492–530; Chatsworth House, Bolton MS 180.

65. R.W. Stewart, *The English Ordnance Office* (Royal Historical Society, Woodbridge, 1996), p. 71.

66. Firth, *Cromwell's Army*, pp. 145–6.

67. ROP, I, pp. 318–19.

68. Firth, *Cromwell's Army*, p. 151.

69. ROP, I, pp. 218; II, pp. 257, 339.

70. Parker, *Military Revolution*, p. 33; Grosjean, thesis, p. 173 n. 150; S. Murdoch, *Robert Scott*, in *DNB* forthcoming.

71. Murdoch, *Scott*.

72. Ibid.

73. Grosjean, thesis, pp. 173–5; Terry, I, p. lxxxviii; John Spalding, *The History of the Troubles*, I (Edinburgh, 1828), p. 88.

74. Parker, *Military Revolution*, pp. 33–5; Firth, *Cromwell's Army*, p. 147; Grosjean, thesis, pp. 173–5; PRO, SP 28/346, no. 346.

75. Carte 6, f. 488; Carte 15, f. 268.

76. Young and Holmes, p. 48; Kenyon, *Civil Wars*, p. 86.

77. M. Atkin and W. Laughlin, *Gloucester and the Civil War: a City under Siege* (Alan Sutton Publishing, Stroud, 1992), p. 83; ROP, I, p. 69.

78. PRO, SP 28/2B, iv, ff. 667–667v.

79. ROP, I, pp. 155, 226.

80. Firth, *Cromwell's Army*, p. 78, 80.

81. Young and Holmes, p. 49.

82. PRO SP 28/145, f. 61.

83. ROP, I, pp. 32–3.

84. Brereton, II, p. 365.

85. Firth, *Cromwell's Army*, p. 168.

86. Firth, *Cromwell's Army*, p. 121.

87. Kenyon, *Civil Wars*, p. 55.

88. Young and Holmes, p. 41.

89. PRO, SP 28/130, iii, ff. 40v–41.

90. ROP, I, *passim*.

91. Firth, *Cromwell's Army*, pp. 71–2.

92. Carlton, p. 99.

93. Ibid.

94. Firth, *Cromwell's Army*, p. 118, n. 1.

95. PRO, SP 28/222, iii.

96. PRO, SP 28/1D, ii, f. 488; SP 28/35, iv, f. 640.

97. For example, Sir Thomas Martin's troop, PRO, SP 28/222, iii.

98. Furgol, pp. 8, 316, 329, 330, 341; Terry, p. xxi; a secret was a piece of defensive armour worn under outer garments; a jack was an item of body armour consisting of a padded coat or one interlined with metal plate or horn.

99. PRO, SP 28/2B, iii, f. 553.

100. Furgol, p. 11; Hodgson, p. 28. I am grateful to Dr Stephen Murdoch for information on the wearing of plaid.

101. Young and Holmes, p. 43, n .4.

102. *CSPD, 1650*, pp. 594, 604; *CSPD, 1651*, pp. 539, 585.

103. PRO, SP 28/1B, I, f. 422; 28/2B, iii, f. 553, 564.

104. PRO, SP 28/131, part 13.

105. Furgol, p. 11.

106. Carte 6, f. 83; Carte 7, f. 65v; Furgol, p. 11.

107. PRO, SP 28/1C, f. 160.

108. PRO, SP 28/253B, f. 91.

109. CIA, II, p. 388.

110. Clive Holmes, *The Eastern Association and the English Civil War* (Cambridge University Press, Cambridge, 1974), p. 152.

111. Firth, *Cromwell's Army*, p. 232.

112. Ibid., pp. 232–3.

113. Holmes, *Eastern Association*, p. 276, n.126; PRO, SP 28/26, ii, f. 136.
114. PRO, SP 28/5, f. 284.
115. Firth, *Cromwell's Army*, p. 233.
116. P. Edwards, 'Logistics and Supply', in J. Kenyon and J. Ohlmeyer (eds) *The Civil Wars: A Military History of England, Scotland and Ireland 1638–1660* (Oxford University Press, Oxford, 1998), p. 239.
117. PRO, SP 28/1A, f. 54.
118. Furgol, p. 11.
119. Edwards, 'Logistics', p. 239.
120. P. Young, *Edgehill 1642* (Windrush Press, Moreton-in-Marsh, 1995), p. 33; Firth, *Cromwell's Army*, pp. 45–6.
121. PRO, SP 28/3A, i, f. 77.
122. PRO, SP 28/225, i, f. 3.
123. PRO, SP 28/29, i, f. 180.
124. Young and Holmes, p. 39; Firth, *Cromwell's Army*, p, 16, n. 2.
125. PRO, SP 28/130, iii, f. 41v.
126. P. Edwards, 'The Supply of Horses to the Parliamentarian and Royalist Armies in the English Civil War', *Historical Research*, 68 (February 1995), 50.
127. Edwards, 'Supply of Horses', pp. 54–6; R.J. Moore-Colyer, 'Horse Supply and the British Cavalry: a Review, 1066–1900', *Journal of the Society for Army Historical Research*, 70 (1992), 251.
128. Edwards, 'Supply of Horses', p. 50.
129. Young and Holmes, pp. 39–40.
130. Edwards, 'Supply of Horses', pp. 50, 54.
131. P. Edwards, *The Horse Trade of Tudor and Stuart England* (Cambridge University Press, Cambridge,1988), pp. 31–46.
132. Young and Holmes, p. 209.
133. Carte 6, f. 26.
134. BL, Harleian MS 6852, f. 50.
135. PRO, SP 28/130, iii, f. 44v.
136. Firth, *Cromwell's Army*, p. 241.
137. Huntingdonshire Record Office, 2091/542.
138. Firth, *Cromwell's Army*, p. 224; Wheeler, Scotland, p. 12.
139. Wheeler, Scotland, pp. 9–10.
140. Carlton, *Wars*, p. 95.
141. H.G. Tibbutt (ed.), *The Letter Books of Sir Samuel Luke* (HMSO, 1963) p. 525, no. 1257.

2. Administration and Supply

1. Stewart, *Ordnance Office*, p. 120.
2. ROP, I, p. 16.
3. Lewis, pp. 24–7; Stewart, *Ordnance Office*, pp. 6–32.
4. PRO, WO 49/73, f. 62; SP 28/39, iv, f. 445.
5. G.E. Aylmer, 'Attempts at Administrative Reform', *English Historical Review*, LXXII (1957), 241.
6. Stewart, *Ordnance Office*, p. 15.
7. Aylmer, 'Administrative Reform', p. 241.
8. Lewis, p. 53.
9. Ibid., pp. 26–7.
10. In 1643 John Pitts sent three consignments of Swedish feathers to Windsor: PRO, SP 28/145.
11. Lewis, pp. 35–7.
12. Lewis, p. 78; PRO, WO 49/75, ff. 89v–90.
13. PRO, WO 49/75, f. 89v; ROP, I, p. 16; G.I. Mungean, 'Contracts for the Supply of Equipment to the "New Model" Army in 1645', *Journal of the Arms and Armour Society*, VI (1968–70), *passim*.
14. John Stow, *The Survey of London* (Dent, 1956), p. 115.
15. PRO, WO 49/76, f. 13; WO 49/75, f. 114.
16. PRO, WO 49/75, f. 89; Lewis, p. 51.
17. PRO, WO 49/75, f. 81; Stewart, *Ordnance Office*, pp. 16, 67–8.
18. PRO, WO 49/69, ff. 23–4.
19. PRO, WO 49/76, f. 6.
20. Aylmer, 'Administrative Reform', pp. 242–4; Fissel, pp. 93–4.
21. Fissel, p. 93.
22. Aylmer, 'Administrative Reform', p. 242; A.Thrush, 'The Ordnance Office and the Navy', *Mariner's Mirror*, 77 (1991), 348–50.
23. Thrush, 'Ordnance Office and the Navy', pp. 348–9.
24. Thrush, 'Ordnance Office and the Navy', p. 349.
25. Fissel, pp. 99–100.
26. PRO, WO 49/71, ff. 8v, 9, 53v, 62v, 64v; 72/86, f. 106.
27. Fissel, pp. 103–6.
28. Aylmer, 'Administrative Reform', p. 245.
29. Fissel, p. 24.
30. Ibid., p. 33.
31. C. Russell, *The Fall of the British Monarchies 1637–1642* (Oxford University Press, Oxford, 1991), pp.142–3; Fissel, p. 116.
32. Ibid., pp. 55, 58, 60; Russell, *British Monarchies*, p. 142.
33. *Supra*, p. 18.
34. *Infra*, pp. 129–37.
35. Russell, *British Monarchies*, p.76; *CSPD, 1638–9*, p. 325.

36. Fissel, p. 94.

37. Ibid., pp. 93–4, 109–10.

38. Ibid., p. 100.

39. Ibid., pp. 2, 47–9.

40. *CSPD, 1638–9*, pp. 406–10.

41. M. Bennett, *The Civil Wars in Britain and Ireland 1638–1651* (Blackwell, Oxford, 1997), p. 43; Fissel, p. 73.

42. *CSPD 1638–9*, January 1638–9, pp. 406–10; NAS, GD 112/39/70/17.

43. Fissel, pp. 75–6.

44. J.R. Young, *The Scottish Parliament 1639–1661: A Political and Constitutional Analysis* (John Donald, Edinburgh, 1996), pp. 23, 44–5, 56.

45. M. Wood, *Extracts from the Records of the Burgh of Edinburgh 1626 to 1641* (Oliver & Boyd, Edinburgh, 1936), pp. 204, 206.

46. Furgol, p. 10; R. Williams, *Montrose: Cavalier in Mourning* (Barrie & Jenkins, 1975), p. 82.

47. Fissel, p. 31, n. 101.

48. Ibid., pp. 32–3.

49. *Infra*, pp. 181–4.

50. Fissel, pp. 75–6; W. Chambers (ed.), *Charters and Documents Relating to the Burgh of Peebles with Extracts from the Records of the Burgh, AD 1165–1710* (Scottish Burgh Records Society, Edinburgh, 1872), pp. 375–6.

51. Fissel, pp. 50–4.

52. Carte, *Ormond*, II, p. 5; Carte 3, f. 476

53. *CSPI, 1633–47*, p. 358.

54. In Elizabeth's reign it consisted of a master of the ordnance, a clerk and assistant clerk, seven gunners and eight artificers: Stewart, *Ordnance Office* p. 116.

55. *CSPI, 1633–47*, pp. 292, 358, 786.

56. Ibid., pp. 765, 773, 780.

57. Ibid., pp. 358, 380.

58. Ibid., p. 341; R. Loeber and G. Parker, 'The Military Revolution in Seventeenth-Century Ireland', in Ohlmeyer, Ireland, pp.73–4; Carte, *Life*, I, p. 347.

59. Carte, *Ormond*, I, p. 349; Carte 2, f. 162.

60. Carte 2, ff. 183, 211; SP 28/1C, iii, f. 258.

61. Hogan, p. 121.

62. *CSPI, 1633–47*, p. 344.5.

63. Russell, *British Monarchies*, p. 416.

64. Ibid., p. 447; ROP, I, pp. 48, 152.

65. *CSPI, 1633–47*, p. 366.

66. Ibid., pp. 361–2.

67. *Infra*, pp. 28, 218; J.R. Powell and E.K. Timings (eds), 'Documents Relating to the Civil War 1642–1648', *Navy Records Society* (1963), 10; B. Capp, 'Naval Operations', in Kenyon and Ohlmeyer, *Civil Wars*, p. 158.

68. PRO, SP 28/139/15; P 28/139/25; SP 28/170.

69. J.S. Wheeler, 'Four armies in Ireland', in Ohlmeyer, Ireland, p. 46.

70. Loeber and Parker, 'Military Revolution', p. 76.

71. Wheeler, 'Four Armies', p. 46.

72. M. Ó Siochru, *Confederate Ireland 1642–1649* (Four Courts Press, Dublin, 1999), p. 27.

73. Ó Siochru, *Confederate Ireland*, pp. 40–1, 44.

74. Gilbert, II, p. 123; Ó Siochru, *Confederate Ireland*, pp. 50–1.

75. *Infra*, pp. 189–93.

76. ROP, I, p. 19.

77. Ibid., pp. 11, 13; Lewis, p. 26; H.C. Tomlinson, *Guns and Government, the Ordnance Office Under the Later Stuarts* (Royal Historical Society, London, 1979), p. 7.

78. Edwards, 'Logistics', p. 241; ROP, I, p. 13.

79. ROP, I, pp. 20, 48.

80. Ibid., I, p. 20.

81. Lewis, p. 305; ROP, I, p. 14; Tomlinson, *Guns and Government*, p.8.

82. Lewis, pp. 26–8.

83. Russell, *British Monarchies*, pp. 464, 512.

84. R. Hutton, 'The Royalist War Effort', in J. Morrill (ed.) *Reactions to the English Civil War 1642–1649*, (Macmillan, 1982), pp. 52–3.

85. HMC Hastings MSS, II, 1930, p. 84.

86. ROP, I, p. 15.

87. Bodl., Fairfax MS 32, f. 23.

88. Stewart, *Ordnance Office*, pp. 126–40; Powell and Timings, 'Documents', p. 10.

89. Kenyon, *Civil Wars*, pp. 60–1; ROP, I, pp. 11, 13.

90. ROP, I, p. 19.

91. C.V. Wedgwood, *The King's War 1641–1647* (Collins, 1958), p. 203.

92. C.H.Firth and R.S.Rait (eds), *Acts and Ordinances of the Interregnum, 1642–60* (HMSO, 1911), pp. 6–9.

93. K. Lindley, *Popular Politics in Civil War London* (Scolar Press, Aldershot, 1997), p. 220.

94. P. Edwards, 'The Supply of Horses to the Parliamentarian and Royalist Armies in the English Civil War', *Historical Research*, 68 (1995), 58.

95. Lindley, *Popular Politics*, p. 220; PRO, SP 28/5, f. 244.

96. P. Tennant, *Edgehill and Beyond: The People's War in the South Midlands 1642–1645* (Alan Sutton Publishing, Stroud, 1992), p. 32.

97. Shropshire Record Office, Ludlow Corporation Records, 556/Box 298.

98. Birmingham Reference Library, Fetherston Correspondence, vol. I, f. 110.

99. Lewis, p. 118; Brenner, *Merchants*, pp. 368, 370–1.

100. Kenyon, *Civil Wars*, p. 97.

101. Lewis, pp. 115–26, 281, 283, 286.

102. ROP, I, pp. 48, 50–1.

103. Ibid., I, pp. 50, 215.

104. Ibid., I, pp. 45; II, p. 385.

105. Ibid., II, pp. 387–8.

106. Ibid., I, pp. 19–20.

107. Ibid., I, p. 19 n. 9; G. Trease, *Portrait of a Cavalier: William Cavendish, First Duke of Newcastle* (Macmillan, 1979), p. 111.

108. *Infra*, pp. 196–8.

109. Ibid., I, pp. 99–100, 107–8.

110. Lewis, p. 249.

111. Ibid., pp. 258–71.

112. Ibid., chs 11–12, *passim*.

113. Ibid., pp. 275–7.

114. Holmes, *Eastern Association*, pp. 150–1.

115. ROP, I, p. 43.

116. F. Kitson, *Prince Rupert*, (Constable, 1994), p. 175.

117. Lewis, pp. 210–11, 218, 253–4.

118. PRO, SP 28/264, f. 28, 31, 33, 42–3, 56, 59, 224, 243–4.

119. Holmes, *Eastern Association*, p. 151.

120. PRO, SP 28/136/26–7; SP 28/137/2; SP 28/247; Warwickshire Record Office, CR 2017/C10, Earl of Denbigh's Letter Books, II, no. 5.

121. PRO, SP 28/15, i, ff. 42, 45.

122. Gloucestershire Record Office, Gloucester Borough Records GBR/B3/2.

123. BL, Add. MS 18981, f. 157.

124. For example, BL, Add. MS 18982, f. 31.

125. ROP, I, p. 53.

126. PRO, SP 28/145, ff. 303, 320, 381, 390–1.

127. ROP, I, pp. 25–6, *passim*; BL, Add. MS, 18981, ff. 71–2; BL, Harleian MS 6852, ff. 32, 88.

128. Lewis, p. 234.

129. PRO, SP 28/240–1.

130. Young and Holmes, p. 44.

131. PRO, SP 28/29, i, f. 231.

132. Warwickshire Record Office, CR 2017/C9, Earl of Denbigh's Letter Books, I, no. 101.

133. PRO, SP 28/24.

134. PRO, SP 28/3; SP 28/128; SP 28/147/2; A.M. Everitt, 'Suffolk and the Great Rebellion', *Suffolk Record Society*, 3 (1960), 89–92, 158.

135. Holmes, *Eastern Association*, p. 151.

136. A.M. Everitt, *The Community of Kent and the Great Rebellion 1640–60* (Leicester University Press, Leicester, 1973), pp. 137, 155, n. 1; PRO, SP 28/130, iii.

137. D.H. Pennington and I.A. Roots, *The Committee at Stafford 1643–45* (Manchester University Press, Manchester, 1957), p. 219.

138. Young, *Scottish Parliament*, *passim*: Stevenson, Finances, pp. 95–123.

139. Stevenson, *Government*, pp. 1–5; Young, *Scottish Parliament*, pp. 105, 114, 122, 125, 138, 267.

140. Stevenson, *Government*, pp. 105–7; Young, *Scottish Parliament*, p. 279.

141. Terry, I, p. xxi.

142. Terry, I, pp. xxi–xxii; TT 245 669, f. 7 (58).

143. Terry, I, p. xxii.

144. Terry, I, p. xxii; J.D. Marwick (ed.), *Charters and Other Documents Relating to the City of Glasgow AD 1175–1649*, vol. I, ii (Scottish Burghs Records Society, Edinburgh, 1894), p. 484, 18 December 1645.

145. *Extracts from the Records of the Burgh of Glasgow AD 1630–1662* (Scottish Burghs Records Society, Glasgow, 1881), p. 90.

146. Argyll and Bute Archive (Lochgilphead), Dumbarton Garrison MSS, f. 12.

147. M. Wood (ed.), *Extracts from the Records of the Burgh of Edinburgh 1642–1655* (Edinburgh, 1938), p. 76.

148. *Infra*, p. 231.

149. NAS, PA 15/3.

150. *Infra*, pp. 183–4.

151. Stevenson, *Government*, p. 17, 64; NAS, PA 16/2/13; NAS, PA 16/3/6, no. 65.

152. NAS, PA 15/3.

153. NAS, PA 15/3; PA 16/3/9, no. 12; NLS, Balcarres Papers 29.2.9, f. 157.

154. *Glasgow Records 1630–1662*, p. 90.

155. Terry, I, pp. 259, 282.

156. NAS, PA 15/3; Terry, I, pp. 15–18.

157. Stevenson, *Government*, p. 89; NAS, PA 15/3.

158. *CSPI, 1633–47*, pp. 464, 490.

159. Ibid., p. 490.

160. Ibid., pp. 503, 517.

161. Ibid., pp. 492, 494.

162. Ó Siochrú, *Confederate Ireland*, p. 84.

163. Ó Siochrú, *Confederate Ireland*, p. 121, n. 17.

164. Ó Siochrú, *Confederate Ireland*, pp. 51–2, 121.

165. Gilbert, VI, pp. 78, 82–3.

166. *CSPI, 1633–47*, pp. 727, 736, 738.

167. Ibid., pp. 735–6.

168. Ibid., pp. 693, 720, 727, 736, 738.

169. Ibid., pp. 619, 717.

170. Gilbert, VI, p. 201.

171. Wheeler, Ireland, p. 50; Wheeler, Scotland, p. 13.

172. Wheeler, Four Armies, pp. 62–3.

173. J. Burke, 'The New Model Army and the problems of Siege Warfare, 1648–51', Irish Historical Studies, XXVII (1990), 8; Loeber and Parker, 'Military Revolution', pp. 78–81.

174. PRO, SP 25/94, f. 318; Loeber and Parker, 'Military Revolution', p. 76; Wheeler, Ireland, p. 41.

175. Burke, 'New Model Army', pp. 10, 16, 17; Wheeler, Ireland, p. 50.

176. PRO, SP 28/61, iv, f. 736; SP 28/62, ii, f. 333; SP 28/63, ii, f. 269.

177. Wheeler, Ireland, p. 48.

178. Ibid., p. 50.

179. Wheeler, Scotland, p. 13.

180. Ibid., pp. 12, 17, n. 68.

181. Ibid., p. 12; J.D. Grainger, Cromwell Against the Scots: the Last Anglo-Scottish War, 1650–1652 (Tuckwell Press, East Linton, 1997), p. 153.

182. Grainger, Last Anglo-Scottish War, pp. 70, 153.

183. Wheeler, Scotland, pp. 9, 11.

184. Ibid., pp. 11–12.

185. Infra, pp. 193–4.

3. The Sinews of War: Financing the War Effort

1. Stevenson, Finances, pp. 122–3.

2. R. Gillespie, 'The Irish Economy at War, 1641–1652', in Ohlmeyer, Ireland, pp. 160–80.

3. Fissel, p. 112.

4. Ibid., pp. 129–37; Russell, British Monarchies, pp. 130–6.

5. Fissel, p. 113, 118, 141.

6. CSPV, 1636–9, p. 500; Fissel, pp. 113–14, 141.

7. Ibid., p. 139, 141.

8. Ibid., pp. 113, 124–9.

9. Ibid., pp. 129–37; J.D. Maltby (ed), 'The Short Parliament (1640) Diary of Sir Thomas Aston', Camden Society, 4th series, 35 (1988), pp. 6–7.

10. Fissel, pp. 140–1.

11. Ibid., pp. 52, 59–60, 116–17.

12. Bennett, Civil Wars, pp. 69–71.

13. M. Bennett, 'Outreiking and Ingathering: Coping with Funding the Scottish Armies 1639–1653', unpublished paper presented at a King's College, London, War Studies Department seminar, 10 March 1999. I am grateful to Dr Bennett for allowing me to make use of this work.

14. P. Donald, An Uncounselled King: Charles I and the Scottish Troubles 1637–1641 (Cambridge University Press, Cambridge, 1990), pp. 282, 300.

15. Bennett, 'Outreiking', p. 6.

16. S. Porter, 'The Economic and Social Impact of the Civil War upon London', in S. Porter (ed), London and the Civil War (Macmillan, 1996), p. 195; H. Hazlett, 'The Financing of the British Armies in Ireland, 1641–9', Irish Historical Studies, I (1938–9) p. 25; J.R. MacCormack, Revolutionary Politics in the Long Parliament (Harvard University Press, Cambridge, Mass., 1973), p. 24–5.

17. CIA, I, p. 463; MacCormack, Revolutionary Politics, p. 38; Hazlett, 'Financing of the British Armies', p. 25.

18. Ormond, new series, II (1903), p .143.

19. K. Lindley, 'Irish Adventurers and Godly Militants in the 1640s', Irish Historical Studies, XXIX (1994–5), pp. 2, 8–10.

20. Hazlett, 'Financing of the British Armies', p. 31; J.R. MacCormack, 'The Irish Adventurers and the English Civil War', Irish Historical Studies, X (1956–7), p. 39.

21. Hazlett, 'Financing of the British Armies', p. 32.

22. Wheeler, World Power, p. 82.

23. Ibid., pp. 40, 45.

24. Edwards, 'Logistics', p. 261.

25. Wheeler, World Power, pp. 85, 106–7, 111.

26. Ibid., p. 111.

27. Brenner, Merchants, pp. 371–4.

28. Porter, 'Impact', p. 194.

29. CSPD, 1644, p. 68; Edwards, 'Logistics', p. 264; Hazlett, 'Financing of the British Armies', p. 34.

30. Tibbutt, Letter Books, p. 385.

31. Wheeler, World Power, p. 105.

32. Ibid., pp. 82, 110; I. Gentles, The New Model Army in England, Ireland and Scotland, 1645–1653 (Blackwell, Oxford, 1992), pp. 28–9.

33. Firth and Rait, Acts and Ordinances, I, pp. 6–9.

34. Wheeler, World Power, p. 102; J.S. Morrill, The Revolt of the Provinces (George Allen & Unwin, London, 1976), p. 85.

35. J. Wroughton, A Community at War: The Civil War in Bath and North Somerset, 1642–1650

(Lansdown Press, Bath, 1992), pp. 138–9; Everitt, *Kent*, p. 156; Pennington and Roots, *Stafford*, p. xxxiii; A. Hughes, *Politics, Society and Civil War in Warwickshire, 1620–1660* (Cambridge University Press, Cambridge, 1987), p. 181.

36. Wheeler, *World Power*, p. 103.
37. Ibid., p. 103.
38. Morrill, *Revolt*, p. 56.
39. Morrill, *Revolt*, pp. 57–8; Bennett, *Civil Wars*, p. 174.
40. Morrill, *Revolt*, p. 69.
41. Wheeler, *World Power*, p. 175.
42. Kenyon, *Civil Wars*, p. 115; Morrill, *Revolt*, p. 85.
43. Wheeler, *World Power*, p. 104.
44. Ibid., pp. 149–50; J.P. Kenyon, *The Stuart Constitution* (Cambridge University Press, Cambridge, 1986), pp. 244–5.
45. Kenyon, *Constitution*, p. 245; M.J. Braddick, *Parliamentary Taxation in 17th Century England* (Royal Historical Society, Woodbridge, 1994), p. 169.
46. Wheeler, *World Power*, pp. 127–8.
47. Ibid., p. 41.
48. Morrill, *Revolt*, p. 79.
49. Ibid., pp. 116–7.
50. Pennington and Roots, *Stafford*, p. xxxix.
51. Wheeler, *World Power*, pp. 104, 107.
52. Ibid., pp. 111–12.
53. Ibid., p. 115.
54. Ibid., pp. 115–16.
55. Ibid., p. 116.
56. Gentles, *New Model Army*, p. 28.
57. *CSPD, 1644*, p. 319; *CSPD, 1644–5*, p. 51.
58. Wheeler, *World Power*, p. 153.
59. Gentles, *New Model Army*, pp. 29–30.
60. Lewis, p. 194.
61. Pennington and Roots, *Stafford*, pp. xxxi–xxxii; Holmes, *Eastern Association*, pp. 75–81.
62. Hughes, *Warwickshire*, pp. 224–8.
63. Wheeler, *World Power*, p. 110.
64. Holmes, *Eastern Association*, pp. 75–81; Carte 5, f. 45.
65. Tibbutt, *Letter Books*, p. 608, no.1568 and *passim*, Edwards, 'Logistics', p. 268.
66. Brereton, I, pp. 89, 98, 126, 152, 172–3, 190, 227, 347; II, pp. 110, 183.
67. Holmes, *Eastern Association*, p. 160.
68. Gentles, *New Model Army*, pp. 28–9.
69. Lewis, pp. 201–2.
70. PRO, SP 28/140.
71. Lewis, pp. 188, 199.
72. Ibid., pp. 186–8.
73. Ibid., p. 202.

74. Ibid., pp. 181, 198.
75. PRO, SP 28/66, iii, f. 481.
76. P. Carter, 'Clerical Taxation During the Civil War and Interregnum', *Historical Research*, LXVII (1994), 121–2; J.E. Engberg, 'Royalist Finances during the English Civil War 1642–1646', *Scandinavian Economic History Review*, XIV (1966), 86; Wheeler, *World Power*, p. 77.
77. Wheeler, *World Power*, p. 78.
78. Hutton, pp. 86–9.
79. Engberg, 'Royalist Finances', p. 78.
80. Hutton, pp. 15, 35, 89; Engberg, 'Royalist Finances', p. 78.
81. ROP, II, p. 468, n. 74; Derbyshire Record Office, D258/41/31X(a).
82. Wheeler, *World Power*, p. 77.
83. M. Atkin, *The Civil War in Worcestershire* (Sutton Publishing, Stroud, 1995), p. 52.
84. Hutton, p. 92.
85. For example, P. Geyl, 'Frederick Henry of Orange and King Charles I', *English Hist. Review*, 38 (1923) 368–9; *CSPD, 1644–5*, pp. 470, 495; and *infra*, pp.
86. Geyl, 'Orange and Charles', pp. 368–9.
87. *CSPD, 1644*, pp. 190, 260, 320; *CSPD, 1644–5*, pp. 499, 502.
88. Edwards, 'Logistics', p. 263; Hutton, p. 30; Engberg, 'Royalist Finances', p. 79.
89. Hutton, p. 30.
90. Carter, 'Clerical Taxation', pp. 122–3.
91. J.W.W. Bund, *The Civil War in Worcestershire 1642–1646* (Sutton, Gloucester, 1905/1979 reprint), pp. 33–45; D. Eddershaw, *The Civil War in Oxfordshire* (Sutton Publishing, Stroud, 1995), p. 50.
92. Hutton, p. 30; Eddershaw, *Oxfordshire*, pp. 56–8; Bund, *Worcestershire*, p. 71.
93. Hutton, pp. 63, 65.
94. Ibid., pp. 36–7.
95. Bennett, *Civil Wars*, p. 179.
96. Edwards, 'Logistics', p. 265.
97. *CSPD, 1641–3*, p. 442.
98. Hutton, p. 93; Bennett, *Civil Wars*, p. 174.
99. Hutton, pp. 89–91.
100. Carter, 'Clerical Taxation', p. 123.
101. *Infra*, p. 52.
102. Powell and Timings 'Documents', p. 125.
103. Engberg, 'Royalist Finances', p. 91.
104. Hutton, p. 172.
105. M. Bennett, '"My Plundered Townes, My Houses Devastation": The Civil War and North Midland Life, 1642–1646', *Midland History*, XXII (1997), 43.

106. Hutton, p. 172.

107. *CSPD, 1644*, p. 27.

108. ROP, I, p. 30.

109. Ibid, pp. 38–9; *CSPD, 1644–5*, p. 511; BL, Harleian MS 6802, f. 250.

110. J.W.W. Bund (ed), 'Diary of Henry Townshend', II, *Worcestershire Historical Society*, (London, 1920), pp. 106, 138–41; M. Wanklyn, 'The King's Armies in the West of England', unpublished Manchester University MA thesis (1966), p. 101.

111. Lichfield Cathedral Library, MS Lich 24, ff. 78–84.

112. M. Bennett, 'A Nottinghamshire Village in War and Peace: the Accounts of the Constables of Upton 1640–1666', *Thoroton Society, Record Series*, XXXIX (1995), *passim*; Wanklyn, thesis, p. 103.

113. Engberg, 'Royalist Finances', pp. 86–7.

114. Engberg, 'Royalist Finances', p. 73.

115. ROP, I, p. 38.

116. Ibid., pp. 23, 33.

117. *CSPD, 1644*, p. 27; ROP, I, p. 39.

118. ROP, II, pp. 388–9.

119. ROP, II, p. 393.

120. Stevenson, Finances, pp. 89–90; Young, *Scottish Parliament*, p. 59.

121. Young, *Scottish Parliament*, p. 25; Stevenson, Finances, pp. 89–90, 94, 101; *Edinburgh Records 1626–41*, p. 219.

122. Cuningham, pp. 84–5.

123. Stevenson, Finances, p. 103; M.P. Rooseboom, *The Scottish Staple in the Netherlands* (Martinus Nijhoff, The Hague, 1910), p. 184; Cuningham, pp. 204–19.

124. Extracts from the Records of the Burgh of Glasgow AD 1573–1642, *Scottish Burgh Records Society* (Glasgow, 1876), pp. 397–8; E.Henderson, *The Annals of Dunfermline* (John Tweed, Glasgow, 1897), p. 305; Stevenson, Finances, pp. 90–1; *Edinburgh Records 1626–41*, p. 238.

125. R. Renwick (ed), 'Extracts from the Records of the Royal Burgh of Stirling AD 1519–1616', *Scottish Burgh Records Society*, (Glasgow, 1887), p. 183.

126. Stevenson, Finances, pp. 90–2, 100–1, 105; Bennett, *Civil Wars*, pp. 193–4.

127. Stevenson, Finances, pp. 108, 115, 121.

128. Ibid., pp. 89–90.

129. NAS, GD 26/12/5/2; GD 26/12/7.

130. Young, *Scottish Parliament*, pp. 44–5; Stevenson, Finances, pp. 98–9.

131. Stevenson, Finances, pp. 100, 102–3.

132. Stevenson, *Government*, pp. 43–6; Stevenson, Finances, pp. 106–11.

133. Stevenson, Finances, pp. 103–4, 111–15; Young, *Scottish Parliament*, p. 80.

134. Stevenson, pp. 105, 109; Young, *Scottish Parliament*, p. 115.

135. Some examples of expenditure are provided in the chapter on hand arms industries.

136. *Edinburgh Records 1642–1655*, pp. 78, 399.

137. Bennett, *Civil Wars*, p. 196.

138. Terry, I, p. xx; Stevenson, Finances, p. 101.

139. NLS, Saltoun MS 17503, f. 24.

140. NLS, PA 16/3/9/4.

141. Stevenson, Finances, pp. 122–3.

142. Ohlmeyer, Wars, p. 175; Stevenson, Finances, pp. 96–7.

143. Terry, I, p. lxxvii.

144. Bennett, 'Outreiking', pp. 13–16, 18.

145. Stevenson, Finances, p. 110; Terry, p. lxxvii.

146. Stevenson, Finances, p. 123.

147. *SRP*, viii, p. 99.

148. Furgol, p. 5.

149. Terry, *passim*.

150. Carte 7, f. 600.

151. *Tanner Letters*, pp. 165, 173–4, 181–2; Carte 7, f. 627.

152. Wheeler, *World Power*, p. 241, n. 23.

153. Stevenson, *Government*, pp. 116, 123, 128, 134.

154. Gillespie, 'Irish Economy', p. 169.

155. Ormond, new series, II, p. 297.

156. Gillespie, 'Irish Economy', p. 171, 175.

157. Hazlett, 'Financing of the British Armies', pp. 32–3.

158. Ohlmeyer, Wars, pp. 175, 177; Gilbert, VII, pp. 343–8.

159. Gillespie, 'Irish Economy', p. 168.

160. Gilbert, II, p. 206.

161. Ó Siochru, *Confederate Ireland*, p. 54; Gillespie, 'Irish Economy', p. 168.

162. Gilbert, VI, pp. 81–2.

163. Gilbert, II, p. 262; also see Franciscan MSS, p. 139.

164. J.I. Casway, 'Owen Roe O'Neill's Return to Ireland in 1642: the Diplomatic Background', *Studia Hibernica*, 9 (1969), 49, 54; Ohlmeyer, 'Ireland Independent', in Ohlmeyer, *Ireland*, p. 109; Wheeler, Four Armies, pp. 54–5.

165. Wheeler, Four armies, p. 54; Ohlmeyer, 'Ireland Independent', p. 109.

166. Gillespie, 'Irish Economy', p. 176.

167. Ohlmeyer, 'Ireland Independent', p. 109.

168. Hazlett, 'Financing of the British Armies', pp. 21–2.

169. Ohlmeyer, Wars, p. 176.
170. Ormond, new series, I, p. 70.
171. D.F. Cregan, 'The Confederate Catholics of Ireland: the Personnel of the Confederation, 1642–9', Irish Historical Studies, XXIX (1994–5), 506.
172. Ó Siochru, Confederate Ireland, p. 53; Gilbert, II, p. 84; Gillespie, 'Irish Economy', pp. 167, 171.
173. Ohlmeyer, Wars, p. 176.
174. Supra, pp. 46, 55.
175. Bennett, Civil Wars, p. 197.
176. Ibid., pp. 199–200.
177. Ohlmeyer, Wars, pp. 176–7.
178. Gillespie, 'Irish Economy', p. 177; Carte 14, f. 2v.
179. Gilbert, VII, p. 214.
180. Ormond, new series, II, p. 320; Ohlmeyer, Wars, p. 177.
181. Carte 9, f. 125.
182. Carte 14, f. 2.
183. Bennett, Civil Wars, p. 197.
184. Ormond, new series, I, p. 70; Ohlmeyer, Wars, p. 177.
185. Gillespie, 'Irish Economy', pp. 176–7.
186. Gillespie, 'Irish Economy', p. 177.
187. Gilbert, VII, p. 215.
188. Ohlmeyer, Wars, p. 177.
189. Ibid., p. 177.
190. Hughes, Warwickshire, pp. 187–8; Eddershaw, Oxfordshire, p. 79.
191. Kenyon, Civil Wars, p. 116; Hughes, Warwickshire, p. 210.
192. D. Underdown, Somerset in the Civil War and Interregnum (David & Charles, Newton Abbot, 1973), p. 71; Tibbutt, Letter Books, p. 599.
193. North Yorkshire Record Office, Scarborough Corporation Minute Book 1621–49, DC/SCB II/1/1/1, MIC 2150/302, f. 163v.
194. Bennett, Civil Wars, p. 171; Holmes, Eastern Association, p. 137.
195. Fissel, pp. 73–4.
196. M. Bennett, 'Contribution and Assessment: Financial Exactions in the English Civil War, 1642–1646', War and Society, 4 (1986), 5, 8; Braddick, Parliamentary Taxation, p. 278.
197. Furgol, pp. 183–6.
198. A. Hopper, '"Tinker" Fox and the Politics of Garrison Warfare in the West Midlands, 1643–50', Midland History, XXIV (1999), 104–7; Tennant, Edgehill, pp. 100–1.
199. Derbyshire Record Office, Gresley of Drakelowe MSS, D803/M/Z9, f. 134.
200. Stevenson, Finances, p. 104.

201. Braddick, Parliamentary Taxation, pp. 168, 175, 177–87; Morrill, Revolt, p. 65.
202. I. Roy, 'The English Civil War and English Society', War and Society, I (1975), 28–9.
203. Hutton, pp. 96–7; Holmes, Eastern Association, pp. 153–4.
204. Bennett, 'North Midlands', p. 47.
205. Morrill, Revolt, p. 80.
206. Hutton, pp. 95–104.

4. Home Supplies: Weapons

1. PRO, WO 49/75, f. 147.
2. PRO, WO 49/71, f. 9.
3. Stern, 'Gunmaking', p. 71.
4. Ibid., pp. 71–89.
5. Ibid., pp. 81–2.
6. PRO, WO 49/69, f. 63.
7. Ibid., ff. 23–57.
8. Ibid., f. 48.
9. PRO, SP 28/4, f. 85; SP 28/35/iv, f. 276.
10. BL, Harleian MS 6804, f. 160; Carte 3, ff. 219, 311.
11. PRO, WO 49/68–75, passim.
12. Fissel, p. 102.
13. PRO, WO 49/71, ff. 55–74.
14. CSPD, 1638–9, p. 237.
15. CSPD, 1636–7, p. 305; Fissel, p. 104.
16. PRO, WO 49/71, f. 9; WO 49/68, f. 59.
17. PRO, WO 49/68, f. 60; Fissel, p. 106.
18. PRO, WO 49/69, f. 79; WO 49/72, f. 47.
19. CSPD, 1639–40, p. 135.
20. PRO, WO 49/71, ff. 55–72.
21. Ibid., ff. 8–9, 53.
22. Stern, 'Gunmaking', p. 60.
23. CSPD, 1639–40, pp. 135–6, 586, 589.
24. Fissel, pp. 101–2.
25. PRO, WO 49/71, ff. 53–74.
26. Stern, 'Gunmaking', pp. 55–6; CSPD, 1638–9, pp. 330–1.
27. CSPD, 1638–9, p. 373.
28. This calculation, like several others in the chapter, is based on an analysis of warrants filed in PRO SP 28.
29. J.U. Nef, The Rise of the British Coal Industry, I (Books for Library Press, New York, 1932/1972 reprint), p. 203, n. 5; PRO, SP 28/262, iii, f. 256.
30. PRO, SP 28/43, I, ff. 162v–163; SP 28/262, iii, f. 256.
31. PRO, SP 28/261–4, passim.
32. PRO, SP 28/261, no. 426; SP 28/262, no. 151–5, 157, 160.

33. PRO, SP 16/498/4.

34. Stern, 'Gunmaking', p. 68.

35. PRO, SP 28/140, iii; Mungean, 'Contracts', *passim*.

36. PRO, SP 28/147, iii, ff. 564–98.

37. *CSPD, 1651*, p. 572.

38. Stern, 'Gunmaking', p. 61; PRO, SP 28/130, iii.

39. W.H.B. Court, *The Rise of the Midland Industries 1600–1838* (Oxford University Press, Oxford, 1938/1953 reprint), p. 46; Stern, 'Gunmaking', p. 61.

40. *CSPD, 1649–50*, p. 20.

41. PRO, SP 28/239.

42. PRO, SP28/145, f. 390; J. Adair, *Roundhead General: a Military Biography of Sir William Waller* (MacDonald, London, 1969), pp. 177–84.

43. Gloucestershire Record Office, Gloucester Borough Records, B3/2, f. 271; Warwickshire Record Office, Earl of Denbigh's Letter Book, II, CR 2017/C10, no. 5.

44. PRO, SP 28 county files.

45. PRO, SP 28/240, ii.

46. BL, Harleian MS 6804, f. 160; ROP, I, p. 13.

47. Stern, 'Gunmaking', p. 88; ROP, I, p. 146; *CSPD, 1651*, p. 580.

48. BL, Harleian MS 6804, f. 160.

49. ROP, I, pp. 25–6. Many of the details concerning suppliers have been taken from ROP, I, with the gaps filled in by reference to the original documents, PRO, WO 55/1661 and BL, Add. MS 34325.

50. ROP, I, p. 179.

51. Ibid., I, p. 66.

52. BL, Add. MS 34325, f. 10v.

53. BL, Harleian MS 6852, f. 88.

54. ROP, I, pp. 200–1; Chatsworth House, Bolton MSS 180–1.

55. ROP, I, pp. 66, 68; BL Add. MS 34325, ff. 19, 21, 29v, 59.

56. BL, Add. MS 34325, ff. 15v, 17v, 19v.

57. Staffordshire Record Office, Dartmouth Papers D(W) 1788/I/i/40.

58. Ibid.; ROP, I, pp. 68, 77, 102.

59. BL, Add. MS 34325, f. 14v; ROP, I, p. 202.

60. ROP, I, p. 68.

61. BL, Harleian MS 6852, f. 88; ROP, I, p. 106.

62. *CSPD, 1641–3*, p. 501; *CSPD, 1644*, p. 27.

63. ROP, I, p. 125.

64. BL, Add. MS 34325, f. 42.

65. TT 12 E.69 (8), 28 September 1643, *Mercurius Civicus*, p. 6.

66. Wanklyn, thesis, p. 95.

67. BL, Add. MS 18980, f. 109; ROP, II, p. 388.

68. ROP, II, p. 392.

69. *CSPD, 1644–5*, p. 511.

70. BL, Add. MS 18982, f. 5.

71. W. Phillips (ed.), 'The Ottley Papers Relating to the Civil War', part 1, *Transactions of the Shropshire Archaeological Society*, VI (1894), pp. 59, 71; part 2, Ibid., VII (1895), p. 253.

72. BL, Add. MS 18982, f. 137.

73. BL, Add. MS 18981, f. 42; Chatsworth House, Bolton MSS 180–1.

74. Atkin, *Worcestershire*, p. 126.

75. *Infra*, pp. 181–4.

76. Grosjean, thesis, p. 151.

77. C.E. Whitelaw, *Scottish Arms Makers* (Arms & Armour Press, 1977), p. 289.

78. Terry, I, p. xxi; *CSPD, 1638–9*, pp. 406–10; NAS, GD 112/39/70/17.

79. NAS, GD 26/12/5/2; GD 26/12/7; NLS, Balcarres Papers, 29.2.9, f. 102–3.

80. W.B. Cook and D.B. Morris (eds), *Extracts from the Records of the Merchant Guild of Stirling, AD 1592–1846* (Glasgow, Stirlingshire & Sons of the Rock Society, Stirling, 1916), p. 55; *Glasgow Records 1573–1642*, p. 397.

81. For example, NLS, Balcarres Papers, 29.2.9, f. 126; 'Peebles Charters and Documents' 30 July 1640 *Scottish Burgh Records Society* (Edinburgh, 1872), p. 376; NAS, GD 112/39/78/12.

82. NLS, Balcarres Papers 29.2.29, f. 102; Furgol, p. 52.

83. *Edinburgh Records 1626–1641*, p. 215; 'Peebles Charters and Documents', pp. 376–7; *Glasgow Records 1573–1642*, p. cccxci.

84. 'Peebles Charters and Documents', p. 376–7; *Edinburgh Records 1626–41*, p. 216.

85. Stevenson, *Government*, pp. 65, 143.

86. *Glasgow Records 1573–1642*, pp. 398, 464; Ibid., 1630–62, p. 66; NAS, North Berwick Burgh Records, B56/16/13.

87. NAS, GD 112/39/70/19.

88. NAS, GD 45/18/1671; for pike heads, Whitelaw, *Arms Makers*, p. 335; *A Breiffe Narration of the Services Done to Three Noble Ladyes by Gilbert Blakhall* (Spalding Club, Aberdeen, 1844), p. 78; *Glasgow Records 1630–62*, p. 193.

89. NLS, Balcarres Papers, 29.2.9, f. 102; *CSPD 1639–40*, p. 491.

90. J. Arthur and D. Caldwell, 'The Doune Pistolmakers', *Guns Review* (April 1976), 183. I am grateful to Dr Steve Murdoch for this reference; Sir John Sinclair, *The Statistical Account of Scotland*, vol. 20 (Edinburgh, 1798), p. 86.

91. Whitelaw, *Arms Makers*, pp. 210–11, 300.
92. Whitelaw, *Arms Makers*, pp. 237, 44; pp. 60–88.
93. Ibid., pp. 18, 24.
94. Ibid., pp. 17, 19, 21; *Glasgow Records 1630–62*, p. 74.
95. Whitelaw, *Arms Makers*, pp. 99, 298.
96. Terry, p. 260.
97. Whitelaw, *Arms Makers*, p. 185.
98. NAS, GD 112/39/69/17; GD 112/39/70/1.
99. Whitelaw, *Arms Makers*, p. 237.
100. NAS, GD 406/1/1203.
101. NAS, PA 15/3, 16/20; *Glasgow Records 1630–62*, pp. 95, 130; NAS, GD 157/1503.
102. Furgol, p.115; Stevenson, *Government*, p. 73.
103. *Infra*, pp. 189–93, 209–10.
104. Carte 2, f. 37, Carte 3, f. 333; NAS, GD 406/1/1455.
105. *Supra*, pp. 24–5.
106. Carte 3, f. 474v.
107. Franciscan MSS, pp. 120, 125, 137, 139.
108. P. Lenihan, 'The Catholic Confederacy 1642–9: an Irish State at War', unpublished University College of Galway PhD thesis (1995). I am grateful to Dr Lenihan for providing me with material from his thesis.
109. Carte 11, ff. 553–4.
110. *CSPI, 1647–60, Addenda 1625–60*, pp. 74–6; Franciscan MSS, p. 157.
111. Loeber and Parker, 'Military Revolution', p. 75.
112. Franciscan MSS, p. 157; Gilbert, II, p. 125.
113. *CSPV, 1640–2*, p. 298; Gilbert, II, p. 283; IV, pp. 125–6.

5. Home Supplies: Ordnance and Munitions

1. P. Edwards, 'Gunpowder and the English Civil War', *Journal of the Arms & Armour Society*, XV (1995),110; *VCH Kent*, III (1932), pp. 386–7.
2. Staffordshire Record Office, Dartmouth Papers, D(W) 1778/I/i/11.
3. PRO, SP 16/489/99.
4. West Suffolk Record Office, Chelsworth Constables' Accounts, HA 525/1/1/4; ROP, I, pp. 160, 163, 183, 460.
5. PRO, SP 28/145, f. 59; ROP, I, p. 242.
6. ROP, I, p. 172.
7. Trease, *Cavalier*, p. 100; ROP, II, p. 491; Brereton, II, pp. 367, 380.
8. Powell and Timings, 'Documents', p. 150.
9. *VCH Surrey*, II (1905), p. 266.
10. Stewart, *Ordnance Office*, p. 73.
11. A.R. Hall, *Ballistics in the Seventeenth Century* (Cambridge University Press, Cambridge, 1952), p. 9; *CSPD, 1650*, p. 480; O.F.G. Hogg, *Artillery, its Origins, Heyday and Decline* (C. Hurst & Co., 1970), pp. 58, 61.
12. *VCH, Sussex*, II (1907), p. 246.
13. *VCH, Kent*, III (1932), pp. 386–7.
14. R. Jenkins, 'Early Gunfounding in England and Wales', *Transactions of the Newcomen Society*, 44 (1971–2), p. 147; P.W. Klein, 'The Trip Family in the 17th Century', *Acta Historiae Neerlandica*, I (1966), 196.
15. Klein, 'Trip Family', pp. 196–9.
16. PRO, WO 49/72/17.
17. PRO, SP 28/30, iii, ff. 240, 245.
18. PRO, WO 49/68, f. 22; SP 28/28, ii, ff. 27,148.
19. ROP, I, pp. 32–3.
20. PRO, WO 49/71/14v.
21. *VCH, Kent*, III, pp. 386–7; Lewis, pp. 153–4.
22. *VCH, Kent*, III, pp. 386–7; Lewis, p. 152; Herefordshire Office, R.O., Foley Papers, E12/VI/2/Bf25.
23. Stewart, Ordnance Office, pp. 74–5.
24. Lewis, pp. 153–4 .
25. PRO, WO 49/69, f. 71.
26. *CSPD 1639–40*, p. 586; PRO, WO 49/75, ff. 220–1.
27. W. Notestein (ed.), *The Journal of Sir Simonds D'Ewes* (Yale University Press, New Haven, 1923), pp. 503–4; M. Jansson, *Two Diaries of the Long Parliament* (Alan Sutton Publishing, Gloucester, 1984) p. 22; C. Ffoulkes, *The Gun-Founders of England* (Cambridge Unversity Press, Cambridge, 1937), p. 75.
28. PRO, WO 55/1660, ff. 13–14, 22.
29. *CSPD, 1644–5*, pp. 607–8, 619; *CSPD, 1645–7*, pp 27–8; *CJ*, 4, pp. 183, 255, 390.
30. PRO, SP 28/35, iii, f. 421.
31. *CSPD, 1650*, pp. 529, 531.
32. Lewis, p. 160.
33. Herefordshire Record Office, Foley Papers, E12/VI/2/Bf3; F/VI/Bf/7127.
34. *CSPD, 1644–5*, p. 633; Young and Holmes, pp. 211–12; *CSPD, 1644*, pp. 508–9.
35. *CSPD, 1644–5*, p. 607.
36. *Military Memoirs of the Great Civil War, being the Military Memoirs of John Gwynne* (Ken Trotman Ltd, Cambridge, 1987), p. 42; Adair, *Roundhead General*, p. 125; PRO, SP 28/190; SP 28/263, f. 269; SP 28/5, f. 369, SP 28/346, no. 189.

37. Lewis, pp. 152–3.
38. PRO, SP 28/139/10.
39. PRO, SP 28/136/27.
40. PRO, SP 28/346, no. 76; SP 28/7, f. 498; SP 28/36, f. 405; Pennington and Roots, *Stafford*, pp. xlv, 24, 179, 208.
41. PRO, SP 28/240/2, nos. 932, 947 and unnumbered; D. Hey, *The Fiery Blades of Hallamshire* (Leicester University Press, Leicester, 1991), p. 17.
42. PRO, SP 28/118, f. 95.
43. Stewart, *Ordnance Office*, p. 72.
44. *Supra*, p. 95.
45. PRO, SP 28/240, ii.
46. *CSPD, 1644*, p. 509.
47. BL, Harleian MS 6804, f. 160.
48. Court, *Midland Industries*, p. 81, ROP, I, p. 9; *CSPD, 1645–7*, p. 4.
49. BL, Harleian MS 6802, f. 138.
50. Eddershaw, *Oxfordshire*, p. 50; ROP, I, p. 27.
51. ROP, I, p. 203; II, p. 473.
52. Eddershaw, *Oxfordshire*, p. 50.
53. BL, Harleian MS 6852, f. 158.
54. Ibid., f. 32; ROP, I, p. 28, n. 7.
55. BL, Harleian MS 6802, f. 218; Hutton. p. 76.
56. Hutton, p. 76; *CSPD, 1645–7*, p. 4; Bund, *Worcestershire*, pp. 5, 73.
57. Ottley Papers, part 2, pp. 288–9; *CSPD, 1641–3*, p. 488; Gloucestershire Record Office, D115/15; BL, Add. MS 18980, f. 115; Hutton, p. 60.
58. ROP, I, pp. 68, 73, 77, 102, 104–5.
59. BL, Harleian MS 6802, f. 138; Add. MS 18981, f. 130.
60. Hutton, pp. 52–3.
61. ROP, I, p. 36.
62. C. Hart, *The Industrial History of Dean* (David & Charles, Newton Abbot, 1971), p. 15; ROP, I, p. 36.
63. Atkin and Laughlin, *Gloucester*, p. 124.
64. ROP, I, pp. 15–16.
65. Terry, I, pp. 15–17; Trease, *Cavalier*, p. 116.
66. Hutton, p. 60.
67. BL, Harleian MS 6804, f. 226.
68. PRO, SP 28/346, no. 76; *CSPD, 1645–7*, p. 4.
69. *Supra*, p. 8.
70. Grosjean, thesis, p. 173; Furgol, pp. 9, 112–13.
71. *CSPD, 1640*, pp. 98–100.
72. Furgol, p. 112–13; Terry, p. lxxxix.
73. Furgol, pp. 297, 360; D.H. Caldwell, *Scotland's Wars and Warriors* (Stationery Office, Edinburgh, 1998), p. 79; Grainger, *Cromwell*, pp. 51–8.

74. Furgol, p. 360; Stevenson, *Government*, p. 112.
75. Argyll and Bute Archive, Lochgilphead, Dumbarton Garrison MSS, ff. 12, 14; Stevenson, *Government*, p. 112.
76. NAS, GD 112/39/68/11, 13, 28; GD 112/39/69/16.
77. *Edinburgh Records, 1642–1655*, p. 421; *infra*, p. 106.
78. NAS, GD 406/1/2512.
79. I.D. Whyte, *Scotland's Society and Economy in Transition, c. 1500–c. 1760* (Macmillan, 1997), p. 142.
80. *Edinburgh Records, 1626–41*, p. 220.
81. *CSPD, 1640*, pp. 98–100; *SRP*, VII, 1637–9, p. 277, VIII, p. 217.
82. Whyte, *Society and Economy*, p. 142.
83. Murdoch, thesis, p 125.
84. ARA, The Hague; ZCA, inv. nr. 2464.
85. Loeber and Parker, 'Military Revolution', pp. 68, 70; *CSPI, 1625–32*, p. 110.
86. *CSPI, 1647–60*, pp. 74–6.
87. Loeber and Parker, 'Military Revolution', p. 70.
88. Ibid., pp. 74–5; Lenihan, thesis, p. 123.
89. *CSPI, 1633–47*, pp. 653, 664, 729, 734.
90. *CSPV, 1640–2*, p. 298; Loeber and Parker, 'Military Revolution', p. 70; Gilbert, VI, pp. 75–7.
91. Carte 12, f. 460; Gilbert, VI, pp. 75–7; Private communication from Dr Pádraig Lenihan.
92. Gilbert, II, p. 282; IV, pp. 125–6.
93. LJRO, Hugh Canter of Holy Trinity, Coventry, probate 14 May 1678.
94. PRO, SP 28/34, i, f. 62; SP 28/30, iii, f. 240; ROP, I, p. 164; Chatsworth House, Bolton MS 181.
95. PRO, WO 49/72, f. 28.
96. PRO, WO 49/71, f. 12; 75/35; 76/35.
97. PRO, SP 28/262, f. 329; SP 28/131/2, f. 3v.
98. PRO, SP 28/45, ii, f. 155; *CSPD, 1651*, p. 569.
99. BL, Add. MS 34315, ff. 43, 58.
100. PRO, SP 28/6, ii, f. 171, *passim*.
101. M. Stoyle, *From Deliverance to Destruction: Rebellion and Civil War in an English City* (University of Exeter Press, Exeter, 1996), p. 77; PRO, SP 28/25, iv, f. 558; SP 28/26, iii, f. 316; SP 28/26, iv, f. 444.
102. PRO, SP 28/134/2; SP 28/136; SP 28/247, no. 152.
103. PRO, SP 28/240; SP 28/229.

104. Tibbutt, *Letter Books*, pp. 375, 385.

105. Derbyshire Record Office, Gell Papers, D 258/34/10; PRO, SP 28/300, i, f. 536.

106. Derbyshire Record Office, Gresley of Drakelowe Papers, D 803M/Z9, ff. 88–91.

107. PRO, SP 28/145.

108. Atkins and Laughlin, *Gloucester*, p. 47; PRO, SP 28/174.

109. ROP, I, pp. 66–148, *passim*; BL, Add. MS 34325, *passim*

110. Bristol Record Office, Bristol Corporation Records, Great Audit Book 1640–4, 04026/21.

111. ROP, II, pp. 389, 392, 420.

112. Terry, I, pp. 16–17; Chatsworth House, Bolton MSS 181, 240; P. Wenham, *The Great and Close Siege of York, 1644* (Session Book Trust, York, 1994), p. 175.

113. *Supra*, p.

114. Trease, *Cavalier*, p. 122; R.T. Spence, *Skipton Castle in the Great Civil War 1642–1645* (Skipton Castle, Skipton, 1991).

115. ROP, I, pp. 65, 69, 130.

116. Atkins, *Worcestershire*, p. 50; NLW, Diocese of Llandaff Results and Orders of Commissioners of Array 1643, LL/MB/17.

117. *CSPD, 1638–9*, pp. 408–10.

118. NLS, Balcarres Papers 29.2.9, f. 102v; T.H. Marshall, *The History of Perth from the Earliest Period to the Present Time* (John Fisher, Perth, 1849), p. 181; NAS, GD 112/39/68/26.

119. Terry, p. xxi.

120. NAS, GD 112/39/68/13.

121. *Edinburgh Records, 1642–1655*, p. 421.

122. Terry, p. 15.

123. Stevenson, *Government*, pp. 116, 123.

124. Whyte, *Society and Economy*, p. 142.

125. *Edinburgh Records, 1626–41*, p. 213; Ibid., *1642–55*, p. 22.

126. Stevenson, *Government*, pp. 116, 128.

127. Terry, I, pp. 18–19.

128. H.F. Morlond-Simpson (ed.), 'Civil War Papers 1643–1650', *Miscellany of the Scottish Historical Society*, I (1893), pp. 157–8.

129. Lenihan, thesis, p. 122.

130. *Supra*, p. 103.

131. *CSPI, 1633–47*, p. 684.

132. Ibid., p. 684.

133. Carte 11, f. 415.

134. Carte 3, f. 333; Carte 6, f. 471.

135. Franciscan MSS, p. 239.

136. B.J. Buchanan, 'The Technology of Gunpowder Making in the Eighteenth Century: Evidence from the Bristol Region', *Transactions of the Newcomen Society*, 67 (1995–6), p. 127; G. and A. Crocker, 'Gunpowder Mills of Surrey', *Surrey History*, IV (1990), 135.

137. P. Edwards, 'Gunpowder and the English Civil War', *Journal of the Arms and Armour Society*, XV (1995) p. 112.

138. Buchanan, 'Gunpowder Making', pp. 130–2.

139. Nef, I, p. 210.

140. Crocker, p. 135.

141. Buchanan, 'Gunpowder Making', pp. 133–4; Edwards, 'Gunpowder', p. 110.

142. Buchanan, 'Gunpowder Making', pp. 131–6; Edwards, 'Gunpowder', p. 110.

143. Edwards, 'Gunpowder', p. 111.

144. *VCH, Surrey*, II, pp. 318–19; Buchanan, 'Gunpowder Making', pp.128, 130.

145. *VCH, Surrey*, II, p. 308.

146. Ibid., pp. 307–8. For an example of the depredations committed, see Gloucestershire Record Office, MF 1395.

147. K. Fairclough, 'The Cordwell Family, Gunpowder Producers at Chilworth 1636–1650', *Surrey Archaeological Collections*, (forthcoming).

148. *CSPD, 1635–6*, p. 390.

149. R. Steele, *Tudor and Stuart Proclamations 1485–1714*, I (Oxford, 1910) nos 209–10 .

150. *VCH, Surrey*, II, p. 320; Fairclough, 'Cordwell Family'; Edwards, 'Gunpowder', p. 111; *CSPD, 1639–40*, p. 424; *CSPD, 1640*, p. 523.

151. *VCH, Surrey*, II, p. 321; Edwards, 'Gunpowder', p. 110.

152. Fairclough, 'Cordwell Family'.

153. *CSPD, 1638–9*, p. 155; *CSPD, 1640–1*, pp. 303, 313.

154. Fairclough, 'Cordwell Family'; SP 16/461, no. 35.

155. Ibid.

156. LJ, 4, p. 316.

157. *CSPD, 1640–1*, pp. 2, 280.

158. Edwards, 'Gunpowder', p. 113; ROP, I, p. 11, n. 6; *CSPV, 1636–9*, pp. 447, 461, 497.

159. Fissel, p. 94.

160. PRO, WO 55/457.

161. ROP, I, p. 12; II, p. 359.

162. CJ, 3, p. 2; PRO, SP 28/264, nos 224, 243–4.

163. *CSPD, 1644–5*, pp. 234, 236; Fairclough, 'Cordwell Family'.

164. CJ, 2, p. 880.

165. Ibid., pp. 880, 960; PRO, SP 28/264, nos 28, 31, 33, 42–3, 56, 59.

166. K. Fairclough, 'Early Gunpowder Production at Waltham', *Essex Journal*, 20 (1985), pp. 11–12.

167. Fairclough, 'Cordwell Family'; *CSPD, 1639–40*, p. 432; *CSPD, 1644*, p. 56.

168. PRO, SP 25/118, f. 113.

169. Fairclough, 'Cordwell Family'.

170. PRO, WO 49/86, ff. 53, 55, 58, 62.

171. *CSPD, 1654*, p. 4.

172. PRO, WO 49/84; for gunpowder, f. 165; for saltpetre, ff. 143, 165, 176, 198.

173. PRO, WO 49/82, f. 3.

174. K. Fairclough, 'John Samyne: 17th-century Gunpowder Maker', *Gunpowder Mills Study Group, Newsletter*, 7 (May 1990), 2–4; PRO, SP 28/33, ii, f. 173.

175. PRO, WO 49/82, f. 84; WO 49/85, ff. 6–7, 9–11, 13, 17, 26.

176. *CSPD, 1649–50*, p. 321.

177. Fairclough, 'Waltham', p. 12.

178. PRO, WO 49/86, ff. 30, 33, 36, 39, 44, 51–2, 57, 66, 105.

179. PRO, WO 49/84, f. 164; WO 49/86, ff. 143, 145, 154–5.

180. PRO, SP 28/45, i, f. 33; SP 28/47, ff. 115, 117; WO 49/82, ff. 99, 106.

181. PRO, WO 47/2.

182. Lewis, p. 147; *CSPD, 1649–50*, pp. 222, 579; PRO, SP 25/118, f. 113; SP 28/60, f. 78; WO 49/83, f. 24.

183. E.B. Sainsbury (ed.), *A Calendar of the Court Minutes of the East India Company 1644–9* (Clarendon Press, Oxford, 1912), p. 5.

184. *CJ*, 3, 1642–4, p. 97; Lewis, pp. 139, 142; *VCH, Surrey*, II, p. 321.

185. PRO, SP 28/28, iii, ff. 220, 234.

186. East India Company Minutes 1644–9, pp. 290, 296; *CSPD, 1649–50*, p. 226.

187. *CSPD, 1649–50*, p. 20.

188. PRO, SP 28/134/12, f. 36; SP 28/152/8, f. 2; SP 28/224; SP 28/225, iii, f. 578, iv, f. 824; Pennington and Roots, *Stafford*, p. 82.

189. PRO, SP 28/152/8, f. 2; SP 28/225, iii, f. 578.

190. Gainsborough: Bodl., Firth C6, f. 153; Gloucester: PRO, SP 28/129, 154, 228–9; D. Evans, 'Gloucester's Civil War Trades and Industries, 1642–46', *Transactions of Bristol and Gloucestershire Arch. Society*, 110 (1992), pp. 138–9; Northampton: PRO, SP 28/238, ff. 68, 202, 238, 595, 765; Nottingham: PRO, SP 28/241; Stafford: Pennington and Roots, *Stafford*, pp. xlvi, 7,

23 36, 66, 84, 206, 224, 317; Warwick: PRO, SP 28/136–7, 184.

191. Pennington and Roots, *Stafford*, pp. xlvi, 7, 224–526.

192. PRO, SP 28/299, i, f. 120.

193. Pennington and Roots, *Stafford*, p. 36; PRO, SP 28/239.

194. PRO, SP 28/247, no. 677; West Suffolk Record Office, Barwell Accounts, 552/11/22.

195. PRO, SP 28/129/5; SP 28/154; SP 28/299, i; Evans, 'Gloucester's Trades', pp. 140–2.

196. Evans, 'Gloucester's Trades', pp. 138–9; PRO, SP 28/238, iii, f. 185.

197. Derbyshire Record Office, Gell Papers, D 258/34/10.

198. Evan's, 'Gloucester's Trades', p. 140.

199. PRO, SP 28/136–7, 184, 247.

200. Edwards, 'Gunpowder', pp. 114–15; A. Clark (ed.) *The Life and Times of Anthony Wood*, I (Clarendon Press, Oxford, 1891), p. 74.

201. ROP, I, p. 29.

202. ROP, I, pp. 186–7, 216; II, p. 469, n. 77; BL, Harleian MS 6552, f. 82.

203. BL, Add. MS 18981, ff. 71–2.

204. ROP, I, p. 362.

205. HMC, Hastings MSS, II (1930), p. 119.

206. ROP, I, pp. 30.

207. Ibid., pp. 30–1.

208. Ottley Papers, part I, p. 49; NLW, Crosse of Shawe Hill Papers, no. 1097, 9 April 1643.

209. *Townshend's Diary*, II, pp. 106, 140–1, 144.

210. NLW, Wynn of Gwydir Papers, no. 1723; Diocese of Llandaff, LL/MB/17; ROP, II, p. 368

211. ROP, II, p. 388–9; HMC, *15th Report*, Appendix, part VII, Somerset MS, p. 69.

212. HMC, *15th Report*, Appendix, part VII, Somerset MS, p. 69; *Townshend's Diary*, II, p. 141; PRO, SP 29/232, no. 193; Ottley Papers, part 1, p. 49; NLW, Wynn Papers, no. 1723.

213. Chatsworth House, Bolton MSS 93, pp. 180–1, 240; PRO, SP 28/261–4; Carte 3, f. 333; for the queen's arms-purchasing activities abroad see below, pp. 197–8.

214. BL, Add. MS 18981, f. 253; *CSPD, 1645–7*, p. 110. The figure given is 2,000 cwt but this is a vast amount and the quantity is probably 2,000 lb. This would still make 300 barrels of gunpowder; Diocese of Llandaff, LL/MB/17.

215. Tennant, *Edgehill*, p. 242.

216. *CSPD, 1644–5*, p. 512.

217. *CSPD, 1644*, p. 17.
218. *CSPV, 1642–3*, p. 269; BL, Add. MS 18980, f. 115.
219. D. Mason (ed.), *Register of PC of Scotland, 2nd Series, I, 1625–7* (Edinburgh, 1899), p. 377.
220. L.B. Taylor (ed.), *Aberdeen Council Letters, I, 1552–1633* (Oxford University Press, Oxford, 1942), p. 271.
221. *Edinburgh Records 1626–41*, pp. 205, 213; NAS, GD 112/39/69/14.
222. Taylor, *Aberdeen Council Letters, II, 1634–44* (Oxford University Press, Oxford, 1950), p. 144; M. Bennett, *The Civil War Experienced: Britain and Ireland, 1638–1661* (Routledge, 2000), p. 83.
223. Murdoch, thesis, pp. 131–4; *KCFB*, 4, pp. 269–70.
224. Cuningham, pp. 54.
225. *Edinburgh Records 1642–55*, p. 47; Cuningham, p. 95; NAS, 15/3; Stevenson, *Government*, p. 10.
226. Terry, I, pp. 260, 425.
227. Terry, I, pp. 15–17.
228. *CSPI, 1625–32*, pp. 296–7, 308.
229. Lenihan, thesis, p. 118.
230. Hogan, *Irish Rebellion*, pp. 3–4; Ormond, new series, II, p. 234; Carte 7, f. 255.
231. Carte 3, f. 333; Carte 8, f. 87.
232. Gilbert, I, p. 71.
233. Franciscan MSS, pp. 186, 199.
234. Lenihan, thesis, pp. 119–20.
235. Casway, 'O'Neill', p. 61; Carte 3, f. 386; Carte 6, f. 159.
236. *Supra*, p. 101.
237. Gilbert, VI, pp. 75–7.
238. Ibid., p. 125.
239. Lenihan, thesis, p. 120.
240. Firth, *Cromwell's Army*, p. 82; Ffoulkes, *Gun-Founders*, p. 36.
241. PRO, SP 28/60, i, ff. 72, 76.
242. Firth, *Cromwell's Army*, p. 83.
243. *CSPD, 1639–40*, p. 135.
244. Ibid., p. 135.
245. PRO, SP 28/129/5; SP 28/154; SP 28/229, i; D. Evans, 'Gloucester's Trades', p. 140.
246. ROP, II, p. 413.
247. PRO, SP 28/242, ii, no. 1065.
248. PRO, WO 49/69, ff. 105, 117, 182; WO 49/71, f. 20; WO 49/72, f. 8; WO 49/75, f. 57.
249. Brenner, *Merchants*, p. 158, n. 147.
250. *CSPD, 1639–40*, p. 135.
251. Ibid., p. 399.

252. For example, PRO, SP 28/263, no. 193; SP 28/264, nos 169, 219, 242, 337, 364.
253. PRO, SP 28, *passim*. ARA, The Hague; ACA, inv. nr. 1388, 1399–1402.
254. PRO, SP 28/17, f. 35.
255. *CSPD, 1644*, p. 393.
256. PRO, SP 28/136–7, 228–9, 240, *passim*.
257. ROP, I, *passim*.
258. Ibid., II, p. 413.
259. ROP, I, p. 114.
260. Wanklyn, thesis, p. 171; Chatsworth House, Bolton MSS 180–1, 240.
261. Ottley Papers, part 2, p. 316.
262. NLW, Brogynton Papers, Clenennau Letters and Papers, f. 609.
263. ROP, II, p. 413.
264. Terry, I, p. 15.
265. NAS, PA 15/3; PA 16/2/2.
266. Carte 3, f. 83; Ormond, new series, II, p. 209.
267. Carte 10, f. 690; Carte 14, f. 158.
268. Gilbert, I, p. 71.
269. Franciscan MSS, p. 239.
270. *Infra*, pp. 216–21.

6. Home Supplies: Clothing and Equipment

1. B. Lemire, *Dress, Culture and Commerce: The English Clothing Trade before the Factory, 1660–1800* (Macmillan, 1997), p. 12.
2. N.V. Sleigh-Johnson, 'The Merchant Taylors' Company of London 1580–1645, with Special Reference to Government and Politics', unpublished London University PhD thesis (1989), pp. 346, 362, 370.
3. Lemire, p. 2.
4. J. McGurk, *The Elizabethan Conquest of Ireland* (Manchester University Press, Manchester, 1997), pp. 210–12; PRO, SP 16/34/112. I am grateful to Professor Mark Fissel for this reference.
5. M. Spufford, 'The Cost of Apparel in Seventeenth-century England', *Economic History Review*, forthcoming.
6. Spufford,' Apparel', quoting PRO, B 32/25/212.
7. PRO, SP 28/31, xiii; SP 28/253B, ii.
8. Ibid.; SP 28, *passim*.
9. B.E. Supple, *Commercial Crisis and Change in England 1600–1642* (Cambridge University Press, Cambridge, 1970), p. 5; P.J. Bowden, *The Wool Trade in Tudor and Stuart England* (Cass, London, 1971), pp. 41–76.

10. Bowden, *Wool Trade*, pp. 55, 60–1, 69, 71; Whyte, *Society and Economy*, p. 141.
11. *Infra*, pp. 143, 145–6.
12. Bowden, *Wool Trade*, pp. 57–60.
13. Bowden, *Wool Trade*, pp. 55, 69.
14. PRO, SP 28/1B, i, ff. 420–1; V.F. Snow and A.S. Young (eds), *Private Journals of the Long Parliament, 7 March–1 June 1642* (Yale University Press, New Haven, 1987), p. 187.
15. CIA, I, pp. 442, 461, 468; II, p. 379.
16. Ormond, new series, II, p. 142; CIA, II, p. 428.
17. CIA, II, p. 392.
18. CIA, I, p. 462; II, 388; PRO, SP 28/170, f. 45–v; SP 28/1B, ii, f. 516; SP 28/1C, ii, f. 194.
19. PRO, SP 28/1C, f. 194.
20. PRO, SP 28/1B, ff. 532, 657; SP 28/170, ff. 26v, 29, 44v.
21. CIA, II, p. 367.
22. Ormond, new series, II, pp. 163, 196.
23. Ibid., p. 174.
24. Wheeler, Four Armies, p. 46; *Tanner Letters*, p. 145.
25. PRO, SP 28/146.
26. Brenner, *Merchants*, pp. 343, 364–5, 373, 397; Lindley, 'Irish Adventurers', pp. 33, 139–42.
27. PRO, SP 28/131, xiii.
28. PRO, SP 28/139/8.
29. PRO, SP 28/131, xiii.
30. *CSPD, 1649–50*, pp. 572–600; *CSPD, 1650*, pp. 570–608; *CSPD, 1651*, pp. 536–88, *passim*.
31. Firth, *Cromwell's Army*, p. 118.
32. PRO, SP 28/253B, ii; SP 28/127, f. 30; SP 28/35, f. 640.
33. PRO, SP 28/253B, ii, *passim*.
34. Ibid., ff. 75, 78–9, 95.
35. Ibid., SP 28/253B, ii, ff. 93, 75.
36. McGirk, *Elizabethan Conquest of Ireland*, pp. 211–12.
37. PRO, SP 28/253B, f. 77.
38. Ibid., f. 76.
39. J.R. McCormack, *Revolutionary Politics in the Long Parliament* (Harvard University Press, Cambridge, Mass., 1973), pp. 98–9.
40. *CSPI, 1633–47*, p. 682.
41. PRO, SP 28/253B, ii, ff. 96–7; SP 28/34, ff. 324v–325.
42. CIA, I, pp. 434, 442, 448.
43. Mungean, 'Contracts', pp. 68–70.
44. CIA, I, pp. 442, 448, 458, 462; PRO, SP 28/253B, f. 93.
45. Mungean, 'Contracts', pp. 75–6, 78, 89, 115.
46. *CSPD, 1651*, pp. 548–9, 552.
47. Mungean, 'Contracts', pp. 75–6; PRO, SP 28/37, ff. 355–7.
48. *CSPD, 1649–50*, pp. 98–9; *CSPD, 1650*, pp. 587, 590, 593–4, 596, 598, 603, 607; *CSPD, 1651*, pp. 537, 548–9, 552, 559, 582–3.
49. PRO, SP 28/139 f. 239.
50. Northamptonshire Record Office, Fermor-Heskith MSS (Baker Collection), FH Baker 704, f. 91.
51. PRO, SP 28/152/7, f. 6.
52. PRO, SP 28/55, f. 267; SP 28/57, f. 300.
53. PRO, SP 28/55, f. 267.
54. W.G. Hoskins, *Provincial England* (Macmillan, London, 1963), pp. 68–85.
55. PRO, SP 28/24, f. 284.
56. PRO, SP 28/26, ff. 314–20v.
57. PRO, SP 28/231.
58. PRO, SP 28/227; Holmes, *Eastern Association*, p. 38.
59. PRO, SP 28/128, ff. 11–37.
60. PRO, SP 28/25, ff. 136, 143–4, 163, 167; SP 28/300, ff. 700–2.
61. PRO, SP 28/41, f. 376.
62. PRO, SP 28/136/26; SP 28/174.
63. PRO, SP 28/49, i, f. 100.
64. Holmes, *Eastern Association*, p. 152; PRO, SP 28/26, f. 136; SP 28/18, f. 234; SP 28/19, f. 257.
65. Bowden, *Wool Trade*, p. 64.
66. PRO, SP 28/21, f. 65; SP 28/225, f. 172; SP 28/134/12; SP 28/147/2.
67. PRO, SP 28/134/12.
68. PRO, SP 28/176; SP 28/128, ff. 11–37.
69. PRO, SP 28/18, f. 234; SP 28/26, f. 136; SP 28/29, f. 200; SP 28/22, f. 284; SP 28/19, f. 257.
70. PRO, SP 28/25, ff. 136, 143–4, 163, 167; SP 28/136/27.
71. PRO, SP 28/49, f. 100; SP 28/136/27.
72. C.E. Long, 'Richard Symonds's Diary of the Marches of the Royal Army', *Camden Society*, old series, 74 1859 (Cambridge University Press, Cambridge, reprint 1997), p. 14.
73. Atkin, *Worcestershire*, p. 6; P. Edwards, 'The Farming Economy of North-east Shropshire in the Seventeenth Century', unpublished Oxford University thesis (1976), p. 299; Morrill, *Reactions*, p. 127.
74. P. Young, *Edgehill 1642* (Windrush Press, Moreton-in-Marsh, 1995). p. 21; Trease, *Cavalier*, p. 93.

75. *Anthony Wood*, pp. 83–4.

76. Bowden, *Wool Trade*, pp. 45–6.

77. Bodl., Firth 6, f .45; Tibbutt, *Letter Books*, p. 186.

78. J. de L. Mann, *The Cloth Industry in the West of England from 1640 to 1880* (Alan Sutton Publishing, Gloucester, 1987 edn), p. 4; Eddershaw, *Oxfordshire*, p. 82.

79. Ottley Papers, part 2, p. 273; ROP, II, p. 518, n. 103.

80. *CSPD, 1644*, p. 4.

81. *Anthony Wood*, p. 103.

82. Stoyle, *From Deliverance to Destruction*, p. 118.

83. BL, Harleian MS 6802, f. 291; Wanklyn, 'King's Armies', pp. 93–4; *CSPD, 1644*, p. 274.

84. Atkin, *Worcestershire*, pp. 44–5, 73.

85. Carte 7, ff. 195, 424.

86. Ibid., f. 38; Hutton, p. 122; NLW, Brogynton MSS, Clenennau Letters and Papers, no. 539.

87. Hutton, pp. 122–3; Carte 7, f. 637.

88. PRO, SP 28/128/12.

89. Furgol, pp. 11, 52.

90. *Stirling Records 1519–1666*, p. 183; *Edinburgh Records 1642–55*, p. 44; Furgol, pp. 120, 397.

91. Furgol, p. 120; NAS, GD 45/14/55.

92. Whyte, *Society and Economy*, p. 134.

93. Furgol, pp. 8, 316, 329–30, 341; Spalding, *Troubles*, I, p. 107.

94. Whyte, *Society and Economy*, pp. 133–5; I. Whyte, *Agriculture and Society in Seventeenth-century Scotland* (John Donald, Edinburgh, 1979), p. 17.

95. Whyte, *Society and Economy*, pp. 133–6; Williams, *Montrose*, p. 160.

96. NAS, PA 16/3/2.

97. Terry, pp. 264–5.

98. Furgol, p. 116.

99. Perth Archive MS67/Bundle 97.

100. Whitelaw, *Arms Makers*, p. 296.

101. Spalding, *Troubles*, I, pp. 204–5, 262; Furgol, p. 64.

102. Stevenson, Finances, p. 97; NAS, GD 26/7/4; *Tanner Letters*, pp. 173, 181, 187.

103. Gilbert, II, p. 29.

104. Ibid., p. 9.

105. Ormond, new series, II, pp. 163, 183, 220.

106. Carte 12, f. 357.

107. Bowden, *Wool Trade*, pp. 69, 71, 203–5; A.P. Wadsworth and J. de L. Mann, *The Cotton Trade and Industrial Lancashire 1600–1780* (Manchester University Press, Manchester, 1931), pp. 6, 11.

108. *CSPI, 1633–47*, p. 311.

109. CIA, I, p. 453, 461; II, pp. 363–4.

110. Ormond, new series, II, pp. 163, 183–4, 196, 232.

111. Carte 14, f. 2v; *CSPI, 1633–47*, p. 311.

112. Carte 6, f. 83.

113. *Infra*, pp. 193–4.

114. Gilbert, II, p. 270; Ormond, new series, II, p. 298.

115. *Tanner Letters*, pp. 214–15; *CSPI, 1647–60*, p. 36.

116. Ohlmeyer, Wars, p. 180.

117. Corporation of London Record Office, Orphans' Court Inventory 274, Henry Keene of St Sepulchre, 1665. I am grateful to Dr David Mitchell for this reference.

118. *CSPD, 1638–9*, p. 108.

119. PRO, WO 49/68/85.

120. *CSPD, 1639–40*, p. 167.

121. *CSPD, 1639–40*, p. 135; PRO, WO 55/455, ff. 3, 10, 26.

122. PRO, WO 55/455, f. 65; WO 49/72, f. 87.

123. ARA The Hague; ACA, inv. nrs. 1388, 1399–1401; PRO, SP 28/261–6.

124. PRO, SP 28/129.

125. PRO, SP 28/168/2; SP 28/300, f. 63, 532, 534; SP 28/130/3, ff. 8, 41, 47v.

126. PRO, SP 28/352; Mungean, 'Contracts', pp. 103–14, *passim*.

127. *CSPD, 1649–50*, p. 599; *CSPD, 1650*, pp. 573, 575, 582.

128. Mungean, 'Contracts', pp. 61, 86, 101, 113, 115; *CSPD, 1649–50*, pp. 581, 583; *CSPD, 1651*, pp. 554, 577.

129. PRO, SP 28/240/2.

130. ROP, I, p. 27; II, p. 433.

131. ROP, I, p. 68; BL, Add. MS 34325, ff. 22v, 45, 60v.

132. ROP, I, p. 74; BL, Add. MS 34325, ff. 28, 44v; WO 55/1661, f. 17.

133. *CSPD, 1638–9*, p. 331; *CSPD, 1639–40*, p. 369.

134. *Infra*, pp. 197–207.

135. ROP, I, p. 103; BL, Add. MS 34325, ff. 49, 51, 53, 56–56v; PRO, WO 55/1661, ff. 91, 96, 99, 103 109, 111.

136. *Supra*, p. 149.

137. ROP, II, p. 388; *CSPD, 1644–5*, p. 511.

138. NLS, Balcarres Papers 29.2.9, f. 126. The one man in three chosen to attend.

139. Terry, p. xxi.

140. NLS, Balcarres Papers 29.2.29, f. 102; NLS, Saltoun MS 17503, f. 45r.

141. NAS, GD 112/39/69/14; GD 45/18/1671.
142. Whitelaw, *Arms Makers*, p. 296.

7. Home Supplies: Horse and Tack

1. Edwards, 'Supply of Horses', p. 51.
2. Ibid., p. 52; BL, Add. MS 18981, f. 270.
3. C.H. Firth, 'The Raising of the Ironsides', in I.R. Christie (ed), *Essays in Modern History* (Macmillan, 1968), pp. 144–55.
4. Edwards, 'Supply of Horses', pp. 54–5; Edwards, *Horse Trade*, pp. 38–46.
5. BL Add. MS 29443, f. 3v.
6. D.M. Goodall, *A History of Horse Breeding* (Hale, London, 1977), p. 236.
7. Edwards, *Horse Trade*, pp. 40–1.
8. Ibid., pp. 45–6.
9. W.C. and C.E. Trevelyan (eds), 'Trevelyan Papers III', *Camden Society*, CV (1872), p. 238.
10. Edwards, *Horse Trade*, p. 45.
11. Edwards, 'Supply of Horses', p. 56.
12. Edwards, *Horse Trade*, pp. 94–5.
13. PRO, SP 46/77/479–81; Cumbria Record Office, Carlisle, D/LONS/L/A1/4, f. 95r; BL, Add. MS 33,146, 7 May 1639.
14. *CSPD, 1638–9*, p. 347.
15. Ibid., p. 539; J. Bruce (ed.), 'Letters and Papers of the Verney Family', *Camden Society*, 56 (1853), pp. 129, 305; Chatsworth House, Curry L/45/39.
16. *CSPD, 1638–9*, p. 387.
17. K. Sharpe, *The Personal Rule of Charles I* (Yale University Press, New Haven, 1992), p. 799; *CSPD, 1638–9*, pp. 461, 466.
18. *CSPD, 1638–9*, p. 347; HMC, De L'Isle MSS, Sidney Papers 1626–98 (1966), p. 190; Institute of Historical Research, London University, Hamilton Muniments microfilm no. 884.
19. Edwards, 'Supply of Horses', p. 56.
20. Sharpe, *Charles I*, p. 803.
21. Edwards, 'Supply of Horses', pp. 56–7; NAS, GD406/1/10491.
22. Northamptonshire Record Office, Finch-Hatton Collection F(M)C 275; Staffordshire Record Office, Dartmouth Papers D(W)1778/I/i/29, 31.
23. Fissel, p. 130, n. 102; M.C. Fissel, 'Scottish War and English Money: the Short Parliament of 1640', in Fissel (ed.) *War and Government in Britain, 1598–1650* (Manchester

University Press, Manchester, 1991), pp. 204–5.
24. Staffordshire Record Office, Dartmouth MSS D(W) 1778/I/i/29, 31.
25. I. Roy, 'The Royalist Army in the First Civil War', unpublished Oxford University DPhil thesis (1963), p. 45; C.V. Wedgwood, *The King's War 1641–1647* (Collins, 1958), p. 124.
26. Edwards, 'Supply of Horses', pp. 56–7.
27. Ibid., p. 58; A. Fletcher, *The Outbreak of the English Civil War* (Edward Arnold, 1981), pp. 337–9.
28. PRO, SP 28/131/3–4.
29. *CSPD, 1641–3*, p. 344.
30. Lincolnshire Archive Office, Monson MSS, MON 27/3/1; *Townshend's Diary*, II, p. 70.
31. Pennington and Roots, *Stafford*, pp. 31–2.
32. PRO, SP 28/130/2.
33. PRO, SP 28/32,i, f. 116; BL, Harleian MS 6802, f. 195; Wedgwood, *King's War*, p. 203; BL, Add. MS 18980, f. 28.
34. Firth and Rait, *Acts and Ordinances*, I, pp. 162–3: Pennington and Roots, *Stafford, passim*.
35. BL, Harleian MS 6802, ff. 192r–192v.
36. Shropshire Record Office, Ludlow Corporation Records 556/Box 298.
37. Edwards, 'Supply of Horses', p. 59.
38. TT E262(1)/6, p. 260.
39. Edwards, 'Supply of Horses', p. 59; P. Tennant, *The Civil War in Stratford-upon-Avon* (Sutton Publishing, Stroud, 1996), p. 145.
40. Chatsworth House, Bolton MS 180, 240; PRO, SP 28/32, f. 66; Firth, *Cromwell's Army*, pp. 241–3.
41. PRO, SP 28/28, iii; SP 28/128/8; SP 28/147/2.
42. Firth, *Cromwell's Army*, p. 241; PRO, SP 28/40; SP 28/43, vii; SP 28/130/3; SP 28/177.
43. A.M. Everitt, 'Suffolk', p. 89; PRO, SP 28/139.
44. Shropshire Record Office, Bridgnorth Corporation Records 4001/no piece no.
45. Edwards, 'Supply of Horses', p. 62.
46. Ibid., pp. 62–3; PRO, SP 28/222/1, i, f. 13v. I am grateful to Gavin Robinson for this reference.
47. PRO, SP 28/17.
48. Berkshire, Buckinghamshire and Oxfordshire: PRO, SP 28/251; Eastern Association: SP 28/35, f. 61, SP 28/147/2; Earl of Essex: SP 28/16, f. 68, SP 28/129/4, SP 28/146, SP 28/227; Kent: SP 28/130/3;

London: SP 28/140/15, SP 28/162; Surrey: SP 28/177; north Wales: SP 28/346; Ireland: *CSPI, 1633–47*, pp. 413, 459, *CSPD, 1649–50*, pp. 577–8, 580–2; Scotland: *CSPD, 1650*, pp. 573, 575–6, *CSPD, 1651*, p. 537.

49. PRO, SP 28/28, ff. 309–10, SP 28/29, i, ff. 164, 166; SP 28/30–3, 36–8, 41, 140/7; *CJ*, IV, p. 99.

50. Edwards, 'Supply of Horses', p. 64.

51. Gentles, *New Model Army*, p. 32.

52. Ibid., p. 44.

53. Edwards, 'Supply of Horses', p. 64.

54. Warwickshire Record Office, CR 1886/411.

55. PRO, SP 28/5, f. 86; Warwickshire Record Office, CR 2017/C9, no. 9.

56. PRO, SP 28/64, f. 781; SP 28/177.

57. Pennington and Roots, *Stafford*, p. 144.

58. M. Toynbee (ed.), 'The Papers of Captain Henry Stephens, Waggon-Master-General to Charles I', *Oxford Record Society*, 42 (1962), p. 14.

59. HMC, Hastings MSS II, p. 125.

60. *CSPD, 1644*, pp. 489, 509.

61. Gentles, *New Model Army*, p. 44.

62. Ibid., p. 54; Edwards, 'Supply of Horses', p. 52.

63. D.M. Goodall, *The Foals of Epona* (Dent, 1962), p. 278.

64. E.M. Furgol, 'Scotland Turned Sweden: the Scottish Covenanters and the Military Revolution', in J. Morrill (ed.), *The Scottish National Covenant in its British Context* (Edinburgh University Press, Edinburgh, 1990), p. 143.

65. *The Memoirs of Henry Guthry late Bishop of Dunkeld* (G. Hamilton and J. Balfour, Glasgow, 2nd edn, 1747), p. 163; Bennett, *Civil Wars*, p. 241; Reid, pp. 40, 106–33.

66. Wheeler, Four Armies, pp. 45–6.

67. Lenihan, 'Celtic Warfare', pp. 118–19, 133–7.

68. Goodall, *Foals*, p. 170; William Camden, *Britannia* (1610), p. 18; J.W. Burns (ed.), *Miscellaneous Writings of John Spreull . . . 1642–1722* (Glasgow, 1882), p. 56; Whyte, *Agriculture and Society*, p. 81.

69. Edwards, 'Supply of Horses', pp. 47–8.

70. NAS, GD 406/1/629, 648.

71. Stevenson, *Government*, pp. 7, 64, 70, 158.

72. Kenyon, *Civil Wars*, p. 91; NAS, PA 16/12/13; *Glasgow Records 1630–62*, pp. 148, 155, 193.

73. NLS, Saltoun Papers MS 17503, ff. 30r–31r, 48r; Perth Archives, MS67/Bundle 97; NAS, GD 16/50/51; Edwards, *Horse Trade*, pp. 55–6; *Edinburgh Records 1642–55*, p. 195.

74. Stevenson, *Government*, pp. 166–7.

75. Thomas Blundeville, *The Foure Chiefest Offices Belongyng to Horsemanship* (1580 edn), f. 6v.

76. *CSPI, 1633–47*, p. 38.

77. Ibid., p. 364.

78. Mary Hickson, *Ireland in the Seventeenth Century or the Irish Massacres of 1641–2, their Causes and Results*, I (Longman, Green & Co., 1884), pp. 203–4.

79. Carte, *Ormond*, II, pp. 325–6; Ormond new series, II, p. 187.

80. Ormond new series, II, pp. 277, 38–9.

81. CIA II, p. 387; *CSPI, 1633–47*, pp. 406, 449, 476–7, 482, 484, 490, 501, 510, 512, 528–9.

82. *Supra*, p. 164.

83. Terry, p. lxxviii; *CSPD, 1640*, p. 615.

84. NLS, Saltoun MS 17503, f. 23r .

85. Stevenson, *Government*, pp. 140, 146.

86. Stevenson, *Government*, p. 42; *Edinburgh Records 1642–55*, p. 259.

87. Ormond new series, II, p. 79.

88. Carte 6, f. 148; Wheeler, Four Armies, p. 63.

89. Wheeler, Four Armies, p. 64.

90. *Infra*, p. 233.

91. PRO, SP 28/130/2.

92. For example, PRO, SP 28/2B, f. 522; SP 28/24, f. 9; SP 28/127/3; Furgol, p. 8.

93. PRO, SP 28/145.

94. Gilbert, V, p. 232.

95. Sharpe, *Charles I*, p. 800.

96. *CSPD, 1638–9*, pp. 315–16.

97. PRO, WO 49/68/62–3, 74, 81.

98. *CSPD, 1639–40*, p. 369.

99. CIA II, p. 387, 391.

100. PRO, WO 49/68/62, 66, 74; CIA II, p. 408

101. PRO, WO 49/68/21.

102. PRO, SP 28/261, i, f. 99; also see ff. 18, 70, 78, 103, 198, 201, 234, 277; SP 28/261, iii, ff. 324, 326; SP 28/262, i, f. 40; SP 28/262, iii, f. 268; SP 28/262, iv, f. 435, 462, 466; SP 28/263, f. 160, 305; SP 264, nos 194, 211, 252, 275, 291, 324, 340.

103. PRO, SP 28/264, f. 115.

104. PRO, SP 28/144/2; SP 28/43, ff. 162v–163; SP 28/300, f. 697.

105. PRO, SP 28/29, f. 188.

106. *CSPD, 1649–50*, p. 591; *CSPD, 1650*, p. 607; *CSPD, 1651*, pp. 553, 559, 570–1, 576, 583.

107. PRO, SP 28/136, 27.

108. PRO, SP 28/223.
109. PRO, SP 28/187.
110. PRO, SP 28/43, f. 944v.
111. Mungean, 'Contracts', pp. 98, 102.
112. Ibid., pp. 67–8; Firth, *Cromwell's Army*, p. 244.
113. PRO, SP 28/23, f. 59.
114. PRO, SP 28/262, iv, f. 438.
115. ROP, I, p. 75; BL, Add. MS 34325, ff. 14, 20, 23, 24v, 28–9, 32v, 37, 41v, 43; Trease, *Cavalier*,p. 98.
116. Chatsworth House, Bolton MS 180; Wenham, *York*, p. 178.
117. Atkin, *Worcestershire*, p. 10.
118. Tennant, *Edgehill*, p. 85.
119. BL, Add. MS 18981, f. 141.
120. J. Thirsk, *Horses in Early Modern England: for Service, for Pleasure, for Power* (Reading University Press, Reading, 1978) p.7 .
121. PRO, SP 28/29, f. 436.
122. Thirsk, *Horses*, p. 7.
123. PRO, SP 28/34, f. 249.
124. PRO, SP 28/177; SP 28/127/3, f. 30.
125. PRO, SP 28/244. I am grateful to Gavin Robinson for this reference.
126. Firth, *Cromwell's Army*, p. 244.
127. I am grateful to Gavin Robinson for supplying me with this information.
128. PRO, SP 28/25, f. 542.
129. Tennant, *Edgehill, passim.*
130. Furgol, pp. 183–4.
131. Edwards, 'Supply of Horses', p. 53.
132. Ibid., pp. 57–8.
133. Furgol, *passim.*

8. Imports

1. Gilbert, I, p. 285.
2. Ohlmeyer, 'Ireland Independent', in Ohlmeyer, *Ireland*, p. 91; Fransiscan MSS, *passim.*
3. ROP, II, p. 381.
4. Cuningham, pp. 221–2, 242, 251; *CSPD, 1644–5*, pp. 430, 448, 502.
5. Carte 9, f. 254; ROP, II, pp. 387; *CSPD, 1644–5*, pp. 469, 480.
6. Franciscan MSS, p. 156.
7. J. Yernaux, *La Métallurgie liégeoise et son expansion au XVIIe siècle* (Thone, Liège, 1939), p. 17–20; C. Gaier, *Quatre siècle d'armurerie liégeoise* (Wahle, Liège, 1977), pp. 31,35–8.
8. Gaier, *D'armurerie*, pp. 18–21.
9. H. Vogel, 'De Republiek als wapenexporteur 1600–1650', in J.P. Puype and M. van der Hoeven (eds), *Het arsenaal van de wereld: Nederlandse wapenhandel in de Gouden Eeuw* (De Bataafsche Leeuw, Amsterdam, 1993), p. 13.
10. S. Groenveld, *Verlopend Getij* (De Bataafsche Leeuw, Dieren, 1984), p. 238.
11. ARA, The Hague; ACA, inv. nr. 1400.
12. V. Barbour, *Capitalism in Amsterdam in the Seventeenth Century* (John Hopkins Press, Baltimore, 1950), p. 35; Gaier, *D'armurerie*, p. 57.
13. Klein, 'Trip Family', p. 196.
14. J.T. Lindblad, 'Louis de Geer (1587–1652): Dutch Entrepreneur and the Father of Swedish Industry', in C. Lesger and L. Noordegraaf (eds), *Entrepreneurs and Entrepreneurship in Early Modern Times: Merchants and Industrialists within the Orbit of the Dutch Staple Market* (Stichting Hollandse Historische Reeks, The Hague, 1955), p. 80.
15. Lindblad, 'Louis de Geer', pp. 78–9; Barbour, *Capitalism in Amsterdam*, pp. 36–7.
16. Klein, 'Trip Family', p. 197.
17. Franciscan MSS, p. 167; *CSPD, 1639–40*, p. 303.
18. ARA, Brussels, Audiëntie, inv. no. 1062, f. 119.
19. PRO, SP 84/157, ff. 240–5.
20. J. Israel, *The Dutch Republic: Its Rise, Greatness, and Fall 1477–1806* (Clarendon Press, Oxford, 1998), pp. 541, 544.
21. Fissel, p. 99; ROP, II, p. 365.
22. ROP, II, p. 413; PRO, SP 28/22, f. 221.
23. Vogel, 'De Republiek', p. 14.
24. ROP, II, p. 515, n. 77.
25. *CSPD, 1641–3*, p. 479; ROP, II, p. 373.
26. ROP, II, p. 413; PRO, SP 28/30, f. 640; SP 28/31, f. 517.
27. NAS, GD 406/1/10491
28. *CSPD, 1638–9*, p. 323; *CSPV, 1636–9*, pp. 494–5.
29. NAS, GD 26/IX/210.
30. Lewis, p. 340.
31. ARA, The Hague; ZCA, inv. nos 2461, 2463–4.
32. NAS, GD 406/1/1115.
33. Murdoch, thesis, pp. 122, 125; S. Mowat, *The Port of Leith, Its History and Its People* (John Donald, Edinburgh, 1993), p. 175; Cuningham, pp. xvi–xvii.
34. ARA, The Hague; ZCA, inv. no. 2464, 18 June 1640; *CSPV, 1640–2*, p. 90.
35. Cuningham, pp. 38–46, 54; Rooseboom, p. 177: Thomas Cunningham was only officially appointed on 10 July 1644.

36. Grosjean, thesis, p. 158.

37. Ibid., pp. 150, 164, 166; *SRP*, VII, 1637–9, pp. 275–7; VIII, 1640–1, pp. 117–20.

38. *SRP*, VII, pp. 274–9.

39. Grosjean, thesis, p. 158.

40. E. Marquard (ed), *Kancelliets Brevbøger 1637–1639* (Copenhagen, 1944,) pp. 672–3.

41. *SRP*, VIII, pp. 117–20, 217, 245, 262.

42. *KB*, *1637–39*, pp. 722–3; *1640–1*, p. 511; Murdoch, thesis, p. 123; *Edinburgh Records 1626–41*, p. 222; 1 centner = *c*. 1 cwt.

43. *SRP*, VIII, pp. 117–20, 217, 245, 262.

44. Murdoch, thesis, pp. 129–30.

45. *KB*, *1637–9*, pp. 722–3.

46. Murdoch, thesis, pp. 111, 115.

47. Murdoch, thesis, pp. 114–16, 118–20, 126–8.

48. *Infra*, p. 206.

49. Cuningham, pp. 37–8, 53–5, 64–8, 95–7, 162.

50. Trip: ARA, The Hague; ACA, inv. nr. 1388, 20 April 1642; De Geer: ARA, The Hague; ACA, inv. nr. 1400, 5 January 1644.

51. Terry, I, pp. 19–23; for native merchants bringing in arms receipts at Leith magazine see PA 15/3.

52. *Edinburgh Records 1642–55*, p. 44.

53. Fissel, p. 98.

54. Fissel, pp. 10, 98; E351/2711: I am grateful to Mark Fissel for this reference.

55. Murdoch, thesis, p. 123; Fissel, p. 99.

56. *CSPD*, *1638–9*, p. 166; ARA, The Hague; ACA, inv. nr. 1385, 23 February 1639.

57. Barbour, *Capitalism in Amsterdam*, p. 113; ARA, The Hague; ACA, inv. nr. 1385, 9 April 1639, 9 June 1639.

58. ARA, The Hague; ACA, inv. nr. 1385, 25 March 1639; Ohlmeyer, *Antrim*, pp. 83–5.

59. *CSPD*, *1639–40*, pp. 303, 368, 375, 559.

60. ARA, Brussels, Audiëntie, inv. nr. 1061, f. 38.

61. *CSPD*, *1640*, p. 272.

62. *KCFB*, 4, 1636–40, pp. 358, 361; Fissel, pp. 172–3.

63. Murdoch, thesis, pp. 120–1; Fissel, pp. 172–3.

64. *CSPD*, *1639–40*, pp. 368, 399.

65. ARA, The Hague; ACA, inv. nr. 1386, 7 and 26 August 1640; 3 August 1640; Ohlmeyer, *Antrim*, p. 94.

66. Spalding, *Troubles*, I, p. 99; *CSPD*, *1638–9*, p. 515.

67. Aberdeen Council Letters, 1633–44, p. 271; Spalding, *Troubles*, I, p. 115.

68. Ohlmeyer, *Antrim*, pp. 147–8.

69. Carte 13, f. 258; Ohlmeyer, *Antrim*, pp. 152–3.

70. *CSPD*, *1644–5*, pp. 374, 546.

71. *CSPD*, *1645–7*, p. 23; Williams, *Montrose*, p. 300.

72. *CSPD*, *1645–7*, p. 31.

73. Murdoch, thesis, p. 153; *CSPD*, *1644–5*, p. 387–8; Morlond-Simpson, 'Civil War Papers', pp. 153–66.

74. Cuningham, p. 162.

75. NAS, GD 406/1/2347; GD 406/1/2418.

76. Cal. Clar. SP, i, p. 438, no. 2879; TT E.465 (34).

77. Kenyon, *Civil Wars*, p. 188; E. Furgol, 'The Civil Wars in Scotland', in Kenyon and Ohlmeyer, *Civil Wars*, p. 64.

78. Williams, *Montrose*, p. 327.

79. S. Murdoch, 'The Search for Northern Allies', in B. Taithe and T. Thornton (eds), *Propaganda: Political Rhetoric and Identity 1300–2000* (Sutton Publishing, Stroud, 1999), pp. 80–3.

80. Murdoch, thesis, pp. 176, 180.

81. Ibid., p. 178; Morlond-Simpson, 'Civil War Papers', pp. 197–8, 211.

82. Grosjean, thesis, pp. 207–11.

83. *SRP*, XIII, pp. 41–3; NAS, GD 40/10/4/1–2.

84. NAS, GD 220/6/2085/2; Carte, *Ormond*, III, p. 455; HMC, *Pepys MSS*, pp. 253, 292; Grosjean, thesis, pp. 214–15.

85. Williams, *Montrose*, pp. 338–9.

86. NAS, GD 220/6/2085/1–3.

87. Williams, *Montrose*, p. 341.

88. Williams, *Montrose*, pp. 336, 341–2; Rooseboom, *Scottish Staple*, p. 185.

89. Murdoch, 'Northern Allies', pp. 83–4.

90. D. Laing, *Correspondence of Sir Robert Kerr, First Earl of Ancram and his Son, William, Third Earl of Lothian, II, 1649–1667* (Edinburgh, 1875), pp. 301, 312, 333–4; Murdoch, thesis, pp. 178–9.

91. NAS, PA 16/3/9/2

92. *CSPD*, *1641–3*, pp. 240, 245; Casway, 'O'Neill', pp. 50–1.

93. *CSPV*, *1642–3*, p. 116.

94. Casway, 'O'Neill', pp. 54–5.

95. *Tanner Letters*, pp. 151–2; TT 21 E.119 (22); *CSPD*, *1641–3*, p. 453.

96. Casway, 'O'Neill', p. 50.

97. Ormond, new series, II, p. 102.

98. *LJ*, 4, pp. 511, 513; *CJ*, 2, p. 377.

99. Ormond, new series, II, pp. 147–8.

100. Ibid., p. 15; W.H. Coates, A.S. Young and V.F. Snow (eds), *The Private Journals of the Long Parliament, 3 January–5 March 1642* (Yale University Press, New Haven, 1982), p. 60.

101. Coates et al., *Private Journals*, pp. 50, 267.

102. Wheeler, Four Armies, p. 44; TT 24 E.135 (2); Coates *et al.*, *Private Journals*, pp. 267, 272; *CSPV, 1640–2*, p. 298.

103. Ormond, new series, II, p. 186.

104. Lenihan, thesis, p. 122; *Tanner Letters*, pp. 150–1; Franciscan MSS, p. 162.

105. Coates *et al.*, *Private Journals*, 173; Ormond, new series, II, p. 80.

106. Franciscan MSS, pp. 157–8.

107. Ibid., pp. 196, 199, 202.

108. TT 23 E.128 (4).

109. Franciscan MSS, p. 199.

110. Casway, 'O'Neill', p. 61; Carte 3, ff. 386, 533v; Carte 6, f. 159; Franciscan MSS, pp. 165, 195; Carte, *Ormond*, II, pp. 356–7.

111. Franciscan MSS, p. 166; Gilbert, II, p. 124.

112. Carte 3, ff. 312, 475; Ormond, new series, I, p. 53.

113. Carte 3, f. 476.

114. Gilbert, II, pp. 262–3.

115. Ibid., p. 340; Ohlmeyer, *Antrim*, pp. 194–5, 280.

116. Wheeler, Four Armies, pp. 52–3.

117. Gilbert, III, pp. 263–4.

118. ARA, Brussels, Audiëntie, inv. nr. 1063, f. 211.

119. Ohlmeyer, Wars, p. 178; Gilbert, V, p. 275: 'Ils m'ont fait dire, depuis, que l'argent leur est plus nécessaire que des armes.'

120. Carte 2, f. 183; Ormond, new series, II, pp. 7, 9.

121. PRO, SP 28/139/15, 25; SP 28/170 and *supra*, p. 24 and *infra*, p. 194; Ormond, new series, II, pp. 321–2; Carte 3, f. 476.

122. Carte 3, f. 476; Hogan, *Irish Rebellion*, pp. 133–4.

123. Ormond, new series, II, p. 320; also n.b. T. Barnard, 'The Protestant Interest, 1641–1660', in Ohlmeyer, *Ireland*, pp. 220–1.

124. Ormond, new series, II, p. 196.

125. Ibid., p. 5; Furgol, p. 65.

126. PRO, SP 28/1B, f. 398; Carte 7, f. 627–v; *Tanner Letters*, pp. 163, 165.

127. *Tanner Letters*, pp. 173–4.

128. Carte 11, f. 419v, Carte 15, f. 567; *CSPI, 1633–47*, pp. 407, 483–4.

129. Ormond, new series, II, pp. 177–8, 226; H.Q. van Ufford, *A Merchant-Adventurer in the Dutch Republic: John Quarles and his Times 1596–1646/7* (V.U. Boekhandel/Uitgeverii, Amsterdam, 1983), p. 74.

130. Ormond, new series, II, pp. 227–8, 322–5.

131. Carte 7, f. 289.

132. Carte 7, ff. 456, 460; Carte 9, f. 65, 322; Carte 10, f. 796–v.

133. Carte 11, f. 258.

134. Carte 15, f. 30.

135. Ohlmeyer, 'The Civil Wars in Ireland', in Kenyon and Ohlmeyer, *Civil Wars*, p. 95; HMC, *Pepys MSS*, p. 248.

136. *Supra*, p. 188.

137. Carte 7, f. 31–v; Carte 8, f. 316.

138. Carte 10, ff. 296, 405v, 431.

139. *Infra*, p. 209.

140. Gilbert, IV, pp. 138–9.

141. Carte 10, f. 556; Gilbert, VII, p. 278.

142. P. Geyl, *Orange and Stuart 1641–72* (Weidenfeld & Nicolson, 1969), pp. 5–19.

143. Groenveld, *Verlopend Getij*, p. 108.

144. Israel, *Dutch Republic*, pp. 540–3; Geyl, *Orange and Stuart*, pp. 13–14.

145. Groenveld, *Verlopend Getij*, p. 110.

146. Ibid., pp. 100–3; Geyl, *Orange and Stuart*, p. 14.

147. TT 27 E.150 (24); TT 669 f. 5, no. 38.

148. ROP, I, p. 15; Powell and Timings, 'Documents', pp. 19–20, 31–2.

149. TT 19 E.109 (12).

150. Groenveld, *Verlopend Getij*, p. 103.

151. TT 27 E.154 (26).

152. ARA, The Hague; ACA, inv. nr. 1388; ZCA, inv. nr. 2463.

153. PRO, SP 28/263, f. 136.

154. Geyl, *Orange and Stuart*, p. 16; Groenveld, *Verlopend Getij*, pp. 104–5.

155. Geyl, *Orange and Stuart*, pp. 16–17; G.G. van Prinsterer, (ed.), *Archives ou Correspondance Inédite de la Maison D'Orange-Nassau, IV, 1642–1650* (Kemink et Fils, Utrecht, 1859), pp. 71–2.

156. Geyl, *Orange and Stuart*, p. 17.

157. Groenveld, *Verlopend Getij*, p. 106.

158. AMA; NA 1066, 233, 5 April 1643.

159. Groenveld, *Verlopend Getij*, p. 237.

160. Ibid., p. 122, n. 60; Geyl, *Orange and Stuart*, pp. 17–18; Israel, *Dutch Republic*, p. 527.

161. Wenham, *York*, p. 8.

162. ROP, I, pp. 41, 44; C.Clar.SP, I, p. 293, no. 2068; Powell and Timings, 'Documents', p. 148; *CSPD, 1644*, p. 157.

163. *LJ*, 6, 1643–4, pp. 619–21; *CSPD, 1644*, p. 320.

164. *LJ*, 6, p. 619.
165. TT 669 f. 5, no. 38.
166. PRO, SP 84/158/16r–16v.
167. ROP, II, pp. 407–8; C.Clar.SP, I, p. 446.
168. *Supra*, p. 72.
169. PRO, SP 28/261, iii, f. 284.
170. PRO, SP 28/261–4, *passim*.
171. PRO, SP 28/250/2.
172. ARA, The Hague; ACA, Freeman: inv. nrs. 1400, 1399; Shuttleworth: inv. nrs. 1388, 1399–1401.
173. PRO, SP 28/26, f. 311; SP 28/130/3, f. 40v.
174. ARA, The Hague; ZCA, inv. nrs. 2463, 2465.
175. PRO, SP 28/25, f. 522; SP 28/28, f. 197.
176. R.A. Stradling, 'The Spanish Dunkirkers, 1621–48: a Record of Plunder and Destruction', *Tijdschrift voor geschiedenis*, 93 (1980), 542–3.
177. ARA, Brussels, Council of Finance, inv. nr. 491, doct. 13.
178. Groenveld, *Verlopend Getij*, p. 155, f. 147.
179. ARA, Brussels, Audiëntie, inv. nr. 1062, f. 132.
180. Groenveld, *Verlopend Getij*, p. 158.
181. Ibid., pp. 165–6; *CSPD, 1644*, p. 234; *CJ*, 2, pp. 620–1.
182. Groenveld, *Verlopend Getij*, p. 165; *CSPD, 1644–5*, pp. 366, 429, 466.
183. ROP, II, pp. 381–2; *CSPD, 1644*, p. 157.
184. ROP, II, p. 381.
185. Ibid., II, pp. 373, 509, n. 30; *CSPD, 1644–5*, p. 366.
186. ROP, p. 513, n. 58; *CSPD, 1644–5*, pp. 366–7.
187. ROP, I, p. 42.
188. Ibid., p. 42, n. 9; C.Clar.SP, I, p. 245, no. 1729; BL, Add. MS 18981, f. 47; Groenveld, *Verlopend Getij*, p. 165; *CSPD, 1644–5*, pp. 469, 494.
189. *CSPD, 1641–3*, p. 500; C. Clar.SP, I, nos 1733, 1912–13; ROP, I, p. 42.
190. *CSPD, 1641–3*, pp. 479, 484; ROP,II, pp. 365, 507, n. 14; Bodl., Firth C6, f. 294v.
191. PRO, WO 55/1660; SP 28/263, ff. 218, 220, 315; SP 28/264, no. 372.
192. *Supra*, p. 202.
193. Groenveld, *Verlopend Getij*, p. 155; ARA, Brussels, Council of Finances, inv. nr. 525; ARA, Brussels, Chambres des Comptes, Affaires Domaniales et Financières, 28 April 1644.
194. *CSPV, 1642–3*, p. 233.
195. Carte 14, f. 373; Wedgewood, p. 353.
196. Brereton, I, p. 313, no. 378, *c.* 30 April 1645, Sir Robert King to Brereton.
197. ROP, I, pp. 45–6.
198. *CSPD, 1644*, pp. 260, 342.
199. PRO, SP 28/22, f. 221v; SP 28/43, f. 944v.
200. TT 23 E.128 (4).
201. *CSPD, 1644*, pp. 56, 342; ROP, *passim*; HMC, *Pepys MSS*, pp. 208, 213.
202. *CSPD, 1644–5*, p. 469.
203. ROP, II, p. 515, n. 78.
204. Carte 14, f. 118.
205. ROP, II, pp. 372–3.
206. Carte 14, f. 237.
207. *Supra*, pp. 183–4.
208. Murdoch, thesis, p. 168.
209. Ibid., p. 145; DRA, TKUA England A II 15.
210. *KCFB*, 8, 1584–1648, pp. 220–2; Murdoch, thesis, pp. 146, 148.
211. *CSPV, 1643–7*, p. 21, 22 January 1644; Murdoch, thesis, p. 149.
212. Murdoch, thesis, p. 150; W.Oldys (ed.), *The Harleian Miscellany*, VII (1811), pp. 568–9.
213. Murdoch, thesis, pp. 146–7.
214. Powell and Timings, 'Documents', pp. 85–6.
215. PRO, SP 28/222, f. 274.
216. Murdoch, thesis, p. 158.
217. Ibid., pp. 147, 162; PRO, WO 55/1660.
218. Murdoch, thesis, pp. 161–3.
219. Ibid., pp. 134, 162, 168.
220. Carte 12, f. 140.
221. Hutton, pp. 122–3; Ormond, new series, II, p. 318; Carte 7, ff. 195, 255.
222. Hutton, pp. 130, 133.
223. Carte 9, ff. 243, 254, 550.
224. Hutton, pp. 134–5.
225. Carte 9, f. 509, Carte 10, ff. 156, 439, 456.
226. BL, Add. MS 18981, f. 191
227. Carte 12, f. 442; Carte 14, f. 106; Brereton, II, p. 365.
228. Carte 15, ff. 671, 690; Carte 16, f. 256.
229. Hutton, p. 194.
230. Carte 9, f. 87.
231. Carte 7, ff. 145, 195, 368.
232. Gilbert, III, p. 88, n. 1.
233. Ibid., III, pp. 87–8.
234. Carte 9, f. 261, 263; Carte 10, f. 30.
235. Carte, 10, f. 30.
236. Carte 10, f. 195v; Carte 14, f. 84.
237. J. Lowe, 'The Glamorgan Mission to Ireland 1645–6', *Studia Hibernica*, 4 (1964), 166.
238. Lowe, 'Glamorgan Mission', pp. 178–9.

239. Lowe, 'Glamorgan Mission', pp. 156–78.
240. Gilbert, V, p. 319; Lowe, 'Glamorgan Mission', pp. 190–1.
241. Wheeler, Four Armies, p. 48.
242. Parker, *Military Revolution*, p. 68.

9. Shipping, Naval Action and Internal Transport

1. Capp, 'Naval Operations', p. 157.
2. TT 245 669 f. 3, no. 50.
3. Capp, 'Naval Operations', p. 167.
4. Powell and Timings, 'Documents', pp. 122–4; Capp, 'Naval Operations', p. 162; TT 245 669 f. 9, no. 36.
5. Capp, 'Naval Operations', p. 162.
6. TT 245 669 f. 9 (58); TT 70 E.446 (24).
7. Capp, 'Naval Operations', pp. 180–6; Wheeler, *World Power*, p. 44.
8. Murdoch, thesis, p. 150. Powell and Timings, 'Documents', pp. 101, 122; J.R. Powell, *The Navy in the English Civil War* (Archon Books, 1962), p. 91.
9. HMC, *Pepys MSS* (HMSO, 1911), pp. 200–1, 204, 263.
10. *CSPD, 1641–3*, p. 499; *CSPD, 1644–5*, pp. 617–18.
11. Capp, 'Naval Operations', pp. 174–5.
12. Ibid., pp. 184–7.
13. Capp, 'Naval Operations', pp. 189–90.
14. *CSPD, 1639*, p. 234; NAS, GD 406/1/1115.
15. *SRP*, VIII, p. 120; Cuningham, p. 54.
16. Stevenson, *Government*, pp. 41–2.
17. Franciscan MSS, pp. 163, 202.
18. Ibid., pp. 123, 169, 202; Loeber and Parker, 'Military Revolution', p. 86.
19. J. Ohlmeyer, 'Irish Privateers during the Civil War, 1642–50', *Mariner's Mirror*, 76 (1990), 120; Loeber and Parker, 'Military Revolution', p. 86; Capp, 'Naval Operations', p. 165.
20. Ohlmeyer, *Antrim*, p. 158; Ohlmeyer, 'Privateers', p. 123.
21. N. Tucker, *North Wales in the Civil War* (Bridge Books, Wrexham, 1992 edn), p. 109.
22. Carte 7, f. 267.
23. Groenveld, *Verlopend Getij*, p. 143.
24. P. Edwards, 'The Low Countries, the Arms Trade and the British Civil Wars', *Journal of European Economic History*, forthcoming; Stradling, pp. 542–3.
25. R. Harding, *The Evolution of the Sailing Navy, 1509–1815* (Macmillan, 1995), p. 64.
26. NAS, GD 112/39/70/3–4, GD 406/1/648, 685–6; GD 406/1/1203, 1115; *CSPD, 1639*, pp. 70–1.
27. Leith, p. 175.
28. Casway, 'O'Neill', p. 50; Ormond, new series, II, pp. 15, 59; *CSPD, 1641–3*, p. 245; *Private Journals 3 January–5 March 1642*, pp. 50, 55.
29. As, for example, TT 24 E.137 (18); TT 27 E.150 (13).
30. TT 245 669 f. 3, (50).
31. Capp. 'Naval Operations', p. 165.
32. Carte 3, ff. 475v–478.
33. TT 23 E.128 (4).
34. Powell, *Navy*, pp. 16–18; Powell and Timings, 'Documents', pp. 23, 85–6; TT 21 E.119 (26).
35. Powell, *Navy*, p. 31; Powell and Timings, 'Documents', pp. 19, 61–7.
36. Powell and Timings, 'Documents', pp. 120–1; Powell, *Navy*, p. 47; Capp, 'Naval Operations', p. 168.
37. Powell and Timings, 'Documents', pp. 122–4.
38. ROP, II, pp. 359–429, *passim*; Powell, *Navy*, p. 28.
39. Capp, 'Naval Operations', p. 173; Edwards, 'Gunpowder', p. 124.
40. Capp, 'Naval Operations', pp. 170–6; Carte 10, ff. 97, 143, 443, 700.
41. Powell and Timings, 'Documents', p. 100; Carte 11, ff. 118–118v; TT E67 [3], p. 261.
42. Carte 11, f. 553; Carte 12, ff. 308, 312, 432.
43. Ohlmeyer, *Antrim*, pp. 143–5.
44. Stevenson, *Government*, p. 9.
45. *Tanner Letters*, p. 177.
46. Powell and Timings, 'Documents', p. 103.
47. Capp, 'Naval Operations', p. 174; HMC, *15th Report*, Duke of Somerset's MSS (1898), p. 68; Powell and Timings, 'Documents', p. 197.
48. *CSPD, 1644–5*, p. 346.
49. Carte 3, ff. 473–475v.
50. Carte 5, f. 187; Ormond, new series, II, p. 296.
51. Capp, 'Naval Operations', p. 177.
52. *CSPI, 1647–60*, p. 30; Wheeler, Four Armies, pp. 60–1; Ohlmeyer, 'Privateers', p. 126.
53. Capp, 'Naval Operations', pp. 188–9.
54. Ohlmeyer, 'Privateers', pp. 126–7.
55. TT 6 E.34 (11).
56. Carte 3, f. 478; Carte 5, f. 553, 559.
57. Ormond, new series, II, pp. 304–5.
58. Carte 10, ff. 725, 730.

59. Powell and Timings, 'Documents', p. 87.
60. CIA, II, pp. 421–2; PRO, SP 21/7, f. 13; *CSPD, 1649–50*, p. 157.
61. Wheeler, *World Power*, pp. 44–5.
62. PRO, WO 49/76, ff. 13,97, 159, 210.
63. PRO, SP 28/145.
64. Ibid.; M. Toynbee (ed.), 'The Papers of Captain Henry Stevens, Wagon-Master-General to King Charles I', *Oxfordshire Record Society*, pp. 15–16.
65. Edwards, *Horse Trade*, pp. 4–5.
66. Ibid.
67. W.C. and C.E. Trevelyan, 'The Trevelyan Papers III', *Camden Society*, CV (1872), pp. 250–1.
68. PRO, SP 28/38, ff. 584–5.
69. Edwards, 'Logistics', p. 259; Edwards, *Horse Trade*, p. 2; Dorian Gerhold, 'Packhorses and Wheeled Vehicles in England 1550–1800', *Journal of Transport History*, 3rd series, 14 (1993), pp. 13–17.
70. Edwards, *Horse Trade*, p. 6.
71. Kenyon, *Civil Wars*, p. 86.
72. PRO, WO 49/76, ff. 13, 97, 159, 210.
73. NAS, GD 406/1/775; Staffordshire Record Office, Dartmouth Papers D(W) 1778/I/i/5.
74. Fissel, p. 109; Staffordshire Record Office, Dartmouth Papers, D(W) 1778/I/i/5.
75. Fissel, pp. 58, 60, 110; Staffordshire Record Office, Dartmouth Papers, D(W) 1778/I/i/5.
76. *CSPD, 1638–9*, p. 602.
77. Ibid., p. 541; PRO, WO 49/68, ff. 33–4; WO 49/76, ff. 55–6.
78. PRO, WO 49/68, ff. 33–4.
79. *Supra*, p. 159.
80. HMC, Earl Cowper MSS, II, p. 306. I am grateful to Howard Usher of Melbourne, Derbyshire, for this reference.
81. CIA, II, p. 406.
82. PRO, WO 49/72, f. 96; CIA, II, pp. 371–2.
83. For example, CIA, I, pp. 421, 428, 436.
84. CIA, I, pp. 410–11, also see CIA II, p. 419; CIA, II, p. 436.
85. Ibid., I, pp. 411, 421, 441.
86. PRO, SP 28/128–9, 154, *passim*; Gloucestershire Record Office, Gloucester Borough Records GBR F4/5, *passim*.
87. Spence, *Skipton Castle*, p. 13.
88. PRO, SP 28/146.
89. Gentles, *New Model Army*, p. 40.
90. PRO, SP 28/30, f. 341.
91. Holmes, *Eastern Association*, pp. 150–1; PRO, SP 28/17, f. 159.
92. Young and Holmes, p. 208; BL, Harleian MS 6802, f. 264.
93. ROP, I, p. 22, II, pp. 332–4.
94. Ibid., I, p. 37; Ottley Papers, part 2, p. 316.
95. ROP, I, p. 47; I. Roy, 'England turned Germany', *TRHS*, 5th series, 28 (1978), pp. 133–4, 137–9.
96. Edwards, 'Logistics', p. 259.
97. ROP, I, pp. 46–7.
98. Ibid., p. 54.
99. PRO, SP 28/152/7.
100. Tennant, *Edgehill*, pp. 121–8; *CSPD, 1644*, p. 24.
101. ROP, I, p. 54; BL, Add. MS 18980, f. 70.
102. ROP, I, pp. 46–7.
103. Ibid., II, pp. 479, n. 157, 412; BL, Harleian MS 6852, f. 50.
104. ROP, I, pp. 22, 213.
105. Everitt, 'Suffolk', p. 92.
106. PRO, SP 28/146.
107. Firth and Rait, *Acts and Ordinances*, I, pp. 653–4.
108. PRO, SP 28/131, ff. 28r–29v; SP 28/130, f. 43v; SP 28/29, f. 126; SP 28/30, f. 293; SP 28/54, ff. 704; SP 28/55, f. 249; *CSPD, 1650*, pp. 572, 581; *CSPD, 1651*, pp. 539, 571, 574.
109. For example, PRO, SP 28/52, f. 17.
110. For examples of the work of John Pitt and Thomas Hodgskins, see PRO, SP 28/28, ff. 184, 186; SP 28/52, ff. 17, 60.
111. PRO, WO 55/1661.
112. Data, based on SP 28, kindly supplied by Gavin Robinson.
113. Lewis, pp. 236–7.
114. Pennington and Roots, *Stafford*, p. 134.
115. Edwards, 'Logistics', p. 260; Tennant, *Edgehill*, pp. 54, 56; SP 28/38, vi, f. 584; Shropshire Record Office,Ludlow Corporation Records 356/Box 298.
116. NLW, Crosse of Shaw Hill Collection, no. 1106.
117. For example, *CSPD, 1644*, p. 143.
118. Edwards, 'Supply of Horses', p. 60.
119. PRO, SP 28/3B, ff. 361, 387; SP 28/34, ff. 509, 567.
120. Shropshire Record Office,Ludlow Corporation Records 356/Box 297, no. 516; 356/Box 298; Chatsworth House, Bolton MSS 93, ff. 180–1, 240.
121. Whyte, *Agriculture and Society*, pp. 176, 223.
122. Carte 11, f. 466v.
123. Stevenson, *Government*, p. 139.
124. Ibid., p. 161 for oxen.

125. Edwards, *Horse Trade*, p. 2; Whyte, *Agriculture and Society*, pp. 174, 225.
126. NAS, GD 45/18/671; Stevenson, *Government*, pp. 114–15.
127. Terry, p. lxxviii.
128. Whyte, *Agriculture and Society*, pp. 174–6; NLS, MS 17503, f. 23r.
129. NAS, PA15/3.
130. Terry, p. 400.
131. Whyte, *Agriculture and Society*, p. 174; *Edinburgh Records 1642–55*, p. 427.
132. NAS, PA 16/3/6, no. 26.
133. NAS, GD 112/39/91/1.
134. Furgol, p. 418; NAS, PA 15/3.
135. For example, Furgol, p. 379.
136. NAS, PA 16/20.
137. *Edinburgh Records, 1642–55*, p. 399.
138. Ormond, new series, II, p. 185.
139. Carte 11, f. 118v.
140. Loeber and Parker, 'Military Revolution', p. 77.
141. Ibid., p. 74.
142. Carte 10, f. 718.
143. Ormond, new series, II, p. 79.
144. CIA, II, pp. 371–2.
145. Wedgwood, *King's War*, p. 124; TT 21 E.118 (48); *Tanner Letters*, p. 145.
146. Ormond, new series, II, p. 192.
147. Carte 6, f. 148.
148. Tanner Letters, p. 204; Wheeler, Four Armies, p. 63.
149. Loeber and Parker, 'Military Revolution', p. 74, 76; Carte 6, f. 26; Gilbert, VI, p. 84.
150. Gilbert, II, p. 260.
151. Carte 7, f. 285; Wheeler, *Cromwell*, p. 74.
152. PRO, SP 25/118; *CSPD, 1649*, p. 536.
153. Wheeler, Ireland, p. 42.
154. Gentles, *New Model Army*, pp. 354, 357.
155. Burke, 'New Model Army', p. 19; Wheeler, Ireland, pp. 43–4, 51.
156. Burke, 'New Model Army', pp. 10, 14–15; Gentles, *New Model Army*, p. 370.
157. Wheeler, Ireland, p. 50; Wheeler, Four Armies, p. 63.
158. PRO, SP 25/118; *CSPD, 1649–50*, pp. 543, 577–8, 580–2; Wheeler, Four Armies, p. 64.
159. *CSPD, 1649–50*, pp. 539, 541.
160. PRO, SP 25/118.
161. Wheeler, Scotland, pp. 4–5.
162. For example, *CSPD, 1650*, pp. 533, 553, 560–3; Grainger, *Cromwell*, p. 18.
163. Wheeler, Scotland, pp. 5, 12.
164. Gentles, *New Model Army*, p. 388; Wheeler, Scotland, pp. 9–14.
165. *CSPD, 1651*, pp. 539, 543, 547, 555–6, 558, 560–1, 571; Grainger, *Cromwell*, pp. 87, 98, 104.
166. For example, *CSPD, 1651*, p. 528.
167. *CSPD, 1650*, p. 581.
168. Ibid., pp. 573, 575–7; *CSPD, 1651*, pp. 537.
169. *CSPD, 1651*, pp. 543, 568–9.
170. *CSPD, 1651*, p. 524.
171. Wheeler, Scotland, p. 12.

Conclusion

1. Edwards, 'Logistics', p. 270.
2. Wheeler, *World Power*, pp. 13–19, 197.
3. Ibid., p. 197.
4. Edwards, 'Supply of Horses', p. 60.
5. Ibid., pp. 57–8, 65–6.
6. Brenner, *passim*; MacCormack, 'Irish Adventurers', p. 22.
7. PRO, SP 29/232.
8. Stevenson, Finances, p. 98.
9. Young and Holmes, *English Civil War*, pp. 74–6.
10. Parker, *Military Revolution*, p. 33.
11. Lenihan, 'Celtic Warfare', pp. 128–9.
12. R. Hutton and W. Reeves, 'Sieges and Fortifications', in Kenyon and Ohlmeyer, *Civil Wars*, p. 195.
13. Hutton and Reeves, 'Sieges', p. 202.
14. Parker, *Military Revolution*, pp. 28; Loeber and Parker, 'Military Revolution', pp. 68, 70; Hutton and Reeves, 'Sieges', pp. 210, 212–15, 221.
15. Hutton and Reeves, 'Sieges', pp. 220–1, 231.
16. Loeber and Parker, 'Military Revolution', pp. 73–4; Hutton and Reeves, 'Sieges', p. 208; Burke, 'New Model Army', pp. 2–3.
17. Burke, ''New Model Army', pp. 3–5; Hutton and Reeves, 'Sieges', p. 209.

BIBLIOGRAPHY

MANUSCRIPT SOURCES

Belgium

National Archives, Belgium
Audiëntie, inv. nrs. 1058, 1061–3
Chambres des Comptes, inv. nr. 1262
Council of Finances, inv. nr. 491, 502, 525, 532
Notarial Archives, inv. nr. 3005
Private Council, Commerce et Industrie, inv. nr. 1324

Denmark

Danish Rigsarkivet, Copenhagen
TKUA England A II 15

England

Birmingham Reference Library
Fetherston Correspondence, vol. I

Bodleian Library, Oxford
Carte MSS 1–17
Fairfax MS 32
Firth Notes, C6–8
Rawlinson MS C125

Bristol City Record Office
Bristol Corporation Records: Great Audit Book 1640–4, 04026/21

British Library
Additional MSS: 18979–82, 29443, 34315, 34325
Harleian MSS: 6802, 6804, 6851–2
Thomason Tracts: TT 6 E.34 (11); TT 12 E.69 (8); TT 19 E.109 (12); TT 21 E.118 (48); TT 21 E.119 (22); TT 23 E.128 (4); TT 24 E.135 (2); TT 24 E.137 (18); TT27 E.150 (13); TT 27 E.150 (24); TT 27 E.154 (26); TT 70 E.446 (24); TT 245 669 f.3, no.50, f.9; TT 669 f.5, no.38; TT E.67 [3] p.261

Chatsworth House
Bolton MSS 93, 180–1, 240
Curry L/45

Cumbria Record Office, Carlisle
Lowther Papers: D/LONS/L/A1/4

Derbyshire Record Office
Gell Collection, D 258/34/10; D 258/41/31X(a)
Gresley of Drakelowe MSS D 803/M/Z9

Gloucestershire Record Office
Gloucester Borough Records GBR/B3/2; GBR/F4/5
Correspondence: D 115/15

Herefordshire Record Office
Foley Papers, E12/VI/2/Bf3,25; F/IV/AD/1–3; F/VI/2/Bf 4,25, 7127–31

Huntingdon Record Office
Earl of Manchester Correspondence, 2091/505–72

Lichfield Cathedral
Accounts of Colonel Richard Bagot, Governor of Lichfield, MS Lich 24

Lichfield Joint Record Office
Probate: Hugh Canter of Holy Trinity, Coventry, 14 May 1678

Lincolnshire Archive Office
Monson Papers, MON 27/3/1

London Corporation Record Office
Orphans' Court Inventory 274, Henry Keene of St Sepulchre, 1665

Northampton Record Office
Fermor-Heskith MSS (Baker Collection), FH Baker 704
Finch-Hatton Collection, F(M)C 275

North Yorkshire Record Office4
Scarborough Corporation Minute Book 1621–49, DC/SCB II/1/1/1, MIC 2150/302

Public Record Office, Kew
Declared Accounts: E351/1748, 2662, 2711, 3518–20, 3522, 3598
Commonwealth Papers: SP 28/1–70, 126–264, 299–305, 352
PROB 11/281/520
State Papers: 25/118; SP 46/77/479–81
War Office Papers: WO 49/68–83; 54/15–6; 55/387, 42–4, 455–60, 1660–6, 1754, 1937

Shropshire Record Office
Bridgnorth Corporation Records 4001/no piece no.
Ludlow Corporation Records, 556/Box 298

Staffordshire Record Office
Dartmouth Papers D(W) 1778/I/i/5, 1788/I/i/11, 29, 31, 40

Warwickshire Record Office
Earl of Denbigh's Letter Books, CR 2017/C9–10

West Suffolk Record Office
Barwell Accounts, 552/11/22
Chelsworth Constables' Accounts, HA 525/1/1/4

Scotland

Argyll & Bute Archive (Lochgilphead)
Dumbarton Garrison MSS

National Archives of Scotland, Edinburgh
North Berwick Burgh Records: B56/16/13
Earls of Leven and Melville Papers: GD 26/7/4; GD 26/12/5/2; GD 26/12/7
Dalhousie Papers: GD 45/18/1671
Breadalbane Letters: GD 112/39
Montrose Papers: GD 220/6/2085/1–3
Hamilton Papers: GD 406/1
Parliamentary Papers: PA 15/3; 16/2/13; 16/3/6, 9; 16/3/9/2; 16/20

National Library of Scotland
Balcarres Papers 29.2.9
Saltoun MS 17503

Perth Archives
Perth Glovers' Corporation MS67/Bundle 97

The Netherlands

Amsterdam Municipal Archives
Nieuwe Kerk, Amsterdam, registers, nr. 421/fo. 210
Notarial Archives: 109–3658 (various)

National Archives, The Hague
Amsterdam Chamber of the Admiralty, inv. nrs. 1385–8, 1399–1402
Resolutions of the Admiralty of Zeeland, inv. nrs. 2461, 2463–7

Rotterdam Municipal Archives
Notarial Archives: 297–440 (various)

Wales

National Library of Wales, Aberystwyth
Brogynton Papers: Clenennau Letters and Papers, f. 609
Crosse of Shawe Hill Papers, nos 1097, 1106
Diocese of Llandaff Results and Orders of Commissioners of Array 1643, LL/MB/17
Tredegan Park MSS, 105/131–151
Wynn of Gwydir Papers: no. 1723

University College North Wales, Bangor

Baron Hill MSS 5362–5380, Viscount Bulkeley's Papers

Bangor MS 1921, Viscount Bulkeley's Papers

PRINTED PRIMARY SOURCES

A Breiffe Narration of the Services Done to Three Noble Ladyes by Gilbert Blakhall (Spalding Club, Aberdeen, 1844)

Barron, D.G., *In Defence of the Regalia 1651–2* (Longman, Green & Co., 1910)

Bennett, M. (ed.), 'A Nottinghamshire Village in War and Peace: the Accounts of the Constables of Upton 1640–1666', *Thoroton Society, Record Series*, XXXIX (1995)

Bergh, S. (ed.), *Svenska Riksrådets Protokoll*, VII, 1637–9 (Stockholm, 1895); VIII, 1640, 1641 (Stockholm, 1898); XIII, 1649 (Stockholm, 1912)

Blundeville, Thomas, *The Foure Chiefest Offices Belongyng to Horsemanship* (1580 edn)

Bricka, C.F. & Fridericia, J.A. (eds), *Kong Christian den Fjerdes Egenhaendige Breve*, 4, 1636–40; 5, 1641–44 (Copenhagen, 1969)

Bricka, C.F. & Udgave, J.A.F., *Kong Christian den Fjerdes Egenhaendige Breve*, 8 (Copenhagen, 1970)

Bruce, J. (ed.), 'Letters and Papers of the Verney Family', *Camden Society*, 56 (1853)

Bund, J.W.W. (ed.), 'Diary of Henry Townshend', II, *Worcestershire Historical Society*, (1920)

Burns, J.W., *Miscellaneous Writings of John Spreull . . . 1642–1722* (Glasgow, 1882)

Calendar of Clarendon State Papers

Calendar of State Papers, Domestic, 1635–51 (12 vols), 1654, 1625–49 Addenda

Calendar of State Papers, Ireland, 1633–47, 1647–60

Calendar of State Papers, Venetian, 1636–43 (3 vols)

Carte, Thomas, *The Life of James Duke of Ormond*, vols 2–3 (Oxford University Press, Oxford, 1851)

Chambers, W. (ed.), 'Charters and Documents relating to the Burgh of Peebles with Extracts from the Records of the Burgh, AD 1165–1710', *Scottish Burgh Records Society* (Edinburgh, 1872)

Clark, A. (ed.), *The Life and Times of Anthony Wood*, I (Clarendon Press, Oxford, 1891)

Coates, W.H., Young, A.S. and Snow, V.F. (eds), *The Private Journals of the Long Parliament, 3 January to 5 March 1642* (Yale University Press, New Haven, 1982)

Cook W.B., and Morris, D.B., (eds), *Extracts from the Records of the Merchant Guild of Stirling, AD 1592–1846* (Stirlingshire & Sons of the Rock Society, Stirling, 1916)

Journals of the House of Commons, vols 2–4

Dore, R.N. (ed.), 'The Letter Books of Sir William Brereton, *Lancashire and Cheshire Record Society*, part 1, CXXIII (1984); part 2, CXXVIII (1990)

Everitt, A.M. (ed.), 'Suffolk and the Great Rebellion', *Suffolk Record Society*, 3 (1960)

Firth C.H. and Rait, R.S. (eds), *Acts and Ordinances of the Interregnum, 1642–60* (HMSO, 1911)

Gilbert, J.T. (ed.), *History of the Irish Confederation and the War in Ireland 1641–53* (7 vols, Dublin, 1882–91)

Henderson, E., *The Annals of Dunfermline* (John Tweed, Glasgow, 1897)

Hickson, M., *Ireland in the Seventeenth Century or the Irish Massacres of 1641–2, Their Causes and Results*, I (Longman, Green & Co. 1884)

His Maiesties Passing Through the Scots Armie (1641)

Historical Manuscripts Commission:

    Twelfth Report, part 2, Earl Cowper MSS (1888)

    Fifteenth Report, Appendix, part VII, Duke of Somerset MSS (1898)

    Manuscripts of the Marquess of Ormonde Preserved at Kilkenny Castle, new series, I (1902), new series, 2 (1903)

    Pepys Manuscripts at Magdalene College, Cambridge (1911)

    Report on the Fransiscan Manuscripts Preserved at the Convent, Merchants' Quay, Dublin (Dublin, 1906)

    Fifteenth Report, Hastings MSS, II (1930)

    De L'Isle MSS, Sidney Papers 1626–98 (1966)

Hodgson, J.C. (ed.), *The Journal of John Aston, 1639* (Pallas Armata, Tonbridge, 1999)

Hogan, J. (ed.), *Letters and Papers Relating to the Irish Rebellion 1642–1646* (Stationery Office, Dublin, 1936)

Holmgaard, J. (ed.), *Kancelliets Brevbøger, vedrorende Danmarks indre forhold 1646* (Copenhagen, 1987); *1647* (Copenhagen, 1989); *1648* (Copenhagen, 1991); *1649* (Copenhagen, 1993); *1650* (Copenhagen, 1950)

Jorgensen, J. (ed.), *Kancelliets Brevbøger, vedrorende Danmarks indre forhold 1644–5* (Copenhagen, 1968)

Kenyon, J.P., *The Stuart Constitution* (Cambridge University Press, Cambridge, 1986)

Lords Journals, vol. 4

Laing, D., *Correspondence of Sir Robert Kerr, First Earl of Ancram and his Son, William, Third Earl of Lothian, II, 1649–1667* (Edinburgh, 1875)

Long, C.E., 'Richard Symonds's Diary of the Marches of the Royal Army', *Camden Society*, old series, 74, 1859 (Cambridge University Press, Cambridge, reprint 1997)

Maltby, J.D. (ed.), 'The Short Parliament (1640) Diary of Sir Thomas Aston', *Camden Society*, 4th series, 35 (1988)

Marquard, E. (ed.), *Kancelliets Brevbøger, vedrorende Danmarks indre forhold 1637–9* (Copenhagen, 1944); *1640–1* (Copenhagen, 1950)

Mason, D. (ed.), *Register of PC of Scotland, 2nd series, I, 1625–7* (Edinburgh, 1899)

McNeill, C. (ed.), *Tanner Letters* (Stationery Office, Dublin, 1943)

The Memoirs of Henry Guthry late Bishop of Dunkeld (G. Hamilton and J. Balfour, Glasgow, 2nd edn 1747)

Military Memoirs of the Great Civil War, Being the Military Memoirs of John Gwynne (Ken Trotman Ltd, Cambridge, 1987)

Morland-Simpson, H.F. (ed.), 'Civil War Papers 1643–1650', *Miscellany of the Scottish Historical Society*, I (1893)

Mungean, G.I., 'Contracts for the Supply of Equipment to the 'New Model' Army in 1645', *Journal of the Arms and Armour Society*, VI (1968–70)

Oldys, W. (ed.), *The Harleian Miscellany*, VII (London, 1811)

Olsen, G. (ed.), *Kancelliets Brevbøger, vedrorende Danmarks indre forhold, 1642–3*, (Copenhagen, 1957)

Pennington D.H. and Roots, I.A., *The Committee at Stafford 1643–45* (Manchester University Press, Manchester, 1957)

Phillips, W. (ed.) 'The Ottley Papers Relating to the Civil War', *Transactions of the Shropshire Archaeological Society*, part 1, VI (1894), pp. 59, 71; part 2, VII (1895)

Powell J.R. and Timings, E.K. (eds), 'Documents Relating to the Civil War 1642–1648', *Navy Records Society* (1963)

Roy, I., 'The Royalist Ordnance Papers', *Oxfordshire Record Society*, part 1, 43 (1963–4); part 2, 49 (1971–3)

Sainsbury, E.B. (ed.), *A Calendar of the Court Minutes of the East India Company 1644–9* (Clarendon Press, Oxford, 1912)

Scottish Burgh Records Society

    Charters and Documents Relating to the Burgh of Peebles with Extracts from the Records of the Burgh, AD 1165–1710, ed. Chambers, W., (Edinburgh, 1872)

    Extracts from the Records of the Burgh of Glasgow AD 1573–1642 (Glasgow, 1876)

    Extracts from the Records of the Burgh of Glasgow AD 1630–62 (Glasgow, 1881)

    Extracts from the Records of the Royal Burgh of Stirling AD 1519–1616, ed., Renwick, R. (Glasgow, 1887)

    Charters and Other Documents Relating to the City of Glasgow AD 1175–1649, vol. I, ii, ed., Marwick, J.D. (Edinburgh, 1894)

Snow, V.F. and Young, A.S. (eds), 'Minute Book of the Commissioners for Irish Affairs (4 April–1 June 1642)', in *Private Journals of the Long Parliament, 7 March–1 June 1642* (Yale University Press, New Haven, 1987); II: (7 June–12 October 1642), in *Private Journals of the Long Parliament, 2 June–17 September 1642* (Yale University Press, New Haven, 1992)

Spalding, John, *The History of the Troubles*, I (Edinburgh, 1828)

Stevenson, D., *The Government of Scotland under the Covenanters 1637–1651* (Edinburgh, 1982)

Stow, John, *The Survey of London* (Dent, 1956)

Taylor, L.B. (ed.), *Aberdeen Council Letters, I, 1552–1633* (Oxford University Press, Oxford, 1942); *II, 1634–44* (Oxford University Press, Oxford, 1950)

Terry, C.S. (ed.), 'Papers Relating to the Army of the Solemn League and Covenant 1643–1647', *Scottish Historical Society*, 2nd series, 16 (2 vols, 1917).

Tibbutt, H.G. (ed.), *The Letter Books of Sir Samuel Luke* (HMSO, London, 1963)

Toynbee, M. (ed.), The Papers of Captain Henry Stephens, Wagon-Master-General to Charles I', *Oxford Record Society*, 42 (1962)

Trevelyan, W.C. and C.E. (eds), 'Trevelyan Papers III', *Camden Society*, CV (1872)

Wood, M. (ed.), *Extracts from the Records of the Burgh of Edinburgh 1626 to 1641* (Edinburgh, 1936); *1642 to 1655* (Edinburgh, 1938)

SECONDARY SOURCES

Adair, J., *Roundhead General: a Military Biography of Sir William Waller* (MacDonald, London, 1969)

Arthur, J. and Caldwell, D., 'The Doune Pistolmakers', *Guns Review* (April 1976)

Atkin, M., *The Civil War in Worcestershire* (Sutton Publishing, Stroud, 1995)

—— and Laughlin, W., *Gloucester and the Civil War: a City under Siege* (Alan Sutton Publishing, Stroud, 1992)

Aylmer, G.E., 'Attempts at Administrative Reform', *English History Review*, LXXII (1957)

Barbour, V., *Capitalism in Amsterdam in the Seventeenth Century* (John Hopkins Press, Baltimore, 1950)

Barnard, T., 'The Protestant Interest, 1641–1660', in Ohlmeyer, J. (ed.), *Ireland from Independence to Occupation 1641–1660* (Cambridge University Press, Cambridge, 1995)

Bennett, M., 'Contribution and Assessment: Financial Exactions in the English Civil War, 1642–1646', *War and Society*, 4 (1986)

——, *The Civil Wars in Britain and Ireland 1638–1651* (Blackwell, Oxford, 1997)

——, '"My Plundered Townes, My Houses Devastation": The Civil War and North Midland Life, 1642–1646', *Midland History*, XXII (1997)

——, *The Civil Wars Experienced: Britain and Ireland, 1638–1661* (Routledge, 2000)

——, 'Outreiking and Ingathering: Coping with Funding the Scottish Armies 1639–1653' (unpublished paper presented at a King's College, London War Studies Department seminar on 10 March 1999)

Bowden, P.J., *The Wool Trade in Tudor and Stuart England* (Cass, 1971)

Braddick, M.J., *Parliamentary Taxation in 17th Century England* (Royal History Society, Woodbridge, 1994)

——, *The Nerves of State: Taxation and the Financing of the English State, 1558–1714* (Manchester University Press, Manchester, 1996)

Brenner, R., *Merchants and Revolution* (Cambridge University Press, Cambridge, 1993)

Buchanan, B.J., 'The Technology of Gunpowder Making in the Eighteenth Century: Evidence from the Bristol Region', *Transactions of the Newcomen Society*, 67 (1995–6)

Bund, J.W.W., *The Civil War in Worcestershire 1642–1646* (Alan Sutton Publishing, Gloucester, 1905/1979 reprint)

Burke, J., 'The New Model Army and the Problems of Siege Warfare, 1648–51', *Irish Historical Studies*, XXVII (1990)

Caldwell, D.H., *Scotland's Wars and Warriers* (Stationery Office, Edinburgh, 1998)

Camden, William, *Britannia* (London, 1610)

Capp, B., 'Naval Operations', in Kenyon, J. and Ohlmeyer, J. (eds), *The Civil Wars: A Military History of England, Scotland and Ireland 1638–1660* (Oxford University Press, Oxford, 1998)

Carlton, C., *Going to the Wars* (Routledge, 1992)

Carte, Thomas, *The Life of James Duke of Ormond*, vols 2–3 (Oxford University Press, Oxford, 1851)

Carter, P., 'Clerical Taxation during the Civil War and Interregnum', *Historical Research*, LXVII (1994)

Casway, J.I., 'Owen Roe O'Neill's Return to Ireland in 1642: the Diplomatic Background', *Studia Hibernica*, 9 (1969)

Court, W.H.B., *The Rise of the Midland Industries 1600–1838* (Oxford University Press, Oxford, 1938/1953 reprint)

Cregan, D.F., 'The Confederate Catholics of Ireland: the Personnel of the Confederation, 1642–9', *Irish Historical Studies*, XXIX (1994–5)

Crocker, G. and A., 'Gunpowder Mills of Surrey', *Surrey History*, IV (1990) de Lacy Mann, J., *The Cloth Industry in the West of England from 1640 to 1880* (Alan Sutton Publishing, Gloucester, 1987 edn)

Donald, P., *An Uncounselled King: Charles I and the Scottish Troubles 1637–1641* (Cambridge University Press, Cambridge, 1990)

Eddershaw, D., *The Civil War in Oxfordshire* (Sutton Publishing, Stroud, 1995)

Edwards, P., *The Horse Trade of Tudor and Stuart England* (Cambridge University Press, Cambridge, 1988)

——, 'The Supply of Horses to the Parliamentarian and Royalist Armies in the English Civil War', *Historical Research*, 68 (February, 1995)

——, 'Gunpowder and the English Civil War', *Journal of the Arms and Armour Society*, XV (1995)

——, 'Logistics and Supply', in Kenyon, J. and Ohlmeyer, J. (eds), *The Civil Wars: A Military History of England, Scotland and Ireland 1638–1660* (Oxford University Press, Oxford, 1998)

——, 'The Low Countries, the Arms Trade and the British Civil Wars', *Journal of European Economic History*, (forthcoming)

Engberg, J.E., 'Royalist Finances during the English Civil War 1642–1646', *Scandinavian Economic Historical Review*, XIV (1966)

Evans, D. 'Gloucester's Civil War Trades and Industries, 1642–46', *Transactions of the Bristol and Gloucestershire Archaeological Society*, 110 (1992)

Everitt, A.M., *The Community of Kent and the Great Rebellion 1640–60* (Leicester University Press, Leicester, 1973)

Fairclough, K. 'Early Gunpowder Production at Waltham', *Essex Journal*, 20 (1985)

——, 'John Samyne: 17th-century Gunpowder Maker', *Gunpowder Mills Study Group, Newsletter*, 7 (May 1990)

——, 'The Cordwell Family, Gunpowder Producers at Chilworth 1636–1650', *Surrey Archaeological Collections*, (forthcoming)

Ffoulkes, C., *The Gun-Founders of England* (Cambridge University Press, Cambridge, 1937)

Firth, C.H., *Cromwell's Army* (Methuen, 1962)

——, 'The Raising of the Ironsides', in Christie, I.R. (ed.), *Essays in Modern History* (Macmillan, 1968)

Fissel, M.C., 'Scottish War and English Money: the Short Parliament of 1640', in Fissel (ed.) *War and Government in Britain, 1598–1650* (Manchester University Press, Manchester, 1991)

——, *The Bishops' Wars* (Cambridge University Press, Cambridge, 1994)

Fletcher, A., *The Outbreak of the English Civil War* (Edward Arnold, 1981)

Furgol, E., *A Regimental History of the Covenanting Armies 1639–1651*(John Donald, Edinburgh, 1990)

——, 'Scotland turned Sweden: the Scottish Covenanters and the Military Revolution', in Morrill, J. (ed.), *The Scottish National Covenant in its British Context* (Edinburgh University Press, Edinburgh, 1990)

——, 'The Civil Wars in Scotland', in Kenyon, J. and Ohlmeyer, J. (eds), *The Civil Wars: A Military History of England, Scotland and Ireland 1638–1660* (Oxford University Press, Oxford, 1998)

Gaier, C., *Quatre siècle d'armurerie liégeoise* (Wahle, Liège, 1977)

Gentles, I., *The New Model Army in England, Ireland and Scotland, 1645–1653* (Blackwell, Oxford, 1992)

Gerhold, Dorian, 'Packhorses and Wheeled Vehicles in England 1550–1800', *Journal of Transport History*, 3rd series, 14 (1993)

Geyl, P., 'Frederick Henry of Orange and King Charles I', *English Historical Review*, 38 (1923)

Gillespie, R., 'The Irish Economy at War, 1641–1652', in Ohlmeyer, J. (ed.), *Ireland from Independence to Occupation 1641–1660* (Cambridge University Press, Cambridge, 1995)

Goodall, D.M., *The Foals of Epona* (Dent, London, 1962)

——, *A History of Horse Breeding* (Robert Hale, 1977)

Grainger, J.D., *Cromwell against the Scots: the Last Anglo-Scottish War, 1650–1652* (Tuckwell Press, East Linton, 1997)

Groenveld, S., *Verlopend Getij* (De Bataafsche Leeuw, Dieren, 1984)

Hall, A.R., *Ballistics in the Seventeenth Century* (Cambridge University Press, Cambridge, 1952)

Harding, R., *The Evolution of the Sailing Navy, 1509–1815* (Macmillan, 1995)

Hart, C., *The Industrial History of Dean* (David & Charles, Newton Abbot, 1971)

Hazlett, H., 'The Financing of the British Armies in Ireland, 1641–9', *Irish Historical Studies*, I (1938–9)

Hey, D., *The Fiery Blades of Hallamshire: Sheffield and its Neighbourhood, 1660–1740* (Leicester University Press, Leicester, 1991)

Hogg, O.F.G., *Artillery, its Origins, Heyday and Decline* (C. Hurst & Co., 1970)

Holmes, Clive, *The Eastern Association and the English Civil War* (Cambridge University Press, Cambridge, 1974)

Hopper, A., '"Tinker" Fox and the Politics of Garrison Warfare in the West Midlands, 1643–50', *Midland History*, XXIV (1999)

Hoskins, W.G., *Provincial England* (Macmillan, 1963)

Hughes, A., *Politics, Society and Civil War in Warwickshire, 1620–1660* (Cambridge University Press, Cambridge, 1987)

Hutton, R., 'The Royalist War Effort', in Morrill, J. (ed.), *Reactions to the English Civil War 1642–1649* (Macmillan, 1982)

——, *The Royalist War Effort 1642–1646* (Longman, 1984)

——, and Reeves, W., 'Sieges and Fortifications', in Kenyon, J. and Ohlmeyer, J. (eds), *The Civil Wars: A Military History of England, Scotland and Ireland 1638–1660* (Oxford University Press, Oxford, 1998)

Israel, J., *The Dutch Republic: Its Rise, Greatness, and Fall 1477–1806* (Clarendon Press, Oxford, 1998)

Kenyon, J., *The Civil Wars of England* (Weidenfeld & Nicolson, 1988)

Kenyon, J. and Ohlmeyer, J. (eds), *The Civil Wars: A Military History of England, Scotland and Ireland 1638–1660* (Oxford University Press, Oxford, 1998)

Kitson, F., *Prince Rupert*, (Constable, 1994)

Klein, P.W., 'The Trip Family in the 17th Century', *Acta Historiae Neerlandica*, I (1966)

Lemire, B., *Dress, Culture and Commerce: The English Clothing Trade before the Factory, 1660–1800* (Macmillan, 1997)

Lenihan, P., '"Celtic Warfare" in the 1640s', in Young, J.R. (ed.), *Celtic Dimensions of the British Civil Wars* (John Donald, Edinburgh, 1997)

Lindblad, J.T., 'Louis de Geer (1587–1652): Dutch Entrepreneur and the Father of Swedish Industry', in Lesger, C. and Noordegraaf, L. (eds), *Entrepreneurs and Entrepreneurship in Early Modern Times: Merchants and Industrialists within the Orbit of the Dutch Staple Market* (Stichting Hollandse Historische Reeks, The Hague, 1955)

Lindley, K., 'Irish Adventurers and Godly Militants in the 1640s', *Irish Historical Studies*, XXIX (1994–5)

——, *Popular Politics in Civil War London* (Scolar Press, Aldershot, 1997)

Loeber, R. and Parker, G., 'The Military Revolution in Seventeenth-century Ireland', in Ohlmeyer, J. (ed.), *Ireland from Independence to Occupation 1641–1660* (Cambridge University Press, Cambridge, 1995)

Lowe, J., 'The Glamorgan Mission to Ireland 1645–6', *Studia Hibernica*, 4 (1964)

MacCormack, J.R., 'The Irish Adventurers and the English Civil War', *Irish Historical Studies*, X (1956–7)

——, *Revolutionary Politics in the Long Parliament* (Harvard University Press, Cambridge, Mass., 1973)

Malcolm, J.L., *Caesar's Due: Loyalty and King Charles 1642–1646*, Studies in History, 38 (Royal History Society, 1983)

Marshall, T.H., *The History of Perth from the Earliest Period to the Present Time* (John Fisher, Perth, 1849)

McGurk, J., *The Elizabethan Conquest of Ireland* (Manchester University Press, Manchester, 1997)

Moore-Colyer, R.J., 'Horse Supply and the British Cavalry: a Review, 1066–1900', *Journal of the Society for Army Historical Research*, 70 (1992)

Morrill, J.S., *The Revolt of the Provinces* (George Allen & Unwin, 1976)

Mowat, S., *The Port of Leith, Its History and its People* (John Donald, Edinburgh, 1993)

Murdoch, S., 'The Search for Northern Allies', in Taithe, B. and Thornton, T. (eds), *Propaganda: Political Rhetoric and Identity 1300–2000* (Sutton Publishing, Stroud, 1999)

——, 'Robert Scott', in *Dictionary of National Biography* (forthcoming)

Nef, J.U., *The Rise of the British Coal Industry*, I (Books for Library Press, New York, 1932/1972 reprint)

Ohlmeyer, J., 'Irish Privateers During the Civil War, 1642–50', *Mariner's Mirror*, 76 (1990)

——, *Civil War and Restoration in the Three Stuart Kingdoms: the Career of Randal MacDonnell, Marquess of Antrim* (Cambridge University Press, Cambridge, 1993)

——, (ed.), *Ireland from Independence to Occupation 1641–1660* (Cambridge University Press, Cambridge, 1995)

——, 'The Wars of Religion, 1603–1660', in Bartlett, T. and Jeffery, K. (eds), *A Military History of Ireland* (Cambridge University Press, Cambridge, 1996)

——, 'The Civil Wars in Ireland', in Kenyon, J. and Ohlmeyer, J. (eds), *The Civil Wars: A Military History of England, Scotland and Ireland 1638–1660* (Oxford University Press, Oxford, 1998)

Ó Siochru, M., *Confederate Ireland 1642–1649* (Four Courts Press, Dublin, 1999)

Parker, G., *The Military Revolution* (Cambridge University Press, Cambridge, 1989)

Porter, S., 'The Economic and Social Impact of the Civil War upon London', in Porter, S. (ed.), *London and the Civil War* (Macmillan, 1996)

Powell, J.R., *The Navy in the English Civil War* (Archon Books, 1962)

Reid, S., *The Campaigns of Montrose* (The Mercat Press, Edinburgh, 1990)

Rogers, C.J., (ed.), *The Military Revolution Debate* (Westview Press, Boulder, 1995)

Rooseboom, M.P., *The Scottish Staple in the Netherlands* (Martinus Nijhoff, The Hague, 1910)

Roy, I., 'The English Civil War and English Society', *War and Society*, I (1975)

——, 'England turned Germany', *TRHS*, 5th series, 28 (1978)

Russell, C., *The Fall of the British Monarchies 1637–1642* (Oxford University Press, Oxford, 1991)

Sharpe, K., *The Personal Rule of Charles I* (Yale University Press, New Haven, 1992)

Sinclair, J. *The Statistical Account of Scotland*, vol. 20 (Edinburgh, 1798)

Spence, R.T., *Skipton Castle in the Great Civil War 1642–1645* (Skipton Castle, Skipton, 1991)

Spufford, M., 'The Cost of Apparel in Seventeenth-century England', *Economic History Review* (forthcoming)

Stern, W.M., 'Gunmaking in Seventeenth-century London', *Journal of the Arms and Armour Society*, I, v (March 1954)

Stevenson, D., 'The Financing the Cause of the Covenants, 1638–51', *Scottish History Review*, 51 (1972)

Stewart, R.W., *The English Ordnance Office* (Royal History Society, Woodbridge, 1996)

Stoyle, M., *From Deliverance to Destruction: Rebellion and Civil War in an English City* (University of Exeter Press, Exeter, 1996)

Stradling, R.A., 'The Spanish Dunkirkers, 1621–48: a Record of Plunder and Destruction', *Tijdschrift voor geschiedenis*, 93 (1980)

Supple, B.E., *Commercial Crisis and Change in England 1600–1642* (Cambridge University Press, Cambridge, 1970)

Tennant, P., *Edgehill and Beyond: The People's War in the South Midlands 1642–1645* (Alan Sutton Publishing, Stroud, 1992)

——, *The Civil War in Stratford-upon-Avon* (Sutton Publishing, Stroud, 1996)

Thrush, A., 'The Ordnance Office and the Navy', *Mariner's Mirror*, 77 (1991)

Tibbutt, H.G. (ed.), *The Letter Books of Sir Samuel Luke* (HMSO, 1963)

Tomlinson, H.C., *Guns and Government, the Ordnance Office under the Later Stuarts* (Royal Historical Society, London, 1979)

Trease, G., *Portrait of a Cavalier* (Macmillan, London, 1979)

Tucker, N., *North Wales in the Civil War* (Bridge Books, Wrexham, 1992 edn)

Underdown, D., *Somerset in the Civil War and Interregnum* (David & Charles, Newton Abbot, 1973)

van Prinsterer, G.G., (ed.), *Archives ou Correspondance Inédite de la Maison D'Orange–Nassau, IV, 1642–1650* (Kemink et Fils, Utrecht, 1859)

van Ufford, H.Q, *A Merchant–Adventurer in the Dutch Republic: John Quarles and his Times 1596–1646/7* (V.U. Boekhandel/ Uitgeverii, Amsterdam, 1983)

Victoria County Histories
   Kent, III (1932)
   Surrey, II (1905)
   Sussex, II (1907)

Vogel, H., 'De Republiek als wapenexporteur 1600–1650', in Puype, J.P. and van der Hoeven, M. (eds), *Het arsenaal van de wereld: Nederlandse wapenhandel in de Gouden Eeuw* (De Bataafsche Leeuw, Amsterdam, 1993)

Wadsworth, A.P. and Mann, de L., *The Cotton Trade and Industrial Lancashire 1600–1780* (Manchester University Press, Manchester, 1931)

Wedgwood, C.V., *The King's War 1641–1647* (Collins, 1958)

Wenham, P., *The Great and Close Siege of York, 1644* (Session Book Trust, York, 1994)

Wheeler, J.S., 'Logistics and Supply in Cromwell's Conquest of Ireland', in M.C. Fissel (ed.), *War and Government in Britain, 1598–1650* (Manchester University Press, Manchester, 1991)

——, 'The Logistics of the Cromwellian Conquest of Scotland 1650–1651', *War and Society*, 10 (1992)

——, 'Four Armies in Ireland', in Ohlmeyer, J., *Ireland from Independence to Occupation 1641–1660* (Cambridge University Press, Cambridge, 1995)

——, *The Making of a World Power: War and the Military Revolution in Seventeenth-century England* (Sutton Publishing, Stroud, 1999)

——, *Cromwell in Ireland* (Gill & Macmillan, Dublin, 1999)

Whitelaw, C.E., *Scottish Arms Makers* (Arms & Armour Press, 1977)

Whyte, I., *Agriculture and Society in Seventeenth-century Scotland* (John Donald, Edinburgh, 1979)

——, *Scotland's Society and Economy in Transition, c. 1500–c. 1760* (Macmillan, 1997)

Williams, R., *Montrose: Cavalier in Mourning* (Barrie & Jenkins, 1975)

Wroughton, J., *A Community at War: The Civil War in Bath and North Somerset, 1642–1650* (Lansdown Press, Bath, 1992)

Yernaux, J., *La Métallurgie liégeoise et son expansion au XVIIe siècle* (Thone, Liège, 1939)

Young, J.R., *The Scottish Parliament 1639–1661: A Political and Constitutional Analysis* (John Donald, Edinburgh, 1996)

Young, P., *Edgehill 1642* (Windrush Press, Moreton-in-Marsh, 1995)

—— and Holmes, R., *The English Civil War: a Military History of the Three Civil Wars 1642–1651* (Eyre Methuen, London, 1974)

THESES

Edwards, P., 'The Farming Economy of North-east Shropshire in the Seventeenth Century', unpublished PhD thesis, Oxford University, 1976)

Grosjean, A., 'Scots and the Swedish State: Diplomacy, Military Service and Ennoblement 1611–1660' (unpublished PhD thesis, Aberdeen University, 1998)

Lenihan, P., 'The Catholic Confederacy 1642–9: an Irish State at War', (unpublished PhD thesis, University College of Galway, 1995)

Lewis, D.E., 'The Office of Ordnance and the Parliamentarian Land Forces 1642–1648' (unpublished PhD thesis, Loughborough University, 1976)

Murdoch, S.W., 'Scotland, Denmark–Norway and the House of Stuart 1603–1660: a Diplomatic and Military Analysis' (unpublished PhD thesis, Aberdeen University, 1998)

Roy, I., 'The Royalist Army in the First Civil War' (unpublished DPhil thesis, Oxford University, 1963)

Sleigh-Johnson, N.V., 'The Merchant Taylors' Company of London 1580–1645 with Special Reference to Government and Politics' (unpublished PhD thesis, London University, 1989)

Wanklyn, M. 'The King's Armies in the West of England' (unpublished MA thesis, Manchester University, 1966)

INDEX